INDIAN NARRATORS AND INTERPRETERS:

Julia Badger, Tom Badger, Charley Batiste,
Tom Batiste, Maggie Christensen, Lizzie Grover,
Prosper Guibord, Frank James, Anna Johnson,
Maggie Lamorie, Alec Martin, Eleanor Martin,
Louis Martin, Pete Martin, John Mink,
John Moustache, Delia Oshogay, Charley Smith,
Elizabeth Taylor, Sam Whitefeather

WISCONSIN CHIPPEWA MYTHS & TALES

and their relation to Chippewa life

Based on folktales collected by Victor Barnouw,
Joseph B. Casagrande, Ernestine Friedl,
and Robert E. Ritzenthaler

VICTOR BARNOUW

THE UNIVERSITY OF WISCONSIN PRESS

Published 1977
The University of Wisconsin Press
Box 1379, Madison, Wisconsin 53701

The University of Wisconsin Press, Ltd.
70 Great Russell Street, London

First printing

Printed in the United States of America

For LC CIP information see the colophon

ISBN 0-299-07310-6

Contents

Preface

The myths and tales in this collection were taken down from Chippewa narrators in northern Wisconsin between 1941 and 1944 by four field workers who were then graduate students in anthropology at Columbia University and later received its Ph.D. degree: Joseph B. Casagrande, Ernestine Friedl, Robert E. Ritzenthaler, and myself. The Wisconsin Chippewa field project was sponsored jointly by the Columbia University Department of Anthropology and the Milwaukee Public Museum. The collection of folklore was only an incidental part of the ethnographic program, for field notes were taken about all aspects of Wisconsin Chippewa culture and social organization. One set of our combined field notes is on file in the Department of Anthropology at the Milwaukee Public Museum; another is at the Columbia University Department of Anthropology. Most of this research was carried on at the Lac Court Oreilles reservation, but some was done by me at the nearby Lac du Flambeau reservation, where the lengthy origin myth, given in chapter 2, was taken down.

For each story in our collection I have given the year and place of its recording, the name of the narrator, the name of the interpreter when there was one, and the name of the field worker. Except in the cases of Tom and Julia Badger, correct names are given, not pseudonyms. Brief bibliographies of five of the principal narrators are given in Appendix B.

I would like to express my thanks to the three anonymous critics who read and evaluated the original manuscript for the University of Wisconsin Press. Their constructive suggestions resulted in considerable improvements in the text. I would also like to thank Donald Temple of the Cartographic Services Laboratory at the University of Wisconsin—Milwaukee for his work on the maps.

V. B.

Milwaukee, Wisconsin
November 1976

WISCONSIN CHIPPEWA
MYTHS & TALES

CHAPTER ONE

Introduction

In 1823 Lewis Cass, governor of Michigan Territory, sent a questionnaire about Indian customs to traders, military men, and Indian agents under his jurisdiction. One of the questions was, "Do they relate stories, or indulge in any work of imagination? Have they any poetry?"

One of the persons who received this questionnaire was Henry Rowe Schoolcraft (1793–1864), an Indian agent at Sault Ste. Marie. Schoolcraft, who married a Chippewa (or Ojibwa)[1] woman, was one of the first persons to make a systematic study of Indian customs. One of the things he found out was that the Chippewa did indeed tell stories and had an extensive mythology. This came to him as a great surprise, as he recorded in his journal: "The fact, indeed, of such a fund of fictitious legendary matter is quite a discovery, and speaks more for the intellect of the race than any trait I have heard. Who could have imagined that these wandering foresters should have possessed such a resource? What have all the voyagers and remarkers from the days of Cabot and Raleigh been about, not to have discovered this curious trait, which lifts up indeed a curtain, as it were, upon the Indian mind, and exhibits it in an entirely new character?" (1956, p. 308).[2]

Schoolcraft made his discovery known in two books, published in 1825 and 1834, which contained some Chippewa tales. But a fuller collection appeared in his *Algic Researches*, published in 1839, which includes some aspects of the Chippewa Wenebojo or Manabozho cycle.[3] It was from this source that Henry Wadsworth Longfellow drew the material that made up his epic poem *Hiawatha* (see Osborn and Osborn, 1942). Chippewa folklore, then, was one of the first extensive collections of American Indian folklore to become known to the outside world. Most of the Chippewa folklore that has been published since comes from north of Lake Superior (Skinner, Jones, Laidlaw, Radin, Reagan, Landes, Morriseau), Michigan (Schoolcraft, Blackbird, Kinietz), or Minnesota

---

1. Chippewa and Ojibwa are two names for the same people, two spellings of alternate English pronunciations of the same Algonkian word. "Chippewa" is the official designation for these Indians adopted by the Bureau of American Ethnology.

2. Cass's questionnaire is reproduced in Schoolcraft (1956, pp. 289-93).

3. For Schoolcraft's bibliography, see Hallowell (1946).

(de Jong).[4] As far as I know, the present volume offers the first published collection of Wisconsin Chippewa myths and tales. The Wisconsin collection includes many of the same tales that are told in Canada, Michigan, and Minnesota, but it also contains stories told in the Plains and other parts of North America, for Wisconsin was a crossroads center open to contacts with different culture areas. Many stories crossed barriers of language and culture.

Reasons for the Study of Myths and Tales

What can we gain from reading a collection of stories such as these? First of all, some aesthetic satisfaction, the enjoyment of a tale for its own sake, which is one of the main reasons, after all, why they are told. But stories are also told to convey information, which suggests another reason for their study. From these stories we can learn something about the belief systems of the people who told and listened to them. Although the Wenebojo origin myth seems strange to us, the Chippewa believed in it. For them Wenebojo was a real person whom they respected, although they also laughed at his antics.

Our word "myth" has the connotation of error. We say, "That's just a myth," meaning that it is unlikely to be true. But in folklore studies a myth is defined as a sacred story which is usually accepted as true in the society in which it is told. Some folklorists distinguish the myth from the folktale, which is a more secular story dealing with the adventures of a hero or trickster. In practice, I think it is hard to separate these two forms. The origin myth about Wenebojo fills the definition of a myth, but there are many stories about Wenebojo which qualify as folktales. A. Irving Hallowell wrote that the northern Ojibwa have no category of fiction, since they consider their tales and myths to be true (1947, pp. 547–48). This should make the investigation of Chippewa myths and tales a good approach to an understanding of their conceptions of reality.

Apart from aesthetic satisfaction and the investigation of native belief systems, there is a third reason for studying a collection of folktales: historical reconstruction. We may examine the stories for clues to past routes of migration, contacts with other peoples, and other past events. Many problems come up in the course of such investigations. Why, for example, do we find a story told by the Wisconsin Chippewa, "The

4. Chippewa myths and tales appear in the following sources: Kohl (1860); Blackbird (1887); Skinner (1911, pp. 1-177); William Jones (1917, 1919); de Jong (1913); Laidlaw (1914-25); Radin and Reagan (1928); Kinietz (1947); Morriseau (1965); Landes (1968).

Turtles' Relay Race," which is also told in Africa? It will be seen later that independent invention is unlikely to account for this; hence diffusion of the tale from one continent to the other must have taken place. But what were the paths of this diffusion? Questions such as these are raised when we examine the folklore of a particular society and find parallels in other bodies of folklore.

The analysis of folklore may also contribute to an understanding of past conditions of social life. In connection with the Chippewa there has been much debate in academic circles about the nature of their social organization in precontact and early postcontact times. We will see later what light our oral narratives may throw on this issue.

A fourth reason for studying a collection of folktales lies in their value as psychological documents, clues to prevalent personality patterns. The psychoanalyst Abram Kardiner, for example, regarded the mythology of a society as part of its "projective screen," the nature of which is influenced by the patterns of child rearing current in the society. Since the patterns differ from one society to another, the mythical themes should also differ from one society to another. Kardiner would not assume that an Oedipus complex is found to the same degree in every society. Its presence or absence would depend upon the nature of the family organization and the kinds of relationships which the parents have with one another and with the child. Thus Oedipal themes might be expected to appear in some societies, like our own, but not in others which have different forms of family organization. From this point of view the presence of certain themes in folklore in a particular society should have some diagnostic significance, perhaps indicating the presence of certain kinds of tension in that society. The best way to highlight the distinctive features in the folklore of a society is to compare it with the folklore of another society which has contrasting features in social structure or family type.

The aims set forth above will be pursued in my analysis of Wisconsin Chippewa oral narratives. I will try to elucidate the attitudes and values implicit in the stories as well as clues to the nature of Chippewa social organization and personality patterns as expressed in the narratives.

Chippewa Culture and Social Organization

The Chippewa are Algonkian-speaking Indians who lived in the region of the Great Lakes with hunting, fishing, and gathering as their bases of subsistence, supplemented by the raising of corn and squash in summer, harvesting of wild rice in the fall, and (at least in historic times) the tapping of maple trees for sugar in the spring. This cycle involved a nomadic or seminomadic way of life. Dome-shaped wigwams were constructed which could be built rather quickly by the women, who carried rolled strips of birchbark from one camp site to another. Travel was on foot or by birchbark canoe, or by toboggan in winter.

Chippewa Social Organization

Summer was the time of village life. The Midewiwin, or Medicine Dance, was held in the spring, when people assembled in the villages, and again in the fall before the bands split up for the winter hunt. This separation provided for the most efficient exploitation of food resources in winter time. This was especially true of the northerly regions, where lakes and streams were frozen for six months of the year. Early in the nineteenth century Peter Grant wrote: "It is customary for them, in the beginning of winter, to separate in single families, a precaution which seems necessary to their very existence, and of which they are so sensible that when one of them has chosen a particular district for his hunting ground, no other person will encroach upon it without a special invitation" (1890, pp. 326–27).

Ruth Landes has described the same state of affairs among the Chippewa Indians of Ontario in the 1930s. During the summer months between three and fifteen families came together and made up a village, but there was no village organization, and village membership was fluctuating. People did not always return to the same settlements. "Almost any circumstance may cause people to drift to a given village or leave it" (Landes, 1937b, p. 3).

A man and his wife formed a relatively self-sufficient unit; hence their mobility. The man was responsible for the hunting, trapping, and other nondomestic work. The woman did the cooking, made clothes, looked after the children, set out fish nets, and trapped rabbits. She tanned leather, made sinew thread, bark utensils, and mats. Since an individual family had much mobility and could readily leave a community, it was difficult for chiefs to impose political sanctions, and they did not have much political authority. There was no regular council of chiefs as there was among the Cheyenne and other Plains Indian tribes, although there may have been a tendency in that direction among the southwestern Chippewa, resulting from their long conflict with the Dakota.

Europeans first encountered Chippewa Indians in the seventeenth century at Sault Ste. Marie and in the Upper Peninsula of Michigan. Hence they were often called Saulteurs or Saulteaux. In the seventeenth century Chippewa were moving down into Wisconsin, where they established themselves at Chequamegon, Lac du Flambeau, Lac Court Oreilles, and other settlements.

The Chippewa social order has often been called "atomistic." The term refers to a loose form of social organization in which corporate organization and political authority are weak. It is not difficult for the component units to break away from the larger society of which they are a part. There are not many mechanisms for reinforcing larger-group social solidarity.[5] Bernard J. James (1954) and Harold Hickerson (1962, 1967) have both criticized the attribution of social atomism to the southwestern Chippewa, which include the Chippewa of Wisconsin. They maintain that the southern Chippewa lived under very different conditions from those in the north. There were larger settlements in the south, and there was warfare with other tribes, which led to greater political organization and social cohesion. Moreover, Hickerson believes that the precontact Chippewa had cohesive communal bands, whose cooperative way of life was disrupted by the fur trade and the incursions of the whites. Thus, if some groups of Chippewa have become atomistic in the last few centuries, that was because of the impact of outside forces.

Most writers on the subject are in agreement that the patrilineal clans which were generally, although not always, present among the Chippewa, served mainly to regulate marriage through the rule of exogamy and had little religious or political significance. This was particularly true of the northern Chippewa; for the southern groups there are indications of a formerly more developed clan system. Dunning believes that the hunting economy prohibited the development of larger groupings and the social elaboration of the clan system in the north (1959, p. 82). Rogers states that the Round Lake Ojibwa have always lacked clans and lineage structures (1962, p. 84). Among the Manitou Reserve Indians, according to Landes, clan functions were slighted whenever private interests dictated (1937a, p. 108). About a dozen clans were referred to at Lac du Flambeau and Court Oreilles reservations in Wisconsin in the 1940s. Those most commonly mentioned were Bear, Wolf, Lynx, Otter, Marten, Bullhead, Catfish, Sturgeon, Loon, Merman, Eagle, and Chicken. Clans are not, however, mentioned in our collection of folktales.

The southwestern Chippewa, including those of Wisconsin, sometimes engaged in war raids against the Dakota. Hickerson has described such raids as follows: "War parties often involved men from two or more con-

5. For the use of the term "atomistic," see Maslow and Honigmann (1970, p. 323). Characterizations of Chippewa society as "atomistic" may be found in Landes (1937a, p. 102); Hallowell (1955, pp. 7, 105, 120, 147); Barnouw (1950, pp. 15–16).

tiguous villages, but in general the warfare was a village rather than a tribal activity. During certain periods, then, villages in one area were at war, while those of another were in a state of truce" (1962, p. 13). Accounts of Chippewa war parties, like those described by John Tanner and Peter Grant, show the difficulty of holding such groups together. Members of these expeditions frequently broke away and returned home.[6]

Chippewa Religion

A crucial experience in the lives of Chippewa individuals, particularly males, was fasting for a dream or vision. Ideally, this should be done before puberty, although Radin refers to the system as "puberty fasting." From around the age of five, boys were periodically sent out to fast in the woods in order to get a dream or vision of a guardian spirit. The expected vision had a rather stereotyped character involving an encounter with a being who often said, "My grandchild, I come to pity you." Here "pity" has the connotation of "to adopt" and "to take care of," as well as "to have compassion" (Landes, 1939, p. 6).

It was from this supernatural being that, theoretically at least, a future shaman learned the secrets of his trade. Before the end of the dream or vision, the guardian spirit assumed an animal form. The guardian spirit was the source of a man's power. This power was not shared with others, except in the case of a godparent who placed a newborn child under the protection of his own guardian spirit until the child was old enough to go and fast for his own guardian spirit. The Chippewa term for spirit, which appears in many of the tales in our collection, is *manido*. The plural is *manidog*.[7] It was from a *manido* that a Chippewa in former days was believed to get his power in life.

One could never tell how much supernatural power a person possessed. A man who seemed to be lazy might really have access to much power. One folktale about a successful hunter concluded: "He could do all this through his early fasting and dreaming. That's how he got to be good. He just made believe he was lazy. When he fasted, the spirit told him to be lazy for a long time, and then to be good." Miscalculation of a person's power often forms a theme in folklore. Although one could never be sure how much power other people had, it might be assumed that successful hunters and shamans had much power.

6. Tanner, (1830, pp. 124–27, 138–42, 204–7); Grant (1890, p. 334); and Jenness, (1935, p. 102).

7. Another Chippewa term often mentioned in our collection is *windigo*, cannibal giant. The plural is *windigog*.

There were two kinds of shamans, or medicine men: sucking doctors and tent shakers. Sucking doctors sucked the sickness out of a person, the sickness being assumed to have a tangible form, something sent into the person's body by a sorcerer. The tent shaker, or conjuring lodge specialist, summoned spirits into a *jizikun*, a barrel-shaped structure covered with hides or blankets. The spirits were asked to give information and advice about problem situations, such as the whereabouts of a missing person. Some shamans were both sucking doctors and tent shakers, and some such men were also Mide priests, priests of the Medicine Dance. John Mink, one of our leading folklore narrators, was both a sucking doctor and a Mide priest. Tom Badger was a Mide priest but not a shaman.

The most important collective religious ritual of the Chippewa was the Midewiwin, or Medicine Dance. While the Medicine Dance seems to be mainly of postcontact origin, it contained many ancient aboriginal features, notably the origin myth about Wenebojo, the Chippewa trickster-culture hero, part of which was told in the course of the ceremony. Only initiated members could take part in the dance. Application for membership in the Midewiwin could result from a sickness or from the death of a close member of the family, spouse, parent, or child. Or it might come as the consequence of a dream which was interpreted to mean that the individual should join the Medicine Lodge. A person could "go through" the Medicine Dance several times, attaining different stages of initiation.

Although Midewiwin rituals differed from community to community, the usual performance consisted largely in parading around the Medicine Lodge in a counter-clockwise direction to the accompaniment of drumming and singing. The climax of the ceremony was introduced when the new initiate was magically "shot" by some selected members of the lodge, who aimed their medicine hides at him and supposedly injected small white shells into his body. The initiate thereupon fell over on his face, as if in a faint. After he was revived the initiate was presented with a medicine hide, which he then pointed at people in the lodge, "shooting" them in turn. Every member of the Midewiwin had a medicine hide (different animal hides being presented at different stages of initiation), and the climax of the ceremony came in a sort of free-for-all in which the members pointed their hides at one another, shooting and getting shot (see Barnouw, 1960).

"Shooting" is the proper term, since the initiators referred to their hides as guns, and it was believed that the magical discharges would be lethal to anyone who was not a member of the Midewiwin. The Indians compared the process to inoculation, except that it was more dangerous.

"If you had a hide pointed at you, you would get sick and die," Tom Badger told me. "The only way you could get well then would be to join the Midewiwin. It's dangerous when they're pointing hides. That's why the two runners watch out—to make sure that no young kids get in [the lodge] by mistake."

Persons who were not members of the Midewiwin, especially Catholicized Indians, often looked with suspicion and fear upon the Midewiwin, suspecting it of being a school for sorcery. There was, indeed, much fear of sorcery among the Chippewa. Hallowell considered this fear to be the psychological explanation for the atomism or individualism of Chippewa society (1955, p. 147).

Chippewa Folklore

As already mentioned, part of the Wenebojo cycle was told in the course of the Medicine Dance ritual. Other stories were supposed to be told only in winter. Charley Bastiste at Lac du Flambeau said that one cannot tell stories unless the frog and snake are in the ground. They are bad spirits which should not hear the stories. It was customary to give some tobacco to the storyteller, who was usually an older person.

Any division of folklore into categories is apt to be somewhat arbitrary, but the stories in this collection have been divided into the following classifications: (1) Wenebojo stories; (2) tales about Matchikwewis and Oshkikwe, mostly cautionary tales told by women to young girls, showing how girls should behave; (3) *windigo* stories about peoples' fights with cannibal giants; (4) animal tales of (*a*) allegedly true stories about peoples' encounters with animals such as bears, giant snakes, and other animals and (*b*) anecdotes, often short and sometimes humorous, involving tricks played by one animal on another, sometimes having explanatory "that's why" elements; (5) tales of spells and magical powers about persons who have come under the magical domination of a powerful evil person; (6) tales of European or mixed origin.

Rationale and Procedure for the Analysis of the Myths and Tales

Does the wide distribution of certain motifs invalidate the attempt to analyze this material for clues to Chippewa world view and personality patterns? If some of these tales were also told in Plains tribes, how can we relate the tales to *Chippewa* culture and social organization? I think that we are on safe ground if we analyze a large collection—all or most of the stories collected within a particular time period — in this case between 1941 and 1944. Characteristic patterns within these tales can then be highlighted by comparison with other large collections, as will be done in chapter 10.

Diffusion of tales of course occurs between societies, but it is still of interest to note which stories are accepted and retained within a body of folklore, and which are not accepted. Even if certain tales are shared with neighbors, there may be differences of emphasis in these collections.

Experiments have shown that individuals change stories slightly in the course of repeating them, and after a number of repetitions the story may be quite changed. Similarly, the members of society A may borrow a story from society B but change it in the process, so that eventually it becomes quite a different story. When a person retells a story, he may repress or omit some aspects of it which may seem either irrelevant or unpleasant to him, and he may elaborate and embroider upon other aspects of the story.[8]

S. F. Nadel (1937) made some cross-cultural experiments with two neighboring West African tribes, the Nupe and Yoruba, in the retelling of stories. He had two matched groups of twenty Nupe and twenty Yoruba schoolboys aged fifteen to eighteen who lived under similar conditions but had rather different cultures. A brief story was read aloud to each group of students in an early morning class. At noon each boy was asked separately to tell this story as he had heard it. Then a week later the students were asked to relate the story again. Rational links and logical explanations were supplied by the Yoruba schoolboys in their retellings but not by the Nupe. The Nupe expanded upon details of time and place which were not important for the development of the plot, and their retellings were more loosely knit.

One would think, then, that the stories told in a given society would tend to be in some harmony with the basic or modal personality type characteristic of that society. Hence, even if neighboring tribes tell some of the same tales, they may have some characteristic differences of emphasis. Franz Boas pointed this out for the Tlingit, Tsimshian, and Kwakiutl: "In the tales of marriages with supernatural beings or animals, the theme of the offended animal seems to belong primarily to the Tlingit, while the theme of the helpful animal is more frequent among the Tsimshian" (1916, p. 874). Again: "The love between husband and wife, between brothers and other members of the family is dwelt upon in Tsimshian tales and forms one of the motives used to develop the plot. This is rarely the case among the Kwakiutl" (1935, p. 174).

8. For accounts of such experiments, see Bartlett (1932, chaps. 5, 8).

In cases where a tale is shared by the Wisconsin Chippewa and a Plains tribe like the Cheyenne, I would look for differences which might reveal something about both groups.

In chapter 2 we will attempt an analysis of the Flambeau origin myth. In subsequent chapters we will see whether patterns found in this origin myth also appear in the other kinds of Chippewa narratives. Then we will compare our collection with some other bodies of North American folklore to see to what extent the patterns found in Chippewa folklore are characteristic of the other groups as well. In this way we may be able to distinguish features which are distinctive of Chippewa folklore as well as features which seem to be characteristic of North American Indian folklore in general. Once we have been able to distinguish features which are distinctive of Chippewa folklore, we can inquire how they are related to Chippewa personality, culture, and social organization.

CHAPTER TWO

The Wenebojo Myth
from Lac du Flambeau

This Wenebojo origin myth is the largest consecutive story in our collection. I have divided it into twenty-seven episodes to facilitate later references.[1] Distributions of the episodes are given in the footnotes. The narrator of the myth was a Mide priest, or priest of the Medicine Dance, to whom I have given the pseudonym of Tom Badger. In 1944 he was in his seventies; his wife Julia, who served as our interpreter, was then thirty-four. Life-history data about Tom and Julia Badger appear in chapter 9 and in Appendix B.

1. The Wenebojo Origin Myth

Collected by Victor Barnouw at Lac du Flambeau in 1944
Narrator: Tom Badger   Interpreter: Julia Badger

1. *The Sun Impregnates a Girl.* The story that I'm going to tell you won't be about this earth. It will be about a different world. There were only two people living in this other world: an old lady and her daughter.

Look how this world looks around us — trees, flowers, and everything. In this other world there was only grass and bushes, no timber.

The old lady's daughter used to go every day into the woods to find something that she could use for food. This was in the summer. She got those early berries that come in the spring. That was their food. She went

---

1. This story was first published in my article, "A Psychological Interpretation of a Chippewa Origin Legend" (1955, pt. 1, no. 267, pp. 78-85; pt. 2, no. 268, pp. 211-23). In reviewing the distributions that follow, our main guides are Stith Thompson's *Tales of the North American Indians* (1973) and his *Motif-Index of Folk Literature* (1955-58). The code letters and numbers used here follow those employed in these standard references. Another source of information on distributions which has been used is Margaret W. Fisher, "The Mythology of the Northern and Northeastern Algonkians in Reference to Algonkian Mythology as a Whole" (1946).

13

into the woods to pick the ripe berries all day long, picking here and there.[2]

Then one day somebody saw her traveling all alone by herself in the woods. That person seemed to take a liking to her. He even wanted to marry her. He knew what to do. When she was out berrying one nice hot day, when there was no wind, at noon-time, she heard a noise like a gust of wind. She looked around in the direction of the noise and saw a wind coming. When the wind reached her, she couldn't pull her dress down for some time, until the gust of wind went by. She didn't think anything of it, because no one was there to see her. She started picking berries again.

Shortly after that, the woman's mother had a queer feeling about her daughter. One day the old lady asked her daughter, "When you go out every day to gather berries, do you ever see anybody out there?"

The girl said, "No, I never see anybody. I'm all by myself all day." But the old lady had a feeling that there was something wrong with her daughter, and she didn't like it. She kept asking about her trips picking berries and whether she ever met anyone. But the girl said she never saw anyone in the woods. The woman's mother didn't like to see her daughter's condition. "There's something wrong," she said. She asked her again; but she said that she saw no one.

Finally the girl got to thinking, "I wonder what's wrong with me?" She began to feel that something must be wrong with her. The only thing she could remember about was that gust of wind. So she told her mother about the time that happened. Then the old lady knew right away who had done it. It was the Sun.[3]

2. *The Girl Gives Birth to Triplets.* It wasn't long afterwards that the girl found out that something else was going to happen. She left that place where she and her mother had been living and went into the woods. There she gave birth to some children — three of them. The first looked just like a human baby boy. After it was born, she held him in her arms. Then she heard a voice from somewhere telling her to put her baby on the ground. She didn't do it. After the person whose voice she heard

---

2. There are some internal inconsistencies in this tale, but that is not at all uncommon in origin myths. Although we are told at the outset that this story took place in a different world where there were no trees, we now learn that the girl went to pick berries in the woods. Later, in episode 4, we are told that the death of Wenebojo's brother was the first time that anybody ever died on the earth, and yet the earth had not yet been created.

3. A girl's impregnation by the sun is not only a Woodland Indian theme but is also found on the Plains (Southern Paiute, southern Ute, Arapaho) and in the Southwest (Navaho and Apache). The motif number is T521, *Conception from sunlight*, or A512.4, *Sun as father of culture hero.* In our version the girl is also impregnated by wind (T524, *Conception from wind.*)

got tired of waiting for her to put her baby down, he spoke to her again, "You don't want to do what I told you to do — put your baby on the ground. If you had done that, your baby would have got up and walked. But since you don't want to do that, it will be a year from the time that he is born that he will be able to walk." That's the way that people of this earth would have done from the time that they were born. They would have walked right away, just like animals. The Indian could have done that too.

Then the next baby was born. This one didn't have human features exactly, but he looked like a human baby to some extent. Just a little while later another one was born. This one didn't look like a human child. This one was stone, *Maskásaswàbik*. Sometimes when I go into the woods I see this stone. It's a very hard stone. I'm just telling you what I heard. It doesn't say that this woman took her babies home. I'm just telling what I heard.

These three boys didn't take long to grow up. They were *manidog* [spirits] Their mother always managed to get something to make bows and arrows for them when they were ready to use them.[4]

3. *Wenebojo Kills His Stone Brother*. Wenebojo, the oldest boy, killed everything he could kill, even the little birds. He brought them to his mother to show her. Wenebojo's mother told him not to kill any little birds. He even tried to kill both big and little *manidog* when he saw them. Wenebojo didn't listen to his mother. He killed everything that he could see.

His little brother, the stone, never went anywhere. He stayed right by the camp where they were living. But the other two boys went together all the time. They traveled just as far as they could go, but they never left their youngest brother alone overnight. They came home every evening.

They were very happy traveling through the woods, but they always came back to camp. At that time the three boys were the only persons living. Well, their grandmother was somewhere, but I'll tell you about her later. Those boys knew all the country around about, but they couldn't go any further.

One day Wenebojo asked his brother if he would do what he was going to ask him. He said, "We can't go any further. We know the country round about now. But it would be very nice if we could go further."

---

4. More often in Algonkian myths, it is twins, rather than triplets. In some versions, as in the one given in the following chapter, the twins quarrel before birth. (T575.1.3, *Twins quarrel before birth in mother's womb*; A511.1.2.1, *Twin culture heroes quarrel before birth*.) In what Margaret W. Fisher has called the Potawatomi type of myth, Wenebojo is the eldest of quadruplets. In Schoolcraft's version he is the youngest of four brothers. Among the eastern Algonkian Micmac and Passamaquoddy, the trickster hero Gluskabe is the eldest of twins.

The other boy said, "What is it you want to ask me?"

Wenebojo said, "If you think it's all right, I will kill our brother, and then we won't have to stay in this one place any more."

The other one didn't say anything. They were walking home to where their youngest brother was waiting. They didn't know how far away he was, but their brother at camp was listening to every word they were saying. While they were walking home through the woods, Wenebojo got tired of waiting for his brother to give him an answer. So he asked him again, "Why don't you say something about what I'm asking you?"

Then his brother answered him, "You're the one that's thinking of what you're going to do."

Wenebojo said, "Yes, I will do what I said."

When the two boys got home, it was just before nightfall. The brother who was at camp spoke to Wenebojo. "Why don't you do what you were talking about? If you can do it, go ahead and start right now."

Wenebojo said, "Yes, I will."

He went to borrow his grandmother's pole-axe. His grandmother lent it to him, and Wenebojo tried to kill his brother with it; but he couldn't even scratch him. He wore the pole-axe out.

Then his brother spoke to him. "You can't do what you're trying to do, unless I tell you how to go about it."

Wenebojo spoke to his brother whom he was trying to kill, "All right, tell me what to do. I'll do whatever you tell me."

"Build a fire, put me in that fire, and when I get to look like a red hot coal, throw some water on me."

Wenebojo said, "All right. That's what I'll do." So he made a fire and put his brother into it. Wenebojo looked at his brother. He was getting to look like a red hot coal. He asked him, "Is it time now?"

"No, not yet."

He built a bigger fire. A little while later, he looked at his brother again. He looked just like a red hot coal. "Is it time now?" he asked.

"Yes, I think it is," said his brother.

Wenebojo poured the water on his brother. Then his brother looked different. The stone cracked in different places. Then there were only two brothers left. When Wenebojo killed his brother, that was the first time that anybody ever died on the earth.[5]

---

5. This does not seem to be a widespread theme in North American mythology. Possibly there is some reference implied here to the sweat lodge or steam house formerly used by the Indians. "Red-hot stones are placed inside and water is poured onto them to give steam" (Morriseau, 1965, p. 55).

After that, Wenebojo and his other brother left that place. They traveled here and there, far and near. Whenever night came, they lay down and went to sleep. They had no special place to come back to now. They traveled all the time.

4. *Wenebojo Causes His Second Brother's Death.* After a while Wenebojo's brother began to get tired. He stayed behind sometimes. He walked slowly, because he was tired and always lagging behind Wenebojo. Wenebojo always waited for his brother to catch up with him. One time Wenebojo wondered how long it would take his brother to catch up. Finally, when he arrived, Wenebojo spoke to him. "Brother, can't you wait for me here a few days? After four days I'll come back."

His brother answered, "All right, you're the one that is thinking of what you are going to do."

"Then I'll leave you here to wait for me."

Wenebojo made a place to put his brother in. He made a hole in the ground. When his brother was inside, Wenebojo covered the place up so that no one would know that he was there. He put a stone at the head of it to let him know where the hole was. Then Wenebojo went away.

He traveled and traveled and traveled. He went just as fast as he could, because there was no one to hold him back now. He was all by himself. Wenebojo was happy, because he could see how the earth looked. He looked all about him. He kept traveling all the time.

Wenebojo forgot that after four days he was supposed to go back to his brother, because he was too busy looking around at the earth, and traveling here and there. Long after the four days were over, he happened to remember his brother whom he had left behind.

He went back to look for him. When Wenebojo got there, he couldn't find his brother any more. He saw his brother's tracks, so he knew that his brother had left. Wenebojo sat down and tried to cry. But he couldn't cry. He tried and tried and tried. Finally he succeeded. I don't know where he was, but his brother heard him. His brother said, "I wonder what is wrong with that fellow." He told Wenebojo not to cry. "I'm here," he said. Wenebojo spoke to his brother. "What did you come back for? Why don't you go back to where you were? The *manidog* have heard me crying already."

Wenebojo's brother said, "You are going to make it hard for the people, your parents, because of what you are saying. I will make a road for the people to travel along when this thing [death] happens to them."

Wenebojo and his brother had only one dish. They ate out of the same dish. The only time they ate was when they were both in the same place. The one couldn't eat unless the other was there too, so they had to eat at the same time. Wenebojo's brother said to him, "I'm leaving you our dish, and this is what the people will do when this thing happens to them. I want you to look at me when I go." He went. He went toward the sunset.[6]

5. *Wenebojo's Brother Makes the Road to the Other World.* As he went along, he made four signs of places.[7] He put four *manidog* along the way. At the first place he put an otter on the right hand side of the road. He went along the road, traveled a long distance, and then put another sign at the left hand side of the road. This was an owl. The Indians say that the owl's eyes are like a looking glass, and he looks just awful. When he speaks of the owl at the last supper with a dead person, sitting next to the coffin, the Mide priest says, "When you see your grandfather's eyes shining like glass, don't be afraid of him. Just go up and offer him your tobacco. He'll take it." They don't say "the owl." They speak of him as "your grandfather."

After he had put the owl on the left hand side of the road, Wenebojo's brother went along the road some more for a long distance, and then he made another sign, on both sides of the road this time. He made it look like two hills when they meet together. They're right on the road there. They're not real hills. They're two snakes with their heads together. When those snakes breathe, fire shoots across the road from their mouths. The road runs between them.

Then Wenebojo's brother kept going along the road for a long ways, and then he put up a fourth sign. He made a river. It wasn't very big or very wide. A man can jump across it, if he's a good jumper. He put a log across the river. It wasn't really a log. It's really a snake. They don't tell this in the story. When it's referred to, it's spoken of as a log; but the Indians know it's a snake.

The water is swift there. The log bobs up and down all the time. On the right hand side of the log, the water is clear. Where the river flows, it's as dark as it can be. You can't see the bottom of it. On the left hand side of the log, the water is black.

Wenebojo's brother kept on along the road. He went up a hill. Later on a strawberry was put there. Wenebojo's brother didn't put it there. The Devil put it there. Near the top of the hill, the road forks in two directions. The strawberry is right there in between the two roads, where they branch off. There's a spoon in the strawberry. When you see it, you hear

---

6. Episodes 3 and 4 are unusual. I have not found them in this form in other collections. In chapter 3 there are more common versions of Wenebojo's fight with his older brother. In the cases in this chapter there is no fight but an acquiescence to death on the part of Wenebojo's brothers.

7. The Chippewa word for "signs" is *kinawájikjikgèt*. Road sign has the same meaning.

a voice saying, "Eat this first." If you eat it, you'll go along the road that branches to the left. That is the road built by the Devil, not by Wenebojo's brother. That road doesn't go far, just a little ways. If you follow it, you won't be able to get a new suit of clothes when the ones that you've got on wear out. The only food you can get there are roots which you have to grub out of the ground with your hands, rooting like a pig. Your fingernails wear out, and your skin wears out too. People who get there always stay there all the time; they can't come back. Once you get there, you stay forever.

Wenebojo's brother kept going along the road. He went up a hill and down the other side. Then he spoke to his brother, Wenebojo. He asked, "Do you see me?"

Wenebojo said, "Yes, I see you."

"Well, I'll tell you what the Indians will call me. They'll call me Nekajíwegìžik." Then he disappeared. Wenebojo couldn't see him any more. That name means "some one who goes down behind the sky, behind the sunset." Wenebojo's brother never had a name before then. He named himself.

Now Wenebojo was all alone by himself. He'd killed his brothers. He was the one who committed the first murders on earth. His brother made a trail for people to go along when they die. His first brother, Maskásaswàbik, never went along that trail. He's still on earth, because he's just a stone.

Wenebojo had that dish that he and his brother ate out of. Now when a child or husband or wife dies, we give the person who is left a dish to keep for the one who has died. The Indian does that, because Wenebojo's brother left him that dish. We call them mourning dishes, bepagwéčinùnk, "something to take your mind off it."

Now that Wenebojo was all alone, he traveled wherever he wanted to go.[8]

6. *Trickster Eats Medicines that Physic Him.* One time when he was walking, he heard a bird making a noise. He didn't listen to that bird. He walked on; he didn't know where he was going. He could hear that bird making a noise all the time. When he heard this bird at first, he thought that he understood what that bird was saying. It seemed to be telling him, "If somebody ate me up, he would shit."

8. This episode could be classified under *Dying culture hero* (A565), in which a culture hero teaches people how to die by dying himself. Thompson gives references to this motif among the Luiseño, Capistrano, and Mohave. The concept of the snake log across the stream has been reported for the Chippewa of Michigan as well as Wisconsin. It is discussed along with snake symbolism in chapter 6. The tempting strawberry is mentioned by J. G. Kohl (1860, pp. 215, 218, 224). Kohl states that those led astray by the strawberry are turned into toads.

Wenebojo kept on walking. He could hear that bird making a noise all the time. Every time the bird made a noise, Wenebojo noticed that the grass was moving. Wenebojo stopped and listened for the bird again. He looked on the ground. When the bird made a noise again, the grass moved.

Wenebojo picked up a piece of grass, put it into his mouth, and started to chew. He said, "Who in the world would shit if he ate this?"

Wenebojo didn't go very far before his stomach started to feel queer. Pretty soon he had to take a crap. The grass that he plucked was *žábusigùn*, an Indian physic.

He started to walk. Pretty soon he wanted to sit down again. He had to keep doing that several times. After a while he got tired of doing that so much, so he started to run. While he was running, he looked for a great big hole. He found a hole and sat right down in it. His bowels kept running. He couldn't get up. The shit came way up to his neck. He put his head back, and the shit came up to around his mouth and nose. When he got through with that, he wondered what he smelled like.

After that, Wenebojo kept on wandering all over the place. He hadn't gone far before he heard a noise. The noise scared him. He stopped. He said to himself, "Look!" Then the noise stopped. He didn't hear it any more. When he got tired of listening, Wenebojo went on. As soon as he took another step, he heard that noise again. He said to himself, "Listen! That must be the South Wind people, *ošáoweno·k*, shooting somewhere." When he took another step, Wenebojo heard that noise again. When he jumped around, the noise went Pom! Pom! Pom! He heard the noise all the time he was jumping around, [faster] Pom-pom-pom! After a while that noise stopped. That noise was the sound of his own farting. He'd never heard it before.[9]

7. *Wenebojo Assumes the Form of a Beaver.* Wenebojo started walking again. He went no place in particular, just kept going on. Then he came to a river. There was a lot of water in that river. He went around the water's edge. After a while he found a beaver dam. He saw a great big beaver house. He hid somewhere nearby and found out who was liv-

---

9. *Trickster eats medicines that physic him* (J2134.2) is a Plains as well as Central Woodland theme, found among the Crow, Wichita, Pawnee, Arikara, Assiniboin, Eastern Dakota, Menomini, Fox, and Canadian Ojibwa. The *Fecal lake* motif occurs in the folklore of the following Algonkian-speaking tribes: Cree, Fox, Menomini, Arapaho, and Gros Ventre. The Winnebago trickster cycle has the same episode about the physic-grass, but it is more elaborate than the Flambeau version. It contains a closer parallel to the later flood episode; since the trickster, in trying to avoid the rising tides of his own excrement, climbs up to the top of a tree but finally falls down into the sea of dung. See Radin (1956, p. 27).

Keewaynah Margaret M. Peschel, a Chippewa authority on ethnobotany, thinks that the purgative grass may be botanically classified as *Isoetes* (personal communication).

ing there. Wenebojo saw the beavers coming out of their house. Then he came out of his hiding place and spoke to them, "Brothers, so this is where you are! I've been looking all over for you! I heard that you were somewhere here. Come here, brothers! I heard that you were here some place!"

Then he got those beavers to come near. Wenebojo said, "When I last saw you, you were little babies. You wouldn't remember me. That was a long time ago." Then he asked them if they couldn't make him look the way they did. "No, I can't do that," said one of the beavers. Wenebojo didn't leave them alone. He kept on begging and begging them to make him look like them. Those beaver people got tired of him after a while. Finally one of them said, "Well, I'll try." Wenebojo said, "If you can make me look like you, I want a big wide tail, bigger than I am."

They told Wenebojo to throw himself into the water. So he did so. The story doesn't say how far he went in the water, but when he came out, he was just like a beaver. Wenebojo looked at himself. He had a great big tail, bigger than himself. That's what he had wanted. Wenebojo said, "I knew that you could make me look like a beaver!" He had the biggest tail of all the beavers.

Wenebojo started to work now. He made the beaver dam bigger, and he put a big door in it, so that he could get in and out. He stayed there and worked along with the other beavers. In the fall they gathered their food for the winter. It turned cold. The water froze to ice. They were underneath the water then. They had to stay there, because it was winter.

Later on, some people came around, and one of the Indians saw the place where the beaver dam was. When he saw it, he was surprised to see the work of those beavers. This man told the others that he'd seen a big beaver dam. So they decided to go and catch some of them. When they got there, they saw a little nest hanging in the beaver house. One of the Indians said, "What's this little nest hanging here for?" The beavers down below could hear what those Indians were saying. The little nest in the middle was the house of the king, ógima. That's why it was up on top there.

The Indians started to break up the beaver house. The beavers down below could hear them. After chopping away for some time, they got it thinned down. There was a lot of mud there, and the Indians cleaned it out. Meanwhile the beavers in the bottom could see the axe coming through the top of the beaver house. They all started to swim away. But in all the excitement, Wenebojo forgot to go out through his own big door. He tried to get through all the other doors, but they were all too small. He just had to stay there. The people outside were working all the time to break open the beaver house. After they'd broken it down, they saw that big beaver tail sticking out. One of the Indians said, "Here's one!" They dragged Wenebojo out of there and put him on top of the ice. They killed him there.

They were there all day, trying to catch the other beavers too. But while Wenebojo was lying there dead, he was watching those Indians. Towards evening they were through killing beavers. When they killed the biggest beaver, his nose bled. They tied him up in a pack and carried him home. But where that blood fell, Wenebojo rose up again. He came out of that pool of blood.[10]

8. *Wenebojo Turns His Intestines into Food.* So Wenebojo went along the edge of the frozen river once more. He walked along on the ice, and as he was walking, he heard the sound of a little bell tinkling in the distance. He looked and saw a fox coming toward him. Wenebojo jumped behind a bunch of grass by the riverside, because he liked to listen to the noise that the fox made. As the fox came nearer, he got up from behind the grass to surprise him. He said, "My brother, here you are at last! I've been looking all over for you, and now here you are!" Everyone was his brother.

So Wenebojo and the fox carried on a conversation. Wenebojo said, "I saw you last when you were a baby. You wouldn't remember me. I wish you could make me like the way you are; then I could make that sound. I like to hear that sound."

The fox said, "Oh, no, I can't make you like the way I am. They must have made me the way I am. I couldn't do that."

But Wenebojo kept on begging and asking him, "Oh please try to make me like the way you are. I'd like to be like you." He just begged. After a long time, the fox finally said, "I'll try to do what you ask me to do, but first look for a round stone." So Wenebojo looked for one. "Brother," he said, "I can't find that! I thought you would ask me for something else!" But finally he found a round stone and took it to the fox.

When he gave it to him, the fox said, "Now bend over, with your hind end this way." Wenebojo did that, and then the fox took a knife and cut his ass-hole out, just cut all around. I don't know what he did with the round stone, but maybe he tied the ass-hole to the round stone, which hung down behind. I don't know for sure whether he put that stone there or not; but he must have done something with it. "Now," said the fox, "now you can go."

When Wenebojo stood up and made a step forward, it sounded like a lot of bells ringing. Then Wenebojo and the fox left each other. Each

10. Although human-animal transformations are common themes throughout the aboriginal New World, I have not found this particular story elsewhere.

went his own way. Wenebojo ran along. He certainly liked the sound of those bells! Wenebojo ran along on the river. As he ran along, it sounded as if that sound was a long ways off. He couldn't hear it very well any more. He stopped to figure out why he didn't hear the sound of those bells any more. He turned and looked around and saw his guts stretched out a long way into the distance. Then he grabbed his gut, and it broke off in his hands.

On the edge of the river there were a lot of elm trees. Wenebojo pulled in his guts toward him, hauling them in. After he'd pulled some of it in, he threw it up into a nearby elm tree. Then he said, "My aunts will have the benefit of eating this stuff when they are hungry. If they haven't got anything else to eat, they will use this."

The reason he thought of his aunts then was because his mother was an Indian. Wenebojo also gave a name to the stuff that he threw over the tree. He called it *aníbima·-kwèt*, which is the name for the elm tree if the stuff is wound around it. Otherwise you call the tree *aníb*, if there isn't any stuff on it. Wenebojo said, "This is the name that my aunts will use for it as long as the earth lasts."

Then the bells started to ring again, as Wenebojo ran on. After he'd run a long ways, the sound died out again. Then he turned around again and saw his guts stretched out into the distance. He did the same thing, grabbed it, and threw it around a tree. He said, "When my aunts are hungry, they will eat this stuff. And this kind will taste sweet. That's what they'll eat as long as the earth lasts."[11]

9. *Wenebojo Kills a Moose, but Does Not Eat the Meat.* After he got through doing that, Wenebojo went on. He wasn't like the way he was

11. Stories about stones tied to the trickster's intestines by Fisher or Mink (rather than Fox) are reported for the Cree, Potawatomi, Menomini, and Cheyenne. In the Menomini version the jingling sound which pleases the trickster comes from shells attached to Mink's tail. The Menomini version also has tree-food created from the trickster's intestines. See Hoffman (1896, p. 164). The closest parallel to the elm-tree food cited by Thompson seems to be *Trickster's burnt (or scratched) flesh becomes gum on trees* (A2731.1), where the tribes mentioned are Plains (Crow, Wichita, Pawnee, Arapaho, Cheyenne, Gros Ventre, Assiniboin) and Central Woodland (Cree, Fox, Ojibwa). A Canadian Ojibwa text has Wenebojo create tree-food in the form of a vine after burning his anus. "He said, 'These is my guts; my grandchildren will eat this in the later days' " (Laidlaw, 1918, p. 89). Another parallel is in a Mississaga version given by A. F. Chamberlain (1892, pp. 291–92) in which the trickster creates *pemâtig*, a species of climbing vine, for his successors, saying, "They will use it when they have nothing else for food."

A Canadian Ojibwa version given by William Jones is about Fisher and Raccoon. Fisher hears a sound, "Tank, tank, tank, tank!" Raccoon explains, "I have cut open my anus, and therefore my entrails have fallen out into exposure." He makes Fisher the same way as himself, so that his entrails spill out. But he doesn't throw them over a tree, as Wenebojo does in our episode. Later, Fisher finds Raccoon, kills him, and puts his entrails inside of his own anus (Jones, 1917, 1919, pt. 2, pp. 125–27).

before. He didn't walk on the river any more. He was walking in a different place. He had his bow and arrow with him. One time when he was walking, he saw a moose lying down in the brush. He pretended that he didn't see it. The moose saw him first. Wenebojo pretended that he'd only just seen him. He said, "Brother, so this is where you are! I've been looking all over for you! They told me that you were here. Come here! We were brought up by different people when we were small babies, so it's a long time since I last saw you. You wouldn't remember me."

The moose thought maybe Wenebojo was telling the truth, so he went up to him. Wenebojo knew then that they would get along all right. Wenebojo said, "Brother, did you hear about those people, about the two brothers who killed one another?"

The moose said he hadn't heard anything about it.

Wenebojo said, "It happened just a little while ago."

They were both facing each other. Wenebojo said to the moose, "Stand the way that fellow stood when he was killed." He showed him how to stand sideways. Then he told the moose to look straight ahead. "That's how that person looked when he was killed." When the moose turned his head away, Wenebojo shot the moose in the side. The moose said, "What are you doing, Wenebush'? You're killing me."

"Well, I told you two brothers were going to kill one another."

The moose walked away from him and kept going until he fell and died. Wenebojo followed him. He found him dead. Then he skinned the moose and cut him up in pieces. Then he cooked him. He cooked a little bit at a time and put each part aside when it was cooked until it was all done, head and all. He looked all around to make sure that he'd cooked it all. The meat was all lying in a heap. "Now we'll eat!" said Wenebojo. "When I eat, I don't want anybody to disturb me, not even the wind." He wanted it just as quiet as it could be. When he had said that, he listened. Everything was dead still. Then Wenebojo grabbed a chunk of meat, but just as he put it to his mouth, when he was about to bite off a piece of it, he heard a noise. He put the meat down uneaten, because the noise disturbed him. A tree had fallen between the forked branches of another tree. That was what was making the noise. Wenebojo named that noise *gizibákwet.*

Then Wenebojo climbed the tree to loosen the fallen tree from that fork and to take it off. He put one hand on the fork and pulled the tree back with the other hand. But then his hand slipped, and the tree bounced back and caught the other hand in the fork. He tried to pull his hand out, but he couldn't do it. He couldn't do anything about it, so Wenebojo just had to stay there.

Pretty soon a bunch of timber wolves went by. They saw Wenebojo up in the tree. He called to them, "Brothers, the person ran that other way, not this way." He didn't want them to see the meat. An old timber wolf saw that he was stuck up there. He said, "Maybe Wenebojo has got something here." The timber wolves went over to where the pile of meat was. They ate it all up. After they got through eating, they looked to see if they'd left anything. But there wasn't a scrap left on the bones. They'd eaten it all.

Wenebojo spoke to the timber wolves, "Go the other way." He'd filled four birch bark baskets full of moose fat. He told them to go the other way, because he was afraid they'd find it. Those timber wolves understood him, though. They figured there must still be something left; so they looked around and found the four baskets of fat and ate it all up. Then they went on their way.

After they'd gone, Wenebojo gave his hand a little jerk, and his hand came loose easily. Then he climbed down and looked around. He found nothing left but bones lying around on the ground. There wasn't even any gristle left on the bones.[12]

10. *Wenebojo Gets His Head Caught in the Moose's Skull.* He found the skull of the moose, looked inside it up the nose, and found a little piece of meat there. If he'd cracked the moose's head open, he'd have got that meat, but he didn't do it. Wenebojo wanted that little piece of meat very badly; so he did some thinking. "I will become a little snake," he thought. "Then I will be able to get the meat inside there. That's the only way I can get at that meat."

So Wenebojo turned into a little snake and crawled into the moose's skull and started to eat the meat. But before he'd finished eating, Wenebojo began to turn back into his normal shape, and his head got stuck in the moose's skull. There was nothing he could do, because when he tried to pull off that moose's head, it hurt him too badly; so he just walked away from that place. He didn't go very far, because he bumped into a tree. He felt the tree to see what kind it might be. He said, "Brother, what kind of a tree are you?"

The tree said, "I'm a maple tree."

Wenebojo said to the maple, "You used to stand close to the river. Do you know if there's any river close by?"

12. This episode includes the *Creaking limbs* theme (J1872), in which a man is caught between creaking tree limbs and thus loses a feast he has prepared. This motif has a wide distribution among the following tribes: Chipewyan, Arapaho, Cheyenne, Dakota, Pawnee, Ponca, Plains Cree, Plains Ojibwa, Sauk, Saulteaux, Mississaga, Cree, Kickapoo, and Menomini.

The tree said, "No, there's no river around here, Wenebush'."

Wenebojo kept on bumping into trees, all kinds of trees. He kept asking them if there was a river close by. They all said No. After bumping into all those trees, Wenebojo came to one tree that he didn't know. He said, "Brother, who are you?"

The tree said, "I'm a cedar."

Wenebojo said, "You always stand at the edge of the river. Is there any river close by?"

The tree said, "Yes, there is a river close by, Wenebush'. Feel my arm. You go straight along in that direction till you get to the river."

Wenebojo felt along the limb of the tree and then kept on going until he got to the river. There was a big high mountain with a river down below. That's where Wenebojo went. While he was walking along the side of the mountain, his foot slipped, and Wenebojo fell and rolled all the way down to the bottom. As he rolled along, the moose skull cracked open, and he was free of it at last.[13]

11. *Wenebojo Dances with the Rushes.* Wenebojo went on again. He walked on and on, looking around. Finally he came to a lake. He looked around and saw a bunch of Indians dancing. They all had feathers on their heads. Wenebojo said to himself, I guess I'll go dancing too. He turned back to the woods again, and looked around for some bark; and when he found some, he chewed on it. The bark changed color and became red. He made ankle bands and a head band with that. Then he went to join the Indians where they were dancing. He danced there all day long and had a good time.

Towards evening they quit dancing. Wenebojo looked around and wondered why the Indians were becoming so quiet. Then he saw that they weren't Indians at all. They were just a lot of rushes swaying in the wind. That's what he'd taken to be Indians dancing.[14]

12. *Hoodwinked Dancers.* Then Wenebojo went along. I don't know where he went, but he kept on going all the time. Finally he came to another lake. He approached the shore. The lake was full of ducks and geese of all kinds, playing in the water. Wenebojo stopped to figure out how he could catch those ducks. He knew what he was going to do.

13. This tale is more commonly about a buffalo skull (J2131.5.1, *Trickster puts on buffalo skull; gets head caught*). It is told by the Thompson Indians of the Plateau area, various Plains tribes (Arapaho, Crow, Blackfoot, Gros Ventre, Assiniboin), and Central Woodland tribes (Mississaga, Winnebago, and Timagami Ojibwa). The tale normally includes the motif *Blinded trickster directed by trees* (D1313.4). In addition to the foregoing tribes, it is also cited for the Menomini, Fox, Eastern Cree, Plains Cree, Southern Ute, and the Paviotso of California.

14. This episode (J1883) is also reported for the Plains Ojibwa, Canadian Ojibwa, and Menomini.

Along the way he'd come, Wenebojo had seen some grass and hay. He thought, I'll get that hay. He went to get it, cut it up, and put it in a bundle. Then he walked back to the lake. Wenebojo walked along the edge of the water. One of the birds saw him and said, "Look! There's Wenebojo. What is Wenebojo packing?"

Wenebojo paid no attention. He kept right on going.

Then another one spoke up, "Wenebush'! What are you carrying?"

He paid no attention, as if he didn't hear them at all.

Another one spoke out loud, "Wenebush'! They're asking you. What are you carrying?"

Then he turned around, looked toward the woods, looked around again, and pretended that he didn't see anybody. He kept on going.

Then another bird spoke up very loudly. "Wenebush'! What are you carrying?"

He looked in that direction. Wenebojo pretended he hadn't seen those birds before. Then he said, "Brothers, I am carrying songs. I will make a place where you and I can dance. When I'm finished making our dancing place, I'll come and tell you, so that we can dance and have a good time."

It took quite a while for Wenebojo to build a long wigwam. He made it good and strong, with one door in the front. When he was all through and had covered all of the holes in the structure, Wenebojo made a rattle. Then he called the ducks and geese to come and have their dance.

All the bird people came, every last one of them. They filled up that long dance lodge. When the birds were all inside, Wenebojo started to talk to them. He said, "I want you all to close your eyes. Anybody that opens his eyes will have funny-looking red eyes forever." The duck people did just what he told them. He shook his rattle, and they danced. He told those people to holler all they wanted to. Then he sang a song: "Brothers, all of you, close your eyes. If you open them, they'll be red forever." He just kept on singing that over and over.

The last birds that came into the hall were the hell-diver and the loon. The hell-diver stood on one side of the door; the loon stood on the other. Wenebojo kept going around among the birds while he was singing that song. He came up to the geese and started wringing their necks. They made a noise, but everyone else was making a noise too. But the goose whose neck was being wrung made a different kind of sound from the others. Wenebojo was afraid that maybe some of the birds would guess what he was doing, so he told them all to make any kind of noise they wanted to — all kinds of noises.

Those two people were still standing at each side of the door. The hell-diver said to the loon, "Those people are making an awfully funny kind of noise. It sounds queer to me. Do you hear it? You know, Wenebojo does anything and everything. Let's open our eyes. What does it matter if we have red eyes the rest of our lives?" So they both opened their eyes just a little bit. This is what they saw: They saw a pile of dead geese stretched along the dance lodge. The loon and the hell-diver hollered, "Wenebojo is killing us!"

Some birds with sharp beaks were there, and the loon and the hell-diver shouted at them, "Peck him! peck him!" Wenebojo tried to get out of that hall, but he couldn't because he'd made the walls so strong, and he'd made only one door. He was caught there. The birds kept pecking Wenebojo.

The hell-diver and the loon were stepped on and crushed by the other birds. That's why they have flat backs. And they have red eyes, too, because they opened them to see what Wenebojo was doing.

After all the birds had left the lodge, Wenebojo finally got out of there. He picked up the birds he'd killed and looked for a place where he could build a fire. He went to the bank of a river and made a big long fire. Then he dug holes all around the fire place and stuck a bird in each hole with its feet sticking out. After he'd done that, he sat down and waited for them to get all cooked.[15]

13. *Buttocks as Magic Watcher.* While he was sitting on the bank of the river waiting for those birds to roast, Wenebojo felt kind of sleepy. He thought about the South Wind men, so he told his hind end to watch out for them coming down the river. Wenebojo was sound asleep when the South Wind men came down the river. When they came around the bend, they saw Wenebojo with his behind sticking up. Then they pushed their boat back up the river. Wenebojo's rear end farted and warned him. So Wenebojo got up to see if he could see those South Wind men, but he couldn't see anybody; so he went to sleep again.

The South Wind men asked each other if anybody had any red dye. One of them had it, so they held it up when they went down the river. Then they pushed it up Wenebojo's behind, so that it couldn't warn Wenebojo any more.

15. Since *Hoodwinked dancers* (K826) is such a good story, it is perhaps understandable that it has such a wide distribution in different culture areas of North America: the Eskimo of Labrador; the Beaver and Chipewyan of the Mackenzie River district; the Cree, Canadian Ojibwa, Potawatomi, Kickapoo, Menomini, and Fox of the Central Woodlands; the following tribes of the Plains: Southern Ute, Southern Paiute, Comanche, Kiowa, Osage, Arapaho, Gros Ventre, Cheyenne, Omaha, Ponca, Crow, Dakota, Pawnee, Iowa, Blackfoot, Piegan, and Assiniboin; the following northeastern Algonkian tribes: Micmac, Passamaquoddy, and Malecite, Montagnais-Naskapi; the Huron-Wyandot of the Iroquois area; the Cherokee, Caddo, and Creek of the Southeast; and the Jicarilla Apache of the Southwest.

Then the South Wind men ate all of those birds around the fire. When they got through, they stuck the feet back into the ashes again. Then they got into their boats and went on down the river.

When Wenebojo woke up from his sleep, he sat up and looked at his roasted birds, got up, and pulled one of the feet out of the ashes. Then he said, "I guess they've been cooked a long time." He dug up all of the holes and looked into all of them, but he didn't find anything, nothing but feet. A little later he found something in his rear end. He felt around and pulled out the red dye. Then he stuck it back in again, as far as he could stick it, and said to his rear end, "All right, you can have this, if you want it so badly. You can keep it."

He was kind of mad, because he'd got nothing to eat, and his hind end hadn't done what it was supposed to do. It wasn't the South Wind men who made him feel sore. It was his rear end that was to blame. "He'll find out! said Wenebojo. After a while he made a big fire. He was going to give his hind end a lesson. He stood over the fire and burned his ass.

When his behind started to burn, his bones got scorched and made a funny noise like the sound of something getting burned in the oven. "Zizingi," it said. Wenebojo said, "Are you trying to call on Zizingi to help you?" Zizingi doesn't mean anything, it's just the noise the bones made; but Wenebojo thought that his rear end was calling on someone called Zizingi for help.[16]

14. *Creation of Tobacco.* Finally, Wenebojo thought that maybe he was punishing his behind too much, so he left the fire. He walked along until he came to a lot of brush. He walked right into it. After he had passed through the bushes, Wenebojo turned around and looked back. There was a trail of red behind him going through the brush. Then Wenebojo thought of his uncles. He said, "When my uncles are out of tobacco and have nothing to smoke, they can always have these to smoke, and they will call them *bakwéčpakuzìgunen.*" *Bakwéč* means "woods." The word means "a stick that grows in the woods." That's the wild kinnickinnick.

---

16. *Buttocks as magic watcher* (D1317.1; also D1610.6.3, *Speaking buttocks*). Thompson states that this episode occurs in substantially all the tales cited under *Hoodwinked dancers* and does not occur independently. The Cheyenne myth contains *Hoodwinked dancers* but not *Buttocks as magic watcher*. The former episode is combined with the creaking tree limbs theme as an alternate form of oral frustration. See Grinnell (1926, pp. 287–89). This is also true of some Siouan-speaking tribes. See Dorsey (1892, p. 301).

Punishment of the trickster's rear end is reported for the following Algonkian-speaking tribes: Cree, Potawatomi, Fox, Kickapoo, Menomini, Arapaho, Gros Ventre, and Blackfoot. In most of these cases, however, the punishment is effected not by standing over a fire but by thrusting a stick or firebrand into the rectum. See Kroeber (1907, p. 71); Dorsey and Kroeber (1903, p. 60n); Wissler and Duvall (1908, pp. 26, 38–39).

Wenebojo walked on again until he came to a river. There he found some more brush and sticks. He walked through it and then looked back again at the brush he'd been through. His scabs and his sores were hanging on all the sticks and brush. He thought about his uncles again. He said, "They will smoke these, and they will be sweet." He named them *gekádugnugèkwukin*. That means "speckled stick." It's another kind of kinnickinnick, very hard to get around here now. It tastes very good and sweet.

Then Wenebojo walked along again until he came to another bunch of brush. Then he walked spread-legged through it; and when he looked back, it was all red. Those were red bushes three or four feet high. White people sometimes plant them in front of their houses. It's another kind of kinnickinnick. Wenebojo thought about his uncles again. "They can smoke these when they have nothing else to smoke." He named them *memiskwákwakìn miskwabímizìn*. That means "red hardwood stick." The *miskwá* that's repeated in there means "red."

After he got through with that, Wenebojo went on. He came to a mountain. He sat down and slipped down the mountain. I don't know how far he fell down, but when he turned around, he saw a trail of scabs behind him. Right then and there he thought of his aunts. He called that trail of scabs *wa·kúnùg*. He said, "My aunts will cook these when they are hungry." They're a kind of lichen that grows on stones. They're boiled in deer blood or some other kind of animal blood.[17]

15. *Wenebojo Joins a Pack of Wolves.* After that Wenebojo went on walking again through the woods. This was late in the fall. Wenebojo walked until he reached a river that was frozen over. He walked along on the ice until he saw a bunch of timber wolves coming. He hid away

17. The only other sources where I have found a similar explanation for the origin of tobacco are in J. G. Kohl's *Kitchi-Gami* (1860, p. 393) and in Speck's collection of Timiskaming folklore (1915b, p. 14). The Menomini tell the same story about the trickster's burning of his buttocks, but they do not give this as an explanation for the origin of tobacco, and they have a quite different story about its origin. See Hoffman (1896, pp. 164 ff.). Trickster burns his anus in the Winnebago cycle but does not create tobacco as a result. See Radin (1956, pp. 17–18). In a Canadian Ojibwa version recorded by G. E. Laidlaw in 1915, Wenebojo punishes his anus by shoveling hot coals into it and then walks through some trees which become red willows, but not tobacco. Later Wenebojo slides down some rocks which become red granite (Laidlaw, 1915, p. 87).

In the narrative of John Tanner, *wah-ka-nug* (the name given by Tom Badger to the lichen on rocks from Wenebojo's scabs) is identified as "the edible gyrophora," a form of *tripe de roches* (1830, p. 299). Keewaynah Margaret M. Peschel refers to *wakon* as edible lichens which grow from cedars, often eaten by the Indians; *wakonug* (plural) is identified as edible *Polypora serpula*. *Windigo wahkon*, or bad spirit lichen, is said to be a form of rock tripe used by Indian women to thicken stews. It does not grow below 1000 feet above sea level. See also Kohl (1860, p. 365).

from them. The timber wolves kept coming nearer. When they approached, Wenebojo got up from behind the bushes. "Brothers, come here. I've walked all over, looking for you. I heard that you were around here somewhere. The last time I saw you we were babies. You wouldn't remember me."

The timber wolves thought that Wenebojo was telling the truth, so they came up to him. There were five of them — one old one and four young ones. But they all looked alike to Wenebojo, and he couldn't tell which was the oldest one. Wenebojo stood rubbing his eyes, and said he couldn't tell which of them was the oldest and which was the youngest. One of them pointed to another of the wolves and said, "This is our parent." Then Wenebojo went to this wolf and called him his brother. So that made Wenebojo the uncle of the other wolves.

Wenebojo took a good look at these wolves so that he could tell them all apart. They kept on talking; I don't know how long. The wolves had no place they could call home. They traveled just like Wenebojo did. After they'd been talking a while, the wolves told Wenebojo that they wanted to go on now. But Wenebojo asked them not to go yet, for he wanted to stay with them for a little while. He'd been hunting around for them so long, he said, that he didn't want them to go yet. I don't know how long they stayed together, but finally they told Wenebojo that they were going. Wenebojo didn't like that, so he asked if he could go along. The oldest wolf said, "You can't keep up with us, because we travel very fast." Wenebojo said, "We can let the others go ahead. You and I can walk behind and follow their tracks."

The old wolf felt sorry for Wenebojo. He didn't want to leave him behind, since he was so anxious to come along with them. So they let Wenebojo come along too. He and the old wolf walked behind, following the young ones. But the old wolf always kept ahead of Wenebojo, although Wenebojo walked just as fast as he could.

One time the young wolves were chasing a deer. The four young ones had spread out, running in different places. The old wolf and Wenebojo could see their tracks in the snow. Some of the tracks had short steps; others had taken long jumps. The old timber wolf asked Wenebojo, "Who do you think will catch the deer first?"

Wenebojo pointed to the tracks. "The one that jumped the farthest will catch the deer first."

The old timber wolf said, "No, the one that jumped the closest will get there first." Pretty soon there was an argument between those two brothers. They followed the tracks, arguing all the way.

The timber wolf walked ahead. Wenebojo followed behind. When they got a little further, they found that one of the wolves had bumped his nose on a tree. so that his tooth had stuck in the tree. The old timber wolf said to Wenebojo, "Pull that arrow out of the tree, and take it to the one that's lost it." He was referring to the wolf's tooth. Wenebojo looked where that "arrow" was and saw it was only a wolf's tooth. He decided he didn't want to do what the old wolf had said. "What would I want to carry a dog's tooth around for?"

"I've been telling you not to talk so much," said the wolf.

Then the timber wolf pulled the tooth out of the tree, and it was an arrow instead of a tooth. Wenebojo saw the arrow. He said, "I'll carry it." The old wolf gave it to him to carry, and they went along. It wasn't very far before they saw the place where the wolves had killed the deer. There was nothing left there but bones. The wolves were all sitting around with big bellies. The old timber wolf told Wenebojo to make a place where they could put the meat. The old wolf had already started making a place for himself. Wenebojo couldn't see any meat at all, and he didn't see why the old wolf was getting a place ready. But he started doing it too. He didn't do it very carefully, though. When they got all finished fixing up a place, the old wolf spoke to one of his sons, "Give Wenebojo half of that meat." One of the young wolves walked up to where Wenebojo was sitting by the place that he'd got ready. Then the wolf vomited on the place Wenebojo had prepared. The other two wolves did that too, and they did the same thing for the old wolf. Then Wenebojo and the old wolf ate the vomit.

After that the old wolf told his children to make a house. One of them started to make a wigwam. They had nothing to make it out of, but they were going to build a house anyway. One of the wolves walked around in a circle. Then Wenebojo saw a wigwam.

After that they stayed there all the time. The young wolves used to go out to hunt, but Wenebojo and the old wolf stayed at home in the wigwam all the time.

16. *Wenebojo Quarrels with the Wolves.* The wolves brought back meat every day. They also kept gathering the bones of the animals they killed. After a while, the old timber wolf said he wanted to make grease and tallow out of those bones. One of Wenebojo's nephews liked him a lot, but the others didn't care for him so much. One day, when all the wolves were at home, one of them was told to make the tallow and grease. The others were told that they weren't supposed to look at him while he was making it. That's what the old timber wolf told them. He said to Wenebojo, "Please don't look at the wolf that's making the tallow and grease. You're a great one for not obeying orders and for not listening to what you're told. If anybody watches or peeks at the wolf while

he's making grease and tallow, the bone will slip out of his hands and come and hit that person on the eye." The other wolves were all supposed to cover up in their blankets and hide their faces in them, and Wenebojo was supposed to do that too.

After everybody had lain down and covered their heads, the wolf started making the tallow and grease. Wenebojo also had his head covered up. While he lay there, he could hear the wolf chewing and gnawing at those bones. But he didn't peek yet. After a while, though, Wenebojo thought that he'd like to know how that fellow was going about making tallow and grease. Wenebojo's old blanket happened to have a hole in it. Through it he peeked at the wolf who was making that grease and tallow. He saw the grease running down the wolf's mouth as he chewed at the bones. Then the bone slipped out of the wolf's hands, came over, and hit Wenebojo on the eye. Wenebojo got hurt and got up from where he was lying. The others got up too because he got up. He was holding his eye. He told the others that that fellow had hit him on the eye.

The old timber wolf said to Wenebojo, "You must have looked at him. That's why you were hit on the eye."

Wenebojo said, "No, he came and hit me."

Then the wolf who was making the grease and tallow stopped his work. But he'd got a little bit made before Wenebojo peeked at him. Nobody else started making any grease. They didn't have very much grease.

The wolves didn't go any place. They all stayed there, but they went out to hunt every day. They stayed in that one place for one or two months. Then one day Wenebojo told the others that he could make grease and tallow out of bones too. All of the grease and tallow was gone now, so the others said, "Go ahead and make it then."

When he started to make it, Wenebojo said, "I don't want any of you to look at me. You all have to cover up your heads." Wenebojo knew which of the wolves it was that had hit him with that bone. He started to do just what he'd seen the other wolf do when he made the tallow and grease. Wenebojo made a little grease, but not much. Pretty soon he got up from where he was sitting, went over, and hit that wolf on the eye. The wolf hollered and made a lot of noise. Wenebojo said, "He was looking at me!"

After that the old timber wolf got to thinking, "Maybe some day Wenebojo will do something to us." So then he told Wenebojo that they were going away and were going to leave him, but that they were going to leave one wolf behind with him — the one that liked Wenebojo.

Wenebojo was glad, so he let the others go. They all went except for the one that stayed on. This one took care of Wenebojo and got his food for him.[18]

17. *Wenebojo's Nephew Is Killed by the Underwater Spirits.* This wolf was never at home. He was always hunting and traveling in the woods. But he never stayed away late. He was always home before sundown. One night, though, the wolf didn't come home. Night fell, but he still didn't come. Wenebojo got to thinking, "Maybe this wolf is lost somewhere in the woods." When night came, Wenebojo went out to look for a dry stump. He struck the wood, so the wolf could hear if he were lost in the woods anywhere nearby. He hollered, but there was no answer. The wolf didn't come home that night.

Early the next morning Wenebojo started to follow the wolf's tracks, to see where he had gone. He followed the tracks all day long. Towards evening of the same day, he saw a place where the wolf had been chasing a deer. Pretty soon he saw what had happened to his nephew. The deer had jumped across the river, and the wolf had jumped too; but he must have slipped and fallen into the water.

The *manidog* under the water were the ones who had done that, because if they had just let Wenebojo have his own way, there wouldn't have been any wild animals left. That's why that wolf drowned. So Wenebojo saw what had happened to his nephew. He was angry. He was very mad. Wenebojo thought to himself, "I'll do the same thing to those *manidog* that they did to my nephew."

Then Wenebojo went back home. When he got home, he looked at his nephew's bed, and he was mad; and he looked around and discovered his nephew's string of beads hanging up by his bed. He took his nephew's string of beads and kissed them and kept them with him.

The next day he made his bow and arrow. The bow was made from a great big cedar log, split in two. He split it twice, so that it would bend easily. He made two arrows too.[19]

18. *Wenebojo Wounds the Two Underwater Kings.* On warm days the *manidog* from under the water come up to bask and sleep on the beach by the lake. Wenebojo went to that bank and stood on the top of the hill nearby. He decided to become a tree stump that had been burned

18. An episode of the trickster's accompanying a wolf pack is found in the folklore of the following Algonkian-speaking Indians: Passamaquoddy, Montagnais-Naskapi, Cree, Potawatomi, Menomini, and Blackfoot.

The Blackfoot story follows the same sequence; but instead of making tallow, one of the wolves makes pemmican with the injunction of keeping eyes closed. In the Blackfoot version the trickster kills the wolf after the bone hits him, and he is forced to leave the wolf pack with one companion wolf. See Grinnell (1892, pp. 149–50).

19. This is an Algonkian Indian tale. For its distribution, see the table on page 70.

a long time ago. When Wenebojo looked at himself, that's just what he
looked like — an old stump. Wenebojo also asked for warm sunshine for
four days, so that it would be good and hot with no wind. That's how it
was for four days.

The *manidog* knew that it was going to be a nice day, so they went
over to the beach where they had basked before. During those four days
Wenebojo stood on top of the bank and watched the water. He saw it stirring, so he knew that the *manidog* were coming up to bask. Pretty soon
they all came up and lay down along the beach. Wenebojo stood up on
the bank and spotted which one was the head one, the king (*ógima*).
There were two of them together, two great big ones.

One big snake saw the stump there by the edge of the bank. He'd never
seen that stump standing there before. That big snake said, "I've never
seen that stump before. Maybe that's Wenebojo. He does everything."
Another one said, "Ah, that can't be Wenebojo. He isn't enough of a
manido to do that." But the big snake said, "I'm going to find out." He
went up the hill, wrapped himself around the stump, and squeezed and
squeezed. Wenebojo didn't feel it. The snake squeezed a little harder. He
did that four times, harder each time. The fourth time, it began to hurt
Wenebojo, and he was just about to move when the snake let go. Then
the snake went down the hill and said to the others, "That's not Wenebojo."

Soon the *manidog* were all sleeping. It was hot. When Wenebojo was
sure that they were all asleep, he went down the hill. He went up to
where the two kings were lying side by side on the beach. He stepped
over all those *manidog*. When he reached the two kings, he shot one of
them in the side with his bow and arrow. Then he shot the other one.
Then all of the *manidog*, including the two wounded kings, rushed back
into the water.[20]

19. *Wenebojo Curses the Kingfisher*. Wenebojo couldn't do anything
more then, so he followed a stream that went into the lake. While he was
following it, he came to a little bird that was sitting on a tree looking
down into the water. Wenebojo asked the little bird, "What are you doing? Why are you looking down into the water?"

The little bird replied, "I'm looking into the water, because I'm
watching for Wenebojo's nephew's guts to float by. I'm waiting for them
to throw his guts out."

Wenebojo said, "I've got something that they gave me that belongs to
Wenebojo's nephew." He went up to the bird and said, "You might as
well have what was given to me. Lower your head, and I'll put this string
of beads around your neck."

20. For the distribution of this episode, see the table.

The little bird did that, and then Wenebojo put the string of beads around the bird's neck; but just as he was about to strangle the bird, his hand slipped, and the bird flew up into a tree. He still had the string of beads around his neck; but his head was bushy in back, where Wenebojo had grabbed him. Wenebojo said to him, "*Mujiúnim* [you dog, you rascal], you will be good for nothing as long as you live. People will call you *gištumanisi* [kingfisher]." Today his head is still bushy, and he has a necklace of white spots.[21]

20. *Wenebojo Kills the Woman Who Doctors the Two Kings.*
Wenebojo kept on going. I don't know where he went. He was going somewheres through the woods, through the hardwood timber. After a while he saw somebody walking. He went up to the person; and when he came close, he saw that it was an old lady. She looked frightened. She could hardly see. She was packing some basswood bark on her back. That old lady looked scared. She looked at Wenebojo real sharp and said, "You're not Wenebojo, are you?"

Wenebojo said, "No, I'm not Wenebojo. Would you be alive if I were Wenebojo? If you saw Wenebojo, he'd kill you."

Wenebojo was mad, because he'd lost his nephew. Then the old lady believed that it wasn't Wenebojo that was speaking to her. Wenebojo asked the old lady, "*Nóko* [Grandmother], what are you going to do with that basswood bark you're packing on your back?"

The old lady said, "My grandson, I'm going to use this basswood to find out where Wenebojo is. We are going to spread it all over. Wherever this basswood moves, wherever it's lying, they're going to send the water there. The reason they're going to do this, my grandson, is because Wenebojo pretty nearly killed the king. It's on account of me that the kings are still living, because I'm doing everything I can for them."

Wenebojo said, "*Nóko*, what do you do when you doctor these kings?"

"I don't do anything for them; I just make medicine for them."

"Do you sing when you doctor them?"

"Yes, my child."

"How do you sing when you doctor them? What do you call that song?"

"The name of the song is 'Wenebojo' and it goes like this." Then she started to sing for him:

> Wenebojo ho, the notch of the arrow.
> Wenebojo ho, the notch of the arrow.
> I try to suck it out with my mouth.
> I try to suck it out with my mouth.

21. Part of this episode, without the explanatory aspects or the curse, occurs in the Blackfoot story. See Grinnell (1892, p. 151).

Then she told him what she did when she doctored the kings, until Wenebojo knew all about it. Then he asked the old lady which way she was going. She pointed in the direction she was headed. Then Wenebojo said, "All right, *Nóko*, you can go now."

She turned to go, but as soon as her back was turned, Wenebojo hit her on the head and killed her. Then he skinned her. He put her skin over himself. It all fitted his body pretty well, except for around the calves of his legs. So Wenebojo took the old lady's axe and chopped off his calf muscles, so that her skin would fit all right there. When he got through, the old lady's skin fitted well. He put that basswood pack on his back. Then he went in the direction the old lady had pointed.

21. *Wenebojo Kills the Two Kings.* After a while he reached the place where the kings were, a little town. He didn't know which way to go, so he stood there a while. Some little children saw him and said, "Ah, our grandmother has come home!" He went into the wrong place. He didn't go into the old lady's home, because he didn't know where it was. Wenebojo said to the little children, "Ah, my grandchildren, take me home. I can hardly see from traveling all day long." So they took him there. When Wenebojo got to where the old lady lived, it was getting late in the evening. Pretty soon they called him to go and doctor the kings. The kings were getting pretty sick. He went over there and doctored them. He didn't know which house the kings lived in. He went into the wrong place. Someone saw him going in there, and they showed him which way to go.

When he went into the house, he saw the two kings lying there. In the doorway of the king's house there was a wolf's skin hanging. That was the skin of Wenebojo's nephew. Wenebojo went in and sat on one side of the wigwam, and he looked at the door through which he'd come. On both sides of the door inside there were the heads of snakes sticking out. The snakes looked around at Wenebojo and thought that it didn't look much like the old lady that used to come there. They could hardly believe that it was the same person. They kept on watching her. The old lady spoke to them and said, "You'd better not keep watching me like that, because then I can't do much for these kings."

The old lady, Wenebojo, started to doctor the kings then. He took his rattle and sang that song the old lady had taught him:

> Wenebojo ho, the notch of the arrow.
> Wenebojo ho, the notch of the arrow.
> I try to suck it out with my mouth.
> I try to suck it out with my mouth.

When he got ready to start, Wenebojo crawled over to where the kings were lying, and saw his arrows sticking out just a little bit from their bodies. When he got there, he took one of the arrows in his mouth and moved it around and then shoved it further back into the king's body. He killed him that way. After he'd killed the first king, he went over to the next one and did the same thing. Then he got up and started to run out of the king's house. As he was running, Wenebojo ducked under the basswood string that was stretched across his path. In a little while he saw another basswood string. He went under that one too. Pretty soon he saw a lot of that basswood on all sides. He just broke it and kept running on as fast as he could go. As he was running, he heard a voice saying, "That's where Wenebojo is! That basswood is moving." Wenebojo broke through all the basswood strings and ran as fast as he could go.[22]

22. *Deluge.* As he was running, he heard a big noise coming behind him. He knew just what it was that was coming. It was the water that was coming. He looked around for a big high hill. He found one. He ran to the top of a hill where a big pine tree was standing. That's where Wenebojo stopped. In a short time the water got up to the top of the hill. When he saw the water coming that high, he climbed right up to the top of the tall pine tree. He said to the tree, "Brother, stretch yourself to twice the length you are now." The tree did that. Then he climbed some more. This tree stretched four times. That's how long it was. Then the tree told Wenebojo that he couldn't do any more for him. That was as high as he could go. But then the water stopped. Wenebojo was standing on the top of the tree. He had his head back, and the water was up to his mouth. Pretty soon Wenebojo felt that he wanted to defecate. He couldn't hold it. The shit floated up to the top of the water and floated around his mouth.[23]

23. *Earth-Diver.* After a while Wenebojo noticed that there was an animal in the water. This animal was playing around. Wenebojo couldn't see the animal, but he knew that it was there. He tried to look around. Then he saw several animals — beaver, muskrat, and otter. Wenebojo spoke to the otter first. "Brother," he said, "could you go down and get some earth? If you do that, I will make an earth for you and me to live on."

22. These episodes incorporate the motifs of *Sham doctor kills his patients* (K824) and *Disguised flayer* (K1941), both of which have wide distributions in the Plains and Central Woodlands.

23. A deluge (A1010) caused by the hero's revenge for the death of the wolf is found in the folklore of the following Algonkian speaking tribes: Cree, Ottawa, Canadian Ojibwa, Fox, Sauk, and Menomini. Deluge myths are among the world's most widespread folklore themes and are found in all the aboriginal North American culture areas. *Pursuit by water* (D1432) is another theme in this section, found also in the other Algonkian versions.

The otter said to Wenebojo, "I will try. Maybe I can't."

Away he went, down to the bottom of the water. But the otter didn't get halfway to the bottom. He drowned. Then he floated up to the top. Wenebojo tried to reach the otter. He got hold of him finally and looked into the otter's paws and mouth, but he didn't find any dirt. Then Wenebojo blew on the otter, and the otter came to again. Wenebojo asked him, "Did you see anything?"

"No," said the otter.

The next person Wenebojo spoke to was the beaver. He asked him to go after some earth down below and said, "If you do, I'll make an earth for us to live on."

The beaver said, "I'll try," and went down. The beaver was gone a long time. Pretty soon he floated to the top of the water. He also drowned. Wenebojo got hold of the beaver and blew on him. When he came to, Wenebojo examined his paws and mouth to see if there was any dirt there, but he couldn't find anything. He asked the beaver, "Did you see any earth at the bottom?"

"Yes, I did," said the beaver. "I saw it, but I couldn't get any of it."

These animals had tried and failed.

The muskrat was playing around there too. Wenebojo didn't think much about that muskrat, since he was so small; but after a while he said to him, "Why don't you try and go after some of that dirt too?"

The muskrat said, "I'll try," and he dived down.

Wenebojo waited and waited a long time for the muskrat to come up to the top of the water. When he floated up to the top, he was all crippled. Wenebojo caught the muskrat and looked him over. The muskrat had his paws closed up tight. His mouth was shut too. Wenebojo opened the muskrat's front paw and found a grain of earth in it. He took it. In his other front paw he found another little grain, and one grain of dirt in each of his hind paws. There was another grain in his mouth.

When he'd found these five grains, Wenebojo started to blow on the muskrat, blew on him until he came back to life. Then Wenebojo took the grains of sand in the palm of his hand and held them up to the sun to dry them out. When it was all dry, he threw it around onto the water. There was a little island then. They went onto that little island — Wenebojo, the beaver, the otter, and the muskrat. Wenebojo got more earth on the island and threw it all around. The island got bigger. It got larger every time Wenebojo threw out another handful of dirt. The animals at the bottom of the water, whoever was there, all came up to the top of the water and went to the island where Wenebojo was. They were tired of being in the water all that time, and when they heard about the earth that Wenebojo had made, they all wanted to stay there. Wenebojo kept on throwing earth around.[24]

24. *Testing of Earth's Size.* One time, I don't know when, Wenebojo spoke to the *adík*. The *adík* [caribou] is like the moose and the elk, but he runs faster than the others and lives somewhere up north. I've never seen any of them. They've never been in this region. Wenebojo knew that the *adík* could run fast, so he asked him to find out how big the earth was that he had made. This animal did as he was told and went out to look it over. He didn't stay long and came back soon. When the *adík* came back, he told Wenebojo that the earth wasn't big enough to live on yet. It would be too small for whoever wanted to live there.

Wenebojo started to throw more earth around. He threw it here, there, and everywhere, near and far, as far as he could throw it. When he'd thrown enough around, he called the *adík* to see how big the earth was. He sent him out and waited for him. But that animal never came back. He was so tired that he stayed where he is today. His home is in the north.

Wenebojo forgot all about the things that the *manidog* had done to him. He forgot that they had made him angry. After he got tired of waiting for the *adík* to come back, he went away. Wenebojo traveled here and there in every direction, and traveled and traveled and traveled. He didn't know which way he was going. He was just traveling. One day he came to a lake. It was very pretty there, all beach. He couldn't see across the lake. There was nothing but water. Wenebojo saw the water there that they had meant to drown him in. Wenebojo stayed there and played around in the sand. After a while, he went along the edge of the lake, along the beach, and walked toward the south. How glad he was that he was traveling! He forgot that the *manidog* had ever made him angry. He played around some more in the sand by the edge of the lake. I don't know what he used to make it, but he made a pack full of sand; then he made some more. When he was finished making them, he left them here and there. He kept making packs of sand and left the bundles here and there along the beach. That's how that beach looks to-day. People can see it today. That's Wenebojo's work. The place is called *kawapíkwadawangàg.* I don't know what the White people call it. The Indian name means "pile of sand by the beach." I don't know where this place is.

24. The *Earth-Diver* theme (A812) of the creator who sends animals down to the bottom of the waters to bring back soil for the creation of the earth is another widespread theme. One animal succeeds, usually the muskrat, as in our myth. Köngas reports that "Earth-Diver occurs not only in Native North America and in part of native South America, but also in the Pacific Islands, Australia, and in Eastern Europe" (1960, p. 151). For the distribution of this tale in North America, see Map 2.

When Wenebojo got tired of playing there, he went on toward the South. At the North of where we are now there is an ocean [Lake Superior]. On the edge of this ocean you can still see the marks of it. Wenebojo went along this ocean, keeping toward the South. I don't know how far he went, but he went past the sun that goes down over the horizon. He played along by the ocean.[25]

25. *Wenebojo Becomes Depressed and Threatens All the Spirits.* One day, when he was walking along by the ocean, he happened to remember the time when those *manidog* made him angry. Then Wenebojo just sat down by the beach with his feet nearly in the water, and he hollered and cried. He sat there crying, remembering the *manidog* who made him angry, and thought of what he would like to do to those *manidog*. He spoke to the earth and said, "Whoever is underneath the earth down there, I will pull them out and bring them up on top here. I can play with them and do whatever I want with them, because I own this earth where I am now."

The Indians say that this earth has four layers. The bottom layer does not look like the one we are in now. It is night there all the time. That is where the *manido* is who is the boss that rules the bottom of the earth. He rules all four layers. There is no special name for him or for the different layers.

When Wenebojo spoke that time, the *manido*, the boss, heard him. Wenebojo spoke again. This time he spoke to the sky: "Whoever is up there, those *manidog* up there, I will get them and pull them down. I will play with them here and do just as I please with them. I will even knock down the sky." Then Wenebojo took a deep breath, and the earth shrank up. When he sniffed from crying, the sky made a loud noise like the cracking of ice.

26. *The Spirits Try to Appease Wenebojo.* The sky has four layers too. In the top layer of the sky there was a *manido* who is equal in power to the *manido* at the bottom of the earth. It is always day there. It is never night. This *manido* has no name, but you can call him *Gičimánido* [Great Spirit]. There is no name for the top layer. We're right in the middle in between the four earth layers and the four sky layers.

The first *manido* at the bottom of the earth spoke to his runner [*škabéwis*], and told him to go and ask the *Gičimánido* if he had heard what Wenebojo had said. He went there. He asked the great spirit if he'd heard what Wenebojo had said.

Gičimánido said, "Yes, I heard him. He will do just what he said. I told you never to make him angry in any way."

25. The testing of the earth's size is an Ottawa and Cree motif as well as Chippewa.

The runner went back to the *manido* who had sent him and said, "The *manido* says that Wenebojo will do just as he said."

Wenebojo thought to himself, "When I get up, I'm going to do what I said I'd do."

Those *manidog* had no right to this earth that we are living on. Wenebojo owned this earth. The *manido* of the last layer of the earth had no right to this earth that we are living on. The only world that he owned was the old country, the earth that Wenebojo had lived on before. I don't know what layer Wenebojo lived on then; one of the bottom ones, I suppose.

The *manido* from the last layer of the earth in the middle of the old world came up to the old country. After he got to the old country, he spoke to the *Gičimánido*, asking him to come down to where he was. *Gičimánido* took his runner with him, so that there were two *manidog* and two runners — four of them — down there. The *manido* from the bottom spoke to *Gičimánido* and asked him, "Are you willing to give Wenebojo what we are going to give him?"

Gičimánido said, "Yes, I am willing to give Wenebojo this thing, if he is willing to accept it."

The *manido* from the bottom said, "We will call him then."

Gičimánido said, "We will call him if he is willing to come, and if he will listen to us."

The two *manidog* were in a hurry. They didn't know when Wenebojo might get up and start to do what he had said he was going to do. They sent one of the runners to go and get Wenebojo where he was sitting; and this runner said to Wenebojo, "Your grandfathers want you to come." Wenebojo didn't even move his head or his eyes or anything. He just sat there. All of the *manidog* were afraid that if Wenebojo got up, he would do just what he said he'd do. They sent everybody that they could get hold of, but still Wenebojo wouldn't listen to any of them. After all of these people had tried and failed, all of the *manidog* were very scared. They got to talking. Who would Wenebojo listen to? They looked around for somebody.

Somewhere up in the North, where the ocean is, there is an animal that is called an otter. He is white; he isn't the kind of otter that's around here. He's a white otter. He has no arms — just little parts like wings [flippers?]. I've seen them in the museum in Milwaukee, but not white ones. I haven't seen any around here. We call them *misá·kik* [seal?].

The *manidog* looked around and saw the *misá·kik* playing around in the water. Then they sent the runner to him. He went and brought the *misá·kik* back with him to where the *manidog* were waiting. The two *manidog* talked to the white otter. They told him that everyone whom they'd sent to Wenebojo had failed. The otter spoke and said, "I will bring him. He will listen to me." So the otter went to look for Wenebojo.

The otter hollered, and the echo of his voice was heard in the sky. Where Wenebojo was sitting, he heard someone. He didn't know who it was. When the otter came to the middle of the ocean he hollered again. The otter came up to the top of a hill and hollered again. Then he went into the other ocean. There's another ocean there. He went into the water; and when he was half way across the ocean, the otter hollered again. Wenebojo was sitting on the shore of that ocean. That otter hollered again. The water made a sound just like the sound that the otter made. Wenebojo looked in the direction where that sound was coming from and wondered who it was. He couldn't see the otter. A long time later he heard a sound like a waterfall. After a while he finally saw the otter coming. He didn't recognize him until he came close up to him. When the otter came close by, Wenebojo looked at him, and he saw that he was all white, and his eyes were black. The otter spoke to Wenebojo and said, "*Nitáowis* [my cousin], I have come after you. Your grandfathers want you to come."

Wenebojo answered, "Huh! You shouldn't do what they tell you. I suppose that's why they sent you to come and get me, because they know that you and I are related to each other. Well, all right, I will go with you. But I was going to do what I said I would do."[26]

27. *The Spirits Give Wenebojo Some Parents and Establish the Medicine Dance.* The otter took him to where the two *manidog* were waiting. When they got there, the *manidog* pointed to the place where Wenebojo should sit. When he had sat down where they told him to sit, the *manido* from the bottom of the earth spoke to Wenebojo. He said, "You will see what we are going to give you, and if you will accept it, this is what your parents, the people who come after you will do."

Wenebojo had no mother or father.

Wenebojo just sat there and didn't say anything. The *manido* from the bottom spoke to Wenebojo. He built up some clay the size of a human being in length and about one foot high, and placed it in front of him. After he had done that, he placed a shell (*mígis*) on top of the earth-heap. After he had done that, he took his rattle and shook it. Then he talked and shook his rattle as he talked. At one point he stopped shaking his rattle, and the heap of clay in front of him began to take the form of a person. He shook his rattle some more, and kept on talking. When he stopped

26. In a Canadian Ojibwa version recorded in 1885, it is a white otter which brings the trickster to the council meeting. See Chamberlain (1891, p. 200). The Potawatomi and Sauk also have the hero reconciled by the spirits' gift of the medicine rites. The idea of different layers of earth and sky or hierarchy of worlds (A651) has a wide distribution.

again, you could see that it was a person there. Wenebojo sat there and looked at what the *manido* had done. Then the *manido* shook his rattle some more and kept on talking. When he stopped this time, the person was breathing. He started shaking his rattle and talked some more. Then he stopped. The person — it was an Indian — got up to a sitting position. They saw that it was a woman.

The *manido* from the bottom of the earth stopped shaking his rattle and talking then. He spoke to the *Gičimánido* and said, "Now it's your turn to make the thing that we are going to give to Wenebojo." *Gičimánido* started to do the same thing. He heaped up some clay, made it like a figure, and placed the shell on top. Then *Gičimánido* took the last rib of the woman and put it into the clay figure. Then he started to shake his rattle and talk. Finally he stopped. It looked still more like a person. Then he shook his rattle and talked again. When he stopped, the person was breathing. He started shaking his rattle and talking again. When he stopped, the person got up from there. It was a man.

Now there was a pair of them, a man and a woman. Then the *manido* from the bottom of the earth spoke to Wenebojo and said, "You see what we have done. This is the thing we are going to give you, if you will take it." These people that the *manidog* had created, they were the ones that Wenebojo was going to call his parents. They were not really his parents, but he was going to call them that. They looked the way Wenebojo's parents had looked — the Sun and that woman. They had no names. Wenebojo didn't call his parents "mother" and "father." He called them "my uncle" and "my aunt"; but when he spoke of both of them together, he said "my parents."[27]

Then the *manidog* started to talk to Wenebojo. They told him all about the *Midewiwin* [the Medicine Dance]. They said, "This is what the Indians will do." Then they told him all about it. All of the *manidog* in existence were there then; I don't know how many of them.

Those first people, the ones that the *manidog* created then, were made hard, like a shell. They were meant to live forever. They would live for a hundred years; then go into a trance for four days, and then go on for another hundred years. This was decided on by the council of the *manidog*. They all agreed to it. All of the *manidog* from all over the

27. It is puzzling that Wenebojo's "parents" are referred to as his uncles and aunts. If the Chippewa had formerly had an Omaha kinship system, or if they acquired this part of the myth from a tribe that did, this section would make more sense. Writing about Siouan-speaking tribes, including the Omaha, J. Owen Dorsey (1892, p. 293) states that the trickster is always spoken of as living with his grandmother, Earth Woman, the mother of the Indian race. Indian females are her daughters and Trickster's mothers; males are her sons and Trickster's uncles. In the Omaha kinship system, male members of Ego's mother's patrilineal lineage are called by a term equivalent to "mother's brother," while female members are called "mother."

universe were there. They were all invited except for one —
Nekajíwegìžik, Wenebojo's brother, who was way down in the bottom of
the earth somewhere.

This is where *Gičimánido* made his mistake. He should have seen to
it that *Nekajíwegìžik* was present at the council too. Although
Nekajíwegìžik wasn't there, he could hear everything that was going
on. He said, "It's no use to make your plans that way. I've already
made that road [to the other world], and everyone who lives on the
earth will have to follow that road."

Nothing could be done about it. Man had to die, in spite of what
the *manidog* decided. That was where God made his mistake — in not
inviting Wenebojo's brother to the council.

It's only Indians who follow his trail to the other world. White men
have some other kind of trail. I don't know what it's like, but maybe
it's a ladder. There are different roads, but all men go to the other
world after death. You can do whatever you want there; you can
travel to a place as fast as you think about it; and you can be
whatever age you want. If you want to, you can come back to earth
and help the people here. Indians are helping our boys overseas right
now. That's why only two Indians from here have died in this war. It
takes four days for Indians to reach the other world. After that they
have no more troubles.

Wenebojo is still alive and can hear what we're saying right now.
He's probably laughing when he thinks about how he lived when he
was young and about all the foolish things he did. But Wenebojo can't
read our thoughts. Only God can do that.

This story I've told you can be told whenever anybody asks for it —
anybody who belongs to the *Midewiwin*. Part of it is told when
someone is going to join the *Midewiwin* and they tell part of it when
they're giving a mourning bowl to someone. When you're going to
join, you hear the story up to where Wenebojo is sitting by the shores
of the water, thinking about what the *manidog* did to him. The last
part of the story is told to people who have lost a husband or wife or
daughter. They tell it to them to take their minds off their troubles.

Comments

It is evident that many of the episodes and themes of the Lac du
Flambeau Wenebojo myth appear in the folklore of many North
American Indian tribes. Most of the parallels seem to be among adja-
cent Algonkian-speaking tribes: the Cree and Canadian Ojibwa,
Central Woodland tribes such as the Fox, Potawatomi, and Menomini,
Northeastern Algonkians such as Micmac and Passamaquoddy, and

Plains tribes such as the Cheyenne, Arapaho, and Gros Ventre. But the stories cross the barriers of both language and culture area. The Siouan-speaking Winnebago tell many of the same tales in their trickster cycle; the Crow of the Plains tell some of them. Some episodes even appear in California. But one can go still farther afield and find similar themes in the Old World, such as Earth-Diver tales.

The parallels which link the Algonkian-speaking tribes of the Eastern Woodlands and Plains could be accounted for by the migrations of tribes like the Cheyenne and Arapaho from the Woodlands to the Plains, perhaps retaining their folklore traditions. Or they could be due to more recent trade relations or other contacts between Woodland and Plains tribes. The crossing of language barriers could be explained by the exchange of women in peacemaking arrangements between former enemies or by the capture of persons in warfare and the adoption of women or captured children. Still another conceivable explanation is that some of the stories are old enough to have antedated linguistic differentiation between formerly linked groups.

The following Wenebojo story was told separately by Tom Badger on a different occasion, not as part of the origin myth. So, brief as it is, I have numbered it as a separate tale rather than as an episode of the origin myth.

2. Wenebojo and the Cranberries

Collected by Victor Barnouw at Lac du Flambeau in 1944
Narrator: Tom Badger   Interpreter: Maggie Christensen

As Wenebojo was traveling one day, he went along the edge of a lake and saw some highbush cranberries lying in the bottom of the shallow water. He tried to fish them out time and time again, but every time he tried, they just stayed on the bottom. Well, he finally gave up. But he tried to grab them with his mouth by sticking his head in the water. Then he dove down into the water. The little rocks in the bottom hurt his face. While he was holding his face, Wenebojo happened to look up and saw the berries hanging up there. But he was so angry that he just tore the berries off the tree and wouldn't eat any, and he walked away.

Comments

This story of oral frustration is given by E. R. Young in his collection of Algonquin tales and also by Radin in the Winnebago trickster cycle, although in the Winnebago version the cranberries are replaced by plums. The story was also told by the Cheyenne, with plums being the reflected fruit.[28] Stories of *Diving for reflected fruit* (J1791.11) have a very wide distribution in the Plateau region, North Pacific Coast, Plains, Central Woodlands, Northeastern Woodlands, the Southeast, and Southwest.

The same general theme is also found in the Old World, although it is not clear whether the parallels are due to independent invention or diffusion from Europe. In one European version a wolf sees the reflection of the moon in the water. Thinking it to be a cheese, he dives in and drowns (Thompson, 1919, p. 438).

General Comments on the Lac du Flambeau Wenebojo Myth

One's first impression of the Wenebojo origin myth presented in this chapter is that it is made up of a disconnected series of unrelated episodes; but after some examination it seems that there is, after all, not only some relationship between the first episode and the last but also ties between some of the intervening episodes. In the opening episode Wenebojo is conceived; at the end he is given a set of "parents" — apparently the greatest gift which the spirits can bestow. In between the first and last episodes Wenebojo is usually an isolated wandering figure. But there are also some social interludes. Wenebojo's life with the beavers is both communal and sedentary. Later he lives with the nomadic wolves, and on this occasion there is a reversal of an earlier theme. In episodes 3 and 4 Wenebojo is annoyed at being held up by his brothers, who are either immobile or slower than himself. But when he is with the wolves, Wenebojo is slower than they. The wolves, however, are tolerant of this failing, while Wenebojo was not.

In episode 17 Wenebojo not only lives with another person, the wolf "nephew," but is dependent on him for food — a unique situation in this series. The murder of his nephew by the underwater spirits echoes Wenebojo's murder of his own brother. He was not unhappy about his own murders, but he becomes very unhappy at being deprived of the wolf on whom he had become dependent. The wolf is a younger brother of Wenebojo in some Menomini and Sauk versions, which would make the reversal more pointed. One might say that when Wenebojo lives with the wolves, he experiences a reversal of roles and

28. Young (1903, p. 243); Radin (1956, p. 28); Grinnell (1926, pp. 282–83).

learns what it is to be slower than others and to be deprived of a needed ally.

It may be noted that each social episode — when Wenebojo is living with others — ends with a death. In episodes 3 and 4 Wenebojo is responsible for the deaths of his brothers. Then he is alone and happy. In episode 7 Wenebojo is himself killed, but revives. In episode 17 the spirits kill his nephew. Then Wenebojo is unhappy. To remedy this, in episode 27, he is given a set of "parents," and is instructed about the Midewiwin.

The Chippewa origin myth seems to make the point that it is difficult to live with others; then one becomes tied down to people who are slower than oneself. In episode 2 there is an implicit regret that children take so long to mature and reach independence, whereas animals can walk shortly after birth. There may be some pleasure in being dependent on others, as Wenebojo is with his wolf nephew, but loss of the source of such gratification brings dismay and unhappiness.

There is no mention of clans in this origin myth and little reference to communal living except among beavers and wolves. There is also little reference to women. This is a man's world. After the opening sections, no female characters appear in the narrative except for the old woman who is going to doctor the two kings and the first woman created by the spirit from the bottom of the earth at the end of the narrative. In this particular myth Wenebojo never marries, although he is married in some other versions. Wenebojo seems to be happiest when he is completely alone (episodes 4, 23).

Animals in the Myth

Since this tale, told in connection with the Medicine Dance, is evidently conservative and probably very old, it is of interest to see what animals are mentioned in the course of the narrative. One might assume that the animals most depended upon for food would be mentioned in such a myth.

The conservative nature of our Chippewa myth is indicated by the mention of the caribou. There is only one other reference to caribou in our collection of tales. Caribou have long been extinct in northern Wisconsin. Tom Badger did not know the English word for caribou but used the Chippewa term *adík*. He said, "The *adík* is like the moose and elk, but he runs faster than the others and lives somewhere up north. I've never seen one of them. They've never been in this region."

Another reference to a northern animal is the *misá·kik* (in episode 26), which Tom Badger called a white otter.

The moose is also referred to. The last moose was killed in Wisconsin around 1921. There are only two other references to moose in our collection. Moose are more prominent in William Jones's two-volume compilation of tales from north of Lake Superior, in which moose figure in 11 of the 141 stories. Only the bear is mentioned more often — in 14 of Jones's tales.

The moose seems to have been an important source of food for the northern Algonkian Indians: " — moose frequent stream and lake margins — exactly the location of the bulk of the fur animals. Beaver, mink, and otter, the most important fur animals, live either in or on the margins of streams and ponds. Moose hunting is carried on parallel to and in conjunction with trapping without the necessity of any important displacement or modification in either" (Rolf Knight, 1965, p. 40).

An important episode in the Wenebojo cycle is the death of Wenebojo's wolf nephew, who is killed by the underwater spirits while he is hunting game for Wenebojo. In a version collected by Radin and Reagan from Nett Lake, Minnesota, the animal being chased by the wolf is a moose (1928, p. 72). This is also the case in a version cited by Kinietz (1947, p. 183) from Michigan and in the Blackfoot myth given by Grinnell (1892, p. 150). But in our Wisconsin version the animal is a deer.[29] The distribution suggests that the deer version is later than that of the moose and represents a substitution.

Both moose and caribou figured prominently in Chippewa diet during the early contact period. Writing about 1804, Peter Grant remarked that moose was their "staff of life" (1890, p. 341). But between 1810 and 1820 moose and caribou were much reduced in parts of Canada such as northwestern Ontario, although moose later returned to some extent (see Bishop, 1970, 1974).

Deer are mentioned in 5 of our 48 stories (not counting the tales of European or mixed origin), but in only 3 of Jones's larger collection. It seems likely that as the Chippewa moved down into Wisconsin, beginning in the seventeenth century, moose became less important and deer more so. It has been reported that deer were rarely seen on

29. In another version of the Wenebojo origin myth, story number 3, given below, collected by Joseph B. Casagrande, the animal in question is also a deer. However, in a previously published version of this narrative, the Ritzenthalers (1970, p. 142) have changed the species to moose, perhaps because that is the more widespread pattern.

the north shore of Lake Superior in 1870, although they have become more numerous there since then. They were also rare in the northern third of Wisconsin, north of Chippewa Falls. Until the 1880s this area was covered by hardwood and evergreen forests, which are not favored environments for deer. Deer are found more on the edges of forests, marshes, or swamps. Deep snow and timber wolves were among the hazards affecting deer in Wisconsin. Deer were, however, abundant in the southern part of the state. They became more numerous in the north only after the lumber companies began cutting down the forests (see Swift, 1946, pp. 5-25). The Chippewa settlements of Court Oreilles and Lac du Flambeau were in the heart of the forests and hence were not in an optimum hunting area. However, deer were more accessible than moose or caribou and play a correspondingly larger role in the folklore in Wisconsin, in contrast to the folklore of the Canadian Chippewa or Ojibwa.

Timber wolves have a prominent place in our origin myth. Although they are generally described as behaving in human rather than animal fashion, episode 15 suggests a hunter's close observation of wolf behavior; for wolves regurgitate food for their young (see Fox, 1971, p. 170).[30] Chippewa knowledge of this practice is explicitly stated in another version of this story given in the following chapter. The tale thus allows for an identification with an immature wolf cub who is provided with abundant food. It may be noted, too, that wolf packs sometimes accept a lone wolf (see Mech, 1966, p. 64). Conceivably, the episode of Wenebojo's acceptance might also be seen as stemming from observation of wolf behavior. But if so, it is curious that Wenebojo's wolf pack contains no females; that is not a usual feature of wolf packs, but it is in keeping with the male focus of our narrative.

Wenebojo's relationship with his wolf nephew is the closest emotional bond he has in the myth cycle. Choice of the wolf for this role may have been influenced by the fact that wolves and men have much in common, being nomadic creatures who move in groups and hunt the same animals, such as moose and deer. Even in Europe, where there seems to have been more fear of wolves, there was some identification with them in the tradition of werewolves, or lycanthropy, the notion that some men were able to assume the shape of wolves. In our Chippewa tales, wolves do not usually play the evil, demonic role that they do in Europe (as in Little Red Riding Hood, and "Who's

30. For similar behavior in related species, see van Lawick-Goodall (1971, pp. 50, 67, 75, 84, 95, 98, 118–19, 142).

Afraid of the Big, Bad Wolf?"). On the contrary, in the story of
Wakayabide in chapter 6, a wolf is the hero's guardian spirit, who
brings him back to life.

Other animals and birds mentioned in our origin myth are otter,
beaver, muskrat, fox, snake, owl, goose, hell-diver, loon, and
kingfisher. The number of animals mentioned suggests the importance
of hunting in Chippewa life. There is no reference to corn, beans,
squash, or wild rice.

The Role of Wenebojo

Wenebojo seems to be neither a human being nor a god, but
something of both. In a cross-cultural examination of the North
American trickster, Ricketts has observed: "Generally speaking, the
more strongly the tribe has been influenced by an agricultural way of
life, the less important is the place of the trickster-figure in the total
mythology of the tribe, and the more he tends to be known only as a
trickster" (1966, p. 328). This points to his archaic nature, related to
a hunting-gathering way of life. Our own version is in the archaic
hunting-gathering tradition.

In our origin myth the trickster assumes many forms in the course
of the story — a beaver (episode 7), a tree stump (episode 18), a snake
(episode 10), and an old lady (episode 20). These episodes exemplify a
pattern which recurs, as will be seen, in many of the stories that
follow: the deceptive nature of visible forms and the readiness of
human-animal transformations. Another such pattern is the reversibility of life and death, illustrated by Wenebojo's return to life after
the Indians kill him in episode 7. A third recurring pattern is the
presence of a hierarchy of power. Some people and beings have more
power than others. In Wenebojo's case, his status seems to be
vacillating. He creates the world we live on (episode 23) and thus is
something of a god; but he is also a sort of crybaby in his tantrum
against the *manidog* (episodes 25, 26), who appease him by giving
him a set of parents. He has enough power to kill the two underwater
kings (episode 21). Although he creates the world we live on and is
thus higher than human beings, Wenebojo is a lesser being than the
manidog, especially *Gičimánido* and the *manido* at the bottom of the
earth. Thus he seems to fall into Lévi-Strauss's category of mediators
between men and gods. The things he creates, besides the earth, are
limited. Wenebojo creates only elm-tree food for his aunts (episode 8)
and tobacco for his uncles (episode 13), and he discovers a laxative
(episode 6); it is the *manido* from the bottom of the earth who creates

the first woman, while *Gičimánido* creates the first man, and the *manidog* tell Wenebojo about the Medicine Dance (episode 27). Writing about 1804, Peter Grant noted that the trickster-hero is never prayed to or given offerings (1890, pp. 353-61). This is not surprising, considering what a buffoonish and often ridiculous character he is. On the other hand, Alanson Skinner, in writing about the eastern Cree, neighbors of the northern Chippewa with a similar culture, noted that the trickster stories "are not told for the sake of their humor, and his role of benefactor is never forgotten" (1911, p. 82).

Since myths may be, in part, cautionary tales, the appearance of certain motifs may indicate tabooed behavior. Wenebojo's actions are not to be taken as models for imitation; instead, they often indicate what should be avoided. C. G. Jung expressed this in a different way when he suggested that the trickster was a representation of the Shadow, a term Jung used for negative outgrown aspects of the self which have come to be rejected by the ego. The creation of such a Shadow figure in mythology implies that the Indian mythmaker had advanced beyond the psychological level represented by the Shadow. "Only when his consciousness reached a higher level could he detach the earlier state from himself and objectify it, that is, saying anything about it. So long as his consciousness was itself trickster-like, such a confrontation could obviously not take place" (1956, p. 202).

Géza Roheim considered the trickster to be a representation of the id or the life principle. Roheim claimed that the North American Indians were deeply disciplined persons with a strong superego, resulting from strict childhood training. The trickster thus represents a kind of protest against the restrictions of the superego (1952, pp. 190-94). This view is not incompatible with Jung's.

Oral Themes

Reference to the mouth or to food and tobacco appear in various episodes: berries in 1, game in 3, "mourning dish" in 4, the tempting strawberry and the roots in 5, chewing the physic grass in 6, feces around the mouth in 6 and 22, transformation of intestines into food in 8, moose meat in 9 and 10, duck dinner in 12 and 13, creation of tobacco in 14, eating of vomited food in 15, chewing bones for grease in 16, kissing beads in 17, sucking cure in 20 and 21.

Oral frustration is a motif in some of these themes. For instance, after Wenebojo kills the moose in episode 9, he does not manage to eat the much anticipated food. Exactly the same thing happens in the ensuing episode with the ducks (episodes 12, 13). In both cases the food is all ready to eat, but somebody else enjoys the dinner. This may be seen as either punishment for Wenebojo's trickery and aggression or punishment for his stinginess and greed. He attempts to eat an enormous meal all by himself — the moose or the collection of birds. In both cases the food is eaten by a *group* — the wolves or the South Wind men.

Oral frustration is also hinted at in the symbol of the tempting strawberry which has to be avoided (episode 5). Feces around the mouth are referred to in episodes 6 and 22.

Anal Themes

Anal themes appear in episodes 6, 8, 13, 14, and 22, often in conjunction with oral motifs. In episodes 6 and 22 feces come up to Wenebojo's mouth. Tobacco, the Indians' sacred link with the supernatural realm, has its origin in the bloody scabs from Wenebojo's rectum (episode 14). Thinking of his uncles, Wenebojo says, "They will smoke these, and they will be sweet." Products of the anal region are labeled "sweet" in episode 8, when Wenebojo pulls in his intestines and throws them over a tree, for the benefit of his future aunts.

A striking episode in our myth is Wenebojo's punishment of his rear end after he finds that the cooked birds have been eaten. In another version of this story, recorded by William Jones, this self-punishment takes on the aspect of self-castration, since it is stated that he was bloody at the testes. In one Chippewa story Wenebojo pushes a burning stick into his grandfather's buttocks, while the old man is having intercourse with Wenebojo's grandmother. In still another story Wenebojo kills a *windigo* giant by telling a weasel to run up into its anus (see Jones, 1917, 1919, pt. 1, pp. 177, 201, 453). In de Jong's collection of Chippewa tales from Minnesota, Wenebojo gets a weasel to kill a bear by going up into its anus (1913, p. 17).

These stories express the vulnerability of the rectum, its susceptibility to penetration and attack. One story, however, depicts it as a source of power. In one of Jones's tales Wenebojo is given power by a skunk to destroy things by breaking wind at them, but he is warned that he may use this power only twice. Wenebojo experiments by breaking wind at a big tree and a great rock, destroying both. When he tries to kill a moose, he can't do so. But the story ends happily. Wenebojo goes back to the skunk, who breaks wind into him to restore the power, and after that Wenebojo is able to kill many moose

(1917, 1919, pt. 1, pp. 321-31). Here we see aggressive potentialities attributed to the anus, just as speech is attributed to it in episode 13.

Jones presents a story about Wenebojo traveling with his grandmother, in which, once again, links are made between the oral and anal regions. The grandmother wants to defecate. "Do it there," he says, as they are traveling along a path. Then she wants to wipe her anus. "Wipe it with your elbows," he says. Then she wants to clean her elbows. "Lick it with your tongue." Then she wants to spit. "Swallow it!" says Wenebojo (1917, 1919, pt. 1, p. 447). In still another of Jones's stories Wenebojo is defecated on by all the people in a town; " . . . he became engulfed so deep in the dung that he had to purse his lips" (ibid., p. 131).

Alan Dundes has suggested that the Earth-Diver motif is a male fantasy of creation stemming from male envy of female pregnancy and an assumed cloacal theory of birth. In Dundes's view the mud from which the earth is formed is symbolic of feces (1962). This may seem an extravagant hypothesis, but it would be in keeping with the Chippewa myth with its exclusion of women and its striking anal themes.

The idea of creating people from feces occurs in some Chippewa tales. In the seventh story in our series Wenebojo creates some Indian warriors by defecating here and there and sticking feathers into the turds. The story "Dung-Warm Weather" in Jones's collection is about a chief's daughter who rejects all her suitors. These men, in revenge, defecate into a hole, make a human form from the dung, dress it up in fine clothes, and will that it become a human being. The dung man goes to the village, where the chief's daughter falls in love with him. He leaves, and the girl follows his tracks. She finally comes to a pile of dung, where the trail ends (1917, 1919, pt. 2, pp. 415 ff.). In both of these stories males create people by defecating, in line with Dundes's hypothesis.

Themes of Aggression

Themes of aggression are common in the origin myth. Murder is a common theme (episodes 3, 4, 7, 9, 12, 17, 20, 21), the victims being brothers in episodes 3 and 4. In episode 25 Wenebojo makes ominous threats against all the *manidog*. There are also masochistic themes. In episode 3 the stone gives Wenebojo advice on how to kill him; in episode 8 Wenebojo pulls out his own intestines; in episode 13 he roasts his rear end over the fire, and in 20 he chops off his own calf muscles. Concerning aggression and duplicity, there is an implication in these stories that crime does not pay. Wenebojo usually suffers punishment in the trickster episodes. In episode 7 he is killed, in 8 he loses his intestines, in 9 he does not eat the moose's meat, in 10 he gets his head caught in the moose's skull, in 12 he is pecked by the birds, in 13 he is cheated out of his dinner, in 16 he has to leave the wolves, and after the murder of the two kings in episode 21, he nearly drowns. The implicit notion of retribution existed in the old culture in relation to sorcery beliefs. There was the concept that sorcery power could boomerang upon the individual who resorted to it. Moreover, a person who presumed too much invited the attacks of others. Note the reason given for the murder of Wenebojo's nephew by the underwater spirits: "because if they had just let Wenebojo have his own way, there wouldn't have been any wild animals left." In other words, Wenebojo had been going too far and his nephew had become too successful a hunter. This is also expressed in a version of this story told to Ernestine Friedl at Court Oreilles in 1942 by Delia Oshogay, with Maggie Lamorie as interpreter: "Wenebojo knew that all his neighbors didn't like it very well that he always had meat that this wolf got for him. They were jealous of him." The same theme is expressed in a story recorded by William Jones: "Soaring-Eagle, do you know why your child was taken from you? Too many of the fishes have you slain. You have angered the Great Sturgeon. He is the one that has seized your child" (1917, 1919, pt. 1, p. 337).

Although hunting involves aggression against animals, some Chippewa conceptions tended to minimize the aggressive aspect of killing game. This was the notion that animals do not really mind being killed for food, provided that the hunter maintains proper attitudes toward them. After eating the animal, the Indian must drop the bones into a stream; then the animal will come back to life. His death is thus just a temporary interruption, so to speak. Hence the respectful speeches made to recently killed bears, apologizing for the necessity of killing them and asking the bear to return to be killed again.

This set of ideas is reflected in a Chippewa story about a man who married a beaver wife. One day, while looking at his sister-in-law, the man thinks, "I wish I could eat her." The man's in-laws can read his mind. An old man says, "Let him go ahead and eat her." So they kill the sister-in-law and cook her, and the man eats her. Then her bones are collected and thrown into the water, and she comes back to life again. After that the man often eats his in-laws, sometimes his mother-in-law and sometimes his brothers-in-law. In the same way, they let outside human beings eat them. Sometimes human beings say or do

things which annoy them, and then the beavers hide and do not let
themselves be killed. One time, after they had hidden, an old dog
came to look for them. The beavers asked him, "On what do they
feed you?" "Your livers," says the dog. "All right. Then bark at us."
So the dog barks, hunters come, find the beavers, and kill them (Jones,
1917, 1919, pt. 2, pp. 207-41).

In another Chippewa story a runaway boy is adopted by a bear,
who finally takes him back to his parents. As he leaves, before the boy
returns to his village, the bear says, "If at any time you are in need of
food, then do you call upon me. I will feed you." One day the boy an-
nounces, "My grandfather, I wish to eat. Do feed me!" The bear
comes swimming, the boy strikes him with a war club, and kills him.
After that, the boy can always get food that way (Jones, 1917, 1919,
pt. 2, pp. 271-79).

These Chippewa notions seem to minimize the aggressive, ex-
ploitative implications of hunting and impute a kind of reciprocal
relationship between human beings and animals. Related to this set of
ideas was a taboo on making fun of animals or laughing at them. One
might expect retaliation for such an insult.

Themes of Accepting and Rejecting Advice

A recurrent minor theme in our origin myth concerns the acceptance or rejection of advice. In episode 2 the mother of Wenebojo is
told by a voice to put her baby on the ground, but she does not obey.
If she had done so, the baby would have got up and walked. Hence
human beings must now take a long time to grow up. In episode 15
the wolf tells Wenebojo to pull a wolf's tooth from a tree. Wenebojo
ignores this advice. The wolf's tooth turns out to be an arrow, a
presumably valuable item. In episode 16 Wenebojo is warned not to
peek when one of the wolves makes tallow and grease. When he
violates this interdiction, the bone hits Wenebojo on the eye. In each
of these cases there is an implication that the advice should have been
heeded.

In episode 3 Wenebojo accepts his stone brother's advice on how to
kill him. In episode 4 Wenebojo's second brother accepts Wenebojo's
advice about his burial. In episode 9 the moose accepts Wenebojo's
advice about how to stand. The birds accept Wenebojo's advice about
dancing (episode 12). In episode 26 Wenebojo agrees to go to a
meeting of the spirits. Generally, when Wenebojo accepts the advice
of others, the outcome is all right for him, except when he takes the
bird's advice about the physic grass in episode 6. But when others ac-

cept Wenebojo's advice, the outcome is usually unfortunate for them, as one might expect of a trickster. The opposition between accepting and rejecting advice may be related to the opposition between living with others and living alone. Social life involves the giving and taking of advice, while independence is expressed in rejecting it.

Locality

Except for some brief allusions to the Lake Superior region in episode 24, there is no reference to specific places in this myth. The narrative reflects a wandering nomadic way of life. "Wenebojo traveled here and there in every direction and traveled and traveled and traveled. He didn't know which way he was going. He was just traveling." "The wolves had no place they could call home. They traveled just like Wenebojo did." This restless and rootless spirit is characteristic of the narrative.

A contrast may be made between societies like the Chippewa which have Earth-Diver origin stories and societies which have emergence myths of autochthonous origin, like the Trobriand Islanders. Malinowski (1926) pointed out that Trobriand clans were provided with a charter by their myths for a claim to land around their place of emergence. G. S. Kirk has noted a parallel in ancient Greek mythology and belief. "Somewhat similarly did the ancient Athenians claim to be autochthonous, always to have belonged to Attica, never to have migrated or been displaced" (1973, p. 256).

Map 1, based with modifications on a map by Wheeler-Voegelin and Moore, shows the distribution of tribes which have emergence myths (A1631, *Emergence of tribe from lower world*). Not surprisingly, they are often settled horticultural tribes of the south, east, and the Mississippi region; they are often matrilineal. Some hunting-gathering tribes are included, such as the Apache and the Cheyenne, and so are the Menomini, although in most respects Menomini folklore is like that of the Chippewa (see Wheeler-Voegelin and Moore, 1957, p. 68). Settled food-producing societies like the Hopi, which have emergence myths, often have many references to local geographical features, in contrast to the Chippewa.

Earth-Diver motifs seem to be more related to hunting-gathering societies in the New World. Map 2 shows the distribution of societies with Earth-Diver motifs, including such northerly groups as Hare, Dogrib, Kaska, Beaver, Carrier, Chipewyan, Sarsi, Cree, and Montagnais. Although they reach down to the southeast, Earth-Diver tales are found mainly in the north, among hunting-gathering societies. The

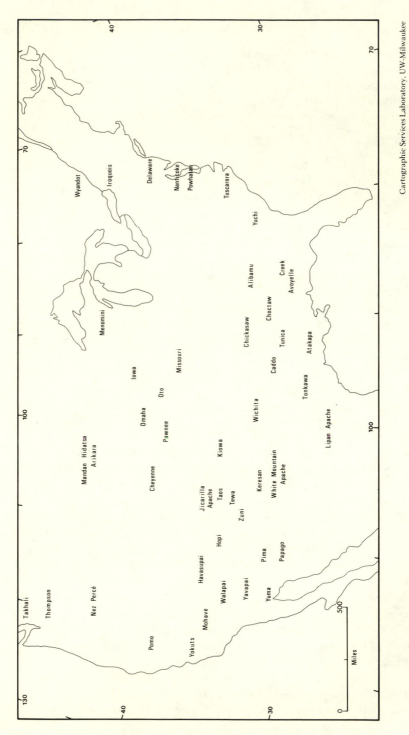

Map 1. Distribution of emergence myths in North America. Based, with modifications, on the map in Wheeler-Voegelin and Moore (1957, pp. 68-69). Many of the tribal locations are according to Map One 1B in Kroeber (1939, in back pocket).

Cartographic Services Laboratory, UW-Milwaukee

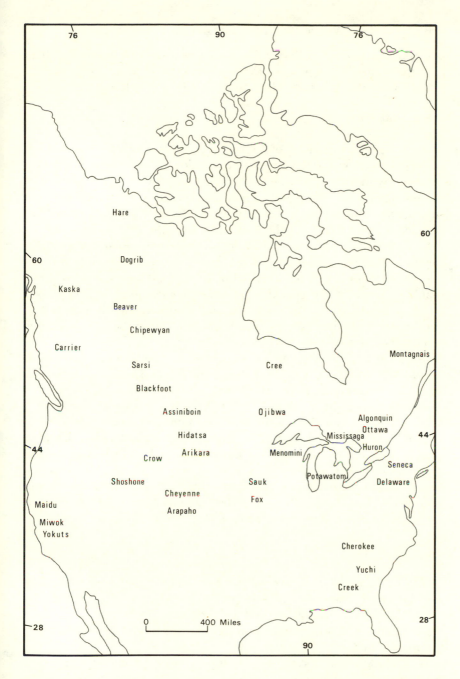

Map 2. Distribution of Earth-Diver myths in North America. The tribal locations are according to Map One 1B in Kroeber (1939, in back pocket).

distribution is quite different from that of the prevailingly southern emergence myths. Some societies have both types of origin myths: Creek, Yuchi, Cheyenne, Arikara, Menomini, Yokuts, and Delaware.

Structural Features

The origin myth consists of a series of episodes which are more or less independent. Some episodes have the following structure: (1) *an encounter*, with a deceptive ingratiating introduction ("My brother, I've been looking all over for you"); (2) *an act of aggression*; (3) *experience of misfortune*. This pattern occurs in the moose episode (9), the hoodwinked dancers (episode 12), and the encounter with the wolves (episodes 15, 16). Part of the same formula is followed in the episodes with the beaver (episode 7) and the fox (episode 8), but these lack acts of aggression.

The structural formula Interdiction/Violation/Consequence is applicable to some of the episodes, as when Wenebojo's mother hears a voice which tells her to put her baby on the ground, and she does not do so (episode 2). Wenebojo is warned not to peek when the wolf is making tallow, but he does (episode 16).

Another structural feature is expressed in the formula Lack/Lack liquidated. Wenebojo wants something and gets it. He wants to look like the beavers and to make a nice tinkling noise like the fox. These wishes are promptly gratified. Wenebojo's sulking fit (episode 25) expresses a lack which is liquidated by the *manidog's* gift of parents (episode 27). When Wenebojo's nephew is killed, he vows revenge (episode 17), and he finally kills the two underwater kings (episode 21). In this case more episodes intervene between the statement of a lack and its liquidation. Alan Dundes contends that American Indian tales usually have fewer intervening motifemes between the statement of a lack and its liquidation than do European folktales (1965, p. 212).

The Personality of the Narrator

Although, as we shall see in the next chapter, Wenebojo tales are similar in the accounts of different narrators, it is likely that individual personality factors affect the ways in which a myth is remembered and transmitted.[31] So a few words about the narrator are in order at this point.

Tom Badger was a reserved, intelligent, mild-mannered man in his seventies, whose biographical sketch is given in the appendix. In the

---

31. See, for example, Boyer (1964).

summer of 1944, I gave him a Rorschach Test and collected two Draw-a-Person drawings.[32] Dr. Werner Wolff made a "blind" interpretation of the drawings (that is, he had no other information about the subject), and he drew attention to the "stuttering" quality of the line, in which there were continuous interruptions. (It should be noted, however, that Tom Badger was illiterate and not accustomed to holding a pencil.) There was also an absence of pressure on the line. The man's head was drawn very large in relation to the rest of the body, and there was a strong emphasis on the mouth, while the arms were weakly depicted. Moreover, although Tom said that the man was naked, he was given no sexual organs. Dr. Wolff suggested that Tom Badger was probably a passive, dreamy person, with sexual inhibitions and that perhaps the frustration in the sexual sphere resulted in a transfer to the oral region.

In an analysis of Tom Badger's Rorschach record, Dr. Pauline Vorhaus remarked that there was evidence of emotional dependency and also some confusion about sex, since Tom's form level was good except for the sexual responses.

The two interpretations suggest the existence of repression, which is also suggested by the origin myth, with its avoidance of women and sex and its recurrent oral and anal themes.

32. These drawings, along with drawings by Julia Badger, are reproduced in my *Culture and Personality* (1973, pp. 357–59).

CHAPTER THREE

Wenebojo Myths from Lac Court Oreilles

In a version of the Wenebojo cycle told to Joseph Casagrande by John Mink at Lac Court Oreilles in 1941 there are some episodes which do not appear in the myth as given earlier. Much of it is the same; so we will have some repetition. But the variations are of interest.[1]

3. *The Court Oreilles Origin Myth*

Collected by Joseph Casagrande at Court Oreilles in 1941
Narrator: John Mink   Interpreter: Prosper Guibord

Wenebojo was coming on the ice across Lake Superior. He saw a bunch of people and went up to them to see who they were. When he came nearer, he saw that they were a pack of wolves. He was surprised to see them and called them his nephews and asked them what they were doing. They said they were hunting. Wenebojo said he was hunting too.

They picked out a place on the edge of the lake to camp. Wenebojo was cold. There were only two logs for a fire. One wolf said, as they were sitting there, "What are you going to do for your uncle? He must be getting hungry." Another wolf pulled off his moccasin, tossed it to Wenebojo, and told him to pull out the sock. Wenebojo looked at it, said he didn't want any stinking socks, and threw it back. The wolf said, "You must be awfully particular if you don't like this food." He reached into the sock and pulled out a deer tenderloin, reached in again and pulled out some bear fat. Wenebojo's eyes popped, and he said, "That's good; give it to me." They put it over the fire to roast. Before he started to eat, Wenebojo took off his old moccasin. He was

---

1. A somewhat different version of John Mink's myth, lacking some of the episodes, appears in Ritzenthaler and Ritzenthaler (1970, pp. 141–45).

going to imitate the wolf. He threw the moccasin at the wolf. The wolf looked into it. There was only dry hay that he used to keep his feet warm. The wolf said that he didn't eat hay. Wenebojo was ashamed.

They all went to sleep. The wolves curled up and were warm, but Wenebojo couldn't sleep and walked around the fire. At about daybreak he hollered at them to get up and go hunting. They all jumped up and went off in different directions; in no time they were out of sight. One old wolf, the father of the young wolves, walked along with Wenebojo. Soon they came to some deer tracks, with wolf tracks following them. One had made awfully long jumps, another short ones. Wenebojo said, "This is the one who is going to get the deer; look how far he jumps." But the old wolf said, "No, this other one is the fast one. He'll get the deer."

Then they came to a place where a wolf had jumped aside and had a shit. The wolf said, "Pick that up. It will make a good blanket."

Wenebojo said that he didn't want any old dog shit and kicked it aside.

The old wolf picked it up and shook it, and it turned into a nice warm tanned wolfskin. Wenebojo wished he could have it. The wolf gave it to him.

The old wolf said, "It isn't far. Soon we'll catch up with them. They've got that deer by now."

They came to a little rise with a hollow down below. There Wenebojo saw some blood, and they soon came to the pack of wolves all lying around asleep with their bellies full. Wenebojo was mad, because the wolves had been so greedy. He picked up the best bones he could find, planning to boil them. They went back to camp. The logs there were burning, just as they'd left them.

The old wolf said to his sons, "Your uncle must be hungry. Give him some meat to cook."

One of the wolves came toward Wenebojo belching and whooping and threw up. A ham came out of his mouth. Another wolf came and threw up some ribs. Wolves have a double stomach; they can carry meat home, unspoiled, for their pups. After that, Wenebojo didn't have to go out. The wolves hunted for him and brought home deer, elk, and moose, and Wenebojo would jerk the meat. He was well fixed there.

Toward spring the old wolf said they'd have to leave, and Wenebojo had enough meat to last until summer. Wenebojo didn't answer. One of the wolves said, "Maybe Wenebojo doesn't like that. He'll be lonesome."

The old wolf agreed and said that they'd leave one wolf with him, the best hunter. Then they left.

The young wolf went up to a ridge under a shade tree and walked round in a circle. Then, when they looked around, there was a nice bark wigwam. After that Wenebojo's nephew hunted only when they needed meat. He would chase a deer close by and kill him, and Wenebojo would pack him.

But one day the *manidog* got jealous of Wenebojo and had a meeting. They decided that they'd have to take that wolf away from Wenebojo.

Wenebojo had a dream about what they were going to do. He told his nephew not to go across a stream while he was hunting, but go around it, even if it was only a tiny spring.

Next morning the wolf went out hunting and had gone only a short way when he scared up a deer and chased it, but he couldn't head him off as usual.

Wenebojo had cooked some meat and was waiting for his nephew, but it got dark and he still didn't come. Wenebojo felt so bad, he didn't eat.

The next morning he started out and followed his nephew's tracks. He could see where he had jumped a deer and tried to head him off. Then he came to a place where he could see his nephew's tracks go back and forth. There was a little stream there. The nephew must have thought of what Wenebojo had told him. But he had taken a long run, being sure he could make it. But he'd fallen right into the water.

Wenebojo knew what had happened. He went home then and thought to himself he'd leave and not take his meat or anything. Then he noticed something hanging up in the wigwam. It was a string of beads, which he put around his neck, saying, "From now on, that's the way the Indians will do." Then Wenebojo set out.

Soon he came to a river and headed downstream. He came to the mouth of a stream where it ran into a lake. There was a big tree leaning over the water. And he saw someone sitting in the tree, looking down into the water. Wenebojo said, "Brother, what are you looking for down in the water?"

The other one said that the *manidog* had taken Wenebojo's nephew away from him, and maybe some of his guts would come floating by.

That made Wenebojo mad. He said, "Look, you can have these beads, if you tell me what you know about him."

"Well, look across the water; there's a big cliff where those *manidog* live. They're mighty, those *manidog*. They killed Wenebojo's nephew, and I'm waiting for a taste of those guts. You can see a sandy beach just this side of that cliff. Day after tomorrow they will come out to sun themselves on the beach. They do that every spring. It will be a nice warm and calm day."

That was all Wenebojo wanted to know. But he was still mad at that fellow. He took off his beads and pretended that he was going to put them around the other's neck. He tried to wring his neck, but the fellow ducked aside and got away. It was a kingfisher, and that's what makes those feathers ruffled around his neck. Wenebojo gave him his name and told him that that would be the only way he could get his food—sit in a tree all the time and wait for it.

Then Wenebojo went to where some Indians lived, close by. He could hear a girl laughing. There was a hut for girls having their first menses. He took one of his arrows and gave it to the older one, Matchikwewis, and told her to rub the point on her lips. Then he took another arrow and told the other girl, Oshkikwe, to do the same.[2]

Then he went down to where the *manidog* would sun themselves. He saw the sandy beach and the cliff. There was a little knoll there, where he decided he would change himself into an old stump.

Next morning the sun came up, and it was nice and calm. Mud turtles and sunfish came close to the shore. They were sent ahead by the *manidog* as guards. Then water began to whirl, and foam came out. A red loon popped out and hollered and dove down again. He told the head *manido* that it was a calm day. The *manido* wanted to be sure; so he sent another bird, a beautiful white loon. He also said it was a nice day. "Well, all right, let's go up," said the *manido*.

They all came up. The whole lake whirled and foamed. A big white bear and a brown one, and a great big snake, and all sorts of animals came out. One took a hide and shook it and laid it down for the king to put his head on. That hide came from Wenebojo's nephew. It was like squeezing his heart to see it; it made him so mad.

2. Chippewa girls at the time of first menstruation had to stay in a seclusion hut; it was believed that at this time their touch might bring about paralysis or death in a child and could destroy berries or crops. Julia Badger spent a month in such a hut. In this context "lips" may refer to the genital labia. If so, Wenebojo's arrows should have been lethal instruments, although, as it turned out, they did not actually kill the kings.

In the following chapter, in story number 14, it is possible that Matchikwewis and Oshkikwe are again in a seclusion hut, since they are described as living on the edge of the village and being visited daily by their mother, who combs their hair. In "Wakayabide," story number 34, there is another reference to a menstrual hut, where a girl is living alone in the woods. There is an implied reference to the lethal effects of menstrual blood in story number 46, "The Girl and the Wicked *Manido*," in which a girl gets power over a wicked *manido* by sticking his head into the waist part of her skirt.

Wenebojo then wished that the turtles and sunfish would go to sleep, and the turtles' legs went limp, and the sunfish lay on their sides.

The king said, "What's that stump over there? I never saw it before. You can't tell about that Wenebojo." So he sent a snake to test it. The snake coiled around the stump twice and squeezed and almost choked Wenebojo. Then he came back and said that he'd seen that stump before. It was all right; Wenebojo couldn't have that much power.

But the king still didn't like it, and he sent over a big bear. The bear scratched the stump up and down, and Wenebojo almost screamed. The bear was so big that he almost sank in the ground when he walked. The bear said, "It's all right; that stump was there before."

Wenebojo wished that all the *manidog* would go to sleep. When they were asleep, he got up. He was a stump no longer. He took his bow and two arrows and shot the king and the next to the king. Someone woke up and called out, "Wenebojo has shot the king!" Wenebojo ran away. The water was boiling and rising up behind him.

Wenebojo came to a woodchuck digging for all it was worth at the side of a hill. Wenebojo said to the woodchuck, "We're going to die." The woodchuck said, "Follow me. You won't die."

The woodchuck dug faster and faster, and Wenebojo crawled in right behind her. He called out to her, "Hey, Big Cunt, you got sand in my eyes." She turned around and said, "What did you say?" Wenebojo said, "I said, 'You're a good digger.' " His job was to fill up the hole after her. After they got through digging, they rested for two days, and then the woodchuck said that she'd dig out and see what it looked like outside. When they got out, everything was quiet, and the water was down to normal again.

When they got out, Wenebojo was still mad and thought to himself he'd keep on going all over the world to see what became of his nephew. It was summer time now. One time, while he was roaming, he heard a voice, and he stopped and listened. Someone was singing and then stopped to cry. Wenebojo drew closer. He heard someone singing, over and over, "Wenebojo shot and killed the king." Wenebojo came to an old woman with a big pack of basswood bark. He said, "Grandma, what are you crying about?"

She put her hands up to her eyes and said, "Oh, I thought it was Wenebojo."

He said, "No, Wenebojo was foolish. He's a long way off. I heard that Wenebojo killed the king, but don't be afraid of him. He isn't close by. But, Granny, what have you got all this bark for?"

She said that they were going to string it up all over the world, and if Wenebojo touched it anywhere, they'd know where he was.

He asked, "Granny, are they dead?"

She said, "No, but they're just about dead." Then she looked at him again and said, "You must be Wenebojo."

He said, "If I were Wenebojo, I'd kill you."

She said, "You know, I'm the one who's doctoring my two boys. No one else can do such a thing. I'd better go. They must be waiting for me." Then she said, "You know, when they killed Wenebojo's nephew, I was the only one who ate him. I have only one paw left now."

That went right to Wenebojo's heart. He said, "You ate my nephew. I'm Wenebojo." He took his bow and hit her over the head and killed her. He took his clothes off and put the old lady's clothes on and wished himself to look like the old woman. He took her pack and started, going in the direction she'd shown him, where her house was.

When he came near the place, he started to sing, "Wenebojo shot and killed the king," and he cried in imitation of the old woman. The children there said, "Grandma is coming."

When Wenebojo heard that, he went off the path. Someone called out to him, "Granny, you're off the road; you'll get lost."

Wenebojo said, "My old eyes can hardly see where they're going." He asked how the boys were; they said, "Pretty bad."

Then he went into the wigwam, and everyone believed that it was their grandma. "Now, children," he said, "close every little hole in the wigwam, so there'll be no light in here. Then you all go outside, as I have to do some supernatural work to try to revive them."

Someone brought his nephew's paw to him, and that hurt him. When he was alone in there, he took the old lady's drum and rattle and started to sing, "Wenebojo killed the king, and I'm going to try to get the arrows out." Then he took the two arrows in his teeth, but instead of pulling them out, he pushed them in further and killed both of them. He took off the old woman's clothes and skinned the king, and he packed the body, going off in a direction where no one would see him. He started to run through the woods.

Outside the wigwam one of the *manidog* said, "Let's see what Granny's doing. She's been a long time in there." When they went in, they found Granny's clothes, and the one next to the king dead, and the king's skin. So they all got mad and chased after him.

As he ran, Wenebojo could hear the earth shake like an earthquake, and he could hear the roar of water. He ran faster, but he could see it coming. The water turned over trees and everything. He looked around and saw a big bluff with a tall pine tree on top of it. He made for that tree. The water came right after him, but he wouldn't let go of the pack. He said to the tree, "Brother, we're going to die." The tree said, "No, just climb up to the top." Wenebojo still hung onto his pack. He climbed up the tree. Soon the water came up to his feet. He said, "Brother, can't you do anything more?" The tree stretched itself its whole length, but the water kept on getting higher. Finally, the tree could do no more.

Wenebojo had to stretch his neck. The water stopped just below his nose. If it had gone a couple of inches higher, he would have drowned. He still had his pack on. Finally he could see all kinds of animals swimming around. He called to them, "There's only one thing that can save us. If any of you can dive down and get a little of the earth, we might live." He said to the loon, "You're a good diver. See if you can dive down and get some dirt." The loon said, "I'll try," and dove down, but he got only about half way and had to breathe and drowned. The loon floated up and gave a few feeble kicks and died. Wenebojo looked around and saw an otter. "Brother, you're a good diver. See if you can get some dirt." The otter tried and went a little further than the loon, but he choked up too and couldn't make it. His body came up dead. Then Wenebojo saw a beaver and asked him to try it. Beaver said, "All right." Down he went, but he didn't make it. Then Wenebojo saw a muskrat and asked him to go down. The muskrat dove down and could see the earth, and he was just able to get his little paws into the mud. He was almost up to the surface when he passed out.

"Poor little fellow, you tried hard," said Wenebojo. Then he saw his closed paws and opened them, and there were a few grains of sand and some mud in them. Wenebojo took it in his hands and started rolling it, and soon he had a handfull. He hollered to the animals to swim closer and help him. Soon he threw some out around him, and there was a little island there, and some of the animals climbed out onto it, and Wenebojo went over onto the island too.

He got hold of a big bird, *Gi-wanasi*, and told him to go round in a big circle, and said that the island would grow as he flew around. He was gone for four days. When he got back, he asked if that was enough. Wenebojo said No, and sent the eagle out. He was gone longer, and when he got back, Wenebojo said that it was now big enough. Wenebojo said, "This is going to be our island. This is where my uncles and aunts and all my relations will make their home."

Then Wenebojo looked around and found a hollow and cut up the body of the king there. He kept one little piece, and that he gave to the woodchuck who had saved his life. Wenebojo said, "You'll have an easy life. You'll just work for your living in the summer time. You'll always be fat. In the winter time make youself a good den and sleep. You won't have to eat. And you'll change your coat for a new one every year."

The rest of the pieces of the king's body turned into oil, and the hollow was half full. Before that almost all animals had lived on grass. Now Wenebojo told all the animals to come and have some oil. The first one that came was a rabbit. He asked if the rabbit wanted some oil. The rabbit said yes, and took a little stick and touched himself high on the back with it. The deer and other animals that eat grass touched themselves on the flanks. But the bear drank some of the fat, and a lot of the smaller animals that eat meat took a little sip of it. Wenebojo told the deer that he could eat moss. Everyone who sipped or touched the fat turned into *manidog*, and those who fast will have them as guardians. Wenebojo told them about plants, roots, and herbs, and named them.

Wenebojo's grandmother has a home some place, and a cedar grows out of her forehead. Wenebojo has a wigwam, but the sticks are rattlesnakes. The lake of fat is still there. I believe it's oil, where kerosene and gasoline come from.

Comments

Although there are various differences between the Flambeau and Court Oreilles origin myths, the main outlines are consistent. Episodes 15–23 of the Flambeau version also appear at Court Oreilles. In both myths Wenebojo joins a pack of wolves, lives with them for a while, and then is left with a single "nephew" who hunts for him so successfully that the jealous underwater *manidog* cause his death. Wenebojo gets revenge by killing one or two underwater "kings," is pursued by rising waters, and finally makes the world we live on in the Earth-Diver episode.

Johannes Gille believes that the Chippewa or Ojibwa were the originators of this string of episodes, which spread from them to the Menomini, who in turn transmitted this cycle to the Sauk, Fox, and Kickapoo. Northward, the cycle spread from the Chippewa to the northern Saulteaux and Cree and eastward to the Ottawa, from whom it diffused to the Mississaga and Montagnais (1939, pp. 75–76).

In John Mink's version, when Wenebojo shoots the king, more animal species are specified than in Tom Badger's account: mud turtle, sunfish, red loon, white loon, white bear, brown bear, and snake,

Distributions of Myth Episodes Among Algonkian Tribes

	Montagnais	Cree	Ottawa	Ojibwa	Potawatomi	Fox	Sauk	Menomini	Blackfoot
Trickster travels with the wolves	X	X		X	X			X	X
The wolf is killed by underwater *manidog*		X	X	X		X		X	X
Trickster kills underwater *manido(g)* in revenge		X	X	X		X	X	X	X
Deluge caused by his revenge		X	X	X		X	X	X	
Earth-Diver and creation of earth	X	X	X	X		X	X	X	X
Testing of earth's size		X	X	X					
Trickster is reconciled by the *manidog's* gift of the Medicine Dance				X	X		X		

This table is based, with modifications, on tables in Fisher (1946, pp. 240–41).

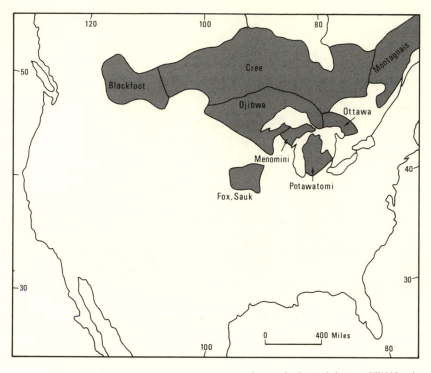

Map 3. Locations of tribal groups listed in preceding table. See also Map 2.

giving more elaboration to this version. This is followed by the rising of the waters and the appearance of a quite new episode concerning the woodchuck, who is reintroduced toward the end of the tale, with the production of oil from the king's body and the creation of fat deposits in different animal species. An episode reminiscent of this one is given by William Carson. The trickster hero boils trout and makes a big pile of fat. He calls Rabbit, Moose, and other animals to come. Rabbit jumps into the fat. Later he dips up fat with a forked stick and rubs it on his neck and under his legs, which accounts for the location of Rabbit's fat deposits (Carson, 1917, p. 492). Later I will discuss the attention given to animal fat in these tales.

John Mink's account does not deal with Wenebojo's sulking fit and the gifts with which the *manidog* sought to appease him, the creation of the first human beings and the rite of the Midewiwin. In the Flambeau version this is the climax of the whole tale. However, this episode seems to have had a restricted distribution and may be a late elaboration, for only the Potawatomi and Sauk are reported to have comparable episodes.

Near the outset of the Court Oreilles origin myth is an episode which may be classed as a *Bungling host* story (J2425), a type of tale reported for most parts of North America and also parts of Micronesia. Jones gives a number of Chippewa stories of this type. In one tale an elk slices meat from the back of his wife to feed his guest Wenebojo. Wenebojo tries to do the same when his former host visits him, but Wenebojo's wife says "Ouch!" when he tries to cut her. The visitor asks if he can do the job and slices Wenebojo's wife's back without causing her pain.

In a similar story Wenebojo visits a woodpecker. The host paints himself red on the forehead and fits a bone-pointed spear into his nostrils, pecks at a post, and raccoons come out. Later the woodpecker visits Wenebojo. Wenebojo paints his nose red, sticks metal into his nose, and pecks at a post. But his nose bleeds, and he loses consciousness. Then the woodpecker pecks the post, and raccoons come out. Wenebojo regains consciousness and eats along with his children.

In a third episode Wenebojo is a guest, as above. His host climbs up a pole, takes an awl, pierces his testes, and bear grease pours out. When the visitor comes to Wenebojo's place, Wenebojo climbs a pole, pierces his testes, and falls down into the fire. Then the guest does it all correctly, and Wenebojo and his children eat (William Jones, 1917, 1919, pt. 1, pp. 299–312).[3]

These stories all concern a failure of reciprocity owing to the fact that different kinds of beings have different faculties or abilities. Under these conditions, a simple return through mechanical imitation of the first host's behavior cannot succeed. This pattern is echoed, in a way, in the episode in the Flambeau origin myth (16) when Wenebojo tries to make grease and tallow with the bone.

4. *Rectum Snake*

Collected by Ernestine Friedl at Court Oreilles in 1942
Narrator: Delia Oshogay   Interpreter: Maggie Lamorie

Wenebojo saw a snake crawling as he looked at a moose he wanted to kill. [This is a version of episode 9 in the origin myth.] He asked

---

3. See also Schoolcraft (1956, pp. 224–27).

the snake to crawl into this moose's rectum and to chew up his innards. He told the snake he'd give him the best part of the meat, if he killed the moose that way.

The snake did so, and Wenebojo got ready to enjoy his feast, but he didn't know where to start. If he went to the rear, people wouldn't think right of him, because he started from the rear end. If he started from the head, people wouldn't think right of him because he started from the head. And if he started from the sides, people wouldn't think right of him either. There were quite a few trees nearby, and he made birchbark dishes and put soup in them, and invited all the trees nearby to eat some soup.

[After that Wenebojo becomes annoyed by the noise made by the rubbing tree branches. He climbs up and gets his hand caught. The episode with the wolves follows, in which his food is devoured by the wolves. As in the Lac du Flambeau version, Wenebojo's head gets caught in the moose's skull, but he is freed in a different way. Wenebojo starts to swim in a lake. Some Indians, thinking that the swimming creature is a moose, shoot at it, and the skull breaks to pieces.]

Comment

The theme of a person being killed by a snake that enters his rectum (G328, *Rectum Snake*) has a wide distribution among Plains tribes such as Arapaho, Hidatsa, Arikara, Pawnee, Crow, Blackfoot, and Gros Ventre. It represents another instance of the theme of penetration of the rectum discussed earlier.

5. *The Incest of Wenebojo's Grandparents*

Collected by Victor Barnouw at Court Oreilles in 1944
Narrator: Elizabeth Taylor

You never hear about Wenebojo's mother or father. I used to wonder where he came from. My aunt told me this story:

Wenebojo's mother was in another land — right straight down from us. There was a woman who had a brother. When this young fellow was there, a woman would come to him at night. He couldn't find out who this woman was. He finally began to suspect his sister. So he put something on his hand. Sure enough, she came during the night. He touched her on the hip and said, "This won't rub out. It'll stay there."

So the next day he stayed in, and his sister was working by the entrance. She kept sitting in one position and wouldn't move. She kept watching him. So he wished that the fire would make her clothes catch fire. Sure enough, her dress was burning. He hollered at her, "Your dress is burning!" So she turned around, and sure enough, his hand-mark was on her hip. So he knew who that woman was, and he was so ashamed of himself that he got sick. So he told his mother to go and build a wigwam for him where he could stay. He stayed there for some time. His mother used to take food to him. So one day he told his mother, "Tell my sister to come over. I want to see her." She went over. When she got there, the boy told her to sit down. Just when she was sitting down, he said, "I used to dream that the earth had a big hole." She went down through it. He said, "How would this world be, if it was like the way you are?" So he got rid of her.

She hollered, but she went down through there. When she came out of the other side, she was in the middle of the sea on a big rock. She couldn't see no land any place. After a while, she noticed this thing was moving that she was on. Then she found out that it was a great big turtle. The turtle spoke to her and told her that she was going to give birth to a girl. "If you promise to marry me to her when she's big enough, I'll save you and take you to shore." So she promised. The old turtle told her to just make a wigwam by the shore. Then he took care of her and supported her. Every morning there'd be something there — fish or muskrat or something. She got this daughter, and she grew up right away, and the turtle married her. When the girl was older, she died in childbirth. She had twins. Wenebojo was the oldest. His brother killed his mother. The brother's name was Flint. Flint disappeared. Long afterwards Wenebojo killed Flint, but that's another long story. This story shows you how Wenebojo came to live with his grandmother.

Comments

Here we have a different story about Wenebojo's paternity and his birth. The story of *Brother-sister incest* (T415) has a wide distribution.[4] In the Chippewa tale the incestuous sister becomes Wenebojo's grandmother. According to William Jones (1917, 1919, pt. 1, p. 431), Wenebojo's grandmother is Mother Earth. She is often called Toad-Woman.

The theme of a woman falling from the sky and landing on a tur-

4. See, for example, the rather similar tale given in Boas (1888, p. 597).

tle's back is an important part of the Iroquois origin myth. This tale involves motif A844.1, *Earth rests on turtle's back* (see Fenton, 1962).[5]

6. *Wenebojo in the Whale and His Fight with His Brother*

Collected by Robert Ritzenthaler at Court Oreilles in 1942
Narrator: Alec Martin   Interpreter: Prosper Guibord

Wenebojo and his twin were talking inside their mother and were wondering who would be born first. The twin said, "I will." But Wenebojo said, "No; if you are, you will kill our mother." While they were arguing, the twin jumped out and disappeared, and so did the mother.[6]

The grandmother was surprised and wondered what had happened. She saw a little speck of blood on the floor, picked it up, and wrapped it in some birchbark and said that that was Wenebojo. Each day she would look at the blood speck, and it seemed like it was growing. Finally she opened it one day, and there was a little rabbit inside the birchbark. She wrapped it up again, and the next day she looked again, and there was a human being in it. It was Wenebojo.

After a while Wenebojo found out where his brother was, so he told his grandmother that he was going to kill a whale and get some oil. She warned him that the whale was a bad fish and could swallow him and his canoe too. But Wenebojo went ahead and made a canoe and went out to sharpen his knife on a big stone. As he rubbed his knife on the rock, it seemed to say, *"Gigá, Gigá, Gigá"* (My mother, My mother, My mother).

He dropped his knife and went in to ask his grandmother where his mother was and why he had never seen her. She told him not to bother about it. She was afraid he would start to search for her too. Finally she told him that a big whale had swallowed her. Wenebojo got mad at this and went out to kill a whale to avenge his mother.

He went out fishing, and when he got out aways, he yelled, "Whale, come and swallow me!" The whale heard him, but they said that it was Wenebojo calling, and he was a bad spirit. Finally, one big whale

---

5. See also Thompson (1973, pp. 14–17).

6. In a version of this story told at Red Lake, Minnesota, in 1911, the three brothers (not just two) were quarreling in the womb about who should be the eldest, and they came to blows. The mother and her wigwam were blown away. The story continues with the grandmother finding a bloodclot, as in this version. See de Jong (1913, p. 507).

got tired of the yelling and opened her mouth and sucked Wenebojo in, his canoe and all.

Wenebojo looked around, and it was just like a wigwam inside. There was a squirrel and a bluejay there, and as Wenebojo could talk to anything, even a rock, he always addressed them as younger brother. He asked the bluejay where he was, and the bluejay told him that they were in the whale's stomach, and he told him where the whale's heart was. Wenebojo was still in his canoe, so he paddled over to the heart and poked it every once in a while with his paddle, until the whale got sick and tried to throw him up. But Wenebojo turned his canoe sideways. Finally he poked the whale's heart and killed it, and the whale turned over on its side.

Then Wenebojo told the wind to blow him over to his grandmother's landing. One morning the grandmother went to get some water, and there lay the big whale on the beach. She let it lie and soon the ravens came and started to eat the flesh until there was a big hole in the middle. Wenebojo, the squirrel, and the bluejay crawled out. He had avenged his mother, so he took all the oil from the whale.

Then he asked, "How was it that the whale didn't get my brother?" She told him that his brother was on a solid rock island surrounded by pitch, and that he was a bad spirit anyway and that Wenebojo shouldn't try to get him. But Wenebojo set out anyway.

He took his canoe and some whale oil and paddled toward the island. All at once his canoe got stuck in the pitch. He put some whale oil on his canoe and paddle and got a little further, and then got stuck again, so he put on some more oil. Finally, after he had used up all the oil, he reached the island. He saw his brother chopping off bits of his leg with a stone axe, and *megis* shells would fly off at each stroke. He didn't know his brother's name; so he called him *Okakwánčagigaùng* (hewing his shin). The brother greeted him and invited him into his wigwam and gave him something to eat. After supper Wenebojo said, "What if someone attacked us? What would you do?"

"I'd fight him first," said the brother.

But Wenebojo said, "No, I'd fight him first."

They argued for a long while, and then the brother lay down and went to sleep. Then Wenebojo went outside and stuck little feathers all around the edge of the island. He told each one to start to whoop and holler just as the sun rose. Then Wenebojo lay down but didn't go to sleep, for he was still afraid of his brother.

At sunrise the feathers started yelling, and the brother ran out to see what the noise was. Wenebojo started to follow him and was shooting arrows into his brother, but nothing happened. A chickadee then told Wenebojo that he would have to shoot his brother in the braid of his hair in order to kill him. Wenebojo shot at the braid, but the arrow glanced off. Wenebojo took his last arrow and waited until his brother turned around. Then he hit him in the center of the braid. The brother fell over dead.

The following story covers much the same ground as the preceding, so this story will be presented first before any comments are offered.

7. Wenebojo in the Whale and His Fight with an Ogre

Collected by Ernestine Friedl at Court Oreilles in 1942
Narrator: Delia Oshogay   Interpreter: Maggie Lamorie

One time Wenebojo and his grandmother were together. One time Wenebojo was around their wigwam, and he found an axe, and he started to sharpen it on a rock. Every time he sharpened it, it'd say, "*Gigá, Gigá*" (Mother, Mother). He got so mad. He thought the axe was talking to him. He wondered what the axe meant. He never knew he had a mother. He got so mad, he turned the axe on the other side. This time the axe said, "*Gus, Gus, Gus*" (Father, Father, Father). Wenebojo said to himself, "I wonder what's the meaning of this. I never knew I had a father or a mother." Then he went home to his grandmother and told her. He asked her what it meant. His grandmother told him, "You had a father who went to battle against the Sioux and never came back. There was a man living across the ocean who got the best of your father. His name was *Okakwandjagigang*. That means chopping-the-shins-with-an-axe. He was more like a beast than a man. He had all kinds of power and could make anything happen where he lived across the lake." Then she told him, "You had a mother. She went out in a boat to go across the lake, and a big fish swallowed her, canoe and all." Then she showed a place to Wenebojo and said, "See that big clearing over there? That used to be your father's village. He was chief of that village, but the bad man got them all."

Wenebojo was mad then; he meant business now. He got ready and made a flat-bottomed ricing boat and went to work and went fishing. He wanted to get even with the one who swallowed his mother. His grandmother told him it was no good, because he'd never get the fish, but he went off anyway. He sang while he was fishing, "*Mišinamégwe*, come on and swallow me." He sang that over and over. The big fish heard him. He was king of the fish. He called one of his helpers, a sunfish. "My flap door, go and see what Wenebojo wants." The sun fish went to see what Wenebojo wanted. Wenebojo told him, "Get out of here. I don't want you. I want *Mišinamégwe*." The big fish sent another fish, the bass, which he called "My door step." He said, "You go and see what Wenebojo wants." The door step went and asked Wenebojo what he wanted. The same thing happened. Wenebojo said that he didn't want him but wanted *Mišinamégwe*. The door step went back and told him. The big fish got mad and went up to where Wenebojo was fishing. Wenebojo saw him coming, and his boat began to swirl around when the mouth of the fish came near. Wenebojo couldn't hold the boat back, and the big fish just swallowed him, boat and all.

When Wenebojo came to, it looked as if he were in a big long wigwam. He looked, and he saw an owl up there. Then he looked again and saw a squirrel. The owl said, "Hey, Wenebojo, we're not going to live, we're dying." Then the squirrel spoke and said the same thing. The owl said that he had been near the shore looking for fish, and that's how he got caught. The squirrel told Wenebojo he had been swimming in the water. Wenebojo started to do everything to that big fish inside. The fish began to feel sick to his stomach. He thought, "I guess I'll go to the shore and throw up Wenebojo." But Wenebojo knew what he was trying to do. He put his boat crosswise in the fish's throat, so the fish couldn't throw him up. *Mišinamégwe* tried another way. He wanted to move his bowels to get rid of Wenebojo. Wenbojo could see something at the other end of the wigwam contracting and expanding. He knew that it was the fish's rectum, but he tied it up so tight that the fish couldn't do anything.

Poor *Mišinamégwe* died from all this. Wenebojo killed him. Wenebojo, the squirrel, and the owl were beginning to get sick inside the fish. Then they heard some kind of a knock on top of the fish's back. It was a raven, that always finds dead meat. He was making a hole through the fish's side, as he was eating it. You could see the sky; there was a big opening in the fish. Wenebojo gave a piece of the meat to the raven and also to the owl and the squirrel.

Wenebojo said, "Let this fish land near my grandmother's shore." Sure enough, *Mišinamégwe* landed on Wenebojo's grandmother's shore. His grandmother ran to the shore. Wenebojo called to her to hurry up quick with a knife, because the insides of the big fish were so hot that it was scalding them. She came with the knife and opened the fish, and they all got out. He gave some fish to the owl and the squirrel. The squirrel couldn't eat the fish, because he was so sick; so Wenebojo just blew on him, and he was better.

Wenebojo and his grandmother started to cook *Mišinamégwe*. He was mostly fat or tallow, so they made grease out of it. They made a rack of wood and put all the fish on it, built a low fire under it, and the smoke made the fish oil. Wenebojo got some birchbark and made some birchbark dishes. They had a kettle hanging from the rack over the fire, and the oil dripped into the kettle. When the kettle was almost full, Wenebojo poured the fish oil into the birchbark dishes.

Wenebojo's grandmother told him that the ogre lived across the ocean. About a quarter of the ocean was full of tar; the ogre had the power to make it that way. You can't get near his place, because you would drown in tar.

When they had the fish oil, Wenebojo made his grandmother dance around the fire to get more fish oil, and he sang to his grandmother as she danced, "Let lots more oil come up," and the kettle filled up more quickly as she danced.

Now Wenebojo was going to kill that ogre. He told his grandmother that he'd be gone ten days. He said that the ocean would be just calm and still from the time he left until he got back. His grandmother cried and wept for him. She said he'd never come back because nobody who goes to fight this ogre ever comes back. But Wenebojo said he'd go and get this fellow's scalp. He made a canoe for his grandmother before he went away.

Just before he started off, his grandmother said, "I have nothing to tell you but there will be an old lady at the place where you land across the ocean. You will stay there overnight with her, and she will tell you what to do to get your enemy." When Wenebojo got into his flat-bottomed boat, his grandmother got into the canoe. She went behind the boat and then came forward to his right side and then back and to his left side. This was a good-bye. In the old days, when they went to fight the Sioux, the women would say good-bye to the men like that.

Wenebojo went on. He finally got across the ocean and arrived at a sort of point. There was an old lady there, and he called her *Nokomis* (grandmother). As he got near her home, he could hear her saying, "My poor grandchild, Wenebojo; he's foolish to come over here to try to kill that enemy."

Wenebojo stayed the night with the woman; she started to get him a meal. She had a tiny kettle as big as a small apple, and she put one kernel of rice in it and one kernel of corn in another kettle. Wenebojo thought,

"That poor old woman, cooking for me; how can I get full on that?" He pitied her. Finally this old woman got the meal ready. Wenebojo started to eat with his wooden spoon, and every time he ate a kernel, there was always another one left, and he never knew where it was coming from. When he was real full, the kettle was empty. Then the old woman said, "Wenebojo, you thought you wouldn't get enough to eat. I knew what you were thinking of me as I cooked."

He stayed all night with the old woman, and she told him what to do. "You will make use of all the fish oil you brought. Go along the shore in your boat, and you'll come to a bay. There will be all kinds of sticks and posts sticking up in the bay. They won't really be sticks; they are walleyed pike guarding the bay. You take some tobacco and speak to those pike. You say, 'Grandfather, let me go by,' and give them some tobacco. They will let you pass. Then you will come to where there's nothing but tar. Take the fish oil and put it all over your boat, inside and out and on your paddle. You will land where there is a big clearing; the ogre lives in the center of the clearing. This is the last place where your father stopped before he went to meet his enemy. As long as I've been here, and it's pretty near all my life, no one ever came back. Either the pike or the tar or the ogre kills them. Your father was the last one who went by here." Wenebojo told the old woman, "I'll be sure to get back. I'll get him. I'll stop here on my way back."

Wenebojo started out. When he came to where the sticks were sticking out of the water, he did as the old woman told him. He took tobacco and said, "Grandfather, won't you let me pass by?" and gave them the tobacco. The pike took the tobacco and went under the water, so Wenebojo could go by. Then he came to that pitch or tar. He followed the woman's orders and put the fish oil all over his boat inside and out and over his paddle. Then he went right along and had no trouble getting by and landing on the shore. As he got up from his boat, he saw a clearing and made for the wigwam. On the way to the wigwam he killed a partridge.

Just as Wenebojo got inside the wigwam, *Okakwan*, the ogre, made for him as if he was ready to fight. Wenebojo called him "brother" and said, "I didn't come to fight you. I came here to visit you." This *Okakwan* couldn't make friends. He wanted to fight. But finally *Okakwan* calmed down and believed that Wenebojo was really there for a visit. He made friends and believed him. *Okakwan* began to cook a meal, because it was evening, and they both ate.

Night came along, and *Okakwan* started fixing up a place for Wenebojo to sleep. He said, "I never sleep. I never slept yet in my life. The only time I'll sleep will be when I'm near the end of my life, and then I'll sleep." They both lay down together. They were telling stories, and when one got finished, the other started in. Wenebojo wished with his power that *Okakwan* would sleep. At the same time he pointed at *Okakwan's* eyes with his finger. He had the power and said to himself that *Okakwan* would sleep. So he did so.

After *Okakwan* had gone to sleep, Wenebojo took his partridge and went outside. He made his bowels move in lots of different places. At each place where he made a little turd, he took the tail of the partridge and took each feather of the tail and dipped it on the turd. All this time *Okakwan* was sleeping. At the same time Wenebojo spoke to all the little outfits he made and told them to yell and make noise in the morning and to become people and come out and make war on both Wenebojo and *Okakwan.* Then Wenebojo went back into the wigwam and lay down next to *Okakwan*, who was still sleeping. But Wenebojo didn't sleep all night.

Toward morning *Okakwan* woke up, and they started talking again. Wenebojo asked, "What would you do if the Indians declared war on us early this morning?" *Okakwan* said, "I'd jump out first." Wenebojo said, "I'd jump first." They kept on that way. So finally the people did declare war on them. Wenebojo had made them look like Indians when he put the little feathers in. They both jumped out of the wigwam, and Wenebojo made for *Okakwan.* It seemed like a big battle, but really Wenebojo and *Okakwan* were the only ones fighting.

One little turd spoke to Wenebojo and said, "If you want to do the right thing, you'll shoot an arrow at *Okakwan's* thick braid. That's where his death is." So Wenebojo shot him in the braid and killed him. Then he scalped him.

Wenebojo went back the way he came. This time there was no tar and no pike. When he got to the old woman's house, she said, "Wenebojo, you're sure smart to have done what you did." He had the scalp right there in front of the boat. She told him he was the first one to get that enemy. She said, "I was real young when I moved here, and I moved here to save someone. Your grandmother is my younger sister. I spent all my life trying to save someone, and now I'm glad I finally saved you." She said now she could move away.

Wenebojo stayed that night and then he left the next morning. It was the tenth day then. This old woman took her boat and went with him a ways and went first to his right side and then to his left to bid him good-bye. When Wenebojo got home to his grandmother, his grandmother saw him coming and saw what Wenebojo had on the stem of his boat. She knew then that Wenebojo had killed the enemy. His grandmother took her canoe and did the same thing, first to his right and then to his left, to welcome him. When they got back to the wigwam, they had a big dance. They danced for four days, Wenebojo and his grandmother. That's the end.

Comments on the Last Two Stories

The two stories cover much the same ground, including the episode of Wenebojo inside the whale and Wenebojo's murder of the shin-chopper. The main theme in both episodes is revenge. In both stories the whale, or big fish, is said to have swallowed Wenebojo's mother; so Wenebojo kills the whale. In the first story the shin-chopper is said to be Wenebojo's brother. In the process of being born, he has killed Wenebojo's mother, so Wenebojo seeks revenge.[7] In the second story the villain is an ogre who had killed Wenebojo's father. In this story, then, Wenebojo seeks revenge for the loss of his parents, first his mother, then his father.

Although the possibility of diffusion of the Jonah tale (F911.4) from European sources should not be ruled out, I think that the big fish, or whale, episode is probably aboriginal. The big fish was originally the sturgeon rather than whale. That is how William Jones (1917, 1919, pt. 1, pp. 207–15, 467–83) translated *Micinamägwä*, which is very close to the *Mišinamégwe* of Delia Oshogay's text. The term "whale" must have been picked up from European-speaking persons and applied to the big fish in the same way in which the words "lion" and "tiger" were applied to the underwater puma or cougar, to be discussed later.

The theme of being swallowed by a whale has often been described as symbolic of return to the womb. J. Stephen Horsley, an English neurologist and psychiatrist, has written (1943, quoted in Woods, 1947, p. 474): "Ever since I began to treat patients by the method of prolonged soneryl narcosis, I have been impressed by the fact that certain dreams are common to the whole human race. I refer particularly to the dream or fantasy of being swallowed by a whale, and to the dream of spiritual or psychological rebirth." Sushruta, a Hindu commentator who lived around 600 B.C., referred to "the patient who dreams of being eaten by a fish, or who fancies himself again entering the womb of his mother" (ibid., p. 55). It has often been suggested that myths originate in dreams. This may be why we find the myth of being swallowed by a great fish in different cultures. In Old World mythology we have the story of Jonah, while in Greece the hero Herakles is swallowed by a monster sent by the

---

7. In a version in de Jong's collection (1913), the grandmother tells him that his twin, the North, was mainly responsible for causing his mother's death, since he was nothing but flint. The subsequent fight with Flint is similar to those in the two preceding stories. No mention is made of turds, however. The whale episode also appears in the de Jong stories.

sea god Poseidon. In more recent times Collodi's Pinocchio is swallowed by a shark. Now we have Wenebojo in the whale. Like the other heroes, he comes out alive. In this case the possible maternal significance of the big fish is strengthened somewhat by the fact that the fish or whale is said to have swallowed Wenebojo's mother. When Wenebojo comes out of the fish, he is met by his grandmother, which seems appropriate. In the second story the fish is said to be scaldingly hot inside, which is suitable for birth symbolism.

Another grandmother figure appears in the second story. This is our first encounter with the theme of the tiny self-replenishing kettle (D1472.1.2, *Magic kettle supplies food*), which often appears in Chippewa stories. Food always keeps coming from the little kettle — an oral wish-fulfillment fantasy, perhaps. In most of the episodes where this theme appears, the food cooked is wild rice. The old woman has a very small kettle, sometimes with only one grain of wild rice in it. Perhaps the magical increase is based on the fact that a small quantity of wild rice does go a long way when water is added; one cup of wild rice can yield three and a half cups of cooked wild rice. This oral wish-fulfillment fantasy is a reversal of the oral frustration episodes with the moose meat and the ducks (9, 13) in the origin myth. In the former cases a promising large meal is not eaten; but in this case an unpromising small kettle yields abundant food.

The brother or ogre with whom Wenebojo fights has the odd characteristic of hewing or chopping at his own shins. Here we have both aggressive and masochistic themes in relations between the brothers, as in the Lac du Flambeau myth. But in the latter version Wenebojo causes the deaths of his brothers without having to fight them. They are acquiescent to their deaths. In the first Court Oreilles story, however, there is a fierce fight between the two brothers (A525.1, *Culture hero fights with his elder brother*).

In the second story Wenebojo creates allies by defecating and sticking feathers into the turds. He tells the "little outfits" to make a lot of noise the next morning. Only feathers are used for this purpose in the first story. In the ensuing battle Wenebojo kills his enemy by shooting at his braid, as advised by a chickadee in the first story, by a turd in the second (D1610.6.4, *Speaking excrements*; D1312.1.1, *Excrements as advisors*).

William Jones (1917, 1919, pt. 1, pp. 451–67) gives a variant of this tale in which Wenebojo visits his grandfather. During the night, as in our second story, Wenebojo goes outside to defecate here and there, sticking feathers into the dung piles and telling them to whoop and holler at dawn. All goes as planned, and Wenebojo kills his grandfather. This story ends in a particularly cruel fashion. Having skinned and packed his grandfather, Wenebojo goes to tell his grandmother to come with him to get the meat. She soon realizes what the carcass is and feels sad. Wenebojo tells her to cook the meat, and when she eats some grease from the ladle, he tells her that she is eating her husband's penis.

This theme has a wide distribution. Knud Rasmussen, for example, gives one version from Eskimo folklore (1929, p. 221). But, as in the Eskimo case, the story usually involves a husband who punishes his wife by making her eat her adulterous lover's penis. In the Chippewa tale we have an odd reversal. The husband is the one who is killed, not the lover, and the murderer is a grandson. This story, then, has Oedipal overtones.

More explicitly Oedipal is an early version recorded by Henry Rowe Schoolcraft (1839, p. 139). In this story Wenebojo is told by his grandmother: "I have nourished you from your infancy, for your mother died in giving you birth, owing to the ill-treatment of your father." "He [Wenebojo] appeared to be rejoiced that his father was living, for he had already thought in his heart to try and kill him." When he finds his father, Wenebojo asks him if he had been the cause of his mother's death. The answer is Yes! But although Wenebojo strikes his father with a rock, he does not kill him in this version. Wenebojo's father buys him off by offering him a portion of the universe to rule.

We have reviewed four Wenebojo stories with similar themes but with different characters in the role of his adversary. They are, respectively, a brother, an ogre, a grandfather, and a father. The brother and the father are said to have caused the death of the mother, and for that reason Wenebojo seeks them out to get revenge. In the second story the ogre is said to have caused the death of Wenebojo's father. Looking at these tales from a Freudian point of view, we could regard the adversary as a father figure, at least in the case of the ogre, grandfather, and father. Since the whale story and the fight with the adversary are so often combined, we may speculate that they jointly express an Oedipal conflict, with a desire to do away with the father and return to the maternal womb.

The Chippewa story of "Filcher-of-Meat" given by Jones provides another example of Oedipal conflict, somewhat reminiscent of the Brazilian Bororo reference myth 1 in Claude Lévi-Strauss, *The Raw and the Cooked* (1970, pp. 35–37). A father tells his son to shoot a ruffed grouse. The son asks, "Where is it?" His stepmother intervenes to say, "At yonder place."

"I myself will go there."

"No, I will go with you," says the stepmother.

His father is made suspicious and angry by this and later strands his son on an island where they have gone to look for eggs. However, the son is carried to shore by a big serpent. After a series of adventures, the son comes back home and finds his beaten stepmother, whose eyes have been punched through by his father. Although the son sets the whole village on fire, he does not kill his father (William Jones, 1917, 1919, pt. 2, pp. 381–99).[8]

8. *The Birth of Wenebojo and His Theft of Fire*

Collected by Ernestine Friedl at Court Oreilles in 1942
Narrator: Delia Oshogay   Interpreter: Maggie Lamorie

One time there was a woman who was very hungry and cold. She had no flint to start a fire. Finally she heard that somebody had killed a moose. It was mostly eaten up, but she thought that there might be some insides left. She went over to see. When she got to the moose, there was no flesh or guts left, just some clotted chunks of blood inside the moose. She had a pair of mittens, and she filled them up with blood clots. Then a voice came from one of the mittens. It was Wenebojo. That's how he was born. He said, "*Noko* (grandmother), we're freezing. I'll go across the ocean to get some fire."

He turned into a little rabbit then. He had the power to make the ice on the ocean smooth and dry like glass and to make the wind go his way so that he could just blow across the ocean. On the other side of the ocean there was an old man and his two daughters. One of the daughters came down to the ice to get some water, just as Wenebojo got there. She thought he looked cute and petted the little rabbit and took him to show to her father. Her father said, "Why did you bring that rabbit in? Haven't you heard about what happened on the other side of the ocean, about how an old lady had a pair of mittens and that Wenebojo was born there? Didn't you know he's a dangerous person? He plays tricks, he's foolish, and he'll do anything. How do you know that that isn't Wenebojo turned into a tiny rabbit?"

Then Wenebojo grabbed some of their fire and started back across the ice and brought the fire to his grandmother.

Comments

A story very similar to this one is given by de Jong (1913, pp. 5–7). The theme of Wenebojo's birth from a speck or clot of blood (T541.1.1, *Birth*

---

8. For a similar Cree story, see "The Son of Aioswé" (Skinner, 1911, pp. 92–95). In the Cree version the father is burned to death in the fire. Frank G. Speck (1915a) gives a Naskapi version of the same story which includes the *vagina dentata* motif. In this version the son turns his father into a frog and his mother into a robin.

from blood clot) appeared in the fourth story given in this chapter. The birth of a hero from a blood clot has a wide distribution in North America among the southern Ute, Arapaho, Ponca, Pawnee, Dakota, Blackfoot, Gros Ventre, Maidu, Winnebago, and Micmac.

Many North American peoples had stories about the *Theft of fire* (A1415) by a culture hero. Such stories are reported for the Eskimo, Carrier, Kaska, Lillooet, Thompson, Tlingit, Haida, Tsimshian, and other Northwest Coast tribes; the Modoc, Shasta, and other California tribes; and the Shoshoni, Paiute, Cherokee, Creek, Jicarilla and San Carlos Apache, and Mohave, among others.

9. *Wenebojo Commits Incest with His Daughters*

Collected by Ernestine Friedl at Court Oreilles in 1942
Narrator: Delia Oshogay   Interpreter: Maggie Lamorie

Wenebojo had two daughters and a son. He'd go out hunting every day with his son. One day, while he was hunting, he thought "How silly I am to be just living with my daughters. Why don't I marry them?"

When he got home, he made believe he was sick. He told his daughters he was going to die. He said, "If I die, and you are poor and have nothing to eat, you should marry the first man who comes along, no matter how old he is, even if he just catches rabbits for you. When I die, put red paint on my cheeks and have food and a knife ready."

Wenebojo died, and his daughters cried. They said to each other, "We don't know how to fix up a dead person." They didn't know how to paint him.

The corpse spoke up: "Around the eyes." He also told his daughters not to come back to his grave for ten days after they buried him.

Wenebojo whittled a stick to make wolf tracks. Then he killed a moose and ate it and put the bones in his grave. Then he made tracks to his grave, so that it looked as if a wolf had eaten him.

On the tenth day after he died, his daughters came to Wenebojo's grave. They saw the bones and started to cry. They said, "He's been eaten up." Then they went home with their little brother.

One day the little boy came home and said that there was a man standing outside. They said, "Oh, we're supposed to marry the first man who comes along; that's what our father said."

The man came in. It was Wenebojo. He sat between his two daughters and married them. The younger girl didn't take to him very well; she mistrusted him. The older one liked him though. One day the younger girl told the older one to look at his head. She said that sometimes he reminded her of her father.

"I was pretty good friends with your father," said Wenebojo.

She said that one of his teeth was missing; that was the way her father was too.

"Yes," he said. "Your father's name was *Wabidozagima* (tooth missing), and my name is *Zagidunezagima* (just like)."

She said, "My father had a scar on his forehead just like you have."

He didn't say anything.

One time he and his brother-in-law were out hunting, and he killed a moose. Every time he spoke to his brother-in-law, he said, "Brother-in-law, my son." He sort of forgot himself.

When the boy got home, he said to his sisters that it was funny what this man always called him. The younger girl said, "That's why I never take to that old man. You know our father was foolish. I bet it's he!"

Sure enough, it was their father. He ran away laughing and said, "Oh, what a trick I played on those two women!"

Wenebojo went away and then he became real ashamed of himself. One time he heard some boys playing lacrosse. He went over and asked them what was new. They said they had some dirty news — Wenebojo had married his daughters.

Wenebojo just said, "What a terrible thing!" and went away, he was so ashamed of himself.

He kept on walking and saw a crowd of girls playing the same game. He asked them what was new, and they said, "Haven't you heard? Wenebojo went and married his daughters!"

He said, "That's dirty news," and walked away. He walked by the shore and saw a big muskie there. He told the muskie to open his mouth, and he crawled in. That's where he is yet.

Comments

Here the theme frankly concerns incest, in this case between Wenebojo and his two daughters (T411.1.2, *Father-daughter incest*). Another version of this story was told to Robert Ritzenthaler at Court Oreilles in 1942 by Louis Martin, with Prosper Guibord as interpreter. In this story Wenebojo is living with his wife and daughter, and he falls in love with his daughter. He pretends to be dying and asks for his body to be placed on a scaffold. He tells his daughter to marry the first man who comes to the wigwam. The story follows much as before, except that in this version it is the mother who discovers Wenebojo's identify from a familiar scar on his head.

William Jones (1917, 1919, pt. 1, pp. 279–99) gives a story which has some parallels with ours, except that Wenebojo wants to marry his sister, rather than his daughter, and pretends to be dead. This general theme has a wide distribution, not only in the Central Woodlands but also in the Plains, Great Basin, California, the Plateau, and Puget Sound (see Schmerler, 1931).

10. *Wenebojo and Madjikiwis*

Collected by Joseph Casagrande at Court Oreilles in 1941
Narrator: John Mink   Interpreter: Prosper Guibord

Wenebojo and Madjikiwis both had their wives with them, and they moved to a place where they could spend the winter hunting and fishing. It was about mid-winter, and there was a blizzard. Madjikiwis decided to spear through the ice and get a lot of trout. He told Wenebojo to go to the end of the big lake, and he would see someone making a hole in the ice. He went there and saw a fellow chopping a hole in the ice with an ice chisel. It was like he was dancing. Wenebojo went right up to him, but he didn't look up. Then Wenebojo hollered. The fellow stopped and asked him where he was going. He said, "Right here." The fellow said, "Take a drink of water, if you're dry." Wenebojo drank, and there were so many little trout he swallowed some. When Wenebojo had had his fill, the fellow said to go home and not to look back, no matter what.

Wenebojo started on the run. He heard voices behind him, but he kept on going and wouldn't look back. The voices were closer and louder and said, "Chase him! He's taking all our fish." They were so loud, he finally looked back but saw nothing. Wind voices came by and twirled him around, and a voice told him to leave the ice and go up over a hill and to a hollow and throw his pack down and then go home. He didn't know he had a pack, but it was all the fish he had swallowed. Wenebojo saw the hollow and threw the pack down, and went on home, which was close by.

When his old lady saw him, she bawled him out — said he was so stubborn he probably didn't do what they told him. He said he did what he was told to do. She asked why he didn't bring anything, then. He said, "Let's go see in the hollow." When they got there, that hollow was full of trout. Madjikiwis came to him and said, "I'm going to leave you. The ice is melting and spring is coming." It was Madjikiwis who had chiseled the hole in the ice.

Comments

This is a story of magical supply of food. Wenebojo is pursued by voices but is given an interdiction not to look back. It is unusual that, although Wenebojo finally violates the interdiction, he suffers no ill effects.

Wenebojo's nagging wife scolds him, but he has brought back a big supply of trout. An implication is that women should not scold their husbands.

The story illustrates a pattern of two families living together in wintertime.

11. *How the Turkey Buzzard Got his Scabby Red Head*

Collected by Robert Ritzenthaler at Court Oreilles in 1942
Narrator: Frank James

Once Wenebojo turned himself into a caribou and lay down and made believe he was dead. All fall and winter birds and animals came and ate from him. But the turkey buzzard knew that Wenebojo was a spirit, so he stayed up on a tree until just bones were left and not much meat. By now he thought that Wenebojo was surely dead, so he flew down. The only meat that was left was around Wenebojo's anus. He started eating there until all of his head was inside. Then Wenebojo closed his rectum and caught the head of the turkey buzzard inside.

Then he got up and walked to the village where the Indians were playing lacrosse. He asked if he could join in the game, and they said "Sure." While he was playing, he tripped and fell. The turkey buzzard slipped out and got away, but in the process his head and neck were scraped. So that is why the buzzard has a red and scabby neck today, and why he smells so bad.

Comments

Here is another anal story, which involves the theme of penetration of the rectum, of which a number of examples were given earlier. The following tale is a variant of the foregoing, in which Wenebojo's trapping of the turkey buzzard is seen as an act of revenge. The first part of the story contains motif K1041, *Trickster carried by birds and dropped.* Versions containing both segments of the tale are given by

Jones (1917, 1919, pt. 1, pp. 133–39; 1915, pp. 9–13), Young (1903, pp. 224–29), and Hoffman (1896, p. 202), although they do not include the concluding lacrosse episode.

12. *Wenebojo and Winango*

Collected by Ernestine Friedl at Court Oreilles in 1942
Narrator: Delia Oshogay   Interpreter: Maggie Lamorie

One time, when Wenebojo was walking along near a lake, he met Winango, the turkey buzzard. Wenebojo asked Winango to carry him up high into the sky. Winango said that Wenebojo wouldn't get along well up there, since he had no wings, but Wenebojo wouldn't leave him alone. So Winango showed him how to use his arms like wings, and they both went up into the sky. Then Winango went down again, leaving Wenebojo up in the sky.

Wenebojo didn't know how to come down. He decided that he'd have to jump. He made a speech to himself, saying, "I'm a hero. I'm not afraid of anything. I won't get killed." Then he jumped and came down in the water near where he started from.

When Wenebojo got back to land, he saw a dead moose lying there. He decided to make himself look like a dead moose too. Pretty soon the birds came to eat him. Winango, who had left him up in the sky, came to eat him too. Pretty soon he was eating right in the moose's rectum. Then Wenebojo held him there and got up.

He was walking to a village where some boys were playing lacrosse. Wenebojo covered up Winango with a bear hide which he used like a blanket. The boys asked him to play, so he joined the lacrosse game. Pretty soon the boys saw the bird flopping every time Wenebojo ran. They asked, "Wenebojo, what have you got there?" Then Wenebojo dropped the bear hide, and let go of Winango. That's the end of the story.

13. *How Wenebojo Gave the Indians Maple Sugar*

Collected by Robert Ritzenthaler at Court Oreilles in 1942
Narrator: John Mink   Interpreter: Prosper Guibord

One day Wenebojo was standing under a maple tree, and all of a sudden it began to rain maple syrup — not sap — right on top of him. So

Wenebojo got a birchbark tray and held it out until it was full. Then he said to himself, "This is too easy for the Indians." So he threw the syrup away. He decided that first the Indians would have to give a feast, offer tobacco, and put out some of the birchbark baskets, as many as they wanted filled, and someone would speak to God. The Indians would have to tap the trees and get sap and boil it before they could have syrup.[9]

General Comments on the Court Oreilles Wenebojo Myths

Of the eleven Court Oreilles stories in this chapter, two deal with incest — one concerning brother and sister and the other father and daughters. This theme is not mentioned in the longer Lac du Flambeau Wenebojo cycle, in which there are no male-female relations except for the sun's impregnation of Wenebojo's mother. In a society having small scattered family units, incest could be a potential problem. Such tales could then function as a warning.

The social units depicted in all these stories are small; one has a brother-and-sister pair. In three stories Wenebojo lives with his grandmother. In one tale Wenebojo steals fire from an old man and his two daughters. In another, Wenebojo lives with his son and two daughters, and in a third two husband-wife pairs are together during winter. There are no references to clans or village life.

The theme of human-animal transformations recurs in the temporary appearance of Wenebojo as a rabbit in two of the tales and his transformation into a caribou in the turkey buzzard story. Wenebojo is dead or seems to be but comes back to life in two of the tales.

The point of many of the tales seems to be that one character has more power than others. *Bungling host* stories suggest that different persons or species have different powers. Wenebojo has more supernatural power than the brother or ogre whom he seeks out to challenge and kill. In the tale about the theft of fire, the girls' father says to them, "Didn't you know that he's [Wenenbojo is] a dangerous person? . . . How do you know that that isn't Wenebojo turned into a tiny rabbit?" In "Wenebojo and Madjikiwis" Wenebojo magically supplies lots of trout for food.

Themes of aggression are notable: first in the *Rectum snake* killing of the moose. Fighting between brothers is a prominent theme in this

---

9. This story also appears in Ritzenthaler and Ritzenthaler (1970, p. 145). A similar tale is given in Blackbird (1887, p. 72) and in Hoffman (1896, pp. 173–74).

chapter, echoing the similar themes in the Lac du Flambeau myth. A masochistic motif is also repeated in the brother who chops at his own shin. Since this brother is often known as Flint, there may be a relationship between this tale and that of Wenebojo's stone brother in the Flambeau myth. Both probably refer to the use of chipped flint in stone technology, although this is not made specific in either story.

In the brother-sister incest tale, the brother punishes his sister by making her fall through the earth. In one story Wenebojo kills an ogre.

Oral themes appear in the *Bungling host* episode, with the meals of deer, tenderloin, and bear fat along with the frustrating dry hay. Oral themes also occur in the sipping of oil or fat by the animals, the swallowing of the big fish, the self-replenishing kettle motif, the swallowing of trout in "Wenebojo and Madjikiwis," and the rain of maple syrup. The theme of oral frustration appears in the dry hay meal in the *Bungling host*. Wenebojo sees to it that the Indians will have to work for their maple syrup.

Anal themes appear in the rectum-snake killing of the moose, the "little outfits" created by Wenebojo, and the tale of how the turkey buzzard got his scabby red head.

Thus, similar patterns are found in transformational, oral, anal, and aggressive themes in both the Court Oreilles and Lac du Flambeau Wenebojo tales.

The animals mentioned in this chapter include bear, deer, moose, caribou, wolf, turtle, muskrat, mouse, squirrel, woodchuck, rabbit, snake, big fish or whale, muskie, pike, trout, sunfish, bass, chickadee, owl, raven, partridge, and turkey buzzard.

Except for one reference to corn in story number 7, there is no reference to any agricultural crops, but there is a story about maple syrup. The picture is thus characteristic of a hunting-gathering way of life. There are no references to specific localities.

CHAPTER FOUR

Stories about Matchikwewis and Oshkikwe

Two sisters, Matchikwewis and Oshkikwe, figure in the stories in this chapter. John Mink, a conservative old medicine man at Court Oreilles, told Robert Ritzenthaler that they were the daughters of Wenebojo. In his collection of Chippewa tales William Jones refers to them as the Foolish Maidens. Of the two, the older one, Matchikwewis, is supposed to be the more foolish and impulsive, while the younger one, Oshkikwe, is often represented as having more common sense and prudence. Stories about these two sisters were told by women. They sometimes served a cautionary purpose, showing what sort of behavior should be avoided by young girls.

Bebukowe, who figures in the first of the following tales, is an ugly old hunchback, described as follows by one informant at Court Oreilles: "He looks awful. He's humped way over. And he's everlastingly got the dirtiest nose. His snot hangs way down."

14. *Bebukowe the Hunchback*

Collected by Robert Ritzenthaler at Court Oreilles in 1942
Narrator: Louis Martin   Interpreter: Prosper Guibord

Once there was a brother and sister living off in the woods all alone and far from anyone. He was a good hunter, and they always had plenty to eat. He had a little flute around his neck, and when he blew it, turkeys would come. One day he got curious and asked his sister if they were the only people in the world, and she said No. He decided he would set out on a journey the next day and find a wife to come and live with him and help his sister with the work.

The next day she gave him a new pair of moccasins and some lunch and told him which direction to take to find people, and he set off. He walked all day through the woods. That evening, as he was looking for a place to camp, he saw a wigwam with smoke coming out. He went over and pulled aside the blanket over the doorway, and saw an old lady sitting there. She never looked up but said, "Come in, grandson."

He sat down, and she told him that she would fix him something to eat. She hung a tiny kettle about an inch in diameter over the fire and put in a few grains of wild rice and a few dried blueberries. Then she gave him a tiny dish and spoon, and when the rice was cooked she handed it to him. He took his spoon and dipped out all the rice and ate it, and then he saw that the dish was full again, and he ate some more. He kept on eating until he was full, and then the dish was empty.

She said, "I suppose you thought there was just one mouthful there." She had read his mind and saw his surprise. She told him to sleep there that night. In the morning she fed him the same way as the night before. Then she told him that it would take two more days for him to reach his destination. On the way he would find two more wigwams with his grandmothers in them who would feed him and take care of him as she had done, and the last one would tell him what to do.

So he started out again, and that night he came to another wigwam with an old lady in it, and she fed him, and the next night it was the same. In the morning the third old lady told him that at around noon he would meet a bad man by the name of *Wejgiwekwané*, who would talk to him. She said that he should not answer him but go right on to the lake, and across that lake he would find a wife.

So he set out, and at about noon he met a homely hunchbacked man who asked him who he was and where he was going. But he didn't answer and kept on going. The fellow followed him and got him mad; so he told the hunchback to be quiet. As he spoke, he couldn't move any farther.

The hunchback told him to sit down, and they would smoke for a while. He pulled out a beaver, and they ate and smoked. The hunchback would point his pipe at the sun, and it would go down a little, but the young man would also point his pipe at the sun, and then it would pull up again. Finally it got dark, and the young man fell asleep. Then the hunchback heated his iron walking stick in the fire and shoved it down the young man's throat, bending it so that he got a hunchback. The hunchback became handsome like the young man and changed clothes with him. In the morning the young man saw that the hunchback had become straight and handsome and that they had changed clothes. He now had a hunchback.

The bad old man led him to the lake and told him that the village was straight across on the other side. They hiked across on the ice. When they reached the other side, they came to a big village. The chief came down and welcomed the handsome man and asked why he had brought the hunchback along. The kids all pitched onto the hunchback, beat him up, and finally killed him.

Then the old chief turned to the bad Indian and said that he had heard of his reputation as a hunter and led him to his wigwam and told him that he knew he hadn't come for nothing and gave him his daughter for a wife.

The next day the men went out hunting, but all the bad Indian got was a rabbit and a prairie chicken. They all thought that this was odd, that such a good hunter should get such small game. They kept on going out hunting every day, but the bad man only got a little game.

Meanwhile, the trampled body of the hunchback had been thrown into a little creek nearby, and one day Oshkikwe saw it lying there. Oshkikwe and Matchikewis were two sisters living on the edge of the village. Each morning their mother would come over and comb their hair. Oshkikwe had a certain power; she knew that the hunchback didn't have his real body. So she dragged him out of the creek and built a sweat lodge and put four hot stones in it and dragged the body inside.

Then she took a little of her hair oil and dropped it on the stones, and the steam went up, and the corpse moved a little. She did it again, and at the third time the corpse said, "You are bringing me back to life. Do you have a little more oil?"

Matchikwewis, who was standing outside, heard him and said that she had some, but Oshkikwe had some too, and she put some more oil on the stones. Then the Indian came back to life. He got up and was very handsome and straight. The iron came up out of his mouth.

Matchikwewis said, "He will be our husband."

But Oshkikwe said, "No, he will be our brother."

The young man walked out of the sweat lodge and went a little way and took the little flute from around his neck and blew it. A lot of turkeys came, and he killed them and brought them back. He showed Oshkikwe all the turkeys, and she was pleased and carried them inside. The young man wanted her for his wife.

The next day the girls' mother came over to comb their hair, and she saw all the turkey feathers. When she peeked in, she saw the handsome young man and all the turkey meat. She picked up some of the feathers and rushed home. She tripped in her excitement and fell into the wigwam. She showed the feathers to her husband and whispered the news to him. Madjikiwis,[1] their son, was there, and when he heard them

1. We encountered this name in the previous chapter in the story of Wenebojo and Madjikiwis. Here Madjikiwis is the brother of Matchikwewis and Oshkikwe. Henry Rowe Schoolcraft says (1839, 1:130) that the name is "indicative of the heir or successor to the first place in power."

whispering together, he got mad and swung his war club at them, but missed. He said that he wanted to hear the news; so they told him that he had a new brother-in-law. Then he quieted down.

The handsome young man missed his tobacco pouch that the hunch-back had taken when he changed their clothes. It was a special kind of bag like a medicine bag made from a fisher's hide. It would bite the other man every time he tried to take tobacco from it. He picked up the iron cane and went over to the other man's place. He had certain powers too. He put the other fellow to sleep. Then he heated the cane in the fire and thrust it down his neck and bent it worse than before. Then he took the tobacco pouch, and it was so glad to see him again that it wiggled.

He went out into the woods and killed a lot of turkeys and then invited the whole village to come to a feast at his wigwam. He invited the old humpback too. When everybody had got there, he asked the humpback to tell the people what he had done. The humpback refused, so the young man took his war club and got up and told the whole story. Then he raised his war club and hit the hunchback on the hump, opening up a big hole from which a partridge flew out. That was his spirit which flew out. Then the young man told the people that he had a sister back at his wigwam. He said that he had been away from her for a long time and he wanted to see her. Madjikiwis volunteered to go along, as soon as he heard that there was a sister. Oshkikwe said that she would go too.

Oshkikwe said that she would shorten the distance, which would normally take three days. She took a small square of buckskin and threw it into the fire. It puckered up, and she said that that would shorten the distance. Then they started out, and by noon they had already got near the wigwam. The young man left his wife and brother-in-law some distance from the wigwam and went on alone, because he sensed that there was something wrong.

When he got there he saw that all his storage racks were empty. When he looked inside, he saw his sister lying in the dirt all covered with ashes and filth. He said, "It is your brother who has come back."

She said, "You always say that, you animals."

He talked to her and convinced her that he really was her brother. Then she cleaned the dirt out of her eyes and looked at him. He asked her who had been mistreating her, and she said, "The animals come every day and say that it is my brother returning, and then they throw dirt on me and urinate on me and make fun of me. Only the brown marten doesn't hurt me."

He told her to lie down again and said that he would hide in the wigwam. He said that when the animals came in, she should say, "I wish my brother were here." Then he'd come out and fix them. So he hid himself, and pretty soon the animals came, led by the wolf. They filed into the wigwam, and the wolf said, "It is your brother returning." Then they started throwing dirt on her again. She said, "I wish my brother were here." With that he came out of his hiding place and blocked the doorway. He asked if anyone had been good to her. The wolf said, "I have been good to her," but the brother answered that he had been the worst one.

He let the brown marten get out, and then he built a fire and took each animal and held him over the fire and singed off all the hair and threw them outside. Then he got some water and washed his sister and combed her hair and cleaned up the wigwam. He told her that he had left some friends nearby.

He went and brought his wife and brother-in-law back to sit next to his sister. He gave the sister as a wife to his brother-in-law. She was very pretty, and Madjikiwis was very happy about it, but he was very bashful and hid his face from her, because she was so beautiful. The two men went hunting the next morning and got a lot of turkeys which Madjikiwis packed home.

The sister had certain powers, and she asked her brother what had happened to him. So he told her about the humpback. She told him that she knew about those spirits and that they were coming soon to try to kill them.

Her brother built a log fort around the wigwam, and the next day she said that they would soon be there. Sure enough, a great horde of those humpback spirits came. The brother and sister kept killing them one at a time. Madjikiwis tried to help, but the spirits knocked him down every time. Each time Oshkikwe revived him with some medicine she had. Finally all the *bebukowe* were dead except for one, and the brother told him to go up to the north and never come back. So to this day there is just one *bebukowe*, and he lives in the north.

Comments

Apart from the story involving brother-sister incest discussed in the preceding chapter, this is the first story in our collection to deal with a brother-sister relationship. This time there is no incest. The brother decides to set out and find a wife who will live with them and help his sister with her work. In a much shorter version of this Bebukowe story told at Court Oreilles, the sister is at first reluctant and says to her brother, "Don't bother. I don't mind working and being busy. You don't have to go for a wife." But he goes anyway.

Economic motives were often used when a young man was persuaded to marry. John Tanner's Indian "mother" (he was a captured white child who was raised as an Indian) spoke to him as follows: "My son, you see that I am now old; I am scarce able to make you your moccasins, to dress and preserve all your skins, and do all that is needful about your lodge. You are now about taking your place as a man and a hunter, and it is right you should have someone who is young and strong, to look after your property, and to take care of your lodge" (1830, p. 64).

As a cooperative complementary team, a Chippewa man and wife formed such an organic social unit that absence of either partner brought about the danger of starvation. This may be illustrated by another quotation from Tanner's narrative. By this time his wife had deserted him on the way to the hunting grounds. He describes the difficulty of living in the woods without a wife: "I had no pukkwi, or mats, for a lodge, and therefore had to build one of poles and long grass. I dressed moose skins, made my own moccasins and leggins, and those for my children, cut wood and cooked for myself and my family, made my snow shoes, &c. &c. All the attention and labour I had to bestow about home, sometimes kept me from hunting, and I was occasionally distressed for want of provisions. I busied myself about my lodge in the night time. When it was sufficiently light, I would bring wood, and attend to other things without; at other times I was repairing my snow shoes, or my own or my children's clothes. For nearly all the winter, I slept but a very little part of each night" (Tanner, 1830, p. 160).

This shows that a viable social unit should contain a male able to hunt and a female able to do the other work. This did not necessarily have to be a husband-wife team. It could consist of a brother and sister or a man and his mother or grandmother. At any rate the complete freedom enjoyed by Wenebojo in the Flambeau origin myth was not realizable in actual life. A man needed a woman to make the wigwam, haul wood and water, prepare his hides and moccasins, and keep the fire going at home. While a baby was still in the cradleboard, it could be taken along without too much trouble and carried on the woman's back. But after the first year or two, the child became a handicap. It could no longer be carried easily and was unable to keep up with the others on foot. Consequently, during the hunting season the child was often left with grandparents, either the mother's or the father's parents. Those too old and too young to hunt stayed behind in relatively settled communities, stocked with provisions, while the active mature members of the group ranged through the woods in search of game. This may help to explain why grandmothers play such prominent roles in Chippewa folklore.

Our present story, "Bebukowe the Hunchback," starts out with a brother-sister pair living alone. Although the central part of the story deals with the villainous old hunchback, his transformation of the hero, and the latter's ultimate success, the story continues with the young man's return to his sister, bringing with him not only a bride but also a brother-in-law, a husband for his sister. Here we have Lévi-Strauss's formula: incest is shunned in favor of reciprocity and brother-sister exchange.

Ruth Landes has given an interesting description of the brother-sister relationship among the Chippewa (1939, pp. 14–15, 17). She describes them as having a good deal of mutual interdependence. The brother brings his sister meat and furs; she mends for him and makes his moccasins. "In spite of the economic and sentimental exchange between brother and sister, there are no intimate contacts. 'They never speak to one another, as though they are shy.' . . . This 'shyness' is initiated by the one who first shows signs of pubescence."

An adult brother-sister pair like that described at the beginning of the Bebukowe story meets all the qualifications for an economically viable social unit, but no sexual satisfaction is possible. Apparently, suppression or repression is achieved. This may help to explain the subsequent experiences of the young man and his sister after they separate but before they marry. The young man is overwhelmed by the old hunchback, and the girl is tormented, dirtied, and teased by wild animals. In both cases we might interpret their experiences as the return of the repressed, an emergence of instinctive drives.

Ernest Jones has argued (1948, pp. 93, 94) that the male genital organ is often depicted as a "little man," a dwarf, gnome, or goblin — deformed, ugly, and wicked men with magical powers. The character of Punch, with his long hooked nose, projecting hump, and pointed cap, is cited as an example. Note the similarity between Punch and Bebukowe, not only in the hump but in the prominent nose, which Freudian literature often terms a phallic symbol, being the only other protrusion beside the penis in the midline of the body. In the southwest of the United States there were stories about a humpbacked flute player called Kokopelli who seduced girls. There may perhaps be a historical link between Kokopelli and Bebukowe, since Kokopelli is considered by Elsie Clews Parsons to have been an insect, perhaps a locust,[2] while Julia Badger described Bebukowe as looking like a grasshopper around the nose and referred to him as "the grasshopper man".[3] Kokopelli's hump was said to contain babies, or blankets, belts, and seeds which he gave as presents to the girls he seduced. He was thus a symbol of fertility, associated with another such symbol, the snake (see Wellman, 1970).

2. Hawley (1937); Parsons (1938); Titiev (1939).
3. For Julia Badger's account about Bebukowe, see chapter 9.

Still another character of Jones's *Little man* type (F451.2.1.4) is the Zulu figure of Tokoloshe, a priapic hairy creature who comes from rivers to assault women sexually. Laubscher has depicted Tokoloshe as follows (1937, p. 8): "He is described as a dwarf-like little man with short limbs and a powerful thick-set body. He wears a sheepskin wrapped round his shoulders. One of his outstanding physical characteristics is his huge penis."

The young man in our story has to accept the sexual side of his nature if he is going to get married. Let us say that the handsome young man represents the ego; then Bebukowe would represent the unrecognized, rejected, alien id impulses. The two are the same person. Something similar happens to the sister who suffers the persecution and insults of the wild animals before she marries Madjikiwis. I suggest that this may be the latent meaning of this story.

Schoolcraft (1956, pp. 84–86) has an Ojibwa story called "Bokwewa the Humpback," which is quite different in most respects, although it echoes some of the themes in our story. In this tale Bokwewa the humpback is a good person. He lives alone with a brother who is normal and well built. Bokwewa has more supernatural power and directs his brother in hunting game. One day the normal brother says that he wants to find other people and get a wife. He sets off, like the hero in our story, and finally comes to a place where there are some dead bodies on scaffolds. One is the corpse of a beautiful young woman whom the man wants to marry. He carries her back to Bokwewa and begs him to bring her back to life. Bokwewa does so, and the three live happily together. The young man continues to do the hunting under the direction of Bokwewa, who stays at home with the wife.

One day a tall man appears and abducts the woman. When his brother returns, Bokwewa tells him what happened. After a period of depression the young man decides to go off in search of her. Bokwewa tries to dissuade him. He warns that his brother may be led astray by dissolute, effeminate people on the way and may forget his errand. He must remember not to eat part of a large grapevine lying across his path; it is really a snake. He must also avoid something that looks like bear's fat; it is frog's eggs.

Of course these interdictions are violated; on his journey the brother eats the tabooed substances. Later he comes to a village full of friendly, gaily dressed people. Soon he is beating corn, a woman's occupation, and has forgotten all about his wife.

Bokwewa waits several years for his brother's return and then sets off to look for him and for the abducted woman. He avoids the temptations to which his brother succumbed. Bokwewa finds the abducted woman and turns himself into a hair snake in the river where she comes to draw water. When her abductor asks for water to drink, he swallows the hair snake, which kills him. Bokwewa then resumes his former shape and goes to beg his brother to come back with him. The brother refuses to listen. So Bokwewa leaves and disappears forever.

Although this story is so different from our tale, they may be related through inversions of themes. Both tales have the polar pairs of hunchback and handsome young man. The hunchback has supernatural power in both tales, but it is evil power in the Court Oreilles story and not in Schoolcraft's. Both tales involve bringing people back to life. Oshkikwe restores the murdered young man to life and to his former shape. Bokwewa brings a young woman back to life. These restorations precede marriages..

The two stories begin the same way, with two siblings living together, one of whom decides to go off in search of a wife. Boy gets girl in both tales, but boy finally loses girl in Schoolcraft's tale.

The latter story seems to be about the loss of virility. When the brother is separated from his wife and from Bokwewa, he becomes a woman, and takes up a woman's occupation, beating corn. He will not listen to Bokwewa, after the latter has killed his wife's abductor.

The two brothers may again be seen to stand for a single person. It is Bokwewa who brings the girl back to life and who tries to reunite the brother and his wife. When the effeminate man refuses, the ties between the brothers and between husband and wife dissolve.

Later, in chapter 9, I will present Julia Badger's fantasies about Bebukowe, which seem to have erotic overtones, in agreement with the suggested phallic symbolism of this character.

It may be noted that Julia Badger believed that Bebukowe rescued her when she was on the road to the other world and brought her back to life. That is also what happens in the story of Bokwewa; he brings a woman back to life so that she can marry his brother. When Bebukowe rescued Julia Badger, he promised her that she would "play around" with a lot of men.

15. *Star Husband*

Collected by Victor Barnouw at Lac du Flambeau in 1944
Narrator: Julia Badger

There were two sisters who used to go out in the woods and pick berries. One was always trying to get ahead of the other; she was inquisitive

and liked to talk. That was Matchikwewis. She said, "I've found a porcupine. But if you don't help me to get him, I won't give you any of his
quills." The porcupine was in the hollow of a stump. Matchikwewis put
her face in the hole in the stump. They say that the porcupine has his
belly against the hole. She said to her sister, "That feels awfully good.
Why don't you put your face in there and rub it against the fur? The
hairs are nice and soft." The other sister didn't do it.

Then the porky said, "If you cut the hole a little more, you'll have
some nice straight quills to feel. If you give me a dress, I will do a lot for
you afterwards."

Matchikwewis asked her sister to take her dress off.

Oshkikwe said, "No, why should I? Why don't you take *your* dress
off?"

Matchikwewis took off her dress and stuck it in the opening and gave it
to the porky. The old porcupine put it on. Then he ran out of the hole. It
was old Wenebojo himself. Matchikwewis ran after him and threw her
axe at him, but he escaped, laughing at them. She must have got another
dress somehow.

They went along in the woods. It was time to look for a place to sleep.
They didn't go to sleep right away. Matchikewis looked up at the stars
and said, "Do you see that star that doesn't shine very much? That's an
old man. And the star that shines real bright is a young man. I don't care
for that old man. I'd like to have the young one."

Oshkikwe said that she didn't care. She'd rather have the old man than
the young one. But it worked out just the opposite. That night the old
man came and slept with the older sister, and the handsome young man
came and slept with Oshkikwe.

The next evening they slept under the stars again. This time those two
fellows came and took them up to their hut above the clouds. There was
an old lady there sitting on the floor with her legs stretched out, making
twine on her lap by rubbing it against her knee. She told them to come
in. She put a tiny kettle on the fire and spoke to the kettle, saying, "What
shall we give these people to eat?" She put some rice into the kettle and
told it to boil.

Matchikwewis said, "My, what a little bit! Is that all they're going to
feed us?"

Oshkikwe said, "It's better than nothing."

Soon the kettle was boiling, rice was set in front of them, and they
were told to eat. Then the old lady told them that she'd help them get
back to earth. She took the big ball of twine she'd been working on and a
cedar woven bag. She told the older sister to get into the bag first. She

said, "Don't look out of this bag. Keep right on going." Then Oshkikwe got into the bag.

While they were going down, Matchikwewis said, "Let's look out to see how far we are."

"Be still," said the younger sister. "We're getting along fine."

They went sailing along. After a while, though, the older sister peeked out. Then they fell down onto the top of a tree. They had to stay up there. Finally a wolverine came along. Matchikwewis called out to him, "Come up here and get us. I want to go first."

The wolverine said, "No, let your sister come first." He carried Oshkikwe down.

While he was bringing down the older sister, she said, "I want to make water. Let me go." But he didn't let her go, so she urinated on him, and he jumped. Matchikwewis fell down the rest of the way and broke her leg.

The younger sister made a place for them to stay. One day, while she was cutting wood, a mouse said to her, "Your sister wants to marry you."

Oshkikwe said, "What are you saying? If you explain what you're saying, I'll give you some of the tallow I put on my hair to make it look nice."

The mouse laughed and said, "Your sister is getting ready to marry you."

Then Oshkikwe brought in all the wood she had been cutting — enough for three days. The next day she went out with her axe and carrying strap, as far as you could still hear the noise of wood chopping. Then she told her axe and packing strap to keep on cutting wood all day, and she went off as fast as she could go.

This was in winter time. She went across a lake and found a man chopping a hole in the ice. She told this man that somebody was bothering her and chasing her. The man told her to go in between his legs. She went right through his legs and then thanked him.

Her sister had been following her and came to the man on the ice. She asked him if an old lady had gone by.

The man said, "I didn't see an old woman go by here. Are you crazy? I did see Matchikwewis' sister go by."

"Which way did she go?" asked Matchikwewis.

She went between his legs, and the man hit her with the pole with which he was chopping the hole in the ice, and she went down through the hole.

The man said, "That's where you belong. What sort of world would it be if people did what you wanted to do — marry your own sister?" As he said this, the hole closed up, and Matchikwewis was caught under the ice. That's where she stayed. Now on cold winter days, when you hear ice cracking and making noises, that's Matchikwewis. But when you see a beautiful sunset on a winter evening, that's Oshkikwe.

Comments

The *Star husband* tale (A762.1) had a very wide distribution in aboriginal North America. Stith Thompson (in Dundes, 1965) has analyzed its variant forms in considerable detail. He concludes that the basic form must go back at least to the eighteenth century. It is found from southern Alaska to central California, in the western plateau and plains from the southwest to far into Canada, around the Great Lakes and east to Nova Scotia, with versions found in Oklahoma, Texas, and Louisiana.

Our Chippewa version differs from those discussed by Thompson in emphasizing the differences between good Oshkikwe and bad Matchikwewis. Matchikwewis initiates all the bad action, while Oshkikwe is modest and good. This is also true in the preceding tale about Bebukowe. It is Oshkikwe who rescues the handsome young man and brings him back to life. When she does so, Matchikwewis, being forward, says, "He will be our husband." The more demure Oshkikwe says, "No, he will be our brother." However, it is she who eventually becomes his wife.

There is something vaguely erotic in the conversation between Matchikwewis and the porcupine at the beginning of this story. This is emphasized by the porcupine's request for a dress, which makes Matchikwewis disrobe. Paul Radin gives a version similar to this story, except that the animal is a raccoon instead of a porcupine, and both of the girls take off their clothes. Radin comments: "It is considered a most shameful thing for women to undress in public" (1956, p. 56). William Jones gives a version of this story in which both girls say they want the porcupine for a husband (1917, 1919, pt. 1, p. 135).[4]

In our version the story about the porcupine is not connected with the *Star husband* tale. They seem to be separate, unrelated episodes. In some Plains tribes, however, the two episodes are more organically tied together. The older sister, who wants a porcupine husband, follows him up a tree which takes her into the sky.

4. See also de Jong (1913, pp. 19–20).

Our version seems to show little interest in the celestial husbands, who disappear from the story after the girls get up there. Attention now shifts to the old woman who gives them a meal. Matchikwewis displays her usual bad manners by commenting on the small amount of food, while Oshkikwe is more tactful.

Then the old lady helps them to get back to earth. The episode about the animal at the foot of the tree, including the fall of one sister, is characteristic of the Ojibwa region. It is not part of the basic *Star husband* tale. Stories of this type are found in Canada from the Kaska in the west to the Micmac of Nova Scotia. Stith Thompson (in Dundes, 1965, p. 453) states that this episode is never found south of the Canadian border, but here he is wrong, as our Wisconsin version shows.

The last part of the story deals with the incest theme again, this time concerning two sisters. Oshkikwe runs away from Matchikwewis in the same way in which Wenebojo's sister runs away from her brother in a story given by William Jones (1917, 1919, pt. 1, pp. 279–99). Both are protected by a man who is chopping a hole in the ice and who tells the girl to go between his legs. In the Jones tale this person is identified as Coot, a long-legged bird, who is described as standing on one leg. Coot tells passersby to go between his legs (a set phrase, according to Jones), but this is manifestly impossible. When Wenebojo tries to go through, Coot drops a frozen human body on him and kills him, although Wenebojo characteristically comes back to life again. Both Matchikwewis and Wenebojo are thus punished in the same way for attempting incest.

A recurrent structural aspect of the Matchikwewis-Oshkikwe stories is the formula Interdiction/Violation/Consequence, which is related to Lack/Lack Liquidated. Matchikwewis wants something which she shouldn't want; she gets it and then is punished, while Oshkikwe is rewarded, or at least not punished, for abstaining from the tabooed action. The interdiction is often unstated but implicit. The following violations and consequences occur: Matchikwewis takes off her dress and loses it. She wishes for a young star husband but gets an old one, while Oshkikwe is paired with the handsome young man. Matchikwewis looks out of the bag, which she was told not to do, and the bag falls into a tree. She urinates on the wolverine and breaks her leg. She wants to marry her sister and is pushed under the ice.

The following Wenebojo story is inserted here because it contains the episode of the two women and the porcupine. Instead of this being followed by the *Star husband* tale, the sequel is Wenebojo's masquerade as a woman in the clothes with which the women have plugged up the hole. This version seems to lack the erotic overtones of Julia Badger's narrative, except for the fact that the women take off their dresses. But their motive in doing so is apparently to trap the porcupine, so that they can catch him later, after they have collected wood.

16. *Wenebojo and the Chief's Son*

Collected by Ernestine Friedl at Court Oreilles in 1943
Narrator: Delia Oshogay   Interpreter: Maggie Lamorie

There was a chief's son who didn't care for women at all. Lots of women tried to get his attention, but he was too proud to bother with them. Wenebojo heard about this and decided to play a trick on him; so he turned himself into a porcupine and hid in a tree stump.

Two women came along, on their way to cut wood. They saw the porcupine go into the tree and tried to catch him, but he was safe inside. They decided to plug up the tree hole with their dresses, so that they could get him after they had cut their wood. Then they went away.

Wenebojo crawled out and put on their dresses. Looking like a woman, he set out for the chief's home. When he got there, the chief's son fell in love with him right away. He proposed marriage, so Wenebojo stayed there. After a while Wenebojo pretended that he was going to have a baby. He went out and got a little marten, and made believe that it was his baby. Then he began to collect a lot of meat and stowed it away in a sack which he placed near the door, where he could grab it easily.

One time everybody was inside the wigwam. Then Wenebojo told his "baby" to run away. The marten ran out, Wenebojo chased after him and grabbed the sack of meat. He shouted that he sure had played a trick on that chief's son. That's what he deserved for not wanting to have any girls around.

Comments

Tales of Trickster posing as a woman and marrying a man (K1321.1) are found among the Tlingit, Haida, and Tsimshian of the Northwest Coast; the Nez Percé of the Plateau; the Western Mono and Paviotso of California; the Arapaho, Dakota, Crow, and Southern Paiute of the Plains; and the Menomini and Micmac of the Woodland area.

Apart from serving as a warning to haughty young men, this story may also function as a slapstick release of homosexual tendencies, and it serves to make marriage seem rather ridiculous. This story is a counterpart to the story of the proud chief's daughter who rejects her suitors and then falls in love with the dung man, given on page 54.

17. *The Two Brothers and Oshkikwe*

Collected by Ernestine Friedl at Court Oreilles in 1942
Narrator: Delia Oshogay   Interpreter: Maggie Lamorie

Once there were two brothers. The older one caught whitefish; the younger one hunted for coon. Nearby lived an old woman with three daughters. Matchikwewis was the oldest and Oshkikwe the youngest. They don't tell you the name of the middle one.

One time the old woman wanted some whitefish. She combed her oldest daughter's hair and said, "I want you to go and marry the man that catches whitefish, because I want some whitefish." So Matchikwewis set out. When she got to the camp of the two brothers, there was nobody there. She looked at the place where the whitefish brother   lived. It was dirty and full of scales. She didn't want to stay there. So she crossed the wigwam to where the coon hunter lived. She got his supper ready. When the two brothers came home, the coon hunter was glad that he didn't have to get his own supper ready.

The next night after supper they filled the coon bladders with coon tallow and took them over to her mother. But her mother wasn't satisfied and ordered them out. She said that she didn't want any coons. She wanted whitefish. She threw out everything they'd brought. The man went home, and the girl stayed with her mother.

Then the mother got her second daughter ready, combed and oiled her hair and dressed her up, and told her to marry the man that caught whitefish. But it all happened exactly the same way. She didn't like the whitefish man's place; she got supper ready for the coon man, stayed with him, and brought home coon bladders filled with tallow for her mother. But her mother said that she didn't want coon; she wanted whitefish. The girl stayed home, and her husband went home with his coon bladders.

Then the mother spoke to Oshkikwe, the youngest daughter, and told her to marry the man who caught whitefish. She said angrily, "I guess you'll go and marry the coon man again!" Then she oiled her hair and told Oshkikwe that she wanted whitefish bad.

When Oshkikwe got to the place of the whitefish man, it was terribly dirty. It made her feel gaggy and funny. But she got ready and started to clean it up. She took all the fish scales and dumped them out and fixed everything up neat and tidy. When the whitefish man came home, was he pleased to see what the woman had done! She had supper ready for him too. The next day her husband told her to go over to where she'd dumped the fish scales. When she got there, she found lots of beautiful shells and pretty things to make into bracelets and ornaments. Then she knew that her husband was a good man.

She made all kinds of pretty things to take home to her people. When she first saw her husband, he'd worn a dog turd for a feather headdress. But now she saw that it was a nice bunch of shells. He told her that he'd wanted her instead of her sisters, and that was why they hadn't settled with him.

When she got home with all her presents, her brother said, "I guess she'll be bringing some more coons and coon gut." But when they passed all the presents around, her mother nearly went wild, as if she didn't know what she was doing, she was so tickled. Everybody was pleased.

Oshkikwe and her husband stayed there for a while. Her mother had an older sister living nearby with two daughters. She took one of the fish brought by her son-in-law to give to her sister. When the two girls heard that their aunt had a new son-in-law, they decided to go over and meet him. When they got there, they were just about to lift up the flap of the entrance to go into the wigwam, when the old woman clubbed them and told them to get out. She didn't want anyone to come in and cast their eyes on her son-in-law.

The girls felt very bad and walked home. They told their mother how their aunt had treated them. She found it hard to believe that her sister would treat them that way. She said that she'd go over and find out for herself. When she got to the wigwam, she told her sister that she'd come to see the new son-in-law, but right away her sister began to club her on the head and knocked her out. When she came to, she felt very bad and went home. When the two sisters were young they had promised never to deny each other anything.

That night the older sister decided what to do. She played sick, moaning and groaning, as if she was dying. Her daughters asked her if there was any medicine that would help her. She said there wasn't any. So the two girls went over to their aunt's place and told her how sick their mother was.

She felt sorry about her sister and got dressed to go out. She remembered the promises they'd made to each other when they were young. When she got to her sister's place, she said, "Don't you know of any medicine that would help you get better?"

The sick woman said, "There is only one thing that could keep me from dying. If you cooked your son-in-law and gave him as a feast to all the people, then I'd get well."

The old woman went home and told the story to her daughter and son-in-law. Her daughter was angry. She said, "It's all nonsense. She's just jealous because my mother has a son-in-law. She's not really sick. It's all a fake." She begged her husband not to give up his life.

But he said, "If you do what I tell you, I'll come back to you. I won't be gone for good. Let them boil me, but if you do as I say, I'll come back."

He told his wife that when they had the feast, she should save each of his bones and be careful not to break any of them. After the feast the men would go out hunting. When they brought back a good deer hide, she should clean and scrape it and put all the bones into it and sew it up. The men should then make a little wigwam high up in the trees and put the bag of bones inside it. On the tenth day after the feast, she should go to that place.

When they had the feast she cried and wept, but she did everything he said, and they built the wigwam and put the bag of bones inside it. Just before the tenth day, Oshkikwe heard a noise coming from the tree, and when she went there she saw the bag of bones come out of the wigwam and head toward the south. She went over to her brother-in-law and told him what had happened. She said that she was going to hunt for the bones and not stop until she found them. He told her that he would lie down beside the fire and not do any work; he'd just stay there by the fire until she came back with the bones. He said the fire wouldn't go out.

Oshkikwe set out for the south. Whenever she camped overnight, she put up a stick pointing south, so that she wouldn't lose her way if the sun didn't come out. Finally she came to a village, as it was getting dark, and stopped at the first wigwam she saw. An old woman and her daughter lived there. The old woman heard a noise outside and said to her daughter, "You'd better let your cousin in. She's probably coming to sleep with you again."

The daughter thought that it was her cousin outside, so she invited Oshkikwe in. Then they saw that it was a stranger, but they got supper ready for her.

The old woman and her daughter told Oshkikwe a story while they were busy stringing shells. They said that one evening they were sitting outside, when a bag of bones came near the wigwam and dropped down. The daughter kept the bag of bones, and every evening she and the other women of the village went and played with it. The daughter would go to a certain place and shake out the bag, and lots of shells would come out, so that everyone could help himself. Oshkikwe didn't say anything, but she thought about what she'd do.

The time came for them to go and shake the bag of bones. Oshkikwe went with them. It had started to get dark. They told Oshkikwe to put on an apron, since she could get more shells that way. The women and girls of the village collected. The daughter shook the bag of bones and got a lapfull of shells. Oshkikwe waited for her turn. When she got the bag, she shook it, and some shells came out. She told the daughter to hold her apron. Then, right away, she grabbed the bag of bones and beat it for the woods.

She kept on going until she reached her brother-in-law's place. He was still lying there by the fire. The man told her to take three big rocks and heat them in the coals. Then he told her to build a tiny wigwam, just big enough to hold the bag of bones. She did as he said. He told her to make a fire in the wigwam and put the rocks in the fire and put the bag of bones inside by the edge of the wigwam. Soon they could hear a man breathing in there, and she knew that her husband was coming to. The brother-in-law told her to hand him some tallow, and he put the tallow in there with the bag of bones, and the bag of bones came to life. The man said, "Whoever is making me come back to life, please open up my wigwam." They opened it up, and there was Oshkikwe's husband. She cooked a big meal for him.

After the meal, Oshkikwe's husband said that she should go back home without him, since there was no use for him and his brother to live as persons any more, because people didn't treat them right. They would go back to what they were made of. Oshkikwe burst out crying and said, "I wouldn't have gone through all this if I didn't care for you, and I'll never go home after the way they treated me. Now, after all I've gone through, you want me to go back home."

Her husband said, "Well, then, do as we do, and you can come with us." So they spread their wings and became birds and flew away. They say that whenever you see those birds, there are always three of them, two males and one female.

Comments

Once again, Oshkikwe is obedient and does the right thing, while her older sisters are selfish. Although the whitefish man's place makes her feel gaggy and funny, she cleans it up. Oshkikwe is rewarded by the transformation of the dirty fish scales into beautiful shells and ornaments and by the knowledge that her husband is a good man.

In the previous stories we have had a simple contrast between the impulsive and greedy Matchikwewis on the one hand and the controlled, sensible Oshkikwe on the other. But now a new dimension is added; we have several "bad" women. Although Oshkikwe has apparently behaved correctly in being obedient to her mother, the mother is soon shown to be overly selfish. She wants her daughters to marry the whitefish brother just because she wants to eat whitefish. Moreover, she becomes so overjoyed with her new son-in-law, that she won't let her sister and nieces see him, and she forgets the promises made by the two sisters when they were young. While this is selfish enough, her sister becomes even more demanding by asking for the death of the son-in-law, to which the young man humbly accedes, since he has the power to come back to life again.

This story is reminiscent of the Bebukowe episode in which Oshkikwe brings the handsome young man back to life. In that episode she did it on her own, but here she is instructed by her brother-in-law.

The husband feels that he cannot return to people who have treated him so badly, and Oshkikwe also does not want to return to her mother; so they become birds. The story seems to emphasize the dangers of pride and lack of reciprocity. One can see that this is a woman's story; it contains nine female characters and only two males, a reverse of the situation in the Flambeau Wenebojo myth.

Once again, we find the structural pattern of Interdiction/Violation/Consequence. The first two sisters violate their mother's interdiction about which husband to marry, and so they lose their husbands. Their mother is unkind to her sister and loses her son-in-law.

Although the following story deals with two girls, they are not Matchikwewis and Oshkikwe. I insert it here, however, because it seems to belong to the same general category, involving a foolish girl and a wiser one.

18. *The Two Girls and the Leech*[5]

Collected by Victor Barnouw at Lac du Flambeau in 1944
Narrator: Tom Badger

At Leech Lake there were two young women in a canoe, crossing the lake. One of them began to wonder why the lake was called Leech Lake. While they were paddling, they began to notice that the current was going just like a rapids. The canoe began to stand straight up, and the woman sitting in front took off all her ornaments. Indian girls used to

5. This story also appears in Barnouw (1954, p. 90).

wear a lot of beads. She took them all off and put them into the lake. The other one didn't know that she should do this. That was the one that had been wondering why it was called Leech Lake. She fell out of the canoe. But before she fell off, she saw a great big leech — three or four feet wide. The other girl saw it too. He was coming through the water in big up-and-down motions, like a worm crawling fast. The girl drowned and died. The leech probably took her to the bottom of the lake. But that showed her why it was called Leech Lake. She should have taken off her ornaments and put them in the lake. That story shows why Indians respect everything. If that girl hadn't asked herself "Why is this called Leech Lake?" nothing would have happened to her.

Comments

In this case the girl's sin is intellectual curiosity. The girl shouldn't have wondered why it was called Leech Lake. In traditional Chippewa culture there seems to have been a great emphasis on meekness, docility, and obedience among young girls. These virtues, at any rate, are stressed in the stories about Matchikwewis and Oshkikwe.

In keeping with this emphasis and with the sexual division of labor, there was also a marked sexual segregation. In a brief visit to La Pointe in 1846 Timoleon Ducatel noticed this segregation: "The old women scarcely ever leave the lodges; young women or maidens are never seen intermixed with the men, or participating in their amusements" (1846).

This story again exemplifies the pattern of Interdiction/Violation/Consequence.

19. *Oshkikwe's Baby*

Collected by Ernestine Friedl at Court Oreilles in 1942
Narrator: Delia Oshogay   Interpreter: Maggie Lamorie

Matchikwewis and Oshkikwe were out picking cranberries and staying by themselves. One day Oshkikwe found a tiny pipe with a little face on it. The eyes were looking at her and would wink at her. She showed it to her older sister and said, "Look at this little pipe! I guess we're not really alone in the world. There must be somebody else in the world."

Matchikwewis said that they had once lived in a village and that their father had been the head man. When he died, she took Oshkikwe away, because she didn't want her to be abused by the people.

Matchikwewis knew that her sister was going to give birth to a child because of the pipe. One time, when they woke up, they saw a *tikinagan* (cradleboard) with wraps and everything set for a baby, including a little bow and arrow. Oshkikwe took sick and found a little boy and a little pup.

Matchikwewis took good care of her sister, and everything was going fine. One day Matchikwewis told her sister that she'd had a dream which told her not to leave the baby out of her sight for ten days but always stay with him, for otherwise an old witch would come for him. Once Oshkikwe just went outside to get a stick of wood, and when she came back she could see the swing moving. The pup used to guard the little cradleboard. While she went out, she heard the pup barking. When she got back, both the baby and the pup were gone. All that remained was a piece of the hind quarters of the witch which the dog must have bitten off and a little piece of the *tikinagan* which the pup must have got too.

As soon as she saw this, she said that she'd get ready to look for the child and the pup. She told her sister she'd be gone for ten days. The sister told her to work on her breasts, so they wouldn't run dry. She had been nursing the baby on one breast and the pup on the other. The sister also said that the further the witch went with the child, the bigger he'd get, and soon he'd become a man.

The mother started walking, and she crossed a deer trail. She kept on going and came to another trail: a man's tracks, deer tracks, and a dog's tracks. This was her son's tracks, because the witch had so much power that it didn't take the child long to grow up. Finally, Oshkikwe came to a wigwam. Outside of it, she saw a man who must have been her son already grown up.

The man went into the wigwam to tell his "mother" what he had seen. He told her that he had seen a young woman. But the witch said, "Don't you dare look at that woman, because she's just a dirty old witch. As soon as you look at her, you'll become ugly."

The young man said, "Well, I don't like to see her trying to build a wigwam of old birchbark and things. Why don't you give her some nice birchbark, so it won't rain on her?"

The witch didn't like to do it, but she had to. Whenever this old witch knew that there was a new-born boy, she'd kidnap him, and as soon as they got into her territory, the boy would grow up and go hunting and work for her, so she got all the profit out of it.

This man of Oshkikwe's got home early one afternoon, because he had to make arrows before it got dark. Just as he went by Oshkikwe's wigwam, she had her breasts open. The pup was hanging around Oshkikwe, because he remembered her.

While the young man was whittling his arrows, the first thing he knew

Oshkikwe was sitting on a woodpile, showing her breasts to her son. He knew that there was something he couldn't remember, but he couldn't remember what it was. He suspected something, though. In his dream he made a wish that his "mother" would sleep soundly, so that he could go over and visit this young woman whom his "mother" called an old witch. So his "mother" slept soundly that night. He went to see the young woman, accompanied by the pup. When the pup got there, he went to nurse at the woman's left breast. Oshkikwe said to him, "You are my son, and here is the milk you lived on before this old witch got hold of you."

He couldn't remember, but she told him, and she brought a piece of his cradleboard made of cedar and shells, and also a piece of the old witch's hindquarters, and showed them to her son. He asked his mother how she managed to live and whether the old witch gave her anything to eat. Oshkikwe said, "When she gives me something, she brings only the livers and dirties them on the way." Then the man told his mother he'd go back with her, but not for a while. The minute he'd go back to her, he'd turn right into a baby. At the same time, though, he had to find out the real facts about who his mother was.

That night he pretended to be sick and started to moan. His "mother" asked him what was the matter, and he said he was dying and that the only thing that would save him would be the sight of his old cradleboard. The old lady went out and got a very old cradleboard, but he said that wasn't his. Then she got his real one, with the pretty shells, and he saw that part of it was missing, and he knew then that Oshkikwe was right, since she had the missing part. Then he started to moan again. His "mother" asked him what the matter was. He said he had to taste the milk he used to nurse on. She pulled out her own breast and squeezed out some old yellow stuff and gave it to him to taste. He thought it was funny that he'd ever grown up with such awful stuff for food. He had to find out one more thing. He said, "The only way I can live is if you pull up your skirts high and dance around a little." So she danced for him and lifted up her buckskin dress. He called out, "Higher, ma!" Then he knew that Oshkikwe was right. The old witch went to sleep after that.

The man went back to his mother and told her that he'd go hunting the next morning. He planned to kill a deer and hang it high up on a tree, and then come back and tell the old witch to go and bring it back because his feet were all blistered.

The next morning he came back and told the witch that he'd killed two deer, one near and one far. He told the witch to send Oshkikwe to go and get the more distant deer, and she should get the other one. They both set out, but instead of going on, Oshkikwe came right back.

The old witch had two children. The man banged them both on the head with a club and killed them. Then he stuck two sugar cookies in their mouths and made it look as though they were still alive.

Then he and his mother picked up one stake of the wigwam and went down into that hole a long ways. The man and the puppy got smaller and smaller. By the time the old witch got home, her boy was gone, and here were her two children with sugar cookies in their mouths. She yelled at the kids, because they were eating something she was saving for their brother; but when she got closer to them, she saw that they were dead.

Then she spoke aloud to her son: "Huh! What do you think? This world is too small for you to get away from me!" She found the hole they had gone down and followed them. By this time the man and the puppy had become very small. He told his mother to put him in the cradleboard which she'd brought along. The last thing he managed to tell his mother was that she should make a big mark with his arrow, and there the earth would split. She took the arrow and marked the ground just as the witch came along. Then the witch fell into the split, and that was the end of her. When Oshkikwe got home, she found her sister all dressed up and her hair oiled. She said that if Oshkikwe hadn't arrived that night, she would have gone after her the next day.

Comments

The opening paragraph of the story suggests that some social units could live in considerable isolation from others. Oshkikwe says, "I guess we're not really alone in the world. There must be somebody else in the world." This is reminiscent of story number 14, at the beginning of this chapter, in which the young man asks his sister if they are the only people living in the world.

As in the Wenebojo origin myth, the young girl becomes pregnant through supernatural means, by a pipe this time instead of the sun (T532.1, *Conception from contact with magic object*). The phrase, "Oshkikwe took sick and found a little boy and a little pup," is rather obscure. It suggests that Oshkikwe gave birth to both the boy and the pup. At any rate, she suckles the pup along with her baby. In some societies women suckle young domesticated animals; I don't know whether or not Chippewa women did so.

This story differs from the preceding ones in having no polarity between bad Matchikwewis and good Oshkikwe. Matchikwewis plays a helpful, subordinate role. It is Oshkikwe's story. Usually it is Matchikwewis who violates an interdiction and suffers the consequence. In this case she warns Oshkikwe not to let the baby out of her sight. When Oshkikwe violates this interdiction, she loses her child.

The witch in this story might be a grandmother symbol. Perhaps the story represents a conflict between a woman and her mother-in-law over the affections of a child. Since grandmothers often took care of children, such conflicts might well have developed in the old culture. Maggie Lamorie, for example, took her oldest grandchild, a baby girl, away from her mother when she was only six weeks old, because "her mother wasn't very good to her." Maggie fed the child on condensed milk. Later on she took over a second granddaughter, who had been suckled by her mother up to the age of eight months. She said that her son and daughter-in-law used to go out on binges for several days at a time. When her daughter-in-law returned, she used to want to breast-feed her baby again. "I wouldn't let her," said Maggie. "I didn't want her to kill the child. So I took care of both of my granddaughters after that." The little girls called their grandmother "Mama."

"Indians like to stay with their grandparents," said John Moustache. "I went to stay with my mother's father, when I'd finished my mother's milk. . . . An Indian thinks more of a grandchild than of his own children." Julia Badger lived with her father's parents and came to think of her grandmother as her real mother. Although Julia used to see her own mother occasionally, she claims that she never knew that the woman was her mother. "When I lived with my grandparents," she said, "I didn't see very much of my mother any more. I didn't know she was my mother." It wasn't until Julia was about fourteen that the true situation was explained to her.

There are Chippewa stories about both good and evil grandmothers. As we have seen, good grandmothers are associated with the theme of the self-replenishing kettle. This might be a tribute to the grandmother's ability to conjure up food out of the often scanty provisions with which they were supplied, or an early fantasy to compensate for the child's deprivation of its mother's breast. The old witch in our story has an unrewarding breast, from which she squeezes "old yellow stuff," while Oshkikwe shows her younger and fuller breasts to her son to bring back his memory. The witch in our story is not a provider of food but an exploiter. Through her magic the young man grows very quickly and starts to hunt game, "so she got all the profit out of it." The young man's rapid growth echoes the episode in the Wenebojo origin myth which expresses regret at the slow maturation of human children, in contrast to animals which are able to walk soon after birth.

A tale similar to our story is given by Schoolcraft and also in William Jones's collection, in both of which the witch is called Old Toad-Woman (G261, *Witch steals children*); the woman is not identified as Oshkikwe in either. (Incidentally, Toad-Woman is also the name given to the old woman who tries to heal the *manido* kings in Jones's version of the

Wenebojo cycle.) In the Jones story the young man falls in love with the young woman who is really his mother, and he wants to marry her.[6] This could be seen as an Oedipal tale, although without hostility to the father. In our version the young man seems to be attracted to Oshkikwe, but he does not wish to marry her or try to woo her, as in the Jones story. In our account the young man ends up as a child in the cradleboard — perhaps a fantasy of regression.

The witch tells the young man that Oshkikwe is really a dirty old witch. "As soon as you look at her, you'll become ugly." Here we are reminded of the confusions about Bebukowe and the young man whom he transforms. It is hard to separate illusion from reality. The old witch whom the young man calls "mother" is not really his mother. Attractive young Oshkikwe is said to be really a dirty witch, and the young man is told that he himself will become ugly if he looks at her. It is difficult for him to learn the truth; he has to have proof supplied by the missing pieces of his cradleboard and the hindquarters of the witch. He has been brainwashed by the old woman.

General Comments on the Matchikwewis and Oshkikwe Stories

The stories in this chapter differ from those which have preceded in the presence of courtship themes, the higher incidence of female characters, and the important role of a heroine, Oshkikwe. These features must stem from the fact that these were women's stories, while the Wenebojo tales, related to the Midewiwin, were told mainly by men. The last story, "Oshkikwe's Baby," deals with issues that particularly concern women — a kidnaped baby, rivalry between a mother and a witch over a son, and the theme of suckling.

In the first tale a young man sets out to find a wife and brings back a husband for his sister. In the second tale Matchikwewis and Oshkikwe find star husbands for themselves, although they do not seem to stay with them long. "The Two Brothers and Oshkikwe" deals with marriage and affinal relationships. The initiative in courtship in this case seems to come from the woman. Indeed, it comes mainly from the girls' mother, who wants to eat whitefish and therefore sends her daughters to the men's camp.

Since these are partially cautionary tales for girls, the pattern of Interdiction/Violation/Consequence often appears.

6. Jones (1917, 1919, pt. 2, pp. 427–41); Schoolcraft (1956, pp. 260–62). Another similar Canadian Ojibwa version is given in Laidlaw (1918, p. 79).

The animals mentioned in these tales include turkey, fisher, marten, wolf, porcupine, wolverine, mouse, coon, dog, deer, partridge, whitefish, and leech. There is no mention of farming or agricultural crops, but there are references to wild rice and to picking cranberries. There seems to be an implied specialization in hunting: one brother hunts coon, the other whitefish. One man is a specialist in hunting turkeys.

In this chapter we find, again, the notion that visible forms are deceptive. Wenebojo turns himself into a porcupine and later masquerades as a woman with a marten as his baby. A handsome young man is changed into an ugly hunchback and vice versa. The witch in the last story tells the young man that Oshkikwe is really a dirty old witch. In "The Two Brothers and Oshkikwe" a man who had worn a dog turd for a feather headdress turns out to really have a nice bunch of shells.

Again, related to this, is the theme of the reversibility of life and death. In the first story Oshkikwe brings the murdered young man back to life (J1955.1). In "The Two Brothers and Oshkikwe" she and her brother-in-law bring her dead husband back to life. In these stories hair oil or tallow is used in the process of revivification.

The notion of a hierarchy of power is also present. The young man in the first story has magical power over turkeys, but Bebukowe has power over him and is able to kill him. Nevertheless, the old hunchback does not have good hunting power, and he is eventually defeated.

Most of the social units mentioned in these stories are small. In the first story a brother and sister live in the woods all alone and far from anyone. The two sisters are alone at the beginning of the second story and the last tale. There is, however, reference to village life in the first story, in which the turkey hunter invites the whole village to a feast. In "The Two Brothers and Oshkikwe" all the women and girls of a village meet in the evenings to play with the bag of bones — collective activity. A village chief is referred to in two of the stories, but he is not described as exercising any special power or authority.

Themes of aggression are prominent in this chapter. A young man is killed in two of the Oshkikwe stories. A battle with hunchbacked spirits occurs in the first story. Matchikwewis is shoved under the ice in the second tale. In the last tale Oshkikwe's baby is kidnaped by the old witch; the witch's children and the witch herself are killed.

Among oral themes we have the self-replenishing kettle in the first two stories. In the first tale Bebukowe shoves a heated iron stick down the young man's throat, which comes out of his mouth when Oshkikwe brings him back to life. Wenebojo steals meat in the third story. In "The Two Brothers and Oshkikwe" the girls' mother wants to eat whitefish and sends her daughters off to the camp of the whitefish man. Since she doesn't want to eat coon meat, she throws it out and drives the coon man away. Oshkikwe feels gaggy and funny about cleaning up the whitefish man's place but does so. The sister of the girls' mother says that she can get well only if Oshkikwe's husband is cooked and served as a feast. After Oshkikwe has brought her husband back to life, she cooks a big meal for him. In the last story Oshkikwe is made pregnant by a pipe. Suckling is a prominent theme in this story. Both baby and pup are nursed at Oshkikwe's breast. After the baby has been captured by the old witch, Oshkikwe shows her breasts to the young man he has become. When the old witch suckles him, he gets only yellow stuff. The witch dirties the food which she gives to Oshkikwe. Sugar cookies are stuck into the mouths of the witch's murdered children.

Anal themes are not so prominent in this chapter, but they are present. In the first story, animals cover the turkey hunter's sister with dirt and urine, and Matchikwewis urinates on the wolverine in the second tale. In "The Two Brothers and Oshkikwe" the whitefish man, whose camp is so dirty, wears a dog turd which later turns into a nice bunch of shells. In "Oshkikwe's Baby" the pup bites off a piece of flesh from the old witch's hindquarters, which Oshkikwe saves and later shows to her son.

CHAPTER FIVE

Windigo Stories

In Chippewa usage a *windigo* is a cannibal giant. The term *windigo* has also been applied by anthropologists to a form of mental disorder. There has been much discussion about the so-called *windigo* or *wiitiko* psychosis.[1] Cases of *windigo* psychosis do not seem to have been reported for the Wisconsin Chippewa. The only reference in our field notes to someone "going *windigo*" is in the story of Mary Careful in chapter 9. The Wisconsin Chippewa do, however, have stories about people who become cannibal giants, but these were not considered to be true stories in the 1940s. According to these tales, the only way one can fight a *windigo* is to become a *windigo* oneself. This involves not only assuming giant size but also turning oneself into ice. To return to normal size and to deice oneself, one must drink great quantities of piping hot tallow.

The stories in this chapter were told only as stories in the 1940s, but they were probably believed in a few generations before. The most conservative old-timer at Court Oreilles, John Mink, did not believe in *windigog*.

20. *The Boy Who Defeated a* Windigo

Collected by Ernestine Friedl at Court Oreilles in 1942
Narrator: Delia Oshogay   Interpreter: Eleanor Martin

When kettles started to move, an old medicine man knew that *windigog* were about. He called the people in, filled a pipe with tobacco, and asked each person to smoke it. The one who could puff on the pipe four times and light it without using a match would have the power to kill a *windigo*. One young boy did it, and he told the people to prepare a place for him, so that he could get power to fight the *windigo*. The medicine man said that the *windigo* was going to come with three dogs. When the boy got ready, he had two dogs that came from nowhere.

The boy told the people to prepare a boiling kettle full of tallow. He

1. Landes (1938); Cooper (1933); Parker (1960); Teicher (1960); Fogelson (1965); Hay (1971).

120

said he'd know whether the *windigo* would get the best of him by the way the dogs fought. He turned himself into a *windigo*, fought the cannibal giant, and finally won. The people poured the hot tallow into the *windigo*, and it melted all the bad spirit out of him. He became just like the rest of the people.

21. *The Man with Four Wives*

Collected by Robert Ritzenthaler at Court Oreilles in 1942
Narrator: Pete Martin

There was a man called Makobimide who had four wives. He was very gluttonous. He was a good hunter, but he made his women hunt too. His four wives were sisters, and they all lived in the same wigwam. When he went hunting, he would not come back until he'd got something; sometimes he was gone for four days. He hunted only bear, while his wives hunted rabbits.

When he got home from hunting, his first wife would fix him two rabbits to eat. After he had eaten them, his second wife would fix him up another pair of rabbits. Then his third and fourth wives did the same. He had two stomachs, one on each hip.

One morning he said, "Another man is coming over to see me, and I'll wait for him." His wives knew that this person was a bad man who could turn himself into a *windigo* whenever he pleased.

When the fellow came, Makobimide went out to meet him. The fellow saw him and hollered eight times. Each time he hollered he grew bigger. At the eighth time he was as tall as a tree. Makobimide hollered too for ten times and grew even taller. Then they started to fight, tearing up trees by their roots and hitting each other with them. Finally Makobimide killed him. That man had come to fight Makobimide because he was jealous of his success in hunting. Makobimide killed a number of *windigog*. After each battle one of his wives would melt tallow in a kettle. Makobimide would drink down the tallow while it was boiling, and that would bring him back to normal size.

Comments

Here an oral-incorporative gluttonous hero defeats an oral-incorporative *windigo* villain. The *windigo*'s motivation is interesting; he was jealous of the hero's success in hunting, like the *manidog* who killed Wenebojo's nephew. Evidently this kind of hostile reaction to

another's success was regarded as understandable by a Chippewa audience. One man's success exacerbates feelings of inferiority and resentment in others; so they retaliate against him. In our competitive modern
world we may concede the validity of such a psychological response, but
it seems surprising to find it in an egalitarian hunting-gathering society.

22. *The Little Girl and the* Windigo[2]

Collected by Joseph Casagrande at Court Oreilles in 1941
Narrator: John Mink   Interpreter: Prosper Guibord

One morning the kettle over the fire started to move, and the people
got scared. They went around the village to see if anyone felt strong
enough to fight a *windigo*, but they couldn't find anyone. At one end of
the village there was an old woman living with her granddaughter. The
girl asked what was wrong, and the old woman said, "Someone is coming, and we're all going to die."

The little girl asked someone to bring her a couple of sticks of sumac as
long as her arm, with the bark peeled off. They gave her the sticks, and
she took them home.

Now it turned so cold that they could hear everything cracking. In the
morning the girl told her grandmother to put a kettle full of tallow on
the fire. It kept getting colder and colder outside. When they looked out,
there was a *windigo* as big as a tree. As he walked along, the trees
cracked and ice formed on the lake. He walked right through the ice on
the lake.

The girl had two dogs; he had one. Her dogs killed his in no time. The
girl kept getting larger. She took her sumac rod, which had turned to
copper, and knocked down the *windigo*. Then she hit him with the other
sumac rod and killed him. The girl drank the tallow and got smaller and
smaller. The people chopped up the *windigo*. He was all ice, except in
the center, and there was a regular man. The people were so happy. The
little girl could have anything she wanted.

Comments

Robert L. Hall has commented on the possible symbolic linkage of fire,
copper, and sumac in connection with this tale. Sun and fire are

2. This story is given in somewhat different form in Ritzenthaler and Ritzenthaler (1970,
pp. 151–52).

associated with warmth and red hues, while death is allied to coldness and lack of color. Hall notes that fire greatly aids the germination of sumac, a circumstance which may also have been noticed by the Indians. Sumac was used by the Indians as an herbal remedy for many purposes, such as healing burns, blisters, and sores. This makes it an appropriate life symbol to counter the cold death symbolism of the *windigo*; and copper, with its reddish hue, may have served as an equivalent symbol (Hall, 1976).

23. *The Baby* Windigo[3]

Collected by Robert Ritzenthaler at Court Oreilles in 1942
Narrator: Pete Martin

A young married couple had a baby which they put in a cradleboard. They'd set him between them and fondle him and talk to him. One day he surprised them by talking (he was too young for that). He said, "Where is that Manidogižik who is said to be so powerful? Some day I'm going to visit him." His mother grabbed him and said, "You should not talk about that *manido* that way."

One night they were sleeping with the baby between them, and the mother woke up to find that the baby was gone. She woke up her husband. They built a fire and looked all over the wigwam for the child. They went to their neighbors' wigwams too, but they couldn't find him. Finally they found some tiny tracks leading to the lake. Halfway down to the lake they found the cradleboard. Now they knew that the baby had made the tracks, had crawled out of his cradleboard, and was on his way to see the *manido*. From the cradleboard down to the lake there were very large tracks. Then they knew that he had turned into a *windigo*.

Manidogižik was protected by fifty dwarfs. (When a dwarf threw a rock, it was a bolt of lightning.) The dwarfs heard the *windigo* coming and came to meet him. They fought, and they finally knocked him down with a bolt of lightning. He fell with a noise like a big tree falling. He was dead. When they chopped him up, he was just a big block of ice. They melted down the pieces, and in the middle of the body they found a tiny infant about six inches long with a hole in his head where the dwarf had hit him. This was the baby who had turned into the *windogo*. If they hadn't killed him, he'd have eaten up his whole village.

---

3. See ibid. (pp. 150–51) for the same tale.

24. *The Little Boy and the* Windigog

Collected by Ernestine Friedl at Court Oreilles in 1942
Narrator: Delia Oshogay   Interpreter: Maggie Lamorie

There was a woman who lived with her little brother, whose name was
Manidowiwises. She had a dream that she should make lots of moccasins
and put them on a rack over the fire. She also dreamed that her little
brother should never wade in the nearby river. One time the little boy
walked to the river with his bow and arrows. When he shot an arrow, it
fell into the water, and he had to get it. As he reached over for it, he fell
into a big muskie's open mouth. He hollered to his sister. She ran to the
rack with the moccasins and then ran to the river with them. She held
the moccasins to the muskie's mouth, and the boy reached out and
grabbed them; then she pulled him out. After he was saved, she told him
never to go in a direction she pointed, because there were all kinds of
manidog there who had killed their mother and father and all the other
people in the village.

In the morning after breakfast the little boy ran straight in the direction his sister had told him not to go. He found an ocean and a big island
on the ice. There were lots of very big men fishing through the ice, lying
down with blankets over their heads. He went near where one of them
was fishing and saw a nice big muskie lying on the ice. The little boy
took the fish and hid it. The big man couldn't see him, because he was so
small. He began to miss his muskie and asked another man what had
happened to it. Nobody knew. The big man said, "One of you has my
muskie." He saw one of the other men's muskies and said, "That's mine.
I speared mine in the back, and you speared yours in the neck." Pretty
soon they started to fight. These big men were *windigog*.

Manidowiwises had the power to make himself invisible. He took the
muskie home to his sister. She asked him where he got it, and he said he
found it frozen in the ice. She didn't believe it, because it was fresh.

The little boy made lots of trips to steal fish. Finally he thought he'd let
the *windigo* see him. When the *windigo* saw him, he said, "You're the
one who's been swiping my fish. I've a notion to break your wrist."

"You couldn't do it," said the little boy. "Try it."

The *windigo* tried, but couldn't break his wrist.

Then the boy said, "Now let me break your arm."

The *windigo* told him to go ahead and try and held out his arm. The
little boy broke it. Then a bunch of other *windigog* took him away. The
little boy went home and told his sister that a bunch of *windigog* would
come over to kill them in the morning because of what he'd done to the

big *windigo*. He told his sister to make breakfast early in the morning, since he had to do something to fight back.

She got up early in the morning and made breakfast. Then she called her brother. He asked her if the *windigog* were coming yet and asked her to look. She saw them coming by the point on the ice and told him to hurry. He took his time getting up and getting dressed. He ate his breakfast. His sister was nervous. She kept telling him to hurry up with his breakfast, because the *windigog* were getting closer and closer. But he just ate his breakfast. She said, "The *windigog* are by the landing." The boy had been eating his food out of a shell. Now he turned it upside down, and it became a mountain. He had the power to do that. The little boy told the *windigog* to stop pounding on his house, because it would leak when it rained. But they wouldn't go away. So the little boy had to go out there and kill the big *windigo* with his club. Some of them got away. Two little children, one on the other's back, came and told him to kill them, because they knew they couldn't escape. Instead of killing them, he put some grass into their mouths and told them that they'd be buffaloes for the rest of their lives. So those *windigo* children turned into buffaloes. He said to them, "Instead of you eating people, people will eat you." And so it was.

25. *The Boy, His Sister, and the Giant*

Collected by Robert Ritzenthaler at Court Oreilles in 1942
Narrator: John Mink   Interpreter: Prosper Guibord

There was a giant who had a lot of power.[4] He lived in a big wigwam with twenty women. One was so big that whenever she moved she "pooped." Whenever he heard about a young girl he might like, he'd go and get her and make her his wife. He was too powerful a spirit.

A brother and sister lived alone out in the woods in a wigwam. There were no neighbors around. The boy was just old enough to hunt small game with his bow. He went hunting every day. One evening he got home from hunting and found that his sister was gone. He called outside but got no answer. There was a lot of wood which she had cut but no fire; so she must have gone early in the day. He felt badly and started to cry. Finally he cried himself to sleep.

In the morning he set out without breakfast to look for his sister. He

4. This seems to be a plain, ordinary giant, not a *windigo*. However, this seems to be a suitable place to insert this story.

followed a trail where she had grabbed twigs and branches and broken them. Following this trail, he came to the giant's wigwam, where he saw his sister sitting near the door, near the other women. She asked him why he came. "The giant will kill you and me too," she said. "I don't care. I can't live alone," said the brother.

The giant was out hunting. Every day he killed one elk and slung it over his shoulder and came home. That evening he threw the elk down before the door and went in and said, "Oh, my brother-in-law is here." He seemed to be glad to see him. He told one of the women to take off his moccasins and hang them up to dry.

Nothing happened that night. In the morning the giant invited the boy to go out hunting with him. The giant moved so fast, the boy couldn't keep up with him. So the giant said he would leave a trail of broken twigs. At noon the boy caught up with the giant, who had killed an elk and was roasting one of the intestines over the fire. The giant tossed him the small end of the intestine and said, "Here is your dinner." Then he told him to unstring his bow and make a pack strap of the twisted rawhide string and put the head of the elk on his back. The antlers stuck into the boy's back, and the pack strap cut his forehead. The giant gave him a shove and told him to pack the head home. The boy was halfway home when the giant caught up with him and chided him for being so slow. He shoved the boy aside into the brush. The boy got to the wigwam late that night. Then the giant scolded him for being a poor hunter and for not being able to pack anything properly.

Every day the same thing happened until winter came and the snow was very deep. The giant would often step on the brother with his big snowshoes and push him right down into the snow. During this time the boy was fasting. One day, while he was following the giant's tracks, he came to a big tree, and someone spoke to him. He looked up and saw a well-dressed man, who said, "My nephew, you're having a hard time."

The boy said, "I don't care, because I won't last long under this treatment, but I don't want to leave my sister alone."

The spirit said, "We had a meeting today, and I was sent to help you." He meant the spirits of Thunder and Lightning.

The spirit said, "When you catch up to the giant, he will be cooking that intestine again. When it is ready to eat, you grab it out of the fire and cut off the small end and give it to the giant. Then eat until you are full and throw the rest into the fire, saying, 'I want my uncle to partake of this.' The giant will be very surprised. This time, when he puts the head on your back, hurry back here. Just before he steps on you, you say, 'The giant is very cruel to me. I wish my uncle were here.' "

The boy followed his instructions. When the giant caught up with him, he said, "The giant is very cruel to me. I wish my uncle were here." Then the uncle appeared and grabbed the giant, just as he was about to step on the boy. They fought each other with war clubs. The uncle would knock off the head of the giant, but it would come right back on again. Finally the uncle told the boy to shoot the head as it flew off, and he did so. Finally the giant's body was dead, but his head was still living. The uncle told the head to go home and bite a big piece out of the cheeks of each of his wives, but not to touch the sister. The uncle told the boy that he had fasted long enough and would have success in hunting after that. He was told to pack as much of the elk as he wanted and to go back and get his sister and take her home. The boy did this and was successful in hunting all the rest of his life.

26. *The* Windigo's *Hunting Ground*

Collected by Victor Barnouw at Lac du Flambeau in 1944
Informant: Tom Badger

A man lived with his wife and his dog and went hunting and trapping as far as he could go. There was another man trapping in the woods too — some distance apart. He didn't want anyone to come onto his hunting grounds. He found the first man's tracks, and he was kind of mad. He met the man and said, "Let's take a rest." They sat down. The second man picked up his tobacco pouch and handed a plug of tobacco to the first man and said, "I want to visit you tomorrow."

The first man knew right away what that man meant, because he'd strayed onto his hunting ground. The second man said, "I'll try to be over at your place around about noon."

"All right, I'll wait for you." Then the other fellow went back home.

There was snow on the ground, so the next day the other man could follow his tracks to his home.

When the first man got home, he told his wife that he'd met somebody. He told his wife that he'd gone over onto somebody else's hunting ground. "That fellow will be here tomorrow," he said. He told his wife that she should get up early in the morning so that they'd be ready. "When that fellow comes, he will be a *windigo*," he said.

The next morning they got up before daylight. The man killed their dog. Then he told his wife to singe him, burn off his hair, and cook him. Then he went out to meet the other man, at the point on the lake.

Before he left, he told his wife what to do when he came back. "Before I come back this afternoon, be sure to get ready and cook that dog. When I come home, I'll stop right in front of the door. Keep on boiling that bucket until I get home. When I get to the door, I'm going to kneel down in front of it and I'll open my mouth. You pour the food from the kettle into my mouth."

The woman said, "All right," and this fellow went to meet the other man right there at the point. The other fellow was there; he was a *windigo* already, a great big man. The first man tried to be like that too. They started to fight, pulling up timber just like weeds, and hit each other. I don't know how long they fought there. Both men were mad. After a while the first man killed the other one. Then he collected wood to build a fire. The *windigo*'s body was all ice. The man built the fire to melt his body. He himself was the same way too. He melted the other man's body and then went back home.

When he got home, he knelt down in front of the door, as he'd told his wife. His woman had the kettle with the dog cooking in it. His mouth was open about four feet. The woman took that bucket and poured it all into his mouth. The food was hot, so he melted when he swallowed it down. So he got back to normal size.

Comments

Before commenting on the *windigo* stories in general, I would like to draw attention to the fact that the last story concerns separate family hunting grounds. The Wisconsin Chippewa did not have this institution, but both Landes (1937a, p. 88) and Hallowell (1955, p. 119) have described it for the Canadian Chippewa. When I pointed out to Tom Badger that the story assumes the existence of family hunting grounds, he acknowledged the implication but denied that Chippewa families had such private hunting grounds. The story need not be taken as evidence that such hunting grounds formerly existed in Wisconsin, for the tale may have been brought by the Indians who moved south of Lake Superior, and who may have continued to tell it along with other traditional tales, or the story may have reached Lac du Flambeau by diffusion.

General Comments on the Windigo Stories

The last story suggests the existence of lone family units living in the woods. In "The Brother, His Sister, and the Giant," a boy and his sister also live alone in the woods with no neighbors around. In general, small social units are suggested by these tales, although there is mention of village life in "The Little Girl and the *Windigo*," "The Little Boy and the *Windigo*," and "The Baby *Windigo*," and it is implied in "The Boy who Defeated a *Windigo*."

Each story, of course, contains themes of aggression and orality (cannibalism), fights between *windigo* and man. Transformations are involved in the cases where the protagonist turns himself into a *windigo* and later comes back into his normal shape. The hierarchy of power is also an important theme, for only certain people have the power to kill *windigog*. Moreover, one cannot tell who they are, for they may be mere children — a boy in two of the stories and a little girl in another. On the other hand, a baby in a cradleboard may suddenly become a *windigo*. In the third and fourth stories the *windigo* is all ice and is chopped up by the people after his death. In the center of the ice they find the original person — "a regular man" in the third story. In three of the stories the person who kills the *windigo* has to become a *windigo* himself temporarily and after that has to drink hot tallow or dog broth to melt himself down and bring himself back to normal size.

The reader may have noticed by now that tallow or animal fat plays a rather prominent role in Chippewa folklore. In the origin myth, Wenebojo makes tallow and grease by chewing bones. In the story "Wenebojo in the Whale and His Fight With an Ogre" in chapter 3 it is stated that the whale is mostly fat or tallow, so Wenebojo and his grandmother make grease out of it. This grease or oil is applied to the canoe and paddles of Wenebojo's boat, so that he can get through the sea of pitch that surrounds the ogre's land. In a Wenebojo episode described in story number 3 the pieces of the slain king's body turn to oil, and different animals come to apply the oil to their bodies — the rabbit to his back, the deer to his flanks — while the bear drinks some of the fat. "Everyone who sipped or touched the fat turned into *manidog*, and those who fast have them as guardians."

In "The Two Brothers and Oshkikwe" in chapter 4, Matchikwewis and her sister fill coon bladders with tallow to take to their mother, although the mother does not appreciate either the presents or the son-in-law. More important, Oshkikwe's brother-in-law in the same story uses tallow to bring her brother back to life from a bag of bones. This last episode and the role of tallow in deicing and normalizing *windigog* show that tallow was regarded as a kind of life-giving and nourishing substance.

Schoolcraft has an Ojibwa story about ghosts that have a gluttonous desire for animal fat, and he observes in a footnote that the fat is considered among the choicest parts of animal meat by the Indians (1956, p. 150).

Part of the explanation for this emphasis on the importance of tallow may lie in the fact that many of the northerly North American Indians made use of tallow as preservative for food that was cached in winter time. It was also used in the making of pemmican. Another explanation is suggested in a paper by Vivian J. Rohrl, who argues that nutritional deficiences may have been contributory factors in the genesis of *windigo* psychoses. Rohrl cites two cases from Teicher's collection in which animal fat was given to the "psychotic" person to eat. Rohrl also cites a Cree folktale about a *windigo* woman who had eaten her own children but who was cured by a drink of melted bear's grease. "It should . . . be noted that bear fat is believed to contain vitamin C, or ascorbic acid, probably derived from berries and other foods in their diets. Large doses of this vitamin are currently used as a sedative in some mental cases" (Rohrl, 1970, p. 99). Rohrl cites Steffanson's conclusion that fatty meat is essential to the diet of Eskimos and northern Athapaskan Indians. Fat deficiency leads to headaches and may ultimately lead to death. Nervous ailments caused by hypoglycemia can be corrected by diets of fat and protein.

Rohrl's paper has been criticized by Jennifer Brown, who points to the small number of cases mentioned in which animal fat was actually used as a cure (1971). However, the attention given to animal fat in Chippewa myths and tales suggests that there may have been, as Rohrl intimates, some kind of knowledge, whether conscious or unconscious, of the value of such substances. Note that the animals who sipped or touched the fat from the body of the slain king became the *manidog* who appear to those who fast. Here is a rather direct relationship between food deficiency and animal fat.

A possible latent meaning of the *windigo* tales is a conflict between child and adult, since the giant is so much bigger than the hero, and in some of the cases the hero is a young boy or girl. Admittedly, this explanation would not hold very well for the story of "The Baby Windigo." Seymour Parker (1960) has suggested that *windigo* psychoses stem from frustrated dependency needs in childhood. The prototype of the cannibal giant is the frustrating mother.

To a Freudian the hot tallow might represent milk. It is interesting that old John Mink at Court Oreilles remarked: "I remember the taste of my mother's milk. It tasted rich and good, like bear fat." If we accept Parker's argument that the frustrating mother is a prototype of the *windigo*, it would help to explain why the *windigo* is made of ice. The mother is cold, rejecting. What is needed to counteract that is warm, nourishing liquid food.

The *windigo* may also be seen as a symbol of cold and winter, which devours everything. Gabibonike, who appears later in story number 39, is the spirit of winter. Made of snow and ice, like a *windigo*, he begins to melt when he eats hot rice.

In structure, some of the *windigo* stories in this chapter have the following sequence: (1) premonitory indications of the coming of *windigog*, e.g. moving kettles; (2) a protagonist states his readiness to fight the *windigo* and gives instructions about preparations; (3) the fight with the *windigo*; (4) resumption of normal human size by the protagonist. This scheme applies to the first and third stories and to some degree to the last tale.

CHAPTER SIX

Animal Tales

There are two types of animal tales in this chapter. First (stories 27–32) are some supposedly true stories about people's experiences with such animals as underwater lions, snakes, and bears. A second group (stories 33–43) are stories recognized as fiction. These are usually rather short anecdotes, sometimes humorous, involving tricks played by one animal on another and sometimes having explanatory that's-why elements.

The following story is about a woman who hits an underwater lion's tail with her paddle, cutting off the end of his tail, which is made of copper. As she does so, she says, "Thunder is striking you," thus invoking the hostility believed to exist between thunderbirds and underwater animals.

27. *The Underwater Lion*

Collected by Robert Ritzenthaler at Court Oreilles in 1942
Narrator: Pete Martin

There was a big lake; Indians lived on both sides of it. There was a big island of mud in the center, and if anyone wanted to go to the other village across the lake, they would have to paddle around the edge of the lake. If they tried to go straight across, something would happen to them. A bad *manido* lived there in the island.

One day there was a medicine dance across the lake, and people started around the lake in their canoes. Two women started later, after the others had gone. They were sisters-in-law. One of them was rather foolish. She was steering in the stern and headed straight across. The other warned her not to do it, but in vain. The first girl had a little cedar paddle with her. She never left it out of her sight — always took it along, even when she went out gathering wood. She held it but did not use it for paddling. As they got to the middle, they crossed the mud, and in the center of the mud was a hole of clear water. The water was swirling around the hole, and as they started to cross it, a lion came out of the middle and switched his tail across the boat, trying to turn it over. The girl picked up her little paddle and hit the lion's tail with it, saying, "Thunder is striking you." The paddle cut off the lion's tail, and the end dropped into the boat. When they picked it up, it was a solid piece of copper about two inches thick. They watched the lion running away through the mud, and the steerer laughed hard. She said, "I scared him. He won't bother us again." When they got across, the girl gave the piece of copper to her father, and he got rich through having it. The copper had certain powers. People would give her father a blanket just for a tiny piece of that copper. They would take that bit for luck in hunting and fishing, and some just kept it in their homes to bring good luck.[1]

Comments

This tale is reminiscent of the two girls on Leech Lake, but the outcome is very different. In the former story a girl drowns and is carried to the bottom of the lake because she wondered why it was called Leech Lake. In this story, however, a bold girl gets the upper hand over a powerful underwater spirit and even laughs at him. One never knows who has power or how much.

An important Indian dichotomy was between the birds of the sky and underwater animals. There was a kind of feud believed to exist between these two classes, especially between thunderbirds and snakes, although thunderbirds were also enemies of underwater panthers, lions, or lynxes, termed *micipijin*, which were said to be made partly of copper. These may refer to pumas or cougars (which can swim), found in the Great Lakes region until fifty or more years ago. The name for the animal given in these stories is the term supplied by the narrator or interpreter. The two underwater kings whom Wenebojo kills in the origin myth are not identified with any animal species in our version, but in some other versions they are said to be underwater panthers. In this tale, as well as in some others, the animal is identified as a lion. Selwyn Dewdney has suggested that wherever British influence penetrated in North America, the Indians must have noted representations of the British lion on coins, treaty documents, and so on, and they may have asked what it was. On being told that it was a lion, the Indian might thereupon have identified this beast with *micipijin*, or Missipeshu, to use Dewdney's term. This explanation may account for the widespread use of the term "lion" for this underwater creature (Dewdney, 1975, p. 125).

1. A story like this is given in Laidlaw (1918, p. 100). In this version the two women are mother and daughter. Thunder is not mentioned. The daughter cuts off the hand of the underwater lion which grasps the canoe.

Creatures of the underwater class were feared by the Chippewa. One should reject such spirits, if they appeared in a dream or vision (see Landes, 1968, p. 31). Such spirits as underwater panthers have not been seen much since the coming of the white man, Tom Badger explained to me, because underwater creatures are afraid of thunder and other loud noises. "When they use dynamite or blast canals and things like that, those things go away. They go underground somewhere," he said.

28. *The Horned Snake*

Collected by Robert Ritzenthaler at Court Oreilles in 1942
Narrator: Pete Martin

There was an old fellow who knew some bad medicine. He was a drummer in the Medicine Dance and was always using his drum. Once he went with his drum and his runner and camped on a sandbar in Gurnoe Swamp. He started to drum and call on a big snake, in order to get bad medicine. After a while there was a sound like water coming through, and then water started to come up through a hole and filled the swamp and caused a big foaming whirlpool. The big snake stuck his head out of the water. He was as big around as a log and had horns. The fellow cut a piece of flesh out of the snake with his knife and gave it to his runner to put away. He also took a piece from under each horn. He cut the snake just as if it was butter. This was used as bad medicine by this fellow, who caused many people to die just by wishing they would die, no matter how far away they were. He would just think that the person should die, and he would. This happened a long time ago.

29. *The Mide Priest and the Snake*

Collected by Robert Ritzenthaler at Court Oreilles in 1942
Narrator: Pete Martin

There was a Mide priest who began to save blankets for the Medicine Dance. He saved up for two years and then told people at the feast that he was going after medicine. His runner was away, so he took his daughter along up to Big Sugar Bush near Indian Post. Here there was a tiny lake with black water in it. He left his daughter on the hill, went down to the lake, put his blankets on the shore, and started to drum and sing. The water started rising, and soon the blankets were in the water, and he had to move back. He moved back several times until he was almost back to where his daughter was sitting. Then he took out some medicine, chewed some, and sprinkled it on the edge of the water. Then it stopped coming up. The fellow then made a knife out of cedar, and when the big snake came up, he took this knife and cut some flesh — very easily — from under the horns. . . . This fellow was good and said as he took the flesh that he didn't want to use it to harm anyone, but only to bring good luck in hunting, trapping, and so on. I've used this stuff myself; it was good stuff. I always had good luck, but I had to stop using it, because the old woman who cooked my meat always had to rub some powdered medicine on her hands before she could use it. I was afraid my wife would forget some time. So I gave the medicine away.

30. *Human Sacrifice*

Collected by Ernestine Friedl at Court Oreilles in 1942
Narrator: Delia Oshogay   Interpreter: Eleanor Martin

There was a man who used to kill his babies. Every time his wife got pregnant, he'd take her in a canoe to give birth to the baby near the deepest part of the lake, and he put a stone around the baby's neck and dropped it in as a sacrifice. He did that nine times. His wife pleaded with him, but he wouldn't listen. He told her never to bury him in the regular cemetery. My grandmother and aunt were out picking strawberries there, when they heard a whistling sound. They turned around and saw a great big serpent with a big head of horns. It came from the grave and went straight to the lake. The children came home and told the people. The people came and saw it go down into the lake near the place where the man's children had been drowned. That was the last they saw of it. It colored the lake for a while. Then they dug up that man's grave and found nothing there.[2]

Comments

Snakes were feared by the Wisconsin Chippewa, who used to carry flagroot in little buckskin bags tied to their legs as a protective charm against them. There were some taboos concerning snakes. As mentioned earlier, one should not tell stories in summertime, when frogs or snakes

2. For similar Chippewa stories about horned serpents, see Kohl (1860, pp. 422–25) and Jenness (1935, pp. 35, 39).

are about, but only in winter, while they are hibernating. It was considered a bad omen to see a snake enter a house; this might portend death in the family.

Wisconsin Chippewa in the 1940s sometimes referred to snakes as evil spirits — *macimanidog*. According to J. G. Kohl, one of the early travelers in the Chippewa region of northern Wisconsin, the reason given for boys' fasting for a vision in a nest high up in the trees, rather than on the ground, was that the boys would be removed from the evil spirits' creatures — snakes, toads, and so on (1860, p. 236).

However, the snake does sometimes play a beneficent role in Chippewa folklore. There are some stories in which a serpent safely transports innocent people across a stream away from danger, while malevolent people are drowned. The reader will remember the snake log which one must cross to reach the afterworld and the two fire-breathing snakes on the road which Wenebojo's brother made. Serpents also guard the home of the two underwater kings whom Wenebojo kills. The serpent figures as one of the *manidog* worshiped in the Midewiwin, and a snake hide was given at Lac du Flambeau to someone who went through the Midewiwin for the third time.

Some shamans were believed to get supernatural power by cutting off part of the flesh of giant horned serpents inhabiting lakes or swamps. The snake was believed to be summoned by drumming and the offering of blankets, and was said to churn up black waters into whirlpools, causing them to rise, as in the two stories told above.

A Chippewa Indian from Sault Ste. Marie who claimed to have gone on the road to the other world while in a trance state identified the afterworld snake log with the underwater horned serpent. He said that he crossed the tree, which had its roots in the air. On the other side he looked back "and there was a great snake with horns. . . . That was what I thought was a tree" (see Julia Knight, 1913).

Beliefs about horned serpents associated with sorcery and with floods are found among other American Indian tribes. Elsie Clews Parsons has noted that in a Hopi folktale the horn of a horned snake "is used for bewitchment, to cause floods" (1925, p. 61n). Voth gives a Hopi story in which a piece of a horned snake's flesh is used for magical purposes, though not for sorcery. His data also refer to the association of snakes with floods (1905, pp. 53, 56, 59).

The antiquity of the relationship of the snake to sorcery beliefs in North America is indicated by the wide distribution of notions concerning the horned serpent, similar to those described for the Chippewa. Gatschet informs us (1899) that horned serpent concepts were found among the Wabenaki, Passamaquoddy, the Indians of southeast Maine, the Shawnee, the Potawatomi, and the Creek, among others. The

Kwakiutl of the Northwest coast also had a horned serpent (see Boas, 1895, p. 371; Locher, 1932, pp. 12, 33). The idea that medicine men get supernatural power from snakes appeared among the Iroquois (see Erminnie A. Smith, 1883, p. 70) and similar concepts are attributed to the Huron, the Choctaw, and the Cherokee (see Hastings, 1911, 3:503, 568; 6:885).

The horned serpent complex has been particularly well documented by Skinner for the Menomini. Among the Menomini, as among the Chippewa, we have concepts about the offering of blankets beside the water, the drumming by medicine men to invoke the serpent, the formation of whirlpools, the rising of waters, and the need to sacrifice children to the horned snake (1915a, pp. 184–89). We have the same use of a cedarwood knife to cut flesh from the snake's head. We have the notion of perpetual warfare between thunderbirds and snakes, and the idea that it is a bad omen to see a snake or to dream of one. There is also the idea that some snakes are beneficent (1913b, pp. 81–82; 1921, pp. 31–32, 265, 384). Skinner notes that designs of horned snakes are found on the medicine bags of sorcerers, containing their "poisons." The same writer has collected data about the horned snake from the Sauk Indians of Oklahoma (1928, pp. 161, 169).

Horned serpents are associated with floods among the Creek in the southeastern United States and among the Sumu of Nicaragua, who also have traditions of the enmity between serpents and thunderbirds (see Rands, 1954). (It may be added that beliefs in huge aquatic snakes which inhabit lakes, like the Loch Ness monster, have sometimes been expressed by whites in Wisconsin and other parts of North America.)[3]

The snake plays an erotic role in some Chippewa tales as a lover of girls.[4] This seems to be implied in one of the fantasies of Julia Badger discussed in chapter 9.

31. *The Man and the Grizzly Bear*

Collected by Robert Ritzenthaler at Court Oreilles in 1942
Narrator: Alec Martin   Interpreter: Prosper Guibord

In the old days the Indians were afraid of grizzly bears. Only those with strong powers obtained through fasting could kill them. Bears

---

3. For some reports of sightings of such creatures in Wisconsin, see Charles E. Brown (1941). For a more global survey, see Costello (1974). Reports from the United States and Canada are given in Costello, pp. 208–32.

4. Four stories of this kind appear in Laidlaw (1918, pp. 86, 88, and 1924–25, pp. 68–69). See also Jones (1917, 1919, pt. 2, p. 47); and Jenness (1935, p. 35).

would sometimes track a man to his village and kill the whole village if there wasn't some powerful person there. One time an Indian was out hunting and saw a grizzly bear. He knew that he didn't have the power to kill him, so he climbed an oak tree. The bear started digging at the roots and finally uprooted the tree, and it fell. The Indian got up and ran. He found a hollow log and climbed into it. The bear grabbed the log and tried to crush it but couldn't. Then he lifted the log on end and tried to shake out the man but couldn't. Then he took the log to the top of a hill and let it roll down, but the man stayed inside it. Then he took the log down to the river and put it on the water and ducked the log, but he still stayed in. The bear pushed the log down deeper the next time, and the man swam out and swam across the stream and got away.

When he got back to the village, he told the people what had happened. The head of the village called a council and said, "We are all going to die unless someone has the power to kill the bear." The people sat around in a circle, and one person filled a pipe and passed it around. Anyone who accepted the pipe and smoked it had the power to fight the bear, but no one accepted it. The pipe was passed around once more, and finally one person accepted it. This man took his gun, shot it, and reloaded it after cutting off some of his long hair. He made a wad and rammed it into his gun. Soon they heard the bear coming, and this fellow went up to him and killed him with just one shot.

32. *An Old Man in the Form of a Bear*

Collected by Victor Barnouw at Lac du Flambeau in 1944
Narrator: Tom Badger

The Indians used to go south to hunt deer. At that time there were no deer around here. One old man and his old lady went along with a bunch of Indians. They had no children. The old man could hardly walk; same with the old lady. When the Indians got a deer, they always gave some to the old man and his wife. Sometimes they killed a bear too and gave them meat. They were afraid of the old man. When a hunter came back, the old man would say, "You've got game. You're lucky." Then the man had to give up his whole deer. He couldn't get by otherwise. They were all afraid of him.

One day a young fellow came along with some deer. He saw the old man waiting by the trail, but he didn't give him the deer. The old man said, "All right. You're going to eat that meat as long as you live."

The young fellow didn't feel well the next morning. He was sick for three or four days; then he died. It was the old man who done it.

After the young man died, the people moved camp and went to another place. The young man's parents were in that group. One day his father went back to their old camp site and made a place where he could hide and watch the place where his boy was buried. He wanted to find out for sure what had happened. While he was sitting there, after sundown, he heard an owl speaking and making all kinds of noise. After a while he heard a fox holler. Pretty soon he saw a bear coming along the trail he'd come along. He watched the bear.

The bear stopped by the grave and dug a little bit. In those days they buried people only about two feet down. Then, while the bear was digging, the man shot. The bear started to run back along the trail. The man jumped up and went down the trail after him. It wasn't far before he came upon the old man. He was dead. He wasn't like a bear then.

The man cut him down the middle — two cuts down the sides — and took out that part of the man (stomach and genitals) and took it home. He left the rest of him there. When he got home, he started to cook that meat, cut up into pieces. After it was all cooked, he called the old people in for a feast. He called the old man's wife too. They passed around the meat. The old lady passed her dish, and they gave her his genitals. The man who gave the feast watched the old lady. She was eating like mad. He could see that her mouth looked kind of greasy. When the feast was over, everybody went home. Then they all knew what the man had done.

Early the next morning the old lady came out. She had a piece of string which she held up and shouted, "Hey, you people. Here are your hearts. You're right in blaming the old man. He did it!" There were a lot of hearts strung on the string. Then she went back into her wigwam.

The man who lost his boy went into her wigwam, knocked her on the head and killed her. Then they burned down the wigwam with the old lady in it, and the people moved away as far as they could. That's a true story, told to me by my father-in-law at Lake Vieux Desert. When a medicine man has killed a man that way, he goes to dig up the body to get a small piece of his heart or tongue.[5]

Comments

The bear was regarded as the equal or superior of a human being. "Of all the animals that exist in their forests," wrote Kohl, "the Indians respect the bear the most. They regard it almost in the light of a human being. Indeed, they will often say that the bear is an 'Anijinabe' (Indian)" (1860, p. 408).

After a bear was killed, he was given a special feast and treated as an

5. For tales of a similar sort, see Dorson (1952, pp. 26–37).

honored guest. His head and paws were decorated with beads and ribbons (see Hallowell, 1926).

The first tale depicts a bear behaving somewhat like a human being. A village council is called to pass a pipe around as was done in the *windigo* stories, in which one person who accepts the pipe has the power to kill the bear.

In some stories bears are depicted as humane; reference was made to one tale about a boy who was abducted and brought up by a bear (see above, p. 56). Nevertheless, bears were generally regarded with the greatest fear by the Chippewa for two reasons: first because bears were dangerous and hard to kill, especially with the crude weapons used by Indians before the gun was introduced; and second because of the association between the bear and sorcery. After a sorcerer had killed a man, he might turn into a bear. In this guise the wizard would dig up his victim's grave and add the dead man's tongue to his collection of trophies. The second story deals with this topic.

The stories presented so far in this chapter fall under the heading of tales which are believed to be true. Those that follow are more fictional in character, although it may be that they also were formerly held to be true.

33. *The Village of Animals*

Collected by Robert Ritzenthaler at Court Oreilles in 1942
Narrator: Pete Martin

Once there was a man whose parents had died; so he left his wigwam that winter and started off into the woods. He came to a place where a campfire had already been built, and the coals were still warm; so he lay down and fell asleep by the fire. When he awoke he found a woman standing beside him. She gave him some warm clothing and wrapped his feet in rags. Then she took him home with her.

Her home was at the edge of a village which was inhabited by people who were really different kinds of animals. Whenever a strange man came to the village, they would challenge him to a game; and if he lost, they would kill him. This fellow had fasted, however, and had a lot of power.

The next evening a man came to the wigwam, lifted the blanket, and said to the fellow, "Why don't you and I play a game?"

They went down to the lake where there were two big holes in the snow. He said, "We will stay in these holes all night, and see who comes out alive." So they each got into a hole. About midnight that fellow was freezing, but then a big owl, his guardian spirit, came down and said, "Grandson, are you cold?"

"Yes, Grandfather," said the man. Then the owl wrapped his big wings around him and sheltered him all the rest of the night. After he got all thawed out in the morning, he called to the other man and asked, "Are you asleep?" But he found that the man was really a deer, a buck, who had frozen to death. So he packed him and took him back to the wigwam.

The next day a man announced that he and the stranger would have a race around the edge of the lake. This man turned himself into a hummingbird and got way ahead. The fellow who had come to the village wondered how he could catch up. Then he asked for rain, and it started to rain right away. He soon caught up with the hummingbird, who was battling the rain, and passed him to reach the goal. Then he went back to the bird, saying, "That bird will make a nice decoration for my hat," and he killed it.

The next day another man challenged him to race over the snow. That man became an otter; he would run to the top of a drift and slide down the other side. The stranger was way behind, struggling through the drifts. Then he took his walking stick and carved it into the shape of a snake. When he stood on it, it became a snake, and they rode right through the drifts until he passed the otter and reached the goal. He killed the otter and took it back to the village. The people were all afraid of him now and said that he must be a *manido*. They started to run away. He caught up to one of them, held out a twig and said, "Eat this." The man ate it and became a deer. He caught up to another one and give him some grass to eat, and he became a buffalo. All those people became different kinds of animals and lived in the woods.

Comments

The hero of this story has an owl for a guardian spirit. Normally, the owl is regarded with fear, but we will find other cases of people having fearsome creatures as guardian spirits. Owls are associated with sorcery and death and generally seem to be rather uncanny. One Chippewa informant said that he was hunting in the woods one day, when he came across a great horned owl, which was asleep. He walked up to it, intending to poke the bird with his gun. But suddenly the owl opened its eyes and stared at him. "I couldn't get my eyes off the owl," said the hunter "I felt something hot go through me, and I felt weak. Then I walked away and could still feel those eyes on my back like a hot rag. I thought of what my grandfather used to tell me about the owl. I haven't gone near one since."

When Prosper Guibord's children died and his wife fell sick, his wife said that a certain owl had been disturbing her, so he shot the bird. Later on an old man died, and Prosper concluded that the owl must have been that man.

Another informant told of shooting an owl that had been hanging around his camp in the woods, spoiling his hunting luck. When the hunter and his friends returned to town, they likewise discovered that an old man had just died. Here again the events were linked in a causal relationship: when the hunter shot the owl, he also killed the old man.

It will be remembered that an owl is encountered on the road to the other world.

34. *Wakayabide*

Collected by Victor Barnouw at Lac du Flambeau in 1944
Narrator: Sam Whitefeather

There was a man called Wakayabide, which means "You can see his teeth plain." He had no lips; that's why you could see his teeth. You could see his guts too. He had a wife but no kids.

He went hunting every day with his bow and arrows. He used to bring home meat every day, but only part of a deer, not the whole animal. He never brought the heart and the liver, but that's what his wife wanted. She asked him to bring the heart and the liver. So he said, "All right, I'll bring them tomorrow."

The man didn't kill the deer himself. The wolves did it, and they ate the liver and heart. He used to cut out the rest of the meat. He never told his wife how he hunted. He never ate when he went out. He had very little clothing: just leggings, moccasins, belt, and breech clout.

He got up early in the morning, because wolves kill deer early in the morning. He could run fast. He could chase a deer until he got the wind out of him. He waited in the woods. It wasn't long until a deer came, followed by a wolf. He chased the deer. The animals paid no attention to the man.

While running, the man lost a moccasin. He paid no attention. Then he lost the other one, but he paid no attention. Pretty soon he dropped his leggings too. But he paid no attention. Pretty soon his apron dropped off. He paid no attention and kept on going. Pretty soon it was evening. He kept on running. He wanted that heart and liver for his wife. All he had left was his buckskin belt.

Toward evening the wolf leaped for the deer and grabbed the heart and liver. The man followed the wolf. He chased him and chased him. It was dark. The wolf kept on going. The man couldn't see any more, so he had to stop and camp out. No matches. Nothing to start the fire with. He said to himself, "I shall die for the sake of my wife, who wanted that meat so badly. I'll prepare a place where I can die." There was a big pine log there. It was nice and dry there. He said, "I'll lie here in the leaves and die." It was cold. The wind started to blow. It was too cold to sleep. Long after midnight he was still awake. He could hear footsteps coming from the direction in which the wolf had gone. He thought, "Someone is coming to kill me." Then he heard a voice saying "Wakayabide, you were foolish to follow me. You know well you can't catch me when I'm running. My grandchild, why did you chase me? I've come back to warn you. If I hadn't come back, you'd have frozen to death tonight. I've come back to tell you what to do. I want to give you my life. I want to protect you, my grandchild. Tomorrow morning, when you get up, go straight south from here. You'll find some people there camping. Make friends with those people. One old lady will come to get timber for a night fire. You'll have a nice place to warm yourself when you get there. Tonight, I'll give you my garment, so you can sleep well."

When he looked out from under the log, Wakayabide saw a great big wolf standing there. Then the wolf shook himself. He shook off some of his wool; it was a blanket. "Take this, my grandchild." He gave him the blanket. Then he grew smaller. "Here's another one." He did the same thing. Then he became tiny, an inch long, and lay beside him. The man felt nice and warm and slept well. The next morning the wolf said, "Now I'll take my blankets back, and I'll show you how much power I've got." He shook himself and made himself big again. He was a great big animal. "Anything you ask me, I'll give you the power. Now watch close again." He shook himself until he was as small as your little finger. He said, "Now put me inside your belt. I'll help you for the rest of your life. If you have any trouble, just call on me. I'll help you." The man sewed the animal into his belt. Then he started south as the wolf had directed and kept on running until he came to a fire outside the village. He dropped onto the bare ground and warmed himself.

Down the hill there was a village with all kinds of wigwams. One of them was pretty long; it must have been a *midewigwan*, a Medicine Dance lodge. Pretty soon an old lady came out of the long wigwam and came running up to the fire. She didn't expect to see anyone there, but then she saw Wakayabide and could see his guts in plain sight. She saw his teeth too. She was scared and ran back down the hill and jumped into the wigwam. She nudged her old man, "Ive seen a *manido* by the fire. His guts and teeth are in plain sight; he's naked."

The old man, who was the chief, said, "There's a stranger by the woodpile."

His son, a clever boy, jumped up and said, "Well, well. It can't be my brother-in-law."

Some other old fellows said, "Here, here, young man; don't talk that way. That's a *manido*. If you talk like that, he'll come and kill us some day. Be careful. A *manido* has come to us, so we'd better be good to him."

Some kids said, "I wouldn't call him *manido*. His guts are in plain sight."

The old man said, "Be good to that man! Don't talk like that!"

The young man had three sisters. His name was Madjikiwis. He said, "I'm going to go and look at my brother-in-law." He took up his club. It had a big ball at the end of it; when he picked it up, sparks flew all over the room. That's how powerful he was. There was thunder and lightning.

When he got to Wakayabide, he said, "My friend, I want you to have a new home. When we go into the wigwam, there's a heavy-set woman; that's my sister. The next one is a medium-sized woman. The next is a smaller one. I'll give you the smallest. I want you to be my brother-in-law. When you go into the wigwam, go to my sisters. Pay no attention to what people say. When you get to the first one, the fat one will say, 'Stop here and sit down; I'm the one you're going to marry.' Just keep right on going. The next one will say the same thing. She'll want you to sit next to her. But keep right on going and sit next to the smallest one. That's the sister I want you to marry. All right, get up and follow me."

He got up. People all came and stared at them. The little kids shouted, "Do you call him *manido* with his guts and teeth in plain sight? I don't call him *manido*."

The old fellows said, "Here, here. You be quiet. *Manido* will fix you after a while, if you talk like that."

When they came to the doorway, the young chief went to his place, and the other man turned the way he'd told him to go. The man came to the big fat woman. She said, "Sit down here; that's where you're supposed to sit." He kept right on going. The second one said, "So you've come to me now. Sit right here with me." He kept on until he came to a little tiny woman. She said nothing, and he sat right down.

He looked around at all the things hanging up that Madjikiwis owned. When his brother-in-law hung up his club, he saw the sparks fly out.

His wife started to teach him: "We have all kinds of games here. I want you to be careful. The people here are dangerous. They kill each other. You won't live very long if you play in any of their games."

The three sisters were going with some men, powerful men. Everybody heard that Madjikiwis had a new brother-in-law, so they all wanted to see him. The first man who came said, "I've come to see my brother." He was a great big tall man. There was a great big rock inside the wigwam. This man came and sat on the rock. He was carrying a big tobacco pouch. He talked to the man: "I'm glad you've come; I'm glad to see you. We have a lot of fun here, lots of games. We'd like you to play with us." Then he said, "Now I'm going to show you my power." He picked up the big rock — solid rock — and tossed it up and down. He walked to the man, playing with it to scare him. He almost dropped it. Then he set it down. He said, "That's my power. That's the kind of man I'd be if I stayed with that woman."

Wakayabide filled up his pipe with tobacco. Then he tightened the cord on his bow. He had to get his revenge. This man was naked. Wakayabide was going to shoot him between the legs. He wasn't going to hurt him, just graze him. He pulled the bow, and the arrow just grazed him. The man took his tobacco and ran outside. Outside you could hear him laughing: "Ha ha ha! I've found a man who's better than I am. I give up! He's a *manido*. I won't bother him any more."

The next day another man came to see him. The first man that had come in was a grizzly bear. The next one who came in was a polar bear. Wakayabide found out that those people changed into animals. This man said, "I've come to see my brother." He had a tobacco pouch and a long pipe too. He sat on the big rock there. He said, "I've got to show you my power." He scratched the stone, and you could see flames springing out of it. It didn't bother those people. They just sat there. Rocks flew around. Then he said, "That's how I'd be if I knew I'd have that woman." Then he sat down to fill up his pipe.

Wakayabide got his bow and arrows out and shot this man by the head, just shaved his skull. Then that man jumped up and ran out. Outside he laughed: "My brother is a better man than I am. I'll give up, and I won't bother him any more."

There was one more visitor, who came the next day: a human being this time, a well-built fellow. His wife knew about what would happen and told him: "The men that go with me are going to try out your power. Be careful. Say nothing to anybody."

This man came in. When he raised the curtain of the wigwam, a flood of water came in — red clay water. That's the power he had. The current was strong. Wakayabide was just about to float away, when his wife grabbed him and tied him with a sash and held him. He could hardly get his breath. He was near drowning when the water went down. It dried in no time. The other people in there didn't even feel it. They just sat there. It was nothing to them. Then the man sat on the rock, filled up his pipe, and said, "That's the kind of man I'd be if I married this woman."

Wakayabide got out his bow and arrows again. This time he shot the rock right in the center. He said in his mind, "A little piece of rock will hit that man's body." That's what happened.

That man said, "I can't beat that man! He's too good for me. I give up!"

Three men had tried to drive that man out, but they couldn't do it. He had too much power.

The next day, early in the morning, there was an announcer going around the village. I suppose the wigwams were in a circle. He announced, "Today we have a lacrosse game. Madjikiwis' brother-in-law must play too."

Wakayabide's wife said, "Be careful! I don't want you to go. They'll kill you."

The man laughed. "They can't kill me. I'll go and look on, anyway. If I don't play, I'll look on."

Madjikiwis was losing the game all the time. He lost all of his clothing. He wanted his brother-in-law to play for him. That's what he had figured before, although he hadn't said so.

Everyone was out in the field. Wakayabide stood with his bow and arrow, watching. Pretty soon one of the fellows, the grizzly bear, came over to him. "Here, brother." He gave him a lacrosse stick.

"I don't know how to play. I can't play."

"No, no. You must play."

"All right, I'll try."

He took the lacrosse stick. This man had left his belt in the wigwam, so the wolf wasn't there. Out in the woods the wolf had told him never to leave the belt and always take it along.

The ball was coming. His partner said, "Grab the ball and run!"

He grabbed the ball with his club and ran for the goal. The other man followed. Instead of taking the ball away, the bear jumped on his bare back and tore his skin to the bone. He dropped dead right there. When the game was over, there was no Wakyabide coming home. They must have cut him up into pieces and shared the meat.

The woman was worrying about him. She asked people where he was, but they didn't tell her. That night all the families feasted on that meat. The man's wife was worried. She couldn't sleep. The wolf knew that something was wrong with his master. He started to howl inside the belt.

The woman heard that noise. She kept quiet and listened. It sounded like a wolf howling. At first it was like a wolf way off in the woods. Then she saw that it was coming from the belt. She found a little pocket there. She opened it and found a tiny dog. She set it on the ground. She knew right away that it belonged to that man.

The dog shook and began to grow. Then he dashed outside right away. He ran all over town. He got all the bones and put them together in the shape of a man. There was one joint he couldn't find — the elbow. He ran all over but couldn't find it. Then he saw smoke going up out in the woods. There was a young woman living by herself out in the woods (in a seclusion hut for menstruating girls). She had a piece of meat too — the elbow. The dog ran over there. The woman had the bone he was looking for. He sat by the doorway, looking at the woman, wishing for her to throw the bone down. She chewed and kept saying, "My my! that tastes good. I can't stop chewing." She saw the dog and said, "I guess he wants that bone. I won't give it to him, though; it tastes too good." The dog moved a little nearer, but she said, "Go outside! I want that bone myself."

The dog got tired of waiting; so he jumped at her, grabbed the bone, and dashed off. Now he had all the bones in the shape of a man. Then he hollered. The bones humped together. He hollered again. Flesh came on the bones. He hollered again. Then his eyes opened up.

The people were surprised to hear that dog holler. One of the old fellows, who was trying to make the young people behave, said, "I wouldn't be surprised if that man is coming alive again."

When the wolf hollered the fourth time, Wakayabide's breath began to come. The wolf said, "You didn't listen to me, my grandchild, so I came to save you. That's what happens when you don't listen. Get up now. We'll go home."

His wife was glad to see him again. She said, "I found that little dog in your belt. He's saved your life. Always take him along now."

The next day the announcer went around again: "Today we have another lacrosse game. Madjikiwis' brother-in-law ought to play too."

His wife said to him, "Don't go. They'll kill you again."

He said, "No, I want to go." He wanted to get his revenge on that fellow who had killed him.

That morning he put on his belt and went out. He was looking for that fellow he'd played with the day before. "Hey, brother," he said, "come here. I want to play with you."

The bear said, "Oh, fine!"

The ball came up. The bear said, "I'll show you how to play!" He took the ball. Wakayabide followed him with two arrows in his hands.

They used to play for a live person. That's how they got their food, their meat. They ate each other.

Wakayabide jumped on the bear with his two arrows and buried them in his skin. He tore the bear to pieces with the arrows and killed him. Then he walked away. The other people cut up the bear and cooked him. They passed the meat around to all the families. He had some of it too. It tasted good, nice and fat.

That man came alive again the next day too. He was a powerful man.

Comments

This is the only story in our collection which hints at a social organization involving more than a few families, with wigwams ranged in a circle and a crier going about making announcements about the next day's events. The society is large enough to provide two teams for lacrosse. It would be interesting to know where this story originated. The collections of William Jones, de Jong, and Radin and Reagan do not contain this tale, but a very similar one appears in Henry Rowe Schoolcraft, *The Indian in His Wigwam* (1848, p. 106), and in W. J. Hoffman, *The Menomini Indians* (1896, pp. 182–96).

A striking thing about this story is the amount of aggression in it. Challenges to competition, with death for the loser, was also a theme in "The Village of Animals," but this story has even more violence. The bear people play lacrosse, kill the losers, and eat them. But they come back to life again. This is reminiscent of the Midewiwin, in which the members shoot and kill one another but revive.

The theme of being killed, eaten, and coming back to life was mentioned earlier, in Jones's story about the man who married a beaver wife. The man eats his in-laws, but they revive.

This belief system would seem to draw the teeth out of aggression, to reduce its importance, as in the speech of Krishna to Arjuna in the *Bhagavad-Gita* with the explanation that it is all right to kill one's enemies because everyone undergoes reincarnation.

The name Wakayabide is said to mean, "You can see his teeth plain." He has no lips. You can also see his guts. This suggests that Wakayabide symbolizes death, although his actions in the story don't seem to support such symbolism. However, the story does deal with death and recovery from it. Wakayabide nearly dies when chasing the wolf, but the wolf rescues him and becomes his guardian spirit. Later Wakayabide is killed but brought back to life again. His guardian spirit collects his bones, as Oshkikwe does in the case of her husband, the whitefish man.

Although the dead can come back to life, death is not lightly regarded. Wakayabide's wife warns him, "Be careful. I don't want you to go. They'll kill you." And later, "Don't go. They'll kill you again."

Relative power is another theme in this story. People seem to be ranked in power. Some have more supernatural resources than others. A man makes a display of his power to show what he can do, but he acknowledges the superior strength of another if that is demonstrated.

An incidental lesson in this story is that one should be respectful to strangers. As the old men warn, "Don't talk that way! That's a *manido*. If you talk like that, he'll come and kill us some day."

Another incidental lesson is that women should not be too demanding of their husbands. Because Wakayabide's first wife wanted to eat heart and liver, he almost died, exclaiming, "I shall die for the sake of my wife, who wanted that meat so badly."

35. *The Fox and the Chief's Daughter*

Collected by Ernestine Friedl at Court Oreilles in 1942
Narrator: Delia Oshogay   Interpreter: Maggie Lamorie

A fox and his grandmother were living together. Some people came and told his grandmother that Wagos was digging up graves and eating the contents. The grandmother said it wasn't true, because Wagos went to bed early. One time the people arranged a feast and invited Wagos. His grandmother told him not to go because she said that they all hated him, but Wagos wouldn't listen and went to the feast. When he got there they took turns pushing him into the fire. He burned his feet but just managed to get away and get back home. He told his grandmother what they had done. She said that they had only invited him to hurt him. Wago was laid up a long time with sore feet.

When Wagos got better, he went around the village shouting, "I'm barking at the chief's daughter." Four days after that, the chief's daughter died. All the people in the village then moved away. They put the body up in a little wigwam near a few trees. They told Wagos's grandmother that they were moving away and asked her to leave too; but she said that she couldn't, because her grandchild couldn't walk since his feet were burned so bad. They said, "We don't want Wagos to dig up graves again as he used to." The grandmother said that he didn't dig up graves but went to bed early. So then the Indians moved away.

Wagos got better and set out fish nets. Every night they used to see a light in the wigwam where the dead body was. Every time Wagos looked in his fish net in the morning he'd find just one whitefish. He'd tell his grandmother that he'd left a fish outside, and she'd go out to get it, but the fish would be gone by then.

On the tenth day Wagos got his tenth whitefish. He saw a light up in the wigwam that night, and he went there and found that the chief's daughter had come back to life. She said, "Wagos, here are your fish; they are all cleaned." She told Wagos that she was going to marry him. "In the daytime you'll see me as I am; at night you'll see me as a shadow." She walked with him to his home. All they saw of her at night was a shadow.

Whenever he got fish, his wife and his grandmother started to clean them. His wife would do more, the less the grandmother looked at her. Finally the grandmother stayed out of the way.

It went on, and one time the woman asked Wagos and his grand-mother to build a wigwam where she could take a sweat bath. That's where she got all her human life back again.

Wagos's wife was busy tanning hides, cleaning fish, and the like. They stored a lot of food for the winter. One time her brothers came to look at the grave, and they saw that their sister had come back to life and was working.

They went back and told the people that she had come back to life. Then they all came back to the village again and made Wagos their chief.

Comments

The Chippewa considered it a bad omen to hear a fox bark. It meant that someone in the family would die. Tom Badger told me that his uncle heard a fox barking one day while he was fishing through the ice, and shortly after that his little son died. Hence Wagos in this story brings about the death of the chief's daughter by barking at her. He evidently does so to get revenge on the people for their cruelty toward him. However, Wagos helps to bring the chief's daughter back to life and eventually becomes chief himself.

After the death of the chief's daughter, all the people in the village move away. This expresses another Indian custom. Tom Badger said to me: "While we were at Sugar Camp Lake my father's mother and one of my sisters died. Then we left that place and moved about a thousand feet away, because of those two deaths" (Barnouw, 1954, p. 84). This custom is also suggested by the first sentence of "The Village of Animals," given earlier.

36. *The Turtle's War Party*

Collected by Ernestine Friedl at Court Oreilles in 1942
Narrator: Delia Oshogay   Interpreter: Maggie Lamorie

Mužike, Turtle, got ready to go to war and invited others to join him. A bear came along, but Mužike pushed him aside and said that the bear was no good. A deer volunteered, but Turtle said he wouldn't do; he was too slow. Then some little turtles said that they'd go, and the party of turtles set off. They found a village where two daughters of a chief were sleeping up in a place where you needed ladders to get up there. The turtles went up and cut off the heads of the chief's daughters. Then Mužike hid under a pile of chips. He thought that he would make an old lady come and pee on him to wet him. He had the power to do that. So an old lady did so. Then she realized what she had done and said, "Oh, I've been peeing on Mužike."

He said, "Don't say that but say, 'I'm peeing on the one who murdered right in the center of town.' "

She said that, and then Mužike was arrested. They made a big fire to burn him in, but he said that they'd all burn and he'd kick the coals all over the town; so they decided not to do that. Then they thought that they'd boil him, but he said that that would be even worse, because he'd splash the water all over and kill them all. Someone said, "Let's chop him up!" but Mužike said that they'd just ruin their axes. One old lady suggested that they throw him in the lake and drown him, so they threw him in the lake. Before they threw him in, he grabbed the women's bodies and attached them to the heads he had. They came alive, and he married them. Then he went to the store and ran up a big bill. He went driving logs on the river and got himself a pair of high boots. When he came back he paid his bill and bought a wrapper for a cradleboard.

Comments

Variants of this tale (F1025.2) are widespread. According to Stith Thompson it contains two distinct parts: (1) Turtle takes various companions with him on the warpath, and they get into trouble; (2) when caught, Turtle professes to fear no punishment except drowning. The following have both parts of the tale: Osage, Arapaho, Skidi, Pawnee, Ponca, Cheyenne, Blackfoot, Oglala, Wichita, Plains Ojibwa, Dakota, Kickapoo, Menomini, Peoria, Iroquois, Seneca, and Cherokee. The second part of the story is widespread in the Eastern Hemisphere from China and Indonesia to West Africa (Thompson, 1973, pp. 302–3).

The turtle seems to have been regarded with humorous affection by the Indians. Mužike, or Mikinak, was the medicine man's emissary and "spirit guide" in the shaking tent seance, who was laughingly chided by the audience for being slow on his supernatural errands. "*Mikinak* talks in a throaty nasal voice not unlike that of Donald Duck. It is extremely characteristic and very easily distinguishable from other voices that emanate from the tent. . . . *Mikinak* is good natured and easy going. He is quick witted and loves a joke" (Hallowell, 1942, pp. 44–45).

37. *The Mink and the Fish*

Collected by Ernestine Friedl at Court Oreilles in 1942
Narrator: Delia Oshogay   Interpreter: Maggie Lamorie

Mink found a live pike on the lake shore. He said, "Pike, the muskie is calling you all kinds of names."
"What is he calling me?"
"He says you're wall-eyed."
The pike said, "Well, he's got teeth like a saw blade and a long plated face. He's not pretty either."
There was a muskie nearby, and Mink told him what the pike had said about him. He went back and forth, getting them mad at each other, and finally they had a fight with Mink as referee. They killed each other; so Mink had the laugh on them. He got a big kettle and boiled and dried the meat. Then Mink lay down to rest. He thought about how he was taking life easy. He had the fish eggs in one lump, and all he had to do was open his eyes and put his tongue out. So he dozed off.
Some Indians came by in their canoes and saw Mink lying there with all those fish. They came ashore and cleaned up all the fish, and then they filled the intestines full of rocks and went away. When Mink woke up, he reached with his tongue for the fish eggs, but instead there was a gut full of rocks and stones which broke all the teeth he had. He realized they'd played a trick on him. Mink just simply walked away.

Comments

This theme is much the same as that in episode 13 in the Wenebojo origin myth. A trickster episode which results in the hero getting something to eat is followed by oral frustration and someone else having the benefit of the meal.

38. *The Coon and the Wolf*[6]

Collected by Ernestine Friedl at Court Oreilles in 1942
Narrator: Anna Johnson

Coon came to a settlement of crabs. They were people too and lived in regular wigwams. The crabs were having a dance and a good time. Coon threw himself down by the edge of the water and pretended to be dead.

The crabs found him and thought that he'd been dead many days. They gathered around him. The last one who came out of the settlement was a man with only one arm. He yelled that the same thing had happened many years ago, and that's how he lost his arm. But the others didn't listen. They danced around Coon. Once in a while they'd pinch him with their claws to see if he was alive. Every time he'd almost holler with pain, but then they stopped pinching him. When the whole bunch had surrounded him except for the old man, Coon jumped up and grabbed as many as he could. He had a good meal of the crabs and then ran along the shore.

Then he saw Wolf, Maingan, coming his way. He thought that Wolf would probably ask him for something. So he went into the woods to defecate and put the stuff into a birchbark container tied with basswood. When they met, Wolf said, "You always carry lunch. I've been traveling a long time. Could you give me something to eat?" Coon said he would and gave his package to Maingan. He said that he'd already eaten. So Maingan ate it all.

After Wolf turned to go, Coon shouted at him, "Hey, Maingan, you ate my feces." Wolf turned around, and Coon climbed up a tree. Wolf just missed him. He decided to starve him up there and settled at the bottom of the tree. But Coon had the power to make him fall asleep, and he climbed down, scratching the bark to see if Wolf was really asleep. He defecated on Wolf's face. Then he poked Wolf and said, "It's time for you to get up." Wolf couldn't see. He said to Coon, "If you can help me to open my eyes, I'll make you as pretty as you can be." Coon decided to help open his eyes, because he wanted to be pretty. So he got some rotten bark, rubbed Wolf's eyes with it, and they opened. Then Wolf put stripes on Coon's face and made him look pretty. Wolf told him that from that

6. The first part of this story is given by Schoolcraft in somewhat different form. See "The Raccoon and Crawfish. A Fable from the Odjibwa" (in 1956, pp. 175–76). The same tale, also minus the wolf episode, is given in Skinner (1925, p. 478). Both crawfish and wolf episodes are given in a version collected by Chamberlain (1889, pp. 142–43). See also William Jones (1916, p. 369) and Skinner (1919, p. 293).

time on his fur would be worth something in the world, and that came to be true.

Comments

The word "crab" is commonly used in Wisconsin to refer to crayfish or crawfish. It must be crayfish that the first part of the story is about, rather than crabs, which are generally found in salt water.

39. *The Hell-diver and the Spirit of Winter*

Collected by Robert Ritzenthaler at Court Oreilles in 1942
Narrator: Pete Martin

Every winter the birds went south. One time a hell-diver volunteered to stay for the winter to take care of two birds, an injured whooping crane and a wounded mallard duck, both of whom had broken wings. He got fish for them by diving through a hole in the ice. Gabibonike, the spirit of winter, got jealous of his success at fishing and froze up the water at the hole after the hell-diver had gone below the ice. But the hell-diver swam to shore where there were a lot of bulrushes and pulled one of them down through the ice with his bill. This made a hole, and the hell-diver got out and flew home to his wigwam. Then he saw that someone was peeking in through the door of his wigwam. It was Gabibonike, who was trying to freeze him out. The hell-diver got a warm fire going, but it was still cold in the wigwam. However, the hell-diver mopped his face with his handkerchief and said, "Gee, but it's hot in here!"

One day the hell-diver decided to have a feast. He got some wild rice and sent a duck to invite Gabibonike, but the duck froze to death before he got there. Then he sent Partridge to go, and she went. She got very cold too, but then she dived under the snow to warm up and then go on again. She reached Gabibonike and invited him.

When he came to the feast, it was like a blizzard coming into the wigwam. He had icicles on his nose and face. Hell-diver kept on making the fire blaze up, and it began to get warm. The icicles began melting on Gabibonike's face. He was getting too warm, but he liked the wild rice and wanted to go on eating it.

Hell-diver said, "It's very warm in here. It must be spring already."

Then Gabibonike grabbed his blanket and ran out.

Hell-diver had brought the spring, and there were just patches of snow here and there. Gabibonike had a hard time getting back to his home in the north, where there is always snow.

Comments

A tale like this one is given by Schoolcraft (1956, pp. 244–45).

In view of the terribly cold, long, and dangerous winters experienced by the Chippewa, this tale is a surprisingly light-hearted treatment of this subject. Winter is seen as rather easily subjugated and driven away.

As noted earlier, at the end of chapter 5, Gabibonike is a kind of *windigo*, being made of snow and ice, and he has a voracious appetite.

The hell-diver, or grebe, is a poor flyer but expert diver that can swim underwater like a penguin. The eared grebe is a species commonly found in Wisconsin. In this story he plays the role of bringer of spring and warm weather. Perhaps the hell-diver was chosen for this role since he is one of the last birds to fly south, leaving around the middle of November, after ice has started to form on the lakes in northern Wisconsin.

40. *Jidwe?e the Sandpiper*

Collected by Victor Barnouw at Lac du Flambeau in 1944
Narrator: Tom Badger   Interpreter: Julia Badger

A man and his grandmother lived together all by themselves by the shore of the ocean. The man had a necklace of shells. When he wanted to travel across the ocean, he threw the shells onto the water and stood upon them. He traveled just the way you see the sandpiper going along the ground. His name was Jidwe?e; that means sandpiper.

One day a great big fish swallowed him up. He thought that he had gone into a great big wigwam. He could see nobody there but himself. He could see a red thing hanging there; it was covered with spots. When he touched it, he heard a noise, like someone groaning. He heard a voice saying, "My heart hurts." That was the fish's heart that he had poked with a stick. Jidwe?e thought about his grandmother and wished that she would stretch her shoestring across the ocean. So the old lady did that. Jidwe?e kicked up a lot of disturbance inside the fish; so the fish vomited him up. Out flew Jidwe?e; he grabbed his grandmother's shoestring, and she pulled him to shore. Today the sandpiper has those spots all over his body.

Jidwe?e went along the ocean until he came to a village. There was a log across the trail there; you had to step over it to get to the water.

Jidwe?e got under the log and lay there, wishing that the king's daughter would come to get some water. Pretty soon he got his wish. The king's daughter came along with a pail in her hand, singing, "Jidwe?e is my husband." When she stepped over the log, Jidwe?e jumped up. She hollered and tried to grab him, but he got away. All she caught of him was the red yarn sash belt he wore; it came loose, and she held it in her hands.

Some time later an announcer went around to invite all the men to a feast at the home of the king. The king's daughter had born a little baby, because of that time when she stepped over the log where Jidwe?e was. Jidwe?e was the last to arrive. When he came in, the men shouted, "Look at his skinny legs!" He sat close to the door.

The king got up and said that he did not know who was the father of his grandchild. So all of the men were asked to hold the baby. When the baby pee'd, that would be its father. Some of the men got up and put some water in their mouths. When the woman handed her baby to the man, some of them spat the water out of their mouths, but the people saw what they were doing, so it didn't count.

Nothing happened until they came to the last man by the door, Jidwe?e. Just before they handed him to Jidwe?e, the baby pee'd all over. Then Jidwe?e jumped up, grabbed the woman and the baby, took them down to the ocean, threw down his shell necklace, and they rode on it across the ocean. The men set out to chase him, but they couldn't catch him. So Jidwe?e brought the king's daughter and the baby to his grandmother's wigwam, where they lived together.

One time, when Jidwe?e came home from one of his trips, he knew that someone was going to take his wife away. Before he left the next morning, he told his wife not to go to get any water but ask the grandmother to get it. After a while, the woman got thirsty and asked her to get some water, but soon she wanted some more water, and she decided that she would go and get it herself. She was so thirsty she didn't bother to get a pail. She just put her face down into the water and drank. Then she saw a man's face in the water. That is the man who took her away to a mountain, where his mother and father lived. They urged him to take her back to her husband, because he was a *manido*. But he said that Jidwe?e couldn't do anything to him, and he put copper on the inside of his house.

When Jidwe?e got home, his wife wasn't there. He knew which way she had been taken. He took his long stone pipe, filled it up with tobacco, and called upon his uncles, the thunderbirds, and asked them to go after his wife. There were eight of them. They struck the mountain where the man's wife was. The first time, there was only some smoke; at the sixth time, they made a crack, but at the seventh time the mountain tore in half. The eight men took the woman back to Jidweʔe.

They lived together again, but another time he knew that someone was going to take his wife away again. Jidweʔe had a hell of a time with his wife. Again, he told his wife not to go and get any water but to tell the old lady to get it. After a while the woman got thirsty and asked the old lady to get some water. She couldn't get enough. After she had bothered the old lady so many times, she decided to go and get the water herself. When she looked into the water, she saw the moon there. She went along with him. When Jidweʔe got home, his wife wasn't there. He knew right away where she'd been taken. He looked up at the moon and saw her sitting there. He said to the moon, "If I wanted to do anything to you, I could do it."

She's still up there now. When you look up at the moon, you can see a lady sitting up there. That's Jidweʔe's wife. My father told me this story when I was a little boy.

Comments

The big fish episode repeats rather closely the Wenebojo big fish episode. Both heroes have grandmothers and both poke the fish's heart. But there are no other animals, such as squirrel and bluejay, inside the fish on this occasion. The shoestring plays a role like the moccasins pulled by the sister in the story of the boy who falls into a muskie's mouth (story number 24).

The king's daughter is impregnated in a noncoital hit-and-run fashion, like the impregnation of Wenebojo's mother by the sun. William Jones gives a similar story about Chirper, who makes a chief's daughter pregnant by drawing his finger along her vulva. After she has given birth to a boy, the chief summons all the youths and declares that whoever is wetted by the baby shall marry his daughter (1917, 1919, pt. 2, pp. 707–29).[7]

Tests made by a chief to determine which young man shall marry his daughter appear in other forms. An interesting version is given by Jones (1917, 1919, pt. 2, p. 143). A chief promises to marry his daughter to the man who can touch the inside of a red mussel shell and have the shell stick on his hand. A young man wishes that he had some glue, for he had once dreamt of glue in the past. So glue appears on his hand, and the mussel shell sticks. Freudian symbolism of the red mussel shell as vagina seems particularly applicable in this case.

7. For another reference to the latter theme, see Skinner (1911, p. 104).

Jidwe?e, a humble-looking bird, mocked by the men for his skinny legs, turns out to have access to great power through his relationship to the thunderbirds. However, he cannot control his wife, with her excessive thirst, and she is twice abducted — the second time for good.

41. *How the Beaver Got His Big Tail*

Collected by Robert Ritzenthaler at Court Oreilles in 1942
Narrator: Pete Martin

The muskrat's tail was once like the beaver's, and the beaver had a rat-tail. The beaver said to him, "Brother, let's trade tails. Your tail is too big for your little body, and my tail is too small for my big body. If we trade, we would both look good." So they traded. Each took off his own tail and gave it to the other. Then they swam out in the lake. The beaver made a fine dive with his new tail, but the muskrat couldn't do much with his little one. He got angry, started to cry, and said, "Give me back my tail, Beaver." But the beaver just swam off and never gave Muskrat his tail back.[8]

42. *The Mosquito and Lightning*

Collected by Robert Ritzenthaler at Lac du Flambeau in 1944
Narrator: Charley Batiste

There were two mosquitoes in the woods. One of them was fat and full of blood. The lightning saw his fat red belly and asked him where he got all his food. The mosquito flew up to the top of a Norway pine and showed the lightning the particle of pitch on the trunk and told him that was what he ate. The Lightning decided to eat it too, but every time he tried to do so, he split the top of the tree. That is why so many of the Norway pines have been struck by lightning.

Comments

A similar story is given in Laidlaw (1924–25, p. 54). In this version the thunderbirds ask mosquitoes where they get the blood that makes them

8. A story like this is given in Laidlaw (1915, p. 73). This tale is told as far away from the Ojibwa area as Puget Sound and in Alaska by northern Athapaskan-speaking Indians. See Ballard (1929, p. 68) and McKennan (1959, p. 212).

fat. The mosquitoes don't want to tell them the truth, so they say that they get it from trees. That's why the trees get struck by lightning.

43. The Origin of the Robin

Collected by Robert Ritzenthaler at Lac du Flambeau in 1944
Narrator: Charley Batiste

Robin is a weakling; he flies close to the ground. His father wanted him to fast for seven days. He fasted nine days and then turned into a robin and told his father what had happened.

Comments

This brief tale is included because it was first recorded by Schoolcraft more than a hundred years ago. Schoolcraft's version gives a fuller account, in which the father is overly ambitious for his son and therefore urges him to fast more than twelve days. The boy then turns into a robin and flies away, a victim of over-fasting (1956, pp. 106–8).[9] A similar story was told at Court Oreilles by Alec Martin to Robert Ritzenthaler; in his version the over-fasting son turned into an owl.

General Comments on Animal Stories

The animals dealt with in this chapter include underwater lion, snake, bear, deer, muskrat, beaver, raccoon, mink, wolf, fox, dog, otter, owl, hummingbird, sandpiper, hell-diver, duck, partridge, wren, robin, crab, turtle, whitefish, pike, muskie, mosquito, and bee.

Most of the same animals figure in Canadian Chippewa tales. The following animals are mentioned in Jones's texts from north of Lake Superior: rabbit, hare, weasel, marten, otter, mink, muskrat, squirrel, chipmunk, mouse, raccoon, fisher, fox, wolf, mole, woodchuck, porcupine, beaver, skunk, wolverine, lynx, dog, deer, elk, moose, caribou, bear, buffalo, snake, lizard, turtle, toad, crawfish, sturgeon, whitefish, pike, swan, goose, duck, diver, gull, loon, turkey, buzzard, owl, bluejay, Canada jay, robin, woodpecker, ruffed grouse, kingfisher, raven, and crow.

The animals which are mentioned most often in the stories collected by

9. See also Laidlaw (1915, p. 86).

Jones north of Lake Superior are the bear (in fourteen stories) and moose (eleven stories). Beaver appear in ten stories. So do ruffed grouse, which Jones states were the easiest of all game to get.

Since humans and animals may have interchangeable forms in Chippewa belief, the category of animal tale is somewhat ambiguous. One long story, "Wakayabide," is perhaps better classified under some other heading than animal tale, but it is included here, since the hero lives in a village of bears.

A Chippewa hunter in former days begged pardon of the animals he killed, especially powerful spirits like the bear, and attempted to secure the good will of his victims through ingratiating speeches, so that they would not resent being hunted down. If the hunter's propitiation were sincerely worded, it was believed, the animals would willingly surrender their lives to him again. For animals were always aware of what was said about them. They avenged insults by staying away from hunters and making them starve, but they rewarded others by sacrificing themselves, as was mentioned in connection with Jones's story of the man who married a beaver wife. "If any one regards a beaver with too much contempt, speaking ill of it," runs Jones's text, "one simply (will) not (be able to) kill it, Just the same as the feelings of one who is disliked, so is the feeling of the beaver. And he who never speaks ill of a beaver is very much loved by it; in the same way as people love one another, so is one held in the mind of the beaver; particularly lucky then is one at killing beavers" (1917, 1919, pt. 2, p. 257). According to Jenness, some of the Indians will not cook deer meat when they are hunting deer, lest the animal be offended by the smell and refuse to be killed. A deer may become prejudiced against a certain hunter and never allow him to approach. His "shadow" will watch the hunter's every step and foil his best-laid plans (1935, p. 22). Thus, to keep on killing animals one must remain on good terms with them.

Not only was the psyche of the animals considered to be essentially like that of human beings, but the animals' mode of life as well. Animals had villages of wigwams under hills or deep clear lakes, where they lived just as human beings do. Each species of animal within a given locality had its own chief or boss, who led his followers from place to place. According to Jenness, the boss was larger than the other members of his species and always colored white. (John Mink at Court Oreilles also said that the deer chief was white.) These animal bosses were seldom seen by the Indians, although it was said that a hunter occasionally ran across one of them (Jenness, 1935, p. 23).[10]

10. See also Hultkranz (1961).

CHAPTER SEVEN

Tales of Spells
and Magical Powers

Many Chippewa tales deal with magical powers. Some, like the story of Bebukowe, deal with magical domination, one person's control over another. That is the theme of the first three stories in this chapter, in which there are persons who seem to be under a spell, under the control of a powerful, evil person. The fourth story, "The Beaver Man," involves magical power of a different kind; the hero is able to make himself small enough to crawl into an oak ball and to become invisible. In the last story, "The Boy, his Grandmother, and the King's Daughter," a dead girl is brought back to life.

44. *The Bad Old Man*

Collected by Robert Ritzenthaler at Court Oreilles in 1942
Narrator: Prosper Guibord

There was an Indian village on the shore of a big lake. On the other side of the lake lived a man who had a lot of bad power. The people would hear dogs barking over there now and then, and the next day the old man would come across the lake, enter the village, and say to some person, "I have come for you." That person would be powerless to help himself and would follow the old man and never come back.

Just outside the village lived three brothers. One was only about ten years old. They were orphans, and one of the older brothers would go out hunting while the other stayed home with the youngest brother. One evening they heard the dogs barking across the lake, and the brother who had been out hunting said that he thought the old man would be coming after him the next day. He told his brother to take good care of the youngest one, if he had to go. Early the next morning the old man came and said, "Grandchild, come with me," and the oldest brother went.

After that the youngest boy had to stay alone while his brother went out hunting. Every day he put charcoal on his face and went without

161

eating all day, eating only when his brother came home from hunting. One evening he said, "I wonder why grandfather's dogs aren't barking any more." The older brother warned him that the old man would hear him. Sure enough, the next morning the old man came for the older brother. The younger brother said, "Grandfather, I'm coming too," but the old man said that he would come for him when he needed him.

The younger brother had dreamed that he should wear a copper neck band, and his brother had made one for him. The younger brother followed them down to the lake, where the old man had kept his dugout boat. The boy tried to get into the boat, but the old man threw him out and stunned him. When he regained consciousness, he saw that the boat was halfway across the lake. Then he took his neck band and bent one end and told it to stick in the dugout, and he threw it. The band stuck in the dugout, and he pulled the dugout back, but the old man threw him aside again. Once again they set out in the boat, and once again it was pulled back from about three-fourths of the way across the lake. The old man was becoming afraid now, and so he told the boy to get in.

The boat set off. They didn't have to paddle, because the old man just tapped the side with a big cane which he carried. When they reached the other side, the old man told them to go into a big lodge like a Medicine Dance lodge next to his wigwam. There were a lot of people inside, all sick, and some couldn't even move.

That evening the first brother returned with a deer and dropped it in front of the old man's wigwam. The two other brothers were glad to see him again. The oldest one told them that he had to hunt for the old man, his wife, and the two big dogs which were really his two sons. The people were hungry. The youngest brother sneaked into the old man's wigwam and took a deer. The old man swung his cane at him, but the boy got out and took the meat back to the people. The old man realized then that this boy had a lot of power and that he would have to treat him well.

The next evening the boy told two of the hunters to bring their deer to the big lodge and he made broth for the sick people. Soon there were many who were fit to go hunting again. Each night the boy gave just two deer to the old man and kept all the rest for the people. He went in and talked to the old man; the old man told him to fast and get more power. He thought he could destroy the boy's power that way. The next day the boy put charcoal on his face and made believe he was fasting, but he really kept on eating. He also made believe he was sleeping. The old man's spirit came to him and said he would help him, but the boy wasn't fooled by that.

The next day the old man's wife tried to destroy his power during his fasting; again he wasn't fooled. He told the old man and his wife that he didn't like the spirits that had come to him. The old man warned the boy against an evil spirit by a cliff; he thought that this would tempt the boy into going to the cliff.

The boy went there and found a cave and saw an animal growling inside. He took his neckband, straightened it out, threw it, and killed the lion in there by hitting it right between the eyes. He skinned the lion and took it to the old man. This lion was really his own son, and that made the old man sad. Then he warned the boy about a lake nearby with a bad spirit in it. But the boy went down to the lake and saw it whirling and bubbling. He threw his neckband toward the center of the lake, and it hit a tiger that was causing all the water to swirl, and killed him. The lion and tiger were really the sons of the old man, and the people thought that they were two dogs barking.

The boy skinned the tiger and took it to the old man, who once more was sad. Then the old man told the boy of a big lake with a small rock island in the center on which two evil birds lived. These birds were really the spirits of the old man and his wife. The boy set out for the lake, and when he got there, he made himself small and crawled into an oak ball and asked the wind to blow him to the island.

When he got to the island, he climbed to the top of a tree and found the birds' nest. There were two small birds in it. The boy touched one of them and could hear the old man groan. When he touched the other one, he could hear the old lady groan. He wrapped up the birds and the nest in a cloth and started back in his oak ball.

After dinner that night, he went to the old man and his wife and asked if he could use the old man's drum, because he wanted to sing. He took the drum and started to sing some songs he had learned through fasting, and they were afraid. Then he asked the old folks to dance, but they refused. Then he touched the birds which he had brought along in his shirt. Then the old folks jumped up and began to dance. After they had danced for a while, he crushed the two birds, and the two old people died.

After that all the people danced all night and were glad that the evil spirits had been killed. They buried the old people, and the next day they all went back to their village. They thanked the boy for killing the two spirits.

Comments

The mean old man is the main villain in Chippewa tales. Here he is a "grandfather" who dominates a host of people who have fallen under his spell. There are some parallels in this tale with the Wenebojo episodes discussed in chapter 3. In both cases the hero is one of three orphaned brothers who goes to fight an adversary who seems to be a father or grandfather figure. Like Wenebojo, the hero of this tale slays an underwater spirit.

A common theme in this tale is the deceptiveness of appearances. The lion and tiger are really the sons of the old man. The two small birds in the tree are really the spirits of the old man and his wife. The problem in escaping from a spell is how to distinguish between realities and delusions.

Oral themes are important in this story. The old man and wife are able to dominate others by depriving them of food. The youngest brother steals a deer from the old man and has a broth made for the sick people, who then become well. Soon many are able to hunt again. So independence of the mean old couple depends upon adequate nourishment.

On the other hand, fasting gives the boy power to conquer the "grandfather." But the mean old man tries to weaken the boy by making him fast too much. The hero is not fooled. He pretends to be fasting but keeps on eating. The attitude toward fasting is thus ambivalent, but the moral seems to be that one needs food to gain strength.

45. *The Spell of the Wicked Uncle*

Collected by Ernestine Friedl at Court Oreilles in 1942
Narrator: Delia Oshogay   Interpreter: Maggie Lamorie

A man and his nephew lived together. He had taken care of the nephew since he was a little boy. The nephew went hunting every day. He had never seen women in his life, but one day he could hear some women talking about him while they swam in the lake. He fell in love with them right away and jumped into the lake to grab them. He found that he had caught two frogs, each by one leg. He took them home with him and put them in his bed that night. They must have tickled him. The old man heard his nephew giggling and wondered what was the matter with him.

In the morning the boy got up and tucked the frogs into the blanket. Then he took his bow and arrows and went off hunting. After he left, his uncle started cleaning up the wigwam and took his nephew's quilts to air them out. He found the two frogs, was annoyed at their dirtying his nephew's blankets, and threw them out.

When the boy came home, he found the frogs outside and started crying. He said to his uncle, "Did you ever hear of anyone throwing his in-laws outside?"

The old man laughed and said, "If you want a woman, I'll tell you one thing: a woman wears a dress. What you picked up were frogs." Then he said, "There are two nice-looking women I know. Go and get them." He pointed in a certain direction and told the boy to go there.

The boy set out and came to some tamarack trees. One of them looked as though the top was a man and the bottom was a tree. This tree-man spoke to him and said, "You're my brother, the youngest one. Our uncle is a mean old man. He made me this way, so I can't walk. See that big clearing over there? That was our father's village. But that uncle of ours killed off everybody there. He's a man-eater. Those women he's sending you to are in his power; they have to do whatever he tells them. As you get near the women's place, you'll come to two big snakes blocking the trail with their heads together, breathing out flames. Take some of this tobacco and give it to them. Call them 'Grandfather' and ask them to let you go through and let you come back again later. They'll say 'Ho' — all right. A little further on you'll come to two swans, one on each side of the trail. The old man has them all in his power. Take this red cloth and show it to the swans, so they'll keep quiet and let you pass."

The boy did as his brother told him. When he came to the snakes, he threw tobacco to them, called them "Grandfather," and asked them to let him go by. They said "Ho." Then he came to the swans. Just as they were going to make a noise, he showed them the red cloth he had and put it on their heads and told them not to make any noise as he went by.

Then he came to the home of the two women. They were both good looking. One of them was making a yarn bag, and the other was making a yarn belt with fringes. They were sitting opposite each other with a fire between them. There was a great big kettle, in which water was boiling. Each woman had a pole-axe beside her, a single bladed axe. The kettle was meant for him. When the man came in, he lit his pipe and puffed on it without saying a word. Finally he got up and said, "Well, I came here to flirt, but these women don't pay any attention to me, so I might as well leave." He emptied his pipe and went out. Then the two women started yelling at each other: "I looked at you to get up and grab your axe; why didn't you?" "I thought you were going to grab your axe." The man started to run. He wasn't supposed to look back, and he didn't. When he came to the two swans, they made no noise, and he got by. The snakes also made room for him, so he got way ahead. The women came after him. The women were angry that the swans hadn't made any warning noise, so they killed them both. They also killed the snakes. The tree-man brother yelled that he was getting the best of the two women.

When the boy got to his uncle's home, he found that the uncle had tied up everything; so the only way he could get in was through a place in the top. When he got inside, he cut everything that was tied. Then the two women walked in, and when they did so they came back to normal. All this time they hadn't been in their right minds on account of the uncle's power over them; they just had to carry out his orders. The two women decided to marry the boy and started to live there with the young man and his uncle. They warned him that the uncle would try to get rid of him.

One night the old man played sick. He kept moaning and groaning and said he was going to die. The nephew asked what he could do to help him, but the women said, "Don't listen to the old man. It's all fake; he's just trying to get rid of you." The young man kept on asking how he could save his uncle's life. Finally the old man said, "See that high hill up there? There's a bear up there. If I could give that bear as a feast, I could get well."

The young man said, "All right, I'll go and get the bear."

He climbed the hill and came to the bear's den. He called out, "Come out, grandfather." As the bear came out, he shot him with his bow and arrow right in the forehead and stunned the bear, so that the bear kept just ahead of him all the way home, and there he fell down dead.[1] The young man made a fire and scorched all the hair off the bear, cut him up, and boiled the meat in a kettle. Then he went to tell his uncle that he had it all ready. The old man told him to holler out and invite the *manidog* in the four corners of the world to come to the feast. The spirits all came, but the young man noticed that there were two old ladies sobbing at the west door, saying "We're eating our brother's dogs." After that feast the old man got better. He rested for four days and nights.

On the fifth night he got sick again and started to moan and groan. The women told their husband to pay no attention; the old man was just trying to get rid of him. But the young man couldn't stand it, because his uncle had taken care of him all his life, and he couldn't go against him. The uncle finally said that there was one thing that would save his life. He said that there were two otters in the middle of the ocean, and if his nephew could get them for a feast he'd get well. The young man wished to have ice on the ocean, so it was frozen over. He asked for a strong wind to carry him over the ice. When he got to the middle of the ocean he found two otters, a black one and a white one. When they poked their heads out of the water, he stunned them with his bow and arrows, so that they just followed a little behind him all the way home. He called for a wind to blow him back. When they got near the wigwam, he killed them

---

1. Although this episode is a hunter's fantasy, there may be a partial basis for such stories in the activities of hunting peoples. "An Eskimo may wound a bear and then drive him down to a stream where he can be killed and boated home" (Laughlin, 1968, p. 309).

and cooked them. When the uncle saw the otters, he didn't know what to think and just shivered. He didn't know that the young man had more power than he had. The women kept encouraging their husband and told him that he was getting ahead of his uncle. The young man asked his uncle what to do next. The uncle told him to call on the four corners of the earth and invite spirits to the feast. Everyone came. Again there were two old ladies sobbing on each side of the entrance to the wigwam, saying that they were eating their brother's dogs. After the feast the uncle left the young man alone for four days and four nights.

On the fifth night he started to moan and groan again. The two wives told the nephew not to listen, because they knew that this kind of thing had happened before. But the young man kept thinking of all the things his uncle had done for him, and he couldn't go against him. He asked him if there was anything he could to to help him get well. The uncle then gave out his last order: "If you let me shoot you right square in the chest with the biggest arrow I have, then I'd get well."

"All right, go ahead," said the young man. He had power too. He had more power from his dreams than his uncle had. His wives kept yelling and crying, but the young man told his uncle to shoot him in the chest. When the uncle got ready to shoot, the young man wished that he turn himself into a squirrel. The uncle said that he was shooting his nephew under four layers of the earth. But as he shot, the young man turned into a squirrel and jumped up onto a limb.

One time after that the young man took sick. He kept on moaning and groaning until his uncle asked him what ailed him. The nephew said, "If I could shoot you with my little bow and arrow right through the chest, then I'd get well." The uncle said that that was all right with him and offered him his bow and arrow. But the young man wouldn't take them; he wanted to use his own bow and arrow. As he shot, he said, "I'm shooting you under eight layers of the earth, and you'll never come back." The uncle squealed and yelled at the boy and begged him not to do it. The wives told the boy that if he had said five or six or seven layers of the earth, the uncle might have come back. So the young man killed the uncle, and that was the end of him.

Now they had nothing to fear, so the three of them walked to the brother who was half a tree. The women went to work and pulled up the roots until he was cured and became a whole man. The young man gave one of his wives to his brother. They all got along well. The two men hunted all kinds of game.

One time the brother who had been a tree told his younger brother that they should never speak of their uncle, because then something would happen. One time, the younger brother forgot himself. He came across an animal with good fur, and after he had skinned it, he said to himself, "Oh, if only my uncle could have this as a bed mat."

As soon as he had said that, his uncle appeared and said, "What is it that you wanted me for? What is it that I'm to have for a bed mat?"

When they heard their uncle's voice, the two brothers and their wives ran away all the way home. They got there safely. That's how they got rid of him.

Comments

A household consisting of an older man and a younger one, an uncle and nephew, is unusual, though we saw the same pattern in the case of Wenebojo and the wolf. But that was apparently a happy alliance, while this one is not. In both cases the younger male does the hunting, while the older one presumably has to take over the female roles. Despite his dominance, it is the uncle in this case who cleans up the wigwam, airs the quilts, and throws out the frogs which have dirtied his nephew's blankets.

As in the previous tale, number 44, this story seems to be about a conflict between generations. All the younger characters end up in an alliance against the formerly dominant uncle, who is finally banished from the scene, although he stages a brief, scarey comeback.

The present story has some features in common with story number 14 about Bebukowe. In the beginning in both tales we have a lonely pair — both male in this case. The young man knows nothing about sex, but he finally gets a wife, after severe tribulations. With sexual repression, sexual symbolism is apt to assert itself. In story number 14 we have the phallic symbolism of Bebukowe, while in the present story there are the fire-breathing snakes and the long-necked swans, which seem to be phallic symbols. These creatures are killed by the two castrating females with their pole-axes.

The story contains a recurrent "invalid dominance" theme like that in "The Two Brothers and Oshkikwe" (number 17), in which a person pretends to be sick and makes excessive demands as a price for recovery. In the former story a woman asks her sister to kill her son-in-law and serve him up in a feast. In the present tale the young man is first sent on some dangerous errands and is finally asked to let himself be shot in the chest. In both stories the young man accedes to the excessive demands.

The story of "The Spell of the Wicked Uncle" recalls a northern Saulteaux (Canadian Chippewa) tale about a man and his father-in-law. Since cross-cousin marriage was formerly practiced among the Chippewa, a man's uncle could well be his father-in-law, especially a mother's brother or father's sister's husband. The young man in the Saulteaux story is called Omishus.

One day the young man says to his father-in-law, "I wonder where we could get some gulls' eggs?" Omishus says that he knows a place. They go in a canoe to an island. While the young man is collecting eggs, Omishus leaves, pounding the boat to make it go. He says, "Here you are, gulls. I give you my son-in-law to eat." A big gull approaches to kill the young man, but he says, "I'm not the right kind of food for gulls. Fly over the old man's canoe." He tells the bird to defecate on the old man's face, and the bird does so. Then the young man kills the gull, cuts off its head, and takes home some of its eggs to his children, saying, "When your grandfather arrives, go to meet him and eat eggs at the same time." When the father-in-law comes home, he tells his grandchildren that the gulls have eaten their father, and he is surprised to find that this is not so, for "the gull was the embodiment of one of his dreams."

One day the young man says, "I wonder where I could get sturgeon to make glue?" Omishus says, "I'll show you." When the young man stands up with his bow and arrow to shoot sturgeon, the old man pounds on his canoe, making his son-in-law fall overboard, and he cries out to the great underwater snakes that he is offering his son-in-law to them. But the young man persuades a great underwater snake that he is not fit food for them and is carried by the snake to shore.

A similar episode follows with an eagle and the safe return of the hero to his wives and children, ahead of his father-in-law. Omishus is surprised that the snake and the eagle did not kill his son-in-law, for in each case the animal or bird "had been the embodiment of one of his dreams." After one last attempt by the old man to kill his son-in-law, he is abandoned by the young couple, and they never see him again (Skinner, 1911, pp. 168–73).[2]

The hositility of the old man is given no motivation in either "The Spell of the Wicked Uncle" or "Omishus." He is simply a mean old man who wants to kill his nephew or son-in-law. In both tales the young man is remarkably forbearing and only turns against the old man after the latter has made several attempts to do away with him. The reason given for this forbearance in the first story is that the uncle had looked after the nephew in his youth, and so the young man could not go against him. No reason is given in the second story. In any case, the repeated plots against the young man make his ultimate revenge seem well justified. These stories seem to reflect an emphasis on respect for elders, especially for

2. The same story is given by Schoolcraft in "Mishosha or the Magician of the Lakes" (in 1956, pp. 163–68).

those who have reared one from childhood. At the same time, Chippewa training for boys emphasized independence and self-reliance, which would be apt to create some tension in the boys between the two emphases.

46. *The Girl and the Wicked* Manido

Collected by Ernestine Friedl at Court Oreilles in 1942
Narrator: Delia Oshogay   Interpreter: Maggie Lamorie

Ten brothers lived together with their niece, a little girl. In the mornings they went out to hunt game. The oldest, Madjikiwis, said to her, "You know we'll be gone all day. If you hear a noise, or if somebody is coming, get underneath that wooden bowl, and then no one will ever find you."

After the men had gone, she heard some voices and saw ten men coming; so she jumped into the bowl. She heard the men say that they wanted to fight her ten uncles. When her uncles came back that evening, she told them what had happened. The same thing happened another time; so Madjikiwis said to the others, "Tomorrow we'll stay home and meet those men. They'll never leave us alone anyway."

The next morning the men stayed home, and the girl hid under the wooden bowl. The ten men came along and killed all the little girl's uncles. They cut off their heads and left the bodies behind. In the evening the girl set out to look for where they'd gone. She came to the right village in the dark. An old lady there heard a noise and said to her daughter, "That must be your cousin coming to spend the night; let her in." Then they saw that it was a stranger, but they let her in. The woman told about the men who had killed ten men who lived with their niece. She didn't know that she was talking to the niece. She said that they had brought the ten heads of the dead men to the village. She suggested that they go and look at the ten heads; so she and her daughter and the little girl went to see them.

They were having a dance to celebrate the capture of the ten heads. The little girl joined in the dance. The bad old *manido* who was in charge of the war party fell in love with her. He asked her to step out and have a talk with him. Then she knew that she'd get her revenge on him. One of the things he said, when they talked, was that he would die if a woman's clothes were placed near his head. He also said, "I've never yet slept, and I won't until just before I die."

She started to fool around with his head, and she had the power to make him fall asleep. Then she took off her skirt and placed it on his head. She tied the waist part of her skirt and stuck his head in that part of it. She took her knife and cut his throat, put the bottom part of her skirt together and held the head in a sack. Now the head was in her power. It could still talk and said, "You sure played a trick on me." The rest of his body went back to the dancing place, and everyone he touched dropped dead. The head said to her, "If you let me go, I'll make your uncles come back to life." But she wouldn't be fooled and wouldn't let him go. It took her four days to walk back to her village, carrying the head. She dried it some way and kept it. It was dead. Everyone was happy, because now they had nothing to fear. The chief of the village took the little girl, and she married his son.

Comments

Here, again, we have a young person triumphing over a mean old man or *manido*. In the two preceding stories the protagonist was a young man; in the present tale it is a young girl. The heroine is referred to as a "little girl," which suggests pre-pubescence. But the story seems to refer to the lethal power of menstrual blood, since the waist part of the skirt is placed over the *manido*'s head after the *manido* had told the girl that he would die if a woman's clothes were placed near his head. Besides, the girl marries at the end of the story, which suggests that she cannot be such a little girl after all.

The cut-off head says to the little girl, "You sure played a trick on me" — a real understatement by a man who has been decapitated.

The household described at the beginning of the tale seems unusual and improbable — ten brothers and one girl. Presumably the brothers are unmarried.

47. *The Beaver Man*

Collected by Robert Ritzenthaler at Court Oreilles in 1942
Narrator: John Mink   Interpreter: Prosper Guibord

Once there was a fellow called Asidenigan who lived off by himself and lived on nothing but corn and beaver. He had a lot of corn and was good at trapping beavers. Nearby was a village headed by a chief named Madjikiwis. This village had had bad luck in hunting, and the people were very hungry.

Before Asidenigan went out to hunt he always made a big kettle of corn mush. He would test it every once in a while by putting a peeled stick into the kettle. If it fell over, it was too soupy. Then he would add more corn until finally the stick would stand up by itself in the corn mush. Then it was ready to eat. He could eat a whole kettlefull. Then he took his blanket, belt, war club, and hatchet and went over to the village to join the hunting party just setting out.

Asidenigan said that he wanted to see the chief's daughter, so he was taken to the chief's wigwam, where he was greeted warmly. He said that he wanted to marry the chief's daughter, and the chief said that would be all right, but he told the man how hungry all the people were. So Asidenigan went out and went along a stream, where he saw that there were beaver nearby. He went upstream to a bend and saw a big beaver house. He waded out to it, tore part of the wall down and felt around for the beavers' tails. He had power that helped him to get beavers easily. They just fell over, and he picked them up. He picked up a lot of beavers, packed them back to the village, and dumped them in front of the village. He called to the chief's daughter to come and see what he'd brought. She was very pleased and called her mother, who was pleased too and wanted to give a feast for the whole village. But Asidenigan said that these beavers were just to feed her family, and he would go and get some more for the rest of the village. So he went back, got a lot more, and they had a big feast in the village. He did that every day and always brought back a lot of beaver for the people. Everyone had a storage rack full of dried beaver meat.

Asidenigan did this all fall and winter, but in the spring he didn't come back. The people worried and wondered what had happened to him, for they liked him very much. He got home late that night and told his wife that the beavers around here were getting scarce, and that he had to go farther and farther for them. By this time the people of the village wore clothing made of beaver, had rugs of beaver, and blankets of beaver.

The man told his wife that they would have to go and camp farther up the river; it was too far to come back to the village each night. He told his wife that they wouldn't have to take anything along. So they set off, just taking along one kettle and an axe. The snow was nearly gone by this time. Asidenigan picked a nice camping ground up the river that evening. He just walked around in a circle about the size of a wigwam, and when he got all the way around there was a wigwam already built. It was all fixed up with blankets and everything.

The next morning, while her husband was out hunting, the woman suddenly heard footsteps, and two men looked in. She told them to come in. One of them sat on her husband's bed, over which hung his war club. The wife asked why they had come, and they told her that a mob of people were going to come back the next morning to kill her husband. She had put a kettle of beaver meat over the fire to cook, and one of the men pulled a partridge from his pocket and told her to cook it with the meat. He told her that the mob were bringing a young man for her to marry and that they wouldn't hurt her, and that she should not tell her husband anything.

That day Asidenigan felt uneasy. He got only a few beaver and went home early. He saw the tracks of the men in front of the wigwam and where the men had sat. He asked his wife who had been there. She said "No one." He looked at his war club and said that four eyes had looked at it that day. She still insisted that no one had been there. When she set the cooked partridge in front of him to eat, he asked who had brought it. She said that she had killed it while cutting wood that morning. He told his wife that he knew that she was hiding something. He couldn't eat anything and said that the next morning he wasn't going to hunt beaver. He didn't sleep all night. Early the next morning he asked his wife to get something for him to eat, so that he could get ready to fight the men that were coming. Then she confessed that two men had come and that a mob was coming to kill him. He took down his war club and told his wife to hang onto his belt.

When the men came, he killed quite a few of them with his club, but finally his wife lost her grip on his belt, and some of the men grabbed her and carried her off. The other men ran away then. When Asidenigan saw that his wife was gone, he went into the wigwam and sat down and felt very sorrowful, for he liked his wife. He couldn't eat and felt very lonesome.

After a while he set out to trail them. He found a camping ground where they had tied his wife and danced around her. He camped there for the night and started out again early next morning. He tracked them all day and ended up at the shore of a big lake, where they must have had dances. He could hear drumming in the distance. He got two oak balls about an inch in diameter, tied them together, enlarged the hole in one and made himself small so that he could crawl inside. He set the oak balls on the water and told the wind to blow him across the lake to the village. He landed and got back to normal size, but then made himself invisible. He went up to the gate of the village where they were drumming and dancing. The village was surrounded by a log stockade, and the people gathered inside a long wigwam, dancing. He peeked in and saw a man seated near his wife. He pointed at the man and wished that he would get thirsty, so that she could get water for him. The man did get thirsty and asked her to get some water. He sent two boys along to guard her. When she got outside the stockade, her husband grabbed her and knocked down the two boys and dug their eyes out, he was so mad. She wanted to go right home, but he told her to take the pail of water back. He went inside with her (he was still invisible), and she told the men that her husband was with her. They were afraid and began dancing very hard. They asked for some light, and as the fire blazed up, they saw her husband and captured him. They said that they were going to make him dance. They tied his legs above the knees and tied his arms, and he started to dance. They wanted to give him a rattle, but he said that he had his own rattle, and pulled one out from under his arm. He sang his name song with his rattle.

When he got around to where his wife was seated, he asked her for some meat, so she started to roast a tenderloin. When it was done, she hung it around his chest, and it burned him so badly that he jumped right through the fire hole in the wigwam and landed out of the village. He fell inside of a hollow stump. He was badly burned and had to rest a minute.

Some of the women from the village came out to chop wood, and one woman saw the hollow stump. They started talking, and one woman talked badly about him, but the other one stuck up for him. Then the man broke open the log and killed the one who had criticized him and told the one who had taken pity on him that he would be back in four days.

Then he went home and packed all the beaver he had and took them to his father-in-law's place. He told them what had happened and showed them his burns. He said that he was going back in four days. All the men offered to help him, but he said that he wanted to go alone. He had brought some of the scalps from his fight, and he showed them to the people. Then he spent two days making a new war club.

His brother-in-law wanted to go with him to punish his sister for burning her husband. So they set off; a whole bunch from the village went along. They had fortified the village, but when the man and his bunch arrived, they broke right through. They captured the wife, and her brother burned her to death as a lesson to other women to treat their husbands better. He told the husband that he would give him his younger sister for a wife, and he did that, when they got back to the village. So Asidenigan married the younger sister, and they went off to live by themselves. They took nothing along, and found a camping place and built another wigwam by just walking around in a circle.

Comments

At the beginning of this tale the hero lives alone. He is self-sufficient and eats both beaver and corn mush. This man is able to summon various powers — in hunting beavers, making himself small in size, and becoming invisible. Power seems to be related to appetite in some of our tales. We are told that the beaver man can eat a whole kettlefull of corn mush, just as the *windigo*-killer in story number 21 is said to have a voracious appetite. Conversely, lack of food in story number 44 makes people powerless, under the spell of others.

Despite his self-sufficiency, our hero needs a wife and marries the chief's daughter. He likes her and becomes lonesome after she has been abducted. One might have expected this tale to follow the formula: man gets girl; man loses girl; man gets girl back again. But our story follows a different course. The wife does not behave properly. She does not tell her husband the truth after the two strangers have visited her wigwam; later, in the enemy village, she burns his chest with a roast tenderloin. When the beaver man goes on his last raid on the enemy village, nothing is said about his getting revenge on the enemy, only that the wife is burned to death by her brother "as a lesson to other women to treat their husbands better." But the story ends happily after all. As in the story of Wakayabide, there is a pattern of a man offering his sister as a bride to another man, and so the beaver man marries the younger sister.

48. *The Boy, His Grandmother, and the King's Daughter*

Collected by Ernestine Friedl at Court Oreilles in 1942
Narrator: Lizzie Grover   Interpreter: Anna Johnson

A king who lived in the center of a town had a daughter who got sick and died. They put her body up on a rack. The king sent his servant to spread news of the death all over the town, asking the people to leave and move out of town. They all left except for one old lady who lived on the edge of town with her grandson. She sent her grandson to the king to tell him that they wanted to stay there and to ask him for a seine and a canoe, food and clothing. She also told him to tell the king that they would watch the girl's grave after everyone else had left. The king said that that was all right.

So everybody left except for the old lady and her grandson. The king gave them everything they asked for. They set out the net, and the next morning, when they went to the net, they found it full of fish. They did that every morning, and the net was always full.

One evening, just as it was getting dark, when the boy went to fix his net, he heard someone singing. He couldn't tell where the voice came from. He looked in the direction of the grave and saw a spark there.

When he got back to the wigwam, the grandmother asked him why he was so quiet. He said that there was nothing wrong. The next time he went down to the net again, he heard the same singing. He could understand more. He heard the words, "Little boy, little boy." He saw a fire in the grave. He went home and didn't say a word.

The next time he went to see his nets, he heard a voice saying, "Come over here, little boy." He went toward the grave. It looked like a wigwam now instead of a grave. He went in and saw the woman who had died sitting there. "Sit here, little boy," she said. "I'm the cause of your coming here. I want you to come here. Have a meal with me." There was one dish there full of meat. "This is the food that was offered to me by my folks. Now I'm going to tell you what you should do. I want you to fast for ten days."

He went home and looked back at the grave. It didn't look like a wigwam any more; it looked like a grave. When he came back to his grandmother, he told her that he was going to fast for ten days. He said that he'd turn over on the fifth day. He took charcoal and put it on his face. His grandmother said, "Grandson, you're too small; you'll starve." "No, I'll do as I said I would do. Don't worry."

During the next days the grandmother went to the nets every morning and dried the fish and put them away. On the tenth day of his fast he spoke to his grandmother: "Grandma, make a little wigwam in the corner of this wigwam. Heat up two rocks and put them in there. Take some deer tallow and put it where I'm going to sit, and you go outside."

The boy went into the little wigwam. Every time he poured tallow on the rocks there was a flame. The old woman outside heard this noise — "Whooooo." On the fourth time, when he put the tallow on the rocks, she heard it too. Then he called her in, and she could see how big he was — a great big person with a bow and arrow alongside of him and one drum. Then he got up and sat on his own side of the wigwam, as he used to.

He told his grandmother that he was going to hunt. Soon he came back with a big bear. He made a fire and cooked the whole bear, and put the meat in birchbark baskets. He said that he was going to give a feast to the *manidog*. He went outside and called on everyone to come. He told his grandmother to stay in one corner of the wigwam, cover herself, and not move. She could hear everyone who came in say "Whoooo." The boy got up to speak and said that the feast was given as an offering to the spirits for all the time he'd been fasting.

After the feast he went to the grave, and it looked like a wigwam again. The same woman was sitting there. She said, "I felt proud of you when you did what I told you to do and when you went through with it.

Tell your grandmother not to mind if she hears someone putting wood there."

One day the grandmother heard someone putting wood there. The boy said to his grandmother, "You're going to see someone today."

On the fourth day of the wood dropping, a woman came in and put some wood on the fire. Then she went right over and sat next to the boy. She spoke to the old woman: "I was the one who was in the grave over there and was left here." The boy had a little flute and a drum. Every night he fixed his drum and sang. "You gave me life because you came through everything," she told him. Every time he sang, all kinds of wild animals came around. They could get any amount of food, and she would fix it.

The boy traveled all day long and was home only at night. There were many racks with drying meat. They made tallow and put it in deer hides. Then the woman told the boy that the people who lived out of town were getting hungry and would come back again. She was going to burn a buckskin so that it would shrink, and the earth would shrink just as the buckskin did. Then the people would come back more quickly.

Her brothers were the first to come, and they saw how different everything looked. The boy told them to come in. They said that they thought that the old lady and her grandson would have starved by now. The woman took the big baskets of meat to where the men were sitting. They just couldn't eat; they looked at the woman and thought that she looked like their sister who had died. The tears rolled down their cheeks as they looked at her.

The girl told her brothers that she had come back to life through the help of this old lady's grandson. She told them to eat, because she had come back to life again, and they shouldn't worry. Those men made packs of the dried meat to take back to the other people. All the people began to come back into the town. The boy put the skin into the fire, and again it shrank, so that the people could come back faster. After they had all returned, the young fellow gave some meat to everyone. Then he became the king. After he was king, every time he sang with the drum, the animals gathered, and everyone lived well while he was the king.

Comments

This story is essentially the same as that of "The Fox and the Chief's Daughter" (number 35). It might be thought that this tale should have been included in the chapter of stories of European or mixed origin. But the European aspects of the tale refer only to such terms as "king" and "town" as replacements for "chief" and "village," just as in the story of

"The Bad Old Man" there are references to a lion and a tiger, which must be modern replacements for aboriginal lynx or panther. In both cases I think the basic story is aboriginal.

In the present tale the hero is not identified as a fox, as in story number 35, and he does not cause the girl's death. Nor is the hero an outcast, as in the other version.

At the outset of the story the hero is a little boy; that is how he is addressed by the dead woman. But he rapidly grows up. Fasting was done before puberty by the Chippewa. In the course of his fasting the hero of our tale assumes large size and acquires a bow and arrow. He goes off to hunt, kills a bear, and then makes a feast for the *manidog*.

In former days, after a boy's first kill, a feast was held to celebrate the event. In this tale the hero arranges his own feast-for-the-kill, which is also an offering to the spirits for the time he had fasted. The hero brings the woman back to life, and she becomes his wife — a rapid transition from the little-boy stage. Perhaps, then, this is an Oedipal fantasy, with the woman representing a mother figure.

General Comments on the Tales of Spells and Magical Powers

The Chippewa dislike "bossy" people who try to dominate others, a trait expressed in extreme form in the first three stories in this chapter, in which people are reduced to helpless subjection to a mean old man who holds them in a spell. In each case a young person challenges and defeats the old villain and rescues his zombie-like victims.

The tales about the powerful mean old men must be seen in the light of Chippewa fears about sorcery, which were current in both Canada and Wisconsin. Here is a statement by one of Ruth Landes's informants: "Everwind sent twisted mouth to his own daughter-in-law because she left her man when she found him with another woman. . . . He sickened a woman because she wouldn't give him her canoe. . . . He made a man impotent. And turned another man into a bear . . ." (1968, p. 63).[3]

The symptom of "twisted mouth" as the result of sorcery was noted by Hoffman, who thought that strychnine poisoning might be involved (1891, p. 227). Norval Morriseau described the onset of symptoms as follows: "first he [the victim] would have a sore eye and think it was

---

3. For statements about sorcery by Wisconsin Chippewa informants, see Barnouw (1950, pp. 20–22).

some eye sickness. Then he would feel his skin being drawn down to one side, little by little, until in a week's time his mouth would begin to drop until it was crooked" (1965, p. 48).

Themes of transformation appear in all of the stories in this chapter. In the first story a lion and tiger are really the sons of the bad old man. Two birds are really the spirits of the old man and his wife. The hero makes himself small and crawls into an oak ball, which is blown across the water to an island. In the second story the hero's brother has been transformed into a tree but resumes his normal shape toward the end of the tale. The hero momentarily turns himself into a squirrel. In the third story the heroine is able to make herself small enough so that she can hide under a wooden bowl. In the fourth story, as in the first, the hero is able to make himself small enough to crawl into an oak ball, and is also able to make himself invisible. In the fifth story the hero grows in size in the sweat lodge, and the earth is made to shrink as a buckskin is burned.

Themes of resurrection also occur. Although the bad old man is killed in the second story and sent under eight layers of earth, he reappears when his nephew thinks of him. In the third story the bad *manido*'s head is cut off but continues to speak. In the last story the king's daughter comes back to life.

The hierarchy of power is also an important theme. The bad old man has power over many others in the first story, but the young man turns out to have more power than he. Similarly, in the second story the bad old man has power over others, but his nephew acquires still more power, and is finally shown to be stronger than the uncle, whom he shoots below eight layers of earth. "He had more power from his dreams than his uncle had." In the third story the girl gets power over the wicked *manido* and is able to cut off his head. The beaver man in the fourth story has power over beavers. "They just fell over, and he picked them up." He also exhibits other magical powers which make him superior to others. In the last story a boy becomes king because of his magical powers.

Themes of courtship occur in the second tale. The boy falls in love with some frogs. The uncle gives an interesting definition of womanhood: "a woman wears a dress. What you picked up were frogs." The uncle directs the young man to court two girls who are under his power and who try to kill the young man. These themes express ambivalent attitudes toward the opposite sex. This is also implied in the third story, when the girl gets power over the *manido* by sticking his head in the waist part of her skirt.

Because the beaver man, in the fourth story, is a good hunter, he is given the chief's daughter in marriage, but she is not a good wife and is punished by being burned to death — another expression of ambivalence.

The animals mentioned in this chapter include dog, deer, lion, tiger, bear, beaver, otter, squirrel, frog, snake, swan, and partridge. There are many references to hunting and fishing. There is also one reference to corn; in the "The Beaver Man" the hero makes thick corn mush.

More than in previous chapters, there is mention of village life in this chapter. In "The Bad Old Man" three brothers live just outside a village. One of them gets meat for the sick people dominated by the bad old man. In "The Spell of the Wicked Uncle" feasts are offered to spirits from the four corners of the world. Village life is referred to in "The Girl and the Wicked *Manido*" and in "The Beaver Man." In the latter story, the hero provides food not only for his wife and her family but also for the rest of the village. The village to which his wife is abducted is surrounded by a log stockade, and all the people are gathered in a long wigwam to dance and drum. The last story in this chapter also has reference to village life.

CHAPTER EIGHT

Tales of European
or Mixed Origin

Since myths and tales readily crossed tribal and linguistic boundaries in different geographical and cultural areas in North America, it should not be surprising that European tales often appear in the repertoires of American Indian story tellers. Those collected in Wisconsin in 1941–44 are presented in this chapter. Most of them seem to have come from France. The Chippewa had more contacts with Frenchmen than with other Europeans, through *voyageurs*, traders, and workers in the lumber camps, and there was intermarriage with Frenchmen. The names of the reservations, Lac du Flambeau and Lac Court Oreilles, are French, and there are many family names of French origin, such as Poupart, Guibord, and St. Germain. Some half-breeds, like Prosper Guibord, were bilingual, speaking both French and Chippewa. The Chippewa term of greeting, *boju*, is derived from the French *bonjour*.

In a list of American Fur Company employees for 1818–19 published in the *Wisconsin Historical Collections*, Vol. 12 (pp. 154–69), twenty-nine men were assigned to work at Lac Court Oreilles or Lac du Flambeau as boatmen, interpreters, fishermen, or clerks. These men were generally hired at Mackinac or Montreal and signed up for one to three years' work. Their names are predominantly French: Beaudrieu, Beaulieu, Beudrin, Bourdeaux, Chapeau, Charette, Corbin, Durant, Ebert, Goké, Janvier, Ladebauche, Lalancet, Lamoureux, Laurent, Neumanville, Provost, Prunier, Robert, Rousseau, St. Arno, Varin.

As will be seen, some of the stories in this chapter have references to such European features as kings, queens, princesses, and castles. There are also references to gold coins, pepper, salt, chickens, pigs, horses, oxen, and other items of Old World culture. It is striking that, despite their alien content, these stories closely resemble the tales told in Europe. They have been faithfully transmitted in the Indian setting, although some Indian patterns do intrude. The narrators of these stories seem to have wished to get the details right, just as Tom Badger evidently wished to give a faithful reproduction of the origin myth as he had heard it. This being the case, the tales that follow can be identified according to the

Aarne-Thompson tale types rather than by the motif numbers which have been used up to now. In Stith Thompson's introduction to the six-volume *Motif-Index* (1955–58), he points out that as long as an entire tale complex of European origin remains intact, the Aarne-Thompson index in *The Types of the Folktale* (1961) is useful. Outside of Europe, however, it is of little help; hence the need for constructing the *Motif-Index*. As will be seen, most of the tales in this chapter are clearly identifiable in the Aarne-Thompson index.

49. *The Cat and the Mouse*

Collected by Ernestine Friedl at Court Oreilles in 1942
Narrator: Delia Oshogay   Interpreter: Maggie Lamorie

A cat and mouse who lived together put away food for the winter. One day the cat said, "I just got word that I'm to be sponsor for a baby that's getting baptized; so I have to go."

"Go ahead," said the mouse. "I wish they had invited me too!"

When the cat got back, the mouse asked him, "What kind of a time did you have, being sponsor for the child?"

"We had a great time; we had a big feast."

"What name did you give the child?"

The cat said, "Started-eating-him."

Another time the cat again announced that he was invited to be sponsor for a child. The mouse said, "It's great that they think of you. If anyone asked me, I'd be there right away."

When the cat got back, the mouse asked him what it had been like.

The cat said, "We had a big time. Everyone looked at me holding the baby."

"What name did you give the child?"

"Half-eaten-up."

The cat finally announced that he had a third invitation. When he got back, the mouse asked him what kind of a time he had had. The cat said, "We had a bigger time than ever."

"What is the name of the child this time?"

The cat said, "All-eaten-up."

The mouse thought a little and said, "It couldn't be, could it, that you ate up all the stuff we're saving up for the winter?"

The cat said, "Oh, you little old mouse, if you don't like it, I'll swallow you!" And he swallowed the mouse.

Comments

"The Cat and the Mouse" might seem, at first glance, to be clearly of European origin, since domesticated cats were not present in North America before Columbus. Moreover, baptism is referred to — a Christian introduction. On the other hand, essentially the same tale appears in a Menomini collection, in which the characters are a wolf and fox, rather than cat and mouse (Skinner, 1913a, pp. 72–75). It might be concluded that an aboriginal version concerning wolf and fox was later replaced by the more European pair. As to baptism, conservative Chippewa have a pattern of giving a newly born child a *weˀg*, or godparent, which involves a feast and a brief ceremony. However, this story is Aarne-Thompson's (henceforth abbreviated A-T) tale type 15, motif K372, *Playing godfather*. It has a wide distribution in Europe: it appears in Germany, Scandinavia, and France, and has been reported among the French of Missouri and Louisiana Creoles. One version, "The Wolf and the Fox," told in Franche-Comté, France, is given by Geneviève Massignon (1968, pp. 189–92).

50. *The War of the Birds and the Animals*

Collected by Robert Ritzenthaler at Court Oreilles in 1942
Narrator: John Moustache   Interpreter: Prosper Guibord

One time the animals were going to war upon the birds. The birds heard about it, and the wren, the king of the birds, sent out a bee as a runner to spy on the animal council. At the council the bee learned that the fox was going to lead the animals, and if he held his tail up, the animals were to advance, but if he dropped his tail the animals were supposed to flee. The bee told this to the wren, and told him that he shouldn't worry. On the next day when the animals started their advance, the fox was leading the animals with his tail up. When they got near the birds, the bee circled around the fox and stung him in the tail. The fox dropped his tail in pain, the animals fled, and the birds were saved.

Comments

This story is A-T tale type 222, motif B261, *War of birds and quadrupeds*. Aarne and Thompson summarize it as follows: "Birds win by cleverness. The fox's lifted tail is to be the signal. The gnats stick him under the tail. He drops it and the quadrupeds flee" (1961, p. 72).

The tale has been recorded in Finnish, Estonian, Latvian, and Norwegian versions, as well as Scottish, Irish, French, Spanish, Flemish, Hungarian, Russian, Greek, and Turkish.

51. *The Turtles' Relay Race*

Collected by Robert Ritzenthaler at Court Oreilles in 1942
Narrator: Pete Martin   Interpreter: Prosper Guibord

Wenebojo decided that his daughter should be married, since she was already an old maid; so he sent out his son to act as a runner and announce that the people should all dress up so that no one would know them, not even the son. So they all dressed up and came to his wigwam, one by one. Each would smoke a pipeful of tobacco, after which the daughter would have to name the person. If she couldn't tell who they were, she would have to marry that one. All day they came in, but she recognized them all; so she didn't get married.

Wenebojo said there would be a race the next day, and the first one to reach his daughter would marry her. That night the turtle went out and got a lot of his brothers, who looked just like him. Then he asked the earth where the race would start. The earth pointed to the place and said "Right there." So he buried the turtles all along the race path up to the finish line, where the turtle buried himself. He told the first turtle to go to his home that night, and the next morning he should dig into the ground when the race started.

So they started the race, and the turtle buried himself, and the next turtle came up and went down, and so on until the last turtle reached up and grabbed the hand of Wenebojo's daughter. But he was a little slow, and the raven grabbed her other hand at the same time. Each held on and wouldn't let go; so the turtle told his runner to go home and get his knife. The runner came back with the knife; but the turtle said, "That's the one I scrape bones with. Go back and bring the big one wrapped up in a mat." So the runner brought back the big knife, and the turtle said, "Yes, that's the one."

Then the turtle said, "We'll cut her in half, and we'll each get half of her." So he started cutting down from the top. When he reached her vagina, he said he would cut around that so that he could have that part. The raven objected to that, but finally he said that the turtle could have her all to himself; so the turtle took her to his wigwam and married her.

Comments

"The Turtles' Relay Race" may be classified as A-T tale type 1074, motif K11.1, *Race won by deception: relative helpers.* Another Chippewa version is given by Paul Radin and A. B. Reagan (1928, pp. 124–25).

The distribution of this tale is so widespread as to almost defy analysis. Franz Boas, who recorded it among the Kutenai Indians in 1918, pointed to other versions of the motif among the Jicarilla Apache, Zuni, Caddo, Cherokee, and Asiatic Eskimo. The role of the turtle is sometimes played by other animals. Among the Kutenai the frog is the protagonist. Boas summarized the story as follows: "Frog makes his people lie down along the race course. When Antelope is running, one Frog after another appears ahead of him" (1918, p. 307). This is clearly the same story as ours, with different actors. Elsie Clews Parsons recorded the tale in the Pueblo area, where the protagonist was the mole. She thought that the tale was probably of Spanish origin (1918, pp. 221–22). However, Boas states that the frog is usually the slow animal in Spanish, French, and Italian versions, as it is among the Kutenai. On the other hand, among the Arikara, the Wyandot, and the Salish of Washington the turtle is the protagonist (Boas, 1940, pp. 521–22).

The motif of the buried row of turtles appears in a collection of folktales of the Ila-speaking peoples of Northern Rhodesia published in 1920 (Smith and Dale, 1968, 2:390). Smith and Dale, who recorded the tale, point to the similarity of an Uncle Remus story. The protagonists of the African tale are the hare and the tortoise. The stories of Uncle Remus contain other African motifs besides this one. Tales of African origin were told by slaves, not only in the southern states but also in Brazil, and spread to some American Indian tribes in both North and South America.[1] In North America the tale might have spread from southern slaves to the Creek Indians and from them to more western tribes, but it may be that the tale was also spread by the Spaniards and the French. It seems to be found everywhere in North America.

52. *Oshkikwe's Children*

Collected by Ernestine Friedl at Court Oreilles in 1942
Narrator: Delia Oshogay   Interpreter: Maggie Lamorie

Once there lived three sisters who were so poor that they had to clean up their clothes when they were invited anywhere. They had no father or

---

1. Examples of such diffusion are presented in the introductions of two Uncle Remus books (Harris, 1880, 1883). See also Gerber (1893).

mother. The king announced that he was giving a feast, and they planned to go. One time, while they were cutting wood in the forest, the king hid there and listened to their conversation. Matchikwewis, the oldest sister, said that she would like to marry the king's cook. The second one said that she would like to marry the king's dishwasher. Oshkikwe, the youngest, said that she'd like to marry the king, and she said that if she did, she'd have two sons and one girl. Also she said that the girl, the youngest one, would have golden hair and a star on her forehead. Just then the king drove up and took them to the palace. He had three apartments, one for his cook, one for the dishwasher, and one for himself. He gave Matchikwewis the cook's bedroom suite; he gave the second sister the dishwasher's bedroom suite, and he took the youngest one to his own.

Oshkikwe became pregnant. When her sisters found that out, they managed to get their brother-in-law to go away for a while. While he was gone, Oshkikwe gave birth to a baby boy. Her two sisters got an empty dry goods box and packed the new born child in it and sent it down the river. When their brother-in-law came home, they lied to him and said that the baby had died.

A few miles down the river there was an old man who lived with his wife in a shack. While the old man was getting water in a pail from the river, he saw a dry goods box floating by. He brought it to shore and opened it up. Then he took it to his wife and told her to hurry up and get into bed. He spread the story that his old lady had given birth to a child. The people were surprised to hear it. Some women took baby clothes and supplies to the shack, and when they arrived the old lady was in bed, still groaning.

Some time after that the young king's wife gave birth to another child, a boy. Her sisters were jealous and did the same thing they'd done before; they packed the baby into a basket and floated it down the river. They told their brother-in-law that his wife had given birth to a lung of a lamb.

The old man down the river saw the basket floating by and took it home. He made his old woman go to bed again, slaughtered a pig, and marked up the bed. He went to town and said that his old woman had had another baby. People gave them things again. She moaned and groaned as her husband had told her to do.

Then Oshkikwe had her third child, the girl with golden hair and a star on her forehead. Her two sisters played the same trick on her and told her husband that his wife had given birth to a lung of a lamb. Again the old man down the river saw something floating in the water, picked up the baby and brought it to the old woman.

The children were growing up and getting quite big. One time the little girl went into the flower garden and saw a real little old lady there. The old lady said to her, "My child, as soon as you go into the house, you tell your mother that you want a golden bird that talks. Start crying and don't stop until you get somebody to go after that golden bird that talks."

The girl cried and cried. Her mother asked her what she wanted, and she said that she wanted a golden bird that talks. Her older brother told her to be quiet and said that he'd go the next day to get the golden bird that talks. Their mother burst out crying and said that there wasn't anybody who could get that golden bird. Whoever tried never came back.

The next morning the boy threw his jack-knife against the wall. It stuck, and he told his mother to watch that knife every morning. If it had blood on it, it would be a sign that somebody had killed him. If it was rusty, sickness killed him; but if it stayed the same it meant that he was all right.

He walked a long way looking for the bird. As he walked, he saw an animal with big long legs crossing the road in front of him. The animal told this boy that he was foolish to look for the bird, since nobody who went there ever came back. But the boy kept on walking until he came to a little wigwam. There was an old woman there who gave him a meal. She put one bean and one kernel of rice in a tiny kettle. The boy wondered how he could get full on that. The old woman knew what he was thinking. But he got plenty to eat. The old woman gave him instructions about what to do. When he got to where the bird was, he should go down hill. He would find a place with shiny clear water; that was where the bird was. Opposite from this was a dirty pond full of manure. He was supposed to go to the dirty place, because that's where the bird rested.

The boy did what she told him to do. He didn't bother to go to the beautiful place but went to the dirty water. The old woman had given him a bottle to fill with the dirty water for the bird to drink. The minute he took that water, he had the nest on his shoulder, and the bird flew right into the nest. He went up hill with the bird. All the rocks along the road were dead people. He heard all kinds of voices saying, "Chase him, shoot him, hit him with rocks." Those were the voices of the dead people. He wasn't supposed to turn around until he got to the top of the hill, but he couldn't stand it any more, and he just turned and looked and was changed into a rock. Then the bird went back to its nest again.

Next morning the parents looked at his knife, and it was rusty. They knew that something had happened to him. Then the next brother insisted on going after him. His mother couldn't stop him. Everything happened to him just the same as with the first boy. When they saw that the knife was rusty, the little sister said that she would go after her brothers. Her mother begged and begged her not to go, because nobody who went there ever came back. But the little girl didn't pay any attention. She left the next morning, taking some cotton with her to put in her ear, so that when she lay down no insects could crawl into it.

When she came near the old woman's home, she saw an animal ahead of her talking to her, as he crossed the road. The animal had long legs and a long neck. It said, "Don't you know that nobody who goes in that direction ever comes back?" The little girl didn't answer that animal; she just kept on going. The old woman at the wigwam said the same thing; it was no use for her to try to get the golden bird that talked. From where the old woman lived it was all down hill and all rock. At the bottom of the hill was the bird's nest and the water, and all the rocks were people who had tried to get the bird.

The old woman said, "This is where both of your brothers stopped overnight, and neither came back." She kept the little girl there overnight and cooked a meal with one little kernel of rice and one bean in a tiny kettle. The girl wondered how she could ever fill up on that, but she ate and ate until she was full.

That night they hardly slept, and the old woman gave her instructions and told her to try as hard as she could not to pay any attention to all the noise she heard after she got the nest. The next morning the old woman gave the little girl a tiny bottle of medicine and told her that if she came back safely, she should put one drop of medicine on each rock, and then her brothers would come back to life. I guess she had a hunch that she'd come back all right.

The little girl started out, going down hill. She came to where there was a pond with crystal clear water and another that was dirty with manure. She went to the dirty pond and filled her bottle with the dirty old water. She put a dirty old nest on her shoulder, and the bird flew and landed in it. Then she started up hill. That's when the noise broke out. The little girl took the cotton and put it into her ears, so that she could not hear. She didn't dare look back, because the old woman told her that if she did, she'd turn into a rock, like the others. She finally made it and passed all the rocks. Then she could look back. Everything was still, and the bird was hers. She did as the old woman had told her and sprinkled one drop on each of the last two rocks, and her two brothers got up. She took the little bottle and used it on as many of the other rocks as she could, and that way saved quite a few people.

Then she and her two brothers went to the old woman's house with the golden bird. The old woman said to her, "My dear girl, you are an awfully smart girl. I'm an old woman, and my hair is white. I was a young girl when I first moved here. I've always tried to save somebody, but you're the first one I saved." Now she could leave that place. There was nothing for her to do there now.

She told the little girl that as soon as she got home, she should ask her folks to give a feast and invite everyone, especially the people up the river. She told the girl that she didn't belong to the old folks. After the feast the girl should lock the doors and not let anybody out. She should put chamber pots in the house, and if anyone had to go to the can, they should use the chamber pots. Everybody was supposed to tell his life history at the feast.

They stayed at the old woman's place overnight, and the next morning they had breakfast, and then the little girl and her two brothers and the golden bird started out. When she got home, the mother and father were happy to see them come back home. Her folks got ready and prepared a big feast. They sent out invitations, and everyone who was invited came. They made a kind of boxed-in shelf on the wall where the bird was, and they had a curtain over it, so that nobody knew what was in there.

The king came, and when he walked in and saw the little girl, he fell in love with her right away and thought that it was his wife.

Oshkikwe's sisters had told the king all sorts of lies. They killed the bookkeeper and told him that Oshkikwe had done it. They said that she killed the bookkeeper because he wouldn't sleep with her when she tried to get him to. The king had some men dig a hole, and then they hoisted her down into it, and she was to be there for the rest of her life. Then the king fixed it so that it would smoke down there to make his wife suffer. They threw burning rags into the pit. Oshkikwe just took it, and didn't try to deny anything. The king told his people to throw all the slop into the hole, and they did. But some good-hearted people baked some good stuff to eat and wrapped it up in paper and hoisted it down to her, and that way she managed to live.

The king fell in love with the little girl at the feast and just cried and shed tears. He thought it was his wife. He thought maybe she'd got out of the hole some way. He thought maybe he'd ask her to marry him. He just didn't know what to think. The little girl had golden hair and a star on her forehead; and the king wondered about that, because he remembered what he overheard his wife say before he married her.

When it came time for the little girl to tell her life story at the feast, she said that she couldn't remember her early life, but she had somebody who could tell the story about herself and her two brothers. Then she opened up the shelf, and the golden bird flew onto her shoulder. Then the two old people who claimed to be their parents felt uncomfortable and afraid, and they asked to go to the toilet; but the doors were locked, and they wouldn't let them out but made them use the chamber pots.

The little bird made a bow to everyone in the room and started the story at the time when the three sisters were out cutting wood and told their wishes which the young king overheard. The oldest sister said that she wanted to marry the king's cook, and the second said that she wanted to marry his dishwasher. The little bird knew everything and told everything. Everything was just quiet in there. Everyone sat listening to the little bird. The bird said that Oshkikwe said that she wanted to marry the king, and if she did she'd have three children, two sons and a little girl with golden hair and a star on her forehead. The bird told about how Matchikwewis shot the bookkeeper and blamed it on Oshkikwe. It told about the babies being sent down the river in baskets. The two sisters were getting scared, and so were the two old folks. The bird told the king that his wife was still alive and that when he got home he should take her out, because she was just barely living. The bird told about what the old folks did. The bird told the king to take the old folks to live with him, because they had taken care of his children. The bird said that here were the king's two sons and his daughter.

Now Matchikwewis and her sister and their husbands were trying to get out, but they couldn't because all the doors were locked and the keys put away.

The king took the children and the old people to his home. They hoisted up his wife, and sure enough, she was still alive. She was just skin and bones. They had to use a spoon to feed her. Then she got better. They threw Matchikwewis and her other sister and their two husbands into the hole. That's the end of that story.

Comments

Although the traditional Chippewa characters, Matchikwewis and Oshkikwe, figure here, the tale is wholly European. It conforms in detail to A-T tale type 707, *The three golden sons*. Aarne and Thompson divide this tale into four episodes: (1) *Wishing for a husband*; (2) *Calumniated wife*: the elder sisters substitute dogs for the newborn children, who are thrown into a stream and recovered by a miller or fisher, while their mother is imprisoned; (3) *The children's adventures*: their successive search for the speaking bird. The brothers are turned into marble columns, but the girl brings them back to life and acquires the speaking bird and magic objects; (4) *Restoration of children*: the bird reveals the whole story; children and wife are restored, and her sisters are punished (Aarne and Thompson, 1961, p. 242).

This tale type has been reported for Scandinavia, Ireland, France, Spain, Germany, Austria, Italy, Rumania, Hungary, Albania, Czechoslovakia, Greece, Russia, and Turkey. A Greek version is given in Richard M. Dawkins (1953, pp. 165–74). Subsidiary motifs in the tale include H71.1, *Star on head as sign of royalty*; R13.1.2, *Miller rescues abandoned child*; H133.1.1, *Quest for Bird of Truth*; and H1321.1, *Quest for Water of Life*; and B131.2, *Bird reveals treachery*.

The story must have come to Wisconsin through Canada from France. Here is a French version of the tale, which closely approximates our own: One of three sisters describes the three marvelous children she will have if she marries. Her words are overheard by the king's son, who passes by their open window. The prince enters the house, proposes to the girl, and takes her off to his court, along with her sisters. The prince marries the girl and in time becomes king. At the first birth, while the king is away at war, the sisters substitute a little dog; at the second a cat, and at the third, another little dog. The queen is then locked up in an iron cage.

The three children are found and rescued, successively, by an old man whom they call their father, but when they are between fifteen and twenty years of age, the old man tells them that he is not their true father and describes how he found them.

The oldest son goes in search of The Bird Who Tells the Truth. He leaves behind a token-object on which blood will appear, if he should die; but he fails in his quest, and the second boy sets out, only to meet the same fate. Alone in the world, the little girl now departs on the same quest. Like her brothers, she hears many voices calling after her, but she does not turn back. She gets some water to sprinkle on the stones into which her brothers and other people have been transformed. Among them is her father, the king, who wanted to find the truth about his offspring. The king takes the girl, her brothers, and the bird to his court, where a great feast is served. Here the magical bird tells the true story, after which the queen is released from her iron cage and her sisters are put to death (Delarue and Tenèze, 1963, pp. 633-48).

Although the aboriginal character of virtuous Oshkikwe fits well with the stereotyped European heroine, a nonaboriginal attitude is expressed by Oshkikwe at the beginning of the story, when she states a wish to marry the king, in contrast to Oshkikwe's more humble attitude in the *Star husband* sequence.

Our Wisconsin story closely follows the European original, but there are some Indian embellishments. A traditional Chippewa theme is fitted into the tale: the self-replenishing kettle with the single kernel of rice, presided over by the old woman in the wigwam who gives advice. There are also some anal motifs which do not seem to have been part of the European story. The children are supposed to get water from a dirty pond full of manure, rather than from shiny clear water. Moreover, the heroine has to set out chamber pots for the guests during the feast, for the doors must be locked and no one may go out to the can.

53. *The Bear Girl*

Collected by Ernestine Friedl at Court Oreilles in 1942
Narrator: Delia Oshogay   Interpreter: Maggie Lamorie

There was an old man and his wife who had three daughters. One of them looked just like a bear, with fur and everything. They were very poor. One time when the two older girls were out cutting wood, they decided that they would go away and look for husbands. They didn't want to take the little bear sister along, because they were ashamed of her. So they set out early the next morning. But the bear girl followed them and said that she wanted to go along with them. They ran away, but she caught up with them; so they brought her back and tied her to the door. First thing they knew, she had caught up with them again, with the door on her back. Then they tied her to a big rock. She caught up with them again with the big rock on her back. So they tied her to a big bunch of rushes, and soon she caught up with them with the pack of rushes, earth and all, on her back. Next they tied her to a pine tree. They went on and came to a big wide river which they couldn't cross. Then the bear girl came along with the pine tree on her back. First she put the pine tree across the river and then another big tree, because the pine tree didn't go all the way across. She scolded her sisters. She said she wasn't following them just because she wanted a husband but because she knew that they couldn't get along without her. She told them that after they crossed the stream there was an old witch who would get them. Mako:s, the Bear Girl, instructed them what to do. The old witch, who had two daughters, would start to cook something for them. It would look like a good meal but was really made up of snakes and toads and things like that. She told her sisters not to eat anything until she did.

They came to the witch's home, and as Mako:s predicted, she made supper for them and set the food before them. The oldest sister was about to eat the food but then stopped, because Mako:s didn't eat. Mako:s told the witch that they didn't eat food like that and that she should prepare different food. So she made a new supper, and this time Mako:s began to eat, and her sisters ate too.

After supper the witch told Mako:s that she'd sleep with her, so they could tell each other stories; and the two sisters would sleep with the witch's two daughters. The two sisters had gold earrings, while the witch's daughters had crab claws for earrings. They all went to bed. Mako:s and the old witch told each other stories until the witch fell asleep. Then Mako:s got up and changed the sisters around, so that the witch's daughters were in her sisters' places, and she put her sisters' earrings on the shelf. Then Mako:s made believe that she was asleep. After a while the old witch got up and started to sharpen her knife. She cut the throats of what she thought were Mako:s' sisters, saying to herself what nice earrings her daughters would have and what a nice soft breakfast Mako:s would make. Then she went back to sleep.

Before daylight Mako:s woke up her sisters and told them to take their earrings from the shelf. They set out on their journey. When the old witch found out what had happened, she was so mad that she took the moon from the sky and locked it up in one of her rooms, so that the girls couldn't travel by moonlight. Mako:s and her sisters had to travel in the dark. Then the sun came up. The old witch was still so angry that she took the sun down too and locked it up.

The girls came to a town or city and went to the king's palace. They let them use a little house to live in. By this time the king was just sick because there was no light from the sun and moon. One of the sisters told somebody there that she thought their sister could bring back the sun. The king heard about that and sent for Mako:s, but she said she wouldn't go. Finally the king came to her and asked if she could really get the sun. She said "Yes." He asked her how much money she wanted. Mako:s said that she didn't want any money but she wanted to marry the king's son. The king felt bad about that, but the son said that it would be all right with him. So Mako:s said that she would get the sun. The king asked her what else she wanted, and she said that she needed three gallons of salt, which the king gave her.

Mako:s set out for the witch's house. When she got there, the old lady was stirring cornmeal by an open fire. Mako:s made herself invisible and put salt in the cornmeal. It became too salty for the old witch, so she rolled some birchbark, made a torch, and went out to get water. Mako:s then took her chance and ran in to get the sun and threw it up in to the sky. The old woman had the power to get the sun only once; she couldn't bring it down again.

When Mako:s got back to the king's palace she said that she had to have the king's son, and if he went back on his promise, she'd take the sun back to where she got it from. The king gave her his son, and they had a big feast; but Mako:s fooled them and led the son over to the oldest sister. The king was much relieved.

Now the king wanted the moon. He asked Mako:s if she could get it. She said that she'd get the moon if she could have his second son. It was easy, because they knew that the king's son would marry Mako:s's second sister. She asked the king for five quarts of sugar and set off again. When she got to the witch's house, she did the same thing. The old witch was cooking some wild rice, and Mako:s put the five quarts of sugar in. The witch kept saying, "Something is sweetening my rice, and it needs water." This time, when she went out for water, Mako:s opened the door, ran for the moon, and threw it up in the sky. When the witch got back, the moon was up, and she couldn't do anything about it. Mako:s went to the king's palace, and they went through the same thing. They had a feast and brought the king's son to the second sister. Now she was the only single one.

One time the king dreamed that there was a horse that could go as fast as the wind. He got the idea that he'd like to have such horses. He went to Mako:s and asked if she could get him some. She said that she could and would get them if she could marry his youngest son. The king said that it was impossible and went back to his palace. But the young man told his father he would do it, because he knew that the king wanted those horses so badly. This time Mako:s asked the king for one quart of pepper. She went to the old witch's place again. When she got there, the old lady was cooking hominy. Mako:s poured in the pepper, and the witch began to say "Too much pepper!" She went for some water. Mako:s ran into her room and found the horses, but this time the witch came back and caught her and put her in a sack and hung her up. She put the horses back in the room again. Then she went to look for a good club to beat Mako:s with. While she was gone, Mako:s untied the bag, got out of the sack, and put various things into the sack: the witch's cat, a dog, some chickens and pigs, and all the witch's dishes. Then she made off with the horses.

The witch came back with the stick and began to beat the sack. The dog barked, and she said, "Mako:s, you sound like a dog." The chickens made a noise, and she said, "Mako:s, you sound like chickens," and so on. Finally she said, "Mako:s, now I will have you as soup!" Then she opened the sack and found the animals killed and the dishes in pieces. Now she was finished. She had no power over the horses a second time.

When Mako:s got back to the king's palace, they gave a feast, and she was married to the king's youngest son. After that the three sisters lived together in the palace. But the king's youngest son didn't treat Mako:s right, and she was sorry about it. She would sit by her husband, and he'd start moving away. When they went to bed, her husband bundled himself up in a blanket and turned the other way. She told her husband that she was very sad that he did that. She said, "Since you don't like me anyway, just make a big fire and throw me in. We'll make believe we're having a quarrel; then you throw me into the fire, and don't let my sisters or anyone else take me out. When I'm all burnt up, smooth out the ashes." So they made believe that they were having a quarrel, and he threw her into the fireplace. Everyone came running in. The sisters said that they didn't hate their sister, even though she was so ugly, and they said that they'd go home. But her husband just shoved them away and kept looking at the fire. Then he took the poker and pushed the ashes, and then suddenly a beautiful woman popped out of the fire and fell onto his bed. He was so happy. They sent for clothes, and he dressed her up. She became a queen, but she had no power any more. She had had all her power because she had been ugly. This time, when he used to come near her, she moved away and wrapped herself up in bed away from him. They brought her family to the palace.

I heard this story when I was very young.

Comments

"The Bear Girl" may be seen as another Cinderella tale in which a despised younger sister ends up marrying a prince. These stories suggest that upward-mobility fantasies have entered into Chippewa women's tales as a byproduct of acculturation.

"The Bear Girl" contains themes which have an aboriginal flavor, such as the pursuit of the sisters by the bear girl, but there are many European elements, such as the city or town, the king and the prince, the use of pepper and salt, and the magical horse. In one episode the heroine changes the earrings of her sisters and the witch's daughters, so that the witch kills the wrong girls during the night. This is a European motif (K1611, *Substituted caps cause ogre to kill his own children*) which, according to Thompson, was carried by the French to the New World (1946, p. 37).

A story which is almost identical to ours was collected by Albert E. Jenks at Court Oreilles around the turn of the century. Jenks states that it was told to him by an Ojibwa woman "considerably more than one hundred years old." This tale has a similar twist at the end, after the transformed heroine has sprung from the fire-ashes: "Then this beautiful maiden would not sleep with her husband" (1902).

54. *The Eight-headed* Windigo

Collected by Ernestine Friedl at Court Oreilles in 1942
Narrator: Delia Oshogay   Interpreter: Maggie Lamorie

An old man and his wife lived near a lake; they were very poor. They had a horse and a dog, both female. The old man set nets for fish. One morning he found a little gold whitefish in his net, the only fish he'd got that morning. He was about to club the fish to death, when it spoke up and said, "Old man, before you kill me, please listen to me." The old man said, "You're the first little fish I've ever seen who could talk." The fish said, "Well, I'm the only fish that talks. I'm the chief of all the fish. After you kill me, don't waste a scale of my body. Give my head to the mare, the middle part to your wife, and my tail to the dog. Then scatter all the guts in the garden and leave all the fish scales on the table without cleaning them off."

The old man did as he was told. That night they went to bed. In the morning, when they got up, his wife found a pair of twin boys. They looked exactly alike. You couldn't tell them apart. All the scales on the table had turned into gold coins. The horse in the barn had a pair of twin horses. They were just alike. You couldn't tell them apart. There were two little puppies in the doghouse that looked just alike. Their garden was almost full grown, so they could use it right away.

The two boys grew up to be men right away. They were two smart men. The dogs and colts grew up right away too. The boys took some of the money and built a nice home for their parents right away. Then one brother said that he wanted to go off to see the world. The other brother had to stay and look after the folks, since he'd be gone a long time. The first brother took his knife and put it on the wall. He told his brother to look at it every day. If it had blood on it, that meant that he'd been killed. If it was rusty, he had died of something else. The old man had given one horse and one dog to each of his sons.

The first brother set off and traveled a long time on horseback, followed by his dog. He came to a town that was all dark and black and quiet, as if the whole town had mourning crape. He could hardly see anybody, and he wondered what the trouble was. At the edge of the town he came to a little house with smoke coming out of the chimney. A woman there asked him what he wanted. He asked if he could stay a while, because he was traveling. He said he could provide groceries. The woman was glad to have him. She had a barn where his horse and dog could stay.

He asked the woman why the town was so gloomy and quiet. She told him that the king's daughter was going to be eaten up by a *windigo* with eight heads. He had already eaten up six of his daughters. He had only one daughter left. The *windigo* had told the king that if he didn't let him eat his last daughter, he'd eat up the whole town. The young man thought it was a shame. He said, "Isn't there a man anywhere who could kill the *windigo*?" She said that they had tried already. It wasn't any use to try to kill him. She said that the next morning she would get up early to go to see the regular parade they had when they took the king's daughter. She asked him if he would come too. He said, "No, I'd never go to see a thing like that and just look on. I couldn't."

The next morning they had breakfast, and she said that she was going to watch the parade. He told her to go ahead; he'd stay and keep house while she was gone. She went to the king's house, where they were getting his daughter ready. They had to keep throwing water on the king's face to keep him from fainting, he felt that bad about his daughter.

The people of the town had a parade, with the girl in a carriage with horses. They had to hold up the old king, he felt that bad about his daughter. She was the last daughter he had. They had a sort of platform in the open, where the *windigo* was to find the girl. It had a bed for the girl to lie on and a chair for her to sit on. There was also a little table where she could eat before the *windigo* came to eat her up. After they got to this place, the people went away and left the girl alone.

When the old woman got home, the young man told her that he was going out for a walk. Instead, he took his horse and dog and sneaked to the place where the girl was. She begged him to stay away, because the *windigo* would be there soon and would eat him up. He said that he would protect her, and she finally stopped begging him to leave. She said, "Just listen to that noise. I can hear him coming."

They heard a racket. The trees were just bending, and the giant was tearing off the limbs of the tall trees. When he got there, he said, "Oh, I have four little chickens for my supper. I thought I'd have only one." By four little chickens he meant the girl, the man, the horse, and the dog. The man said, "You're going to sweat first before you eat those four chickens." He took his sword and cut off one of the giant's eight heads. But it jumped right back in place on the giant's head. He chopped it off again, and this time the horse and dog jumped on it and ate it all up. He chopped off a second head, and again the horse and dog chewed it all up. Then the *windigo* begged the boy for a rest for three days, because he sure was tired. The boy agreed, and they rested for three days, and then started fighting again. He got rid of three of the giant's heads. The *win-*

digo begged him for a rest for three days. On the fourth day they started again, and he got rid of two more heads. Now the windigo had only one head left, and that one was the hardest. The *windigo* begged him for a rest for three days again. On the fourth day they started again. As soon as the young man had cut off the head, it would jump back into place again. They fought all day. It was pretty near dark when he finally cut off the last head and the horse and dog finished it off.

After he killed the *windigo*, he was all in. The horse and dog were all in too. The girl had to pour cold water over him to make him come to. After the man and his horse and dog were rested, the girl asked the boy to come home with her, because her father had said that if any man ever killed that *windigo*, he would give his daughter to him in marriage. The young man told the girl that he would marry her but not right away. He told her to go home to her father, and said that he would come back to marry her a year and one day later.

On her way home the girl met a chimney sweep. He told her that she had better go back, or else the eight-headed *windigo* would eat up the whole town. She said, "No, I'm not going back. The *windigo* has been killed." Then the chimney sweep said that she should say that it was he who killed the *windigo*. If she didn't do that, he said that he would take his axe and kill her. He made her promise that, and she agreed.

Meanwhile the young man cut out the *windigo*'s eight tongues and took them home and dried them, so that they would be preserved. After he left, the chimney sweep came and cut off the giant's eight heads, took them away, and hid them.

When the girl got home, she told her father that the chimney sweep had killed the *windigo*. Her father said, "Well, I suppose you'll get married then." The girl said, "Oh no, father. I'll be married just one year and one day from now."

When the young man got back to the old woman's house, he told her that he was going away and would be back just one year and one day later. Then he went off with his horse and dog.

When the year and one day were up, the king's daughter got ready for her marriage. On the same day the young man came back to the old woman's place. She told him that the girl was going to be married that day, and that she had an invitation to the wedding.

They had a feast before the wedding. The chimney sweep sat next to the girl. She paid no attention to him. The king asked if everyone was there for the wedding. The old woman who had come there spoke up and said that there was a young man who had just arrived, who had stayed at her place and left again just one year and one day before. When the girl heard that, she knew that it was that young man she was waiting for. The king said that someone should go and invite that young man to come to the feast. The young man had sent his dog to take some food from the king's plate and bring it back to him. When the girl saw the dog, she recognized him right away. The chimney sweep grabbed the dog, intending to kill him, but the girl stopped him and told him to leave the dog alone.

When the young man got the invitation to the feast, he took the eight dried tongues with him. He sat down right next to the king's daughter. She was sitting between the two men. While they were eating, the king asked if someone could tell a story about what they had seen or done. The chimney sweep spoke up right away. He told about how he had killed that *windigo*. He had the eight heads with him in a sack.

Then the other man told his story, from the time he first arrived at the town, how he fought the giant and how many days they rested up. Then he turned to the chimney sweep and asked, "Did the eight heads you took have any tongues?"

The chimney sweep said, "I suppose they must have had tongues." He looked over his eight heads and found that they had no tongues. The young man showed his eight dried tongues. So they knew who had killed the giant. The young man married the king's daughter, and the king ordered some men to take the chimney sweep and throw him head first into the toilet, and he died.

The young man and his bride lived together for some time. Then one night, while he was talking to his wife, he noticed some kind of red light in the distance. He asked his wife what it was. She said, "Don't look at that light. It's a very bad light. Don't look at it again. Nobody who goes to where that light is ever comes back again." But the man couldn't forget about that light. He took a pin right where he was sitting and pointed it in the direction of the light, so that he would know which way to travel the next day.

In the morning he told his wife that he was going out duck hunting. He had his horse and dog with him, and they traveled in the direction of the red light. A big storm came up, and he ran for shelter to a little house, where there was an old woman who greeted him. He said, "Grandmother, can I come in?" She said, "Grandson, I'm afraid that your horse and dog will eat me up. Please tie them up before you come in." He said, "I don't have any rope to tie them with." The old woman pulled out a strand of her hair and said, "Here, grandson, use this." Just as he took the strand of hair from her, the young man dropped dead and turned into stone. That was the end of him.

When his twin brother back home looked at the knife, he saw that it was rusty. He said that he'd go and look for his brother, and he wouldn't listen to his parents who told him not to go. He went off with his horse and dog. Finally he got to the home of his sister-in-law. She was glad to see him, because she thought he was her husband. She said, "I thought something happened to you, because you went after that light." He thought to himself, "My brother must have gone after a light and got killed." His sister-in-law gave him a meal, thinking he was her husband. He just let her think so. Then he saw the light that his brother had seen, and he asked her what it was. She said, "There you go again. That's why we thought you were gone for good, because you asked about that light." Then the man knew that his brother must have gone for the light. He did the same thing his brother had done; he took a pin and pointed it toward the light so that he'd know where to go the next day. Just before bed time she said, "Aren't you going to put your horse in the barn? What's the matter with you?" Then he looked around and saw the barn and thought, "Oh, that's where the horse is supposed to go." He found the barn and put his horse there.

When they went to bed, he didn't undress; he just sat on the edge of the bed. He wouldn't lie in bed. He wouldn't even cover up. The woman asked him, "What's the matter with you? You act so funny."

The next morning the man headed in the direction that the pin pointed. A big storm came up; the old lady made it like that. He came to her house and asked if he could shelter there until the storm was over. She said, "I'm afraid that your horse and dog might bite me. Please tie them up before you come in." He said that he didn't have anything to tie them with. She pulled out a strand of her hair and handed it to him, but he wouldn't take it. He said, "Oh, you're the one who killed my brother. You take that hair and tie them yourself, but before you do that I want you to bring my brother back to life. If you don't, I'll get my horse and dog to chew you up." The old lady got some medicine from under the floor. She put it on the dead man and his horse and dog, and they all came back to life. Then they got both their horses and dogs to chew up the old lady, and they finished her off completely.

When they were riding back together, the second brother asked his brother to forgive him, because he had partly slept on his bed the night before. The first brother didn't like that, so he shot his brother on the road and killed him. But after a while he thought that it was foolish to kill his brother after he had come all the way to rescue him; so he took the medicine and poured it over him, and he came back to life. When they got back home, the woman didn't know which one was her husband

and which to go to, until her brother-in-law told her. Then he went back home, and the first brother stayed with his wife.

Comments

This story is a perfect combination of A-T tale types 300, *The dragon slayer*, and 303, *The twins or blood brothers*. In Europe these two tale types are often combined in a single story, as in this case. The combined tale also appears in two other collections of Chippewa/Ojibwa folklore: in G. E. Laidlaw (1918, pp. 90–92) and in Alanson Skinner (1916a).

A-T tale type 300 concerns a hero's rescue of a princess by slaying a multi-headed dragon or ogre. In our Chipppewa tale the dragon or ogre has been replaced by a *windigo*. In Europe the standard number of the ogre's heads is seven, while our version has eight, twice the American Indian sacred number four. Both Laidlaw's and Skinner's Chippewa versions, however, still have the standard European number; so this change in re-telling must be recent.

In the standard tale, as in ours, the hero cuts out the ogre's tongues, which later prove that he was the true slayer, despite the claims of an impostor, who is about to marry the princess when the hero shows up.[2]

The following synopsis of A-T 303 by Aarne and Thompson (1961, p. 271) (omitting some irrelevant episodes) shows how closely our combined story conforms to the European tale type.

1. *The twins' origin.* A magic fish which a man has caught tells him to cut him up and give the parts to his wife, his dog, and his horse to eat. Each bears twins.

2. *The life-tokens.* On leaving, one boy sets up a life-token to notify the other of misfortune, e.g., a knife which becomes rusty.

3. *The transformation by witch.* Having rescued and married a princess (tale type 300), the first brother follows a fire which he sees from the window on his wedding night, but he falls under the power of a witch who turns him into stone.

4. *The chaste brother.* When the second brother sees from the rusty life-token that the first is in trouble, he goes in search of him and is mistaken by the brother's wife for her husband, but they do not have sexual relations.

2. For a French version of A-T 300 told in Brittany, see "The Seven-Headed Monster" (in Massignon, 1968, pp. 34–39). See also Delarue (1957, pp. 101–7, 147–60) for distributions of both A-T 300 and A-T 303.

5. *Disenchantment.* He disenchants his brother. The first brother is jealous of his brother for involvement with his wife and kills him, but when he finds out the truth he kills the witch and brings his brother back to life.

For the English translation of a French version which combines A-T 300 and 303, see Paul Delarue's "The Miller's Three Sons" (in 1956, pp. 187–200).

Our Chippewa story fills the above outline very well. A possible Chippewa innovation in our version is the statement by the fish near the beginning of the story, "I'm the chief of all the fish," which seems to reflect the Master of Animals concept of the American Indians.

In Laidlaw's and Skinner's tales the impostors are blacksmiths, while in ours he is a chimney sweep. The common element seems to be a grimy occupation of relatively low status. In the Plains Ojibwa version the impostor is punished by being thrown into the sea, but in our Wisconsin tale he is thrown head first into the toilet, an anal innovation absent in the other accounts. The three Chippewa versions provide striking evidence of conservatism and fidelity in the transmission of this European tale, despite some minor deviations.

The most exhaustive study of A-T tale type 303 is Kurt Ranke's monograph, *Die Zwei Brüder* (1934). Ranke has analyzed more than 700 versions of the tale from different regions, including Scandinavia, France, Holland, Germany, Portugal, Spain, Italy, Rumania, and Czechoslovakia. The well-developed form of the tale seems to be especially characteristic of France, whence it apparently diffused to the New World and to northern Wisconsin.

55. *The Magic Horse*

Collected by Robert Ritzenthaler at Court Oreilles in 1942
Narrator: Prosper Guibord

Once there was a village of white people, and there was a family living there that had a grown boy. When the boy got married, his father gave him a cow, some sheep, some chickens, and the young couple went out to look for a place to stay. That evening they found a nice spot, a hardwood grove in the forest. The young man cleared the land and built a log shack.

They got along good out there, and about a year later they had a baby boy. After the boy had been cleaned up and was nursing, the mother told her husband that they hadn't had any visitors out there in the woods, and that the first person who came to visit them would be the child's *weʔę* (godparent). Soon after that, a stranger came riding up on a horse, nicely dressed up in a black suit and stove pipe hat. He stopped in to see them. They invited him in, and the mother reminded her husband about what they had decided. They handed the baby to the stranger and told him that they wanted him to be the child's godfather. He fondled the baby and praised him but didn't take off his gloves. Then he gave the baby back to the mother, went out to his horse, and took two heavy saddlebags off and brought them in. He laid them on the table and said, "Here is some money for my *weʔę* [a reciprocal term for either godfather or godson]. It will last him a long time." He told the parents that they could buy a horse and other things they needed, and that when the boy was eleven or twelve years old, he should come and visit him. He said that they should then pack a lunch for the boy and have him walk west all day; at sundown he would arrive at the stranger's city — but *he should come alone.*

After the stranger left, the parents opened the bags. One was full of gold and the other full of silver. They were very happy, and they bought a mare to foal, and they lived well.

When the boy was twelve years old, he told his parents that he would like to visit his *weʔę*. They gave him a lunch and told him to walk west until sundown. The tallest house in the city would be the house of his *weʔę*. They told him not to associate with anyone on the way.

The boy started out. At about noon he reached a crossroad, where he saw two boys coming from opposite directions. They stopped to talk. The boys were ragged; they said that they were orphans and hadn't eaten all day. The boy offered them his lunch, and they went to look for water. They found an old well in a deserted farm. They said that he could get a drink if they lowered him down the well, with each boy holding one leg. When the orphans lowered him into the well, they said that they would drop him in unless he let them go along with him. He was to say that they were *weʔę* too. The boy had to consent; so they set out for the city.

At sundown they came to a big city, which seemed deserted. They went to the biggest house, and the door opened. The larger of the two orphans went up to the stranger, greeted him, and told him that he was his *weʔę*. The stranger asked him why he had brought the other two boys. The boy said that they were orphans looking for work. The man said that that would be all right; they could live in a shack nearby.

He took the boy into the house and fed him well and gave him a fine new suit and showed him where to sleep. He said that when a bell rang, he should go to eat; he always had his meals alone. The boy went into his room. Later a bell rang, and he went to eat. There was a fine meal laid out for him, but there was no one around. He slept well that night. In the morning he got dressed, the bell rang, and he went to have breakfast. Then the stranger came in and said that they were going to take the orphans out and give them a place to live out in the woods. He told them to cut wood and said that he would pay them.

Several days later the stranger took the orphan to the forest where the other two boys were cutting wood. The man noticed that the boy who was his real wẹʔẹ looked sad. So he sent the other two boys away and talked to the boy. In that way he found out that the boy was the real wẹʔẹ. He took him back to his house, gave him a fine bedroom, and put the two orphans in the shack. The stranger said that he could have those orphans killed, if he wished; but the boy told him just to send them away. The man did so.

He asked the boy what his parents called him. He said, "Sonny." The man said, "Your real name is Rising Sun." Then he said that the boy should play and enjoy himself but not ask any questions about the place.

One day the stranger said that he was going away for four days and that the boy should stay out of one room in the house. He took the boy out to the barn, where there was a shabby mule and a beautiful horse. He told the boy to feed the mule oats and hay and give him water three times a day, but he was not to feed the horse at all but to whip him three times a day, because he was a mean horse.

The next day the boy fed the mule and then took the whip and just whipped the horse lightly, because he didn't want to hurt him. At noon he did the same thing. This time the horse spoke to the boy and told him that the stranger was a bad spirit who had killed all the people in the city and that the boy was in real trouble if he stayed here. He told the boy to go into the forbidden room, where he would see a kettle full of liquid gold. He was to dip his little finger and his hair in it, and they would become golden, and then he should cover his head with a towel. Then he should take a small empty bottle that was there and also a razor and he should go to his bed and cut open the mattress and pillows and then run fast, for the feathers would follow him. The horse told the boy that he would help him get out of there, but they had to act fast. The stranger was far away now, but he would know it as soon as they started to escape.

The boy did everything the horse told him and just got out before the feathers caught up with him. He ran out to the barn, and the horse told him to saddle him up and to put a brush and a curry comb in the saddlebag. Then they started off very fast. The horse told him to look back. If he saw a big black cloud in the sky that would be the stranger coming after them. The horse said, "If we can stay away from him until sundown, we'll be safe."

After a while the boy looked back and saw a big cloud in the sky. He told the horse about it. The horse told the boy to throw the brush behind him; then there rose up a big mountain covered with trees and brush. That would delay the stranger a while. Around noon the boy looked back and saw the cloud coming again. The horse told him to throw the curry comb behind them. Then there was a sharp ridged mountain behind them. "That will delay him," said the horse. Near sundown the boy saw the cloud again. The horse told the boy to throw the razor behind them. Then a mountain with sharp peaks arose. The horse said that they were safe now. Then they stopped, and the horse told the boy to fill the little bottle with the sweat from under the horse's neck. The boy did so. Then he cleaned up the horse with grass and wiped off all the rest of the sweat and foam from his body. The horse said that they were going to visit a king and that the boy should ask for a job. He was to say that he was an excellent gardener.

They went on again, and as they got near the palace the horse changed himself into an old nag. The boy told the palace guards that he wanted to see the king to get a job. The guards said that the king was very busy because he was engaged in a war that was going badly, but they would take the boy in to see him. The king hired the boy and gave him a little house to live in and a place for the horse.

The horse told the boy that he should take a scythe and cut down all the flowers in the garden and throw them over the wall that evening. The boy did this, and the princess saw him and was dismayed. She called the king about it. The boy told the king to wait until the next morning before he passed judgment on what he had done. The next morning there was a beautiful garden there, much better than the old one. The princess was very pleased with it.

Now the horse told the boy that they should go out and help the king in the wars. The boy took an old rusty sword from the hut, and they started out with the soldiers. They stopped at the gate and let the soldiers go ahead. The horse told the boy to take the little bottle and put a drop of the sweat on his breast and behind the ears of the horse. The horse became beautiful again, and the boy found himself wearing a new suit of armor and having a fine sword.

They rode on and passed the soldiers in battle and rode into the fray and defeated the other side for the day. Then they rode back and changed back to their old clothes and appearance. When the soldiers got back, they talked about the man who had a golden finger and a towel around his head, who had defeated the enemy. They kidded the boy and his old nag and told him that he should have been there to see it.

That night the boy cut the flowers again, and the next morning there was an even more beautiful garden than before.

The next morning the boy and his nag started out again, and the soldiers kidded him. They changed their shapes again by using the bottle. Then they went like the wind and passed the soldiers, beat the enemy, and the horn blew, signaling their defeat.

They did the same thing again the next day, but this time the boy didn't wear his towel. This time the enemy abandoned the fight and went back to their own country. The king tried to capture the boy to see who it was and tried to stop him with his sword. He hit him in the leg, and the point broke off and stuck in the boy's leg. The boy went back, and they changed again.

The king announced that everyone with a sore leg must come to the palace the next day, and the person with the point of the sword in his leg would marry the princess. The next morning all the limping men assembled, and the king examined them all but could not find the point. Then the princess told her father to ask the gardener in, because he was limping too. When the gardener came in, the king put his magnetic sword to the wound, and the point came out and stuck onto the sword. The king was amazed. They boy went out and got his horse, and put the two drops under his ears and a drop on his own chest, and they were both transformed. Then the boy rode into the palace as final proof. The king said that the boy and the princess would be married that night. So they were married.

The next morning the horse said to the boy, "You must help me. You must cut off my head." The boy didn't want to do that, but the horse insisted; so the boy raised his sword and cut off the horse's head. Then a handsome prince appeared. The prince said that that bad spirit was the devil who had changed him into a horse. The prince said that he would be back in a year and a day for final payment of his services.

A year and a day later the princess had a baby boy. Then the prince came back and told him to cut the baby in two, since he demanded half of the baby boy. The boy told him to take the whole baby, but the prince insisted. The boy was just about to cut the baby in half when the prince stopped him and said, "No, I was just testing you. You keep the baby, and good luck to all of you."

Comments

This tale exemplifies A-T tale type 314, *The youth transformed to a horse*, at the start of which the devil becomes a boy's godfather. In return for this, the boy is sent at a designated time to serve in the devil's castle. The hero breaks a taboo on entering one of the rooms, and his hair turns to gold. He has been ordered to look after some horses and to abuse others. The abused horse proves to be an enchanted prince, who advises the hero on how to flee from the devil by throwing a series of magic objects behind him, which become obstacles in the path (D672, *Obstacle flight*). Thus they escape.

The hero takes service in the king's court as a gardener and wins the love of the princess. With the horse's help, he performs several acts of bravery. Then the magic horse is disenchanted.

Our story clearly fits this synopsis. This tale has been reported for the Scandinavian and Baltic countries and for Ireland, France, Holland, Germany, Italy, Greece, Poland, and Russia. In some of the European versions, as in ours, appears the theme that the point of a weapon broken off is later matched with the rest of the weapon, thereby identifying the hero. Also in some European versions, as in our Wisconsin tale, the means of disenchantment of the prince is decapitation (D711, *Disenchantment by decapitation*), a motif which recurs in the story that follows.

Distributions and references for this tale are given in Delarue (1956, pp. 242–63).

56. *The Magic Ox*

Collected by Robert Ritzenthaler at Court Oreilles in 1942
Narrator: Prosper Guibord

Once there was a king who had two sons. When he died the throne went to the older one, although everyone liked and admired the younger brother and hated the older one. The older brother got more and more jealous of the younger brother and finally told two of his henchmen to take the boy out into the woods and kill him and bring back the tip of his tongue as evidence that they had done it.

The next morning the henchmen told the younger brother that they were going for a walk, so the boy got his dog and they started off. They stopped at noon, but neither of the men could bring themselves to kill the boy; so they confessed about their instructions and sent the boy on alone. They killed the dog and took back the tip of its tongue.

The next day the boy came to a farmhouse and asked for work. The farmer said that he needed a sheepherder. He told the boy that every day one of his sheep was missing. He gave the boy a horse and gun, and they went out and counted the sheep. Then the boy took them out to graze. That afternoon the farmer's wife rode up and told the boy that she needed a sheep to pay a debt. The boy didn't want to do it, but finally he gave in, and she took one of the sheep and went over to a saloon and drank. That evening, when the farmer came to count the sheep, he found that one of them was missing. He asked the boy what had happened, but the boy said that he didn't know.

The next day he took out the sheep again, and the wife came in the afternoon and demanded another sheep. This time the boy refused to give her one. He brought in all the sheep that evening, and the farmer complimented him. Later that evening, however, the wife tore her clothes and she started to scream and say that the boy had done it. The farmer turned him out, and the boy had to sleep in the woods that night.

The next day he came to another farm where he applied for work and was hired. He was sent out with a gun and a horse, with instructions to tend the cattle and keep out any strange cattle. Toward evening a big red ox came up to the herd. The boy was about to shoot him, when the ox spoke and told him that he was in bad hands and that he would take him away if he would jump onto his back. The boy got on the neck of the ox, and they started off. They came to a field of flowers, where the ox told the boy not to pick any flowers, but they were so beautiful that the boy finally picked one, and the ox jumped up and started running. The boy picked another flower, and the ox ran faster. When they got out of the field the ox told the boy that they had just had a very close call.

They went on and stopped by a nice lake where they decided to camp for the night. The ox told the boy to pull on his left horn, and it came off, and there were two blankets and a tablecloth inside. He told the boy to spread out the cloth, and there was a full meal on it, and the boy ate. The ox told him to shake the cloth, and then the dishes disappeared, and he put it back in the horn. They slept that night and had breakfast the next morning on the magic cloth.

Then they came to a big city where they learned that there was a king who had to feed his daughter to a three-headed monster in three days' time. The ox told the boy to reach into his horn, and he pulled out a big bouquet of flowers. The ox told the boy to take them and sell them to the king's daughter and to find out what was happening in the palace.

The boy went to the palace and was taken to the princess, who bought the flowers and said that she wanted some more. The next day the boy took another bouquet to the princess, who stopped crying when she saw the flowers. The boy asked the guards what was wrong, and they said that tomorrow they had to leave the princess outside the gates for the three-headed monster. The boy returned and told the ox.

The next day the ox told the boy to pull off his other horn, and there was a little box with a suit and a horse in it. He shut his eyes, and the suit and the horse became full-sized. He put on the suit and got on the horse. The ox told him to go and fight the monster and to keep thinking of him, the ox, all through the fight. The boy rode to the place where the princess had been left, got off his horse, and went up the stairs to talk to her. She told him to go away, or he would be killed, but he refused. Soon they heard a noise and saw the monster come crashing through the trees. They boy got onto his horse, and the fight began. As soon as the boy cut off one of the monster's heads, it would jump right back on again. Finally it stayed off, and the monster called for a truce until the next day.

The boy went back and told the ox what had happened. He confessed that he had not thought of the ox during the fight. The next day the boy took the box from the ox's horn; this time there was a different suit and a big bay horse. He took some flowers and talked to the princess until the monster came, and they fought, but the heads kept jumping back on again. Finally, the monster called for a truce. The boy returned and confessed that he hadn't thought of the ox during the fight.

The next day the boy got a different suit and a white horse, and the ox told the boy to think of him this time; it was his last chance to kill the monster. This time the boy did think of the ox and he cut off the two remaining heads, and they didn't come back on again, and the monster died. The boy then confessed to the princess that he was the flower boy, and he took her back to the palace.

The next morning he put on his old clothes again and took some flowers and revealed his identity to the king, who offered the boy his kingdom.

That night, when the boy went back to the ox, the ox said that he had a favor to ask. He wanted the boy to cut off the ox's head. The boy didn't want to do that to his good friend, but after much persuasion the boy took his sword and cut off the ox's head, and then there appeared a fine prince. The prince told the boy that he had saved his life. A witch had transformed him into an ox.

Several days later the king offered the boy his kingdom, but the boy refused. However, he said that he would marry the princess, and they had a big wedding. The boy and his wife and the prince left the next day for the kingdom ruled by the wicked brother. The two henchmen recognized him and took him to the king, who fell back dead when he saw his brother alive. The people crowned the boy king, and the prince went back to rule the other kingdom.

Comments

So far most of the tales in this chapter have conformed rather neatly to one or more of the Aarne-Thompson tale types, but the foregoing is less easily identified and includes a melange of tale types. The leading one seems to be 511A, *The little red ox*, in which the hero is helped by a magic ox which provides food from a removable horn (also motif B115, *Animal with horns of plenty*, a theme found in French folklore).

At the outset of the tale there is a sort of "Snow-White" motif, with the sexes reversed; a king demands to have his son executed, followed by motif K512.2, *Compassionate executioner: substituted heart* (or substituted tongue-tip in our version). Figuring later in the story is A-T tale type 300, *The dragon slayer*, but without the cutting-out of tongues or the grimy impostor. Then, again, we have motif D711, *Disenchantment by decapitation*.

The ox plays a role like that of the horse in the previous story. Both are transformed princes who help the hero to acquire a princess and to accomplish deeds of bravery. Both of the transformed princes need to be decapitated by the hero in order to resume their former shapes.

57. *The Girl Who Married an Ox*

Collected by Victor Barnouw at Lac du Flambeau in 1944
Narrator: Maggie Christensen

There was a family that lived on an estate, and they didn't know who owned it. They had three daughters — three very pretty girls. One day an ox came and asked the old lady if he could marry the oldest girl. She said, "You've got to ask her yourself." Now how can an ox talk? But he asked her, told her how pretty she was and how crazy he was about her, but the girl said, "No, I won't marry an ox."

"You'll have to get off my place then, if you won't."

"No, I won't marry an ox."

He said, "I'll come tomorrow for an answer."

The next day he came, and she told him the same thing. So then he went to the second girl, and she told him the same thing: "I wouldn't marry an ox. I'm afraid of you."

"All right; then you'll have to get off my place."

Well, they were afraid. He came back the next day. This time he went to the mother to ask if he could marry her youngest daughter. "Oh my!" she said, "my girl is too young to marry, let alone marry an ox."

"Well, then, you'll have to get off my place, and it's a long way to go before you get to another place to live."

This girl must have heard him. "Mother," she said, "I'll marry him."

So she couldn't say anything.

"Well, you'll have to come along with me," said the ox.

He gave her a pair of shoes. He spread a blanket on his back, and she got on and rode off.

The other two girls were scared to death. They didn't know what was to become of their sister. They said, "Let's follow their tracks."

When they got to a wigwam or a house, that's where they stopped. This was to be her home.

The ox said to the girl, "There's one promise I want you to make. I never want you to tell your people that I'm not an ox."

She promised. He said, "I'm going into the other room to change." When he came back, he was a nice-looking man.

Every time her sisters came, he was gone. They didn't see how in the world she could live with an ox. But she'd promised not to tell about him.

The next time they came she had the nicest little baby. Oh, like an angel! Oh, they were just crazy about that baby. Before she'd had the baby, they'd said, "Now if you have a baby, what will you do if it looks like an ox?" But it turned out it wasn't an ox. So she told her sisters, "I've got the nicest looking man you ever saw." She broke her promise. After that, a stately man came into the room, and the girls were surprised that she had such a handsome looking husband. They went home to tell their parents.

"Now I'll have to leave you. You broke your promise," said the ox to his wife, "but I'll give you a pair of iron shoes to wear, and when they wear out, you'll find me. But you'll be well taken care of on your way. At night your feet will be sore, but you'll get along all right."

It took her ten years to get to this wigwam where a wee little woman came out. "Who are you?" she said.

She told her who she was, the wife of the king. She had her little boy with her. She watched while the old woman cooked a meal. There was a fireplace in the center of the wigwam. Over it hung a kettle as big as a thimble. She put one grain of rice in it. The woman thought, "My goodness! How can I get enough to eat from one grain of rice?"

It turned out to be a great big kettlefull of rice. "I can never eat all that!" she said. The woman gave her some to take along for her lunch. She has ten more years to walk. She started the next day and came to the next wigwam. There was another woman in that wigwam who asked her to come in. She didn't give her anything to eat there. The woman just gave her a comb, a pretty red comb. She was never to give it away — always keep it. She said, "I know where you're going. You'll soon be there. But your man is going to be married tomorrow to a princess. Before you get to that place where they live, sit down and comb your hair with that comb." When she unbraided her hair and started to comb, nothing but gold fell out of her hair onto her lap.

The woman that was going to marry her man saw her combing her hair. She came over and wanted to get that comb from her. She said, "No, I'm going to keep that comb. I'm not going to give it away."

"You're the ox's wife, aren't you?"

She said, "Yes."

"If you let me have that comb, I'll let you speak to your husband."

"Well, I'm not going to give it to you until I have a talk with him."

"Well, you can talk to him this evening after dark. He's got his room right in there, where he sleeps."

She saw this woman brewing some kind of tea, put it in a cup. She went in where that ox was. She said he'd rest good if he drank it. He drank it; must have fallen asleep. When his real wife came to talk to him, he was sound asleep. He couldn't hear one word she said. When she came out, she told this woman that she couldn't wake him, so she couldn't give up that comb.

"Well, we'll try it tomorrow night."

She saw her brewing that tea the next night. She went in with that cup. He said, "I don't want to drink it just now. Leave it there on the table, and when I get ready to go to sleep, I'll drink it."

She went out, and he spilled it into a spittoon. Then the woman came in. He was sound asleep. She saw the cup empty and thought he'd drunk it. She called the girl, "You can go in now."

When the girl came in, she said, "Well, do you know me?"

He said, "Yes, but I wouldn't have recognized you right away. I didn't think the twenty years were up yet." He asked her how the little boy was.

The next day they took the other woman and tied her to two horses, one on each leg, and they pulled her apart. She didn't last long. She was a queen too. The king told the girl that they'd always stay together, and so they lived happily ever after.

Comments

This story conforms to A-T tale type 425, *The search for the lost husband*, in which a girl promises herself as bride to a monster whom she disenchants, but then loses him because she betrays his secret to her sisters and must subsequently wander about in iron shoes in search of him. Included here are motifs S215.1, *Girl promises herself to animal suitor*, and L54.1, *Youngest daughter agrees to marry a monster; later the sisters are jealous*.

Toward the end of her wanderings the heroine gets some magic objects from an old woman which help her to disenchant her husband and to become reunited with him.

In our version, the Chippewa motif of the self-replenishing kettle (D1472.1.2, *Magic kettle supplies food*) is introduced in the course of the narrative.

Tale type 425 has had a wide distribution throughout Europe. It has been one of the most widely discussed of European tale types, partly because of its relationship to the tale of Cupid and Psyche. A detailed analysis of tale type 425 has been made by Jan-Ojvind Swahn, who reviewed the works of earlier scholars, including Andrew Lang, Ernst Tegethoff, and Inger M. Boberg. According to Swahn's system of classification, our Wisconsin version of the tale conforms to his sub-type B(2) in which the heroine acquires the right to spend three nights in the same room with her husband. He is given a sleeping draught during the first two nights but avoids it on the third and then recognizes his wife. Swahn concludes that sub-type B probably originated in France, perhaps among the Bretons. (The iron-shoes motif also occurs in the Breton area.) From France, according to Swahn, sub-type B spread to other parts of Europe, including Germany, Scandinavia, the Balkans, Italy, Greece, and Turkey (1955, pp. 31, 287-95).[3] It seems likely that the tale was brought to Wisconsin by men of French origin.[4]

In Europe the animal whom the girl marries may be a bear, dog, snake, swine, wolf, or "monster." Swahn gives a long list of other animals which have filled the same role, but the ox is not among them. This may be a New World modification, probably related to the use of oxen in hauling logs in American lumber camps.

58. *Jijean*

Collected by Victor Barnouw at Lac du Flambeau in 1944
Narrator: Tom Badger   Interpreter: Julia Badger

Jijean (French pronunciation) lived at the edge of the town where the king lived. One day he went to the next town to look for work. While he was on his way, he found some gold coins. At the next town he bought three beautiful horses and brought them back to his home. The king liked those horses and asked if he could buy them, but Jijean wouldn't let them go.

One night the king told his men to go and cut off the tails of Jijean's horses. They did as they were told. Jijean had one man working for him.

---

3. See also Boberg (1938).
4. Some French versions are given in Delarue and Tenèze (1963, pp. 72–109).

The next morning this man went to feed the horses and found they had no tails. He went to tell Jijean. Jijean ordered his man to hitch up the horses anyway. While he rode about town, everybody laughed at him and said, "Look at Jijean's horses!"

The king had some horses too. One night Jijean told the man who worked for him to go and cut those horses' mouths. The horses had to keep their mouths open after that. The king knew who had done it. Jijean denied up and down that he had done it. He said, "When I rode around town, everybody laughed; so maybe those horses laughed so hard that that's why their mouths are open like that."

The king ordered his men to put Jijean in a sack and throw him into the water. But Jijean changed places with one of his men and went away to the next town. They threw this man into the water instead of him. In the next town Jijean bought a beautiful pair of oxen with golden-tipped horns. He came back and drove them through town. The king said, "Where did you get such beautiful oxen?"

Jijean said, "If you'd thrown me still further out in the water, I would have got still nicer oxen."

The king wanted to get some oxen like those, so he had himself tied up in a sack and dumped far out into the water. He drowned. Jijean married the king's daughter.

Comments

This story seems to be based on A-T tale type 1535, *The rich and poor peasant*, especially item 5, involving an exchange of persons in a sack, which fatally deceives the poor hero's rich opponent. Thinking that it will help him to get fine sheep, the rich peasant dives to the bottom of the sea. The same theme appears in motif K842, *Dupe persuaded to take prisoner's place in a sack: killed. The bag is to be thrown into the sea.*

Not only is the story of European origin, but the hero's French name has been preserved. It was originally Petit Jean, often shortened in Canada to Ti-Jean. Franz Boas pointed out this linguistic conservatism in borrowed tales in 1925 (p. 199).

59. *Fourteen with One Stroke*

Collected by Robert Ritzenthaler at Court Oreilles in 1942
Narrator: Tom Batiste   Interpreter: Prosper Guibord

Midaswe lived on the edge of a big town. He had a big family and worked in the town. Every day at quitting time he would buy a bottle and get drunk. His wife would tell him to buy grub for the kids instead of liquor, but he wouldn't listen. One day he decided not to get a bottle; and after he had worked all day, he took the money and started home. But as he passed the tavern where he usually stopped, the bartender came out and said, "Come here, I want to hire you to clear land for me. It's a good job." So he went in, and the bartender set a bottle in front of him and told him to take a drink first. At first the Indian refused, but finally he took one, then another, and then he bought a bottle, got drunk, and went home. His wife saw that he was drunk again and told him so. The next morning she told him that if he got drunk again that day, he shouldn't come home.

He went to work. That evening he got his money and started for home. As he passed the saloon, the bartender called to him, saying he had something to tell him. The Indian went in, got drunk, bought a bottle, and went home; but his wife wouldn't let him in. He sat on the doorstep and thought about how hard his wife worked and how little his kids had. Finally he got up and walked over to the woods in remorse and walked around all night, not caring if he died or not.

Near morning he lay down and tried to sleep, pulling his coat over him, but there were too many mosquitoes. He struck at the mosquitoes on his face and killed a bunch of them. He counted them; there were fourteen. He struck on the other side of his face and killed some more and counted them; there were fourteen. "I killed fourteen again with one stroke," he said. Then he got up and started walking.

In the afternoon he struck the road and walked along it. Then he saw something on the road and picked it up; it was a fifty cent piece. He walked on and saw the metal part of a scythe stuck in a stump. He pulled it out and said, "This will be my sword."

That evening he came to a lumber camp and went to the blacksmith shop. The blacksmith looked at the ragged Indian and said, "Where did you come from?" The Indian said he didn't know, but that he wanted a sword made from the scythe. The blacksmith took the scythe and made a sword out of it. The Indian said that was fine; but now he wanted the words carved on it: "Fourteen with one stroke." So the blacksmith did it. The Indian said, "Now carve the same thing on the other side." The blacksmith did that too and asked if that was all. "No, you have to make a scabbard for it." So the blacksmith made the scabbard and carved the same thing on each side of it. He charged the Indian fifty cents.

That night the Indian stayed at the camp, and the next day he started off. That night he camped in the woods, and the next day he came to a strange town. He asked if there were any soldiers there, and they showed him the barracks. He went in. The soldiers were just sitting down to eat. The ragged Indian sat down too and ate, and then lay down on the floor and slept. The soldiers all noticed the sword with the inscription, "Fourteen with one stroke." They wondered about it and went to tell the president about it. The president sent for the Indian, and the soldiers woke him up and told him that the president wanted to see him. "Why doesn't he come down here?" asked the Indian. But he got up and went over to see the president. The president asked him where he was from. The Indian said he didn't know. The president asked him about the inscription, whether it was true. The Indian said it wouldn't be there if it weren't. The president asked him what he was doing here, and the Indian said that he was looking for a fight. The president said he had had three daughters that were eaten by a *windigo*, and he had only one daughter left. He said that if the Indian would kill the *windigo*, he would give him his daughter in marriage. The Indian said he didn't want to get married; he was just looking for a fight. The president asked, "Will you fight the *windigo*?" The Indian said, "Sure, but I don't want your daughter." The president told him to come back at one o'clock.

The Indian went back to the barracks and lay down on the floor and slept. At one o'clock the soldiers woke him up. He was very mad, but he went over to the president and saw the daughter crying. The president told him it was time to go and gave him directions — go north and then take the west road. The Indian took the girl and started out.

He left the girl at the crossroads and took the road to the west alone and soon came to a big oak lying across the road. He climbed over it and then walked on until he saw the *windigo*. The *windigo* had horns a foot long. When he saw the Indian, he started hollering. The Indian turned tail and ran fast. He climbed over the big oak and fell down on the other side. He heard the *windigo* trying to get over the fallen oak. The Indian wondered what was happening. Finally he raised his head and saw that the *windigo* had fallen and driven his horns into the hard, dry oak. The Indian took a rock and pounded his horns deeper into the oak. Then he walked back to the girl and told her that he couldn't haul the *windigo* away but had driven his horns into the tree. The girl went over and saw the *windigo* and believed the Indian's story.

When the president saw them returning, he was very glad. The Indian told the same story to the president, and the president took some soldiers with him and went to see the *windigo* stuck into the log. Then he said, "You didn't do this." The Indian said, "All right, then, I'll pull them out." He started to pull, but the president said, "No. Stop." He told the soldiers to shoot the *windigo*, and they did.

Then the president said, "There is one more *windigo* on the east road, and if you kill him, you can marry my daughter." The Indian said that he didn't want to get married; he just wanted a fight. He went back to the barracks, and the soldiers wondered about him, still doubting his story. He ate his meals there and slept with his sword showing the inscription, "Fourteen with one blow."

They woke him up at one o'clock, and he was mad again, but went over to the president. This time the daughter didn't cry. He took her to the crossroads and left and took the road to the east. He came to a bridge where there was a hole about the shape of a big iron kettle, but very deep. He crossed the bridge and walked on and then saw the *windigo*. He turned tail and ran. When he crossed the bridge, he fell, and the *windigo* who chased him fell over him and went into the hole. The Indian raised his head and saw that the *windigo* was trapped in the hole. He got up and looked at the *windigo* and saw that he couldn't get out; so he went over and got the girl and told her that he'd thrown the *windigo* into a hole. He took her over there and showed her the *windigo* in the hole, and then they went back to town.

When the president had heard the story, he took some soldiers out there, and when the president asked the Indian if he had thrown the *windigo* into the hole, the Indian said, "Sure I did. Watch, and I'll pull him out for you." The president said "No, don't do that," and told the soldiers to shoot the *windigo*.

They all went home, and the president said, "You have done a big thing here, Indian; but there is just one more thing to do. We are at war with the president of another country, and I want you to go there and fight. If you win, you can marry my daughter." The Indian said he didn't want to get married; he just wanted a fight. The president wanted him to take the soldiers along, but the Indian said he wanted to go alone.

The next day he started off to the east, where he was told that he'd find a big house with gold plates and knives. He was supposed to ride a horse up to the big fence around the house. The Indian had never been on a horse before, and when they put the spurs on his boots he didn't know what they were for. When he got on, he tried to hold himself on by holding his feet tight on the horse, but he was spurring the horse, and the horse ran faster. They ran into the town and around the big fence that surrounded the big house. As they went by a big cross, he grabbed it to try to get off the horse, but instead he pulled it out, and they rode around the fence three times. All the people were wondering who this mad man was and what he was doing. The fourth time around the fence, his horse fell down, and the Indian landed with one foot under the horse. Finally he managed to pull it loose. He got up and saw that the horse was dead, and there were no people around. He saw the big cross and wondered how he could have carried it. He limped over to the gate and walked into the house, from which everyone had fled. He picked up the gold keys and filled a sack with gold knives and forks and things, and then he walked back to the barracks and put down the sack and went to sleep.

At breakfast no one spoke to him, and the soldiers wondered about him. He went to sleep again. The president told the soldiers to bring the Indian to him. The Indian was mad when they woke him up, but he got up and went over to see the president. He told what had happened. The president and all the soldiers went over to check on his story and saw the deserted town and picked up all the gold they could carry. The president gave the Indian a new suit of clothes and a haircut and said that the Indian should stay there and live with him and marry his daughter because he had done so much. The Indian thought about his wife and kids, but finally he decided to marry the daughter. They got married, and the Indian was respected, because now the people believed him.

One night he dreamed and called out the names of his wife and five kids. The daughter wondered about this and went to tell her father. He told her to leave the door open that night, and he would listen. The Indian overheard their plans and made up his mind to stay awake that night. When they went to bed, his wife didn't close the door, and he noticed that. A little later he heard the president at the door. Then the Indian took down his sword and pulled it from the scabbard and started yelling, "Fight, boys!" He made believe he was in battle and started slashing around and cut off the president's ear. The president "woke" up the Indian and said, "Stop. You cut off my ear." The Indian said he had been dreaming and asked what the president was doing in his room. The president said that he suspected that the Indian had another family because he was shouting children's names in his sleep. The Indian said, "No, I don't have any other family." The end.

Comments

"Fourteen with One Stroke" is recognizable as A-T 1640, *The brave tailor*. In Europe, as in our Chippewa version, the protagonist is an antihero who succeeds through dumb luck, despite his cowardice. In Europe the hero is a tailor; in our version he is simply an Indian. The Chippewa version makes him out to be a drunkard who neglects his wife and children, which is not part of the European tale complex. The Indian version also depicts him as being indifferent to the prospect of marrying the president's daughter, although he does marry her in the end and does not return to his wife and children.

The episodes are fairly close to the European sequence. The man kills fourteen mosquitoes and has the inscription "Fourteen with One Stroke" inscribed on his sword. He is then put to various tests by the president (king in Europe). In Europe the tailor tricks a unicorn into running his horn into a tree. In our version the unicorn's place is taken by a horned *windigo*. The battle scene, with the hero seizing a cross, roughly follows European patterns.

In some European versions, after his marriage to the princess, the tailor reveals his tailor's calling by talking in his sleep. The princess reports this to the king, and they place a sentry outside the door to kill the tailor. The tailor learns of this plot and pretends to talk in his sleep, boasting of former deeds of bravery. This has been changed in the Chippewa version. The Indian talks of his former wife and children in his sleep. The president comes to listen and has his ear cut off.

It is interesting that in the narration of this tale the storyteller has evidently accepted the stereotype of the drunken Indian. This theme occupies the opening paragraphs and explains the hero's departure from his wife and children. The problem of drinking does not recur later in the story. However, the hero is described as being ill-tempered, mad at being wakened up, and he describes himself as "looking for a fight."

For some comparative data on this tale, see Laurits Bødker (1957).

60. *The Magic Ring*

Collected by Robert Ritzenthaler at Court Oreilles in 1942
Narrator: Tom Batiste   Interpreter: Prosper Guibord

A chief lived in a village with his two daughters and his son. He was well off and had lots of horses; his son had a pony too. Once the boy heard some of the other fellows talking about a very pretty daughter of a chief in another village. She had power to keep men away from her, and so no one could get to her. She could even see the eye-prints of someone who looked at something. The boy thought about this girl every day, and one day he decided to go and try to see her. He didn't want anyone to know where he was going, so he told his folks that he was just going on a journey and might be gone a long while; so they should not worry, and he would come back. He took his pony and some grub and started out. He didn't know where she lived.

He camped for nine nights on his trip, and on the tenth day he came to a little wigwam with smoke coming out. A voice said, "Come in, grandson, I know what you are looking for, and I will help you." He went in and saw an old lady, who told him to sit down and eat. She gave him some wild rice and dried blueberries cooked together, some maple sugar and venison. She told him that the place he was looking for was hard to find. She said that she would give him some medicine, but he would have to stay for several years and keep on drinking it. She told him that he could hunt and take care of the little garden there and keep his pony there too. The medicine was the root of a flower plant that birds fed on. She would go out during the day and find it, and at night, once a month during the full moon, she would take a birchbark torch and go out and gather it. She could gather it just once a month. She got enough for the winter and went out again in the spring.

The boy took the medicine every day, just a little bit at a time, three times in the morning, three in the afternoon, and three in the evening. He did this for two years. During the third year, in the spring, she told him to leave before sunrise and go in a certain direction through a big forest, until he came to a place where there were a lot of birds. She said that he should wait until the birds woke up and started singing and that he should try to understand what they said.

He followed her instructions. When the birds started to sing, he listened and could understand a little of what two of the birds were saying. He went back and told his grandmother, but she told him that he would have to stay another year and drink more medicine.

The next spring she called him one day and told him to get up early the next morning and go back and try to understand the birds. He took his pony and went back to that place. When the same two birds started to sing, he understood every word they said. One of the birds told the other about the beautiful daughter of the chief who came to bathe in a certain pool once each spring. This bird said that he was going to get the news about when she was coming to the pool. He said that only birds could see her; she was invisible to other eyes.

The boy went back and told his grandmother what he had heard, and she told him to go back the next day for the news about when the girl was going to bathe. He did, and found out that she was going to bathe three days later and that the two birds were going the next day to watch her. He went back to his grandmother and told her that, and she said that he was now ready to leave. She said that he should take his pony the next morning and follow the birds. She said that the birds would go slowly from tree to tree, and when they stopped he should camp nearby.

He set out the next morning and came to where the two birds were. He followed them on their journey to the pool, camping three nights. On the fourth day they came to a beautiful pool. His grandmother had told him to hide behind a tree and watch her secretly while she was bathing, and then to follow her to her wigwam. So he hid behind a big tree, and pretty soon along came the beautiful girl followed by her maid. When they got to the pool, the girl saw the eye-prints in the pool and saw the birds above and asked them who had been there, but they didn't answer.

After she had finished bathing, they started back, and the young man followed along behind on his pony. When they got to her village, the girl went inside a big cave where they lived. They didn't live in wigwams like other people. The young man followed her right in, as his grandmother had told him to do. When the girl saw him, she said that it was strange that he had got in there, since no other man had ever been able to do that. She said that from now on they would be considered married.

They lived together and got along fine, but every day she would disappear for a while and she never told her husband where she went. He was happy and didn't care about that, but one day he asked her maid where his wife went. The maid told him that she had a ring which she put on and which could change her into an eagle or anything she wanted to be, and she could fly away. The ring was kept in an iron box with a lock on it. The young man asked to borrow the ring some time just to see if it really worked, and the maid agreed to let him try. That night, when his wife returned and gave the ring to her maid and went to bed, the husband asked the maid for it, and he put it on and rubbed it. He announced that he wanted to go home, and quick as a flash he was at home. He just stopped to see how his folks were, and he left without anyone seeing him.

Then he decided that he wanted to see a woman in another village who, he had heard, had a magic ring more powerful than his wife's. So he rubbed the ring and found himself in that woman's cave, and he asked her about the ring she was supposed to have. She told him that the ring was lost, and the only person who could get to where it was had to have a ring like it. She knew of only one person who had another one, and that was his wife, and she was afraid that she would not return it once she had found it. She told him that she had lost it one time when she went to a big lake and saw a big ship and got on it, and they took her across the lake to where the white people lived. On the way back they stopped to bathe on an island, and she was in a hurry to get dressed, and she left the ring there. He told her he was leaving but that he would return. He walked out of the village, and when he was in the woods, he rubbed the ring and told it he wanted to go to the island.

He fould himself on the island and looked for the ring, but he couldn't find it. He asked the ring where to look for the other ring, and then he found it and returned home to his wife. He put the ring back in the iron box and made a box out of bone lined with buckskin and put the other ring into it and kept it in his saddle.

Then he decided to go back and visit his folks. He rode on his pony. On the way he stopped and told his grandmother what had happened, except for mentioning that he had found the ring. She told him that on that island where he found the ring, once a month some girls of a different race would come to bathe. When he got home he had been gone four years, and his parents were glad to see him. He told them that he had been married but had left his wife.

He wanted to go to the island to see the girls who came to the island to bathe in the full moon. First, however, he went to his wife's place and got the ring from the maid and went out to a big cliff. He had been told that if he put the ring on a certain finger, he could lift anything. So he did and lifted the cliff and put his wife's ring under it, where he thought it would be safe from anyone. Then he went to the island and there was a big ship there and the girls took him through it. He thought it was a big house at first.

He wanted a big ship like that, so he went back and got four strong men and rubbed the ring and got materials, and they started to build a ship like the big one. Suddenly he realized that the ring could do it, so he just rubbed the ring and wished that the ship was finished, and there it was, all ready to sail.

The four men got in and sailed around for a while. He made one of the men a navigator, one a cook, and one a captain through his ring. As they neared shore, they saw a man listening to the ground with one ear and then the other. The man got off the boat and went over to the fellow and asked him what he was doing. The man said that he was listening to the grass grow. The man asked him if he would like to come along with them, and he accepted. They went on and saw another fellow with a bow and arrow shooting up in the air. They stopped the boat and asked this fellow what he was doing. He told them that he was shooting up through a little hole in the sky and shooting sparrows for practice. They looked, but it was too far away to see with ordinary eyes, and they asked him to come along, and he did.

They sailed some more and saw a fellow looking at the boat, and when he turned his back the boat stopped, and when he turned his face toward the boat it started again. They went over and asked him if he was stopping the boat. He said, "Yes, I have the power to do that by turning my back." So they asked him to come along too. They went a little further and saw another man with an axe, who disappeared into the woods. They stopped the boat and followed him and came to a place where the man had chopped a big pile of wood bigger than a house. The man said that he had done that in just a few minutes. They were surprised and invited him along, and he joined the party, and they went to explore some more.

Soon they came to a big city where white men lived. The king was having a carnival and races. The king sent a messenger to the Indians and invited them to come and participate, so they all went. The first contest was to be a race. The king had a man who could race to the top of the sky and back in no time. The Indian with the bow and arrow decided to challenge him. The man drew his bow and shot an arrow and then grabbed hold of it just as it left the bow, and he went right up to the top of the sky. He and the other man both got up there at about the same time. The Indian said, "Let's rest a while. They'll wait for us down there." He lay down and fell asleep, and the king's man started back while the other man was asleep. When the Indians saw the king's man coming, they wondered what to do, and the man who could stop anything turned his back, so the man up there stopped right in mid-air. Then the man who could hear anything listened and heard their friend snoring. He told the others that their man was asleep, so the man with the axe, who also had a bow, shot an arrow and nicked the sleeper's ear and woke him up. He started coming back and passed the king's man and won the race.

The next day the king said, "Today we are having a wood-cutting contest. Do you have an entry?" They pitted their man with the axe against the king's entry. They were to cut all morning, and the man with the biggest pile would be the winner. They started cutting, and at noon they went out to where the king's man was cutting. He had a huge pile out. Then they went to the Indian's place and saw him sitting on a pile about as big as the king's man's. He told them to come up, and when they got to the top he showed them about a hundred other piles that he had cut; so he won the contest easily. That finished the contests, and the Indians had beaten the whites.

Comments

This rambling story seems to be made up of different tales, with the concluding one conforming to A-T 513, 514, *The helpers*, motif *F601*, *Extraordinary companions. A group of men with extraordinary powers travel together*; and A-T 513A, *The helpers perform various deeds for the hero at the king's court.*

This competition usually ends with the hero marrying a princess, but in our version the point is that the Indians have beaten the whites. So perhaps the last part of the tale functions as a fantasy of power in its New World setting. When the hero finds and marries the girl, that would normally be the climax and end of such a tale. But in this case the hero soon seems to lose interest in the girl and goes on to more adventures.

General Comments on the Tales of European or Mixed Origin

In these stories we have a new world of kings, princesses, castles, and ships, all bearing a European stamp, but some of the traditional Indian themes remain as well. The main ways in which these stories differ in content from traditional Chippewa tales are the references to city life and royalty and the importance of courtship themes. These are Cinderella themes, lacking in aboriginal Chippewa tales.[5] Most of the tales deal with courtship, even the one about Wenebojo's daughter. Bear Girl, Oshkikwe, and the girl in "The Girl Who Married an Ox" all marry a prince or king. The heroes in four of the other tales marry princesses: in "The Eight-Headed *Windigo*," "The Magic Horse," "The Magic Ox," and "Jijean." The Indian in "Fourteen with One Stroke" marries the president's daughter, evidently a New World substitute for a princess. These tales, then, not only deal with courtship but also with upward mobility. Although these themes were lacking in traditional Chippewa tales, there seems to have been no resistance to incorporating them into the Chippewa storyteller's body of tales. At the same time, there is less acceptance of romantic idealization of marriage. The Indian in "Fourteen with One Stroke" is willing to fight *windigog* for the president but doesn't want to marry his daughter. In true European style, the hero in "The Magic Ring" searches for three years for a beautiful girl, but after their marriage he apparently loses interest in her and later tells his parents that he has left her.

Some anal motifs have been inserted into the European tales: the chamber-pots in story number 52 and the punishment of the impostor in story number 54 by having him thrown head first into the toilet.

The Chippewa oral fantasy of the self-replenishing kettle has been introduced into stories 52 and 57. The idea that the hero of "Fourteen With One Stroke" is a drunkard who neglects his wife and children is a prominent new theme in the opening of story number 59.

---

5. But Cinderella tales having parallel themes to European folklore were told in the Northwest Coast of North America among tribes which had social stratification. See Randall (1949).

Consciousness of Indian-ness appears in the latter tale. The president congratulates the hero for killing the *windigog* by saying "You have done a big thing here, Indian." Later, after he has married the president's daughter, "the Indian was respected, because now the people believed him." Story number 60 ends with the Indians beating the whites in a wood-cutting contest.

The influence of the lumber camps of Wisconsin apparently figures not only in the latter episode but also in the prominence given to the ox in some of these stories: number 56, "The Magic Ox," number 57, "The Girl Who Married an Ox," and number 58, "Jijean." The most interesting of these is number 57, the widespread tale of the *Quest for the lost husband*; for the beast or monster in the European tale does not seem to have ever been an ox but instead a bear, wolf, or other creature.

Horses figure in stories 53, 54, 58, and 59, in keeping with the original European tales. Some giants or monsters in European tales understandably become *windigog* in Chippewa re-tellings. In story number 54 the European seven-headed monster, dragon, or ogre has been recast as an eight-headed *windigo*, while in story number 59 the European unicorn has become a horned *windigo*.

Franz Boas long ago pointed out that European folklore is remarkably uniform throughout Europe, having many of the same incidents, plots, and arrangement over a wide territory. "European folklore," wrote Boas, "creates the impression that the whole stories are units and that their cohesion is strong, the whole complex very old. The analysis of American material, on the other hand, demonstrates that complex stories are new, that there is little cohesion between the component elements . . ." (1916, p. 878).

It is the cohesion and consistency of European tales which makes it possible to identify them according to the Aarne-Thompson tale types. We are thus left in no doubt that the stories in this chapter came from the Old World and that France was the probable point of origin for most of them.

The widespread diffusion of European tales among the American Indians makes one realize that Indian-white relations were not always inimical or estranged. The *voyageurs*, fur traders, and lumberjacks evidently spent much time telling their stock of tales to Indian listeners, who were careful to get the details right when they re-told them. Despite prejudice, warfare, and exploitation, there persisted a sort of freemasonry of folklore in which, temporarily at least, the storyteller and his audience were united.

CHAPTER NINE

Chippewa Folklore in Individual Fantasies

Field work at the Wisconsin Chippewa reservations in the early 1940s sometimes elicited stories which were told as true but which had a mythical quality, such as the story about the Mide priest who cut flesh from the head of the giant horned serpent or Tom Badger's tale about the bearwalk. To give another example, in 1942 an Indian informant told Robert Ritzenthaler that he was once chased by a big supernatural snake about six or seven inches in diameter. He managed to reach home and told his wife to fill up his pipe for him. Then he smoked and called upon the thunderbirds for help. Soon some clouds appeared in the sky; then a thunderbolt came down and killed the snake, which was close to the house. Since one of the thunderbirds carried the snake away, no one else saw the carcase.

The term "memorate" has been given to such experiences, reported by individuals as true events. We can see that these experiences must be structured and perceived by a mental set imbued with traditional beliefs. The Indian's encounter with a giant snake and thunderbirds was experienced by him in such a way that he could tell it as a true story. We can also see, from an account like this, how such experiences and reports would reinforce traditional beliefs, providing an empirical basis for Chippewa conceptions of reality. This was particularly true of experiences connected with the vision quest for a guardian spirit. Those who had the appropriate dream or vision reported on what they had experienced, which reinforced the beliefs of those who listened. As Lauri Honko has written, "Memorates are a valuable source for the study of folk religion primarily because they reveal those situations in which supernatural tradition was actualized and began directly to influence behavior" (1964, p. 10).

In the light of these considerations we can consider the story of Mary Careful.[1] Mary Careful was a vigorous old woman, remembered by many old-timers at Court Oreilles in the 1940s. A rich folklore had ac-

---

1. Collected by Ernestine Friedl at Court Oreilles in 1942.

cumulated about her experiences, of which the following provides a summary. (Remember that "folklore" is *our* term for this material.)

Mary Careful was "a brave old lady who feared nothing." She was a good Catholic, and so she got mad one day when a "pagan" woman started to assail her religion at an Indian dance. She gave the woman a licking but got arrested for this and was sent to jail in Madison. After her prison term was over, Mary was placed in a boarding house to earn her fare back to Court Oreilles, but she decided to leave and walk home — a distance of several hundred miles. "They looked for her," said the informant, "but she was invisible. As she came out of there, there were two cops, but she pointed at them and told them that she had power so that they wouldn't be able to see her. They started looking for her. They called up the Indian Farmer at Reserve. They were scared. They thought maybe somebody had killed her. After Mary left the boarding house, she lost her way about ten miles. Then she came to a house where there was an old lady and an old man and their son — white people. She stayed there over night. They wanted her to stay all the time, but she wanted to get home. They gave her lunch and some clothes.

"Then she went on and came to some hunters. They started shooting at Mary. She made herself appear in the form of a deer. Mary had power to do that. Then the deer turned into a wolf. When the hunters saw that, they knew it must be the woman who was lost. They didn't bother her after that.

"Mary went along, walking along a railroad track, and came to a tunnel. She heard a voice calling her, saying 'My namesake!' Mary recognized the voice from her dream. She knew who it was. The voice told her not to be afraid to go through the tunnel, and that she wouldn't have any storms or bad weather on her journey and would get home all right.

"She walked and walked, never made a fire all the way or stopped to drink any water. She was afraid that if she drank any water, she might turn *windigo*. She must have been part *windigo*. She was barefoot by the time she got to Eau Claire. Her boots were all gone, and she wrapped rags around her feet."

Finally Mary reached her destination and told this story to many people. This same old lady was said to have had so much power that she could summon the winds and thunders by puffing her pipe. One time Mary got revenge on some mean neighbors of hers by calling upon the winds to destroy their ricefields. After the storm had caused enough damage, she went outside and shouted "That's enough!" Mary said that she didn't want to cause any more destruction, because she didn't want her grandchildren to suffer retaliation.

Tom Badger's Prenatal Recollections

Tom Badger, narrator of the Flambeau origin myth, whose life history is given in the appendix, began his autobiography with the following account, which provides a link with some fantasies of his wife Julia. Both of their stories concern Bebukowe, who figures in the first tale in chapter 4. As will be seen, however, their accounts of Bebukowe are quite different from the picture of the evil old hunchback of the folktale.

Here is Tom Badger's story:

Before I was born, I was walking towards the sun — not on the earth. I saw something over there that was shining. (The reason I'm telling you these things is that you gave me tobacco before we began.) I was coming from the west. I looked to the north and saw this shining thing. I didn't know what it was.

After I passed the south end of the place where I was walking, half-way to the east, I saw that shining thing. I didn't know what it was, but it was pretty. I turned to look at it and saw that man standing there behind me. He was like a little fellow, like a boy — short. He kept right along behind me, wherever I went. When we went to that shining thing, he was right there.

I walked to that shining thing. When I got near to it, it was a stream or a river. I walked slowly toward the river. The stream looked just like a mirror; it was frozen over. There was no snow on it. When I was right next to that river, the man behind me spoke to me. We had reached a bend in the river, and this man said, "Let's slide across to the bend there."

We slid along the ice. When I reached the bend, I was born. I don't know what the other fellow looked like or what became of him then. His name was Bebukowe.

Julia Badger's Trip to the Other World

When Tom Badger had finished this story, Julia said, "I've seen him too," and told the following story, which I quote from my article, "The Phantasy World of a Chippewa Woman" (1949), from which the foregoing passage about Tom Badger was also quoted.

When I was about two months old I fell very sick. A woman who had lost a child stepped on my bonnet. It must have been lying around. Then I became paralyzed and got sick, so that I could hardly see out of my eyes. My father called his father and mother to come and see what they could do for me. He said, "My daughter can't see. Her eyes seem to have been staying in the same position since yesterday. They aren't straight."

They tried all they could do. They couldn't get them straight. It was all on account of this woman. You know how women are — they like children. She should have been more careful. My father said, "What shall I do? They say I'm going to lose my first baby if I don't get busy and do something for her."

Old Man Otter, who married my grandmother's sister, always lived with us. He said, "Get the men together to make a *jizikun* [conjuring lodge]." They built a wigwam, a big one. Old Man Otter was pretty near to crying. Every sentence he spoke, while he talked about the days when he fasted, he sounded as if he was going to cry. "I'll try to do call I can," he said. "A lot of people never believe in me." He said that before he started so that my parents would give him something — blankets or something. So they gave him what they could. My mother and father believed in him. He's the one that doctored me, and he did all he could for me.

Then he got into the wigwam and started to talk. He said, "Hush up that noise!" to the people outside — mainly my mother and father, who were crying. Then the thing started to shake. He asked my father to hand me in and then he took me in through the door.

At the time that I was taken into the shaking tepee, I was already on the road to the other world. I was on that road that Wenebojo's brother made. I saw the otter in the distance. I didn't go close, because I felt afraid of him. Then I heard something coming behind me, a noise like jingling tin. I wasn't walking fast. I walked slow, but I didn't look back. I kept right on going.

[Did you know where you were going?]

Yes, I knew that I was going along the road that Wenebojo's brother made. I don't know how I knew it, but I knew that that was where I was. That road was hard to travel on. You could see tracks there. All the time that I was walking along this road there was a little bird flying above me in the air on my right-hand side, and it spoke to me now and then, like it was beckoning me to go on.

[Was that the bird that's inside you between your shoulder blades?]

Yes, that's the one. He was leading me. I could also hear this fellow coming behind me. After a while he spoke. He said, "Your people want you to come back." I turned in a semi-circle and looked at that fellow. It was Bebukowe. He said, "It isn't time for you yet." Then he grabbed me by the waist and twisted and turned me around.

I don't know how fast I came back. When I got back home I could hear my mother and father crying. My father was crying the loudest — just screaming. We went through the door. Bebukowe was puffing, like you do when you're tired. He said, "She was half-way. I went and got her half-way." He said that to the people outside. Then he said, "Before we do anything now, I want to dance." So he did.

We went into the shaking tepee then. Bebukowe danced while they were drumming outside. I suppose my spirit went in through the top while my body went the other way. That was the only time I ever went along that road and the only time I ever saw Bebukowe. But I knew that it was him, and he knew that I knew him.

When I was handed in to Old Man Otter, he said to me, "Look over there." I looked where he told me to look. Then he started to talk. He said, "I want you people to help me. You're the ones who told me to do this to help doctor my people. I need you real bad now." [He was speaking to his guardian spirits.] I kept looking over there all the time. Then some people came in, and the wigwam started to go. The old man said, "Now you can look around." I looked around all over.

Wherever the basswood bark was tied, it looked all shining, like shining stars. That was all the people who belong there. From where that shining stuff was I heard voices coming, talking.[2] The top of the wigwam looked just like a door. After a while I heard those bells that they hang up on top. They sounded good. I looked around as fast as I could. I didn't want to miss anything.

Then I saw Bebukowe. He was standing there. He said, "I'd like to dance before we do anything." The old man spoke to those people outside. "Bebukowe wants to dance. Has anybody got a drum out there?" They hadn't drummed before that. The wigwam started to go just the way Bebukowe was going around. I don't know who beat the drum — my father, I guess. Bebukowe looks a lot like a man — except that his face is different. His face is a little like a grasshopper's face around the nose.[3] Bebukowe's face is handsome, though. And when he hollers, he's got a voice on him like any man's. He's dressed up in fine clothes,

2. This is in agreement with Hallowell's description (1942, pp. 50–51): "In point of size the spirits in the tent are reputed to be extremely tiny. They sit on the hoops and when these are full, on the upright poles. To the eye they are said to look like minute sparks or tiny stars." Hallowell also reports that a conjurer may sometimes take a grandson into the tent with him, and from their accounts people learn what the spirits look like.

3. Tom Badger nodded in agreement with this description, as his wife continued.

covered with bells.[4] He likes to dance when he enters. He grabbed me around the waist like this. [Demonstrates.] Then he said, "You're going to play around with a lot of men like this. You can't go now." He said, "I'm a handsome man. You'll see a lot of men like me. You'll play with us too." Sometimes I get tired of playing with men. But that's what he told me I'd do. And I'm like that too. Men are always joshing me and fooling around with me.

He took my bonnet and whirled it around in the air. You could see that cotton flying around. He made like a wind when he did that. The bells started to go, and the wigwam tipped way over. The old man just sat there cross-legged, smoking his pipe. He was looking at Bebukowe. My bonnet was hanging over the doorway, before Bebukowe got hold of it. Two old men and one woman were there too — three *manidog*. My bonnet was hanging up on the pole. I think the woman sitting by the door handed him the bonnet. He said, "I guess I'll wave my flag." Then Bebukowe swung it around. It was like feathers flying around. That was the dirt from the floor that that woman had got into it when she knocked it down — the woman who made me sick. My hair falls out all the time now, still, on account of that. Those three people — they're the ones that shook the wigwam. Then the grasshopper man gave the bonnet to the old woman sitting there. They told us what kind of medicine to use. I don't use it much except now and then when I think of it. They told us I should use it all the time. It helped me a lot. But I couldn't walk for two and a half years.

I was two months old when this happened. I can just picture it now. I remember *just* what they did. The old woman just waved her hand. That's how she fixed the bonnet. She's the one that smoked the bonnet. She named my grandfather and grandmother to get the medicine to use. She said they had some of it. She pointed to the ground. That's where you get it from. She mentioned the name of the medicine and how it's made. She said she was from the South. She had a long dress, long hair. She was dressed like an Indian woman.

The men said that they were from the North. Their hair was white, snow white, and they were dressed in buckskin outfits. They didn't say much. They just smoked. They told me to call them "grandfather." They were the *skabéwisuk* [runners] from the North, and they had come to accept my father's tobacco. These old men were the ones who told my parents to put me through the Midewiwin as soon as they could. They said, "If you lose this one, you'll never get her back." They told them to

---

4. She laughed at this point. Julia derived great pleasure from her own narrative, and spoke about Bebukowe with great affection.

hurry up. There was some wind in the wigwam — just like when leaves move in the air, like someone was fanning. That's how it was inside the wigwam. It kept shaking all the time too.

On a later occasion Mrs. Badger told me about a vision she had had later in her life, in which there seem to be some parallels with the foregoing episode about Bebukowe. Her account follows:

Julia Badger's Vision of the Snake

The third time I went through the Midewiwin, I went through because I had a vision that I should do that. We were living out in the woods at that time. Everything was still and quiet there. I was lying on a bed. I got to thinking of things I'd done way back in my younger days. I thought about my relatives and my friends, my parents who were dead and gone. I had no one to call upon except for my old man [Tom Badger]. I lay still, and my mind was working all the time. Then I said out loud, so that I could be heard: "What is there that I didn't do right? Everything that I can remember I thought I did right. What is wrong with me that I have so many visions of different things and different people?" All that summer I had had visions of people and things. I said aloud again, "Maybe the Almighty has mercy on people who see all these visions."

Then I had a vision that I was walking along a narrow trail through the brush — no tall trees. It was a beautiful day. No wind. Plenty of sunshine. I walked along this trail for about an hour until I heard the sound of tinkling bells in the distance. As I came nearer to the sound, I saw four men sitting around something that was round.[5] Above their heads was something across the sky like a rainbow. One of these men called me his grandchild. He said, "You are supposed to tell the people once in a while when you are in trouble about something you know, something that's in you. Let them know what's in you. Don't pay any attention if people laugh at you. If they do, they're not throwing jokes at you; they're throwing jokes at themselves." One real old white-haired man sat at the far end of that round thing. He pointed to his snow-white hair. He told me that my hair would be just like his some day, if I did what I was told. "We are the ones that asked you to come here, because you are in trouble and don't know which way to turn. There are four things that I want you to remember — North, East, South, and West. On all of these four there

5. A drum. The four men represent the four directions.

sits a man who waits and wants to receive your tobacco. You have a name that you bear, which means a great deal to me. Your name means a whole lot. As you go along, you'll realize this. Your thinking power is working real hard. It will get you somewhere, if you listen to it."

Then another real old man spoke. "It's been a long time since you thought of your grandfather. I like to receive your tobacco once in a while too. I'm the one that suggested to this man the name that you are called by. Don't be afraid of me because I'm big. I will tell you what you are supposed to do once in a while. You are supposed to put out food, like meat and corn, and put some tobacco into the fire or on the ground when I go by. You do your own speaking. [To the spirits.] Nobody else needs to do it. I am the one who will listen."

Then I said, "Oh, I'm the one who made a mistake. I never thought that I would ever make such a big mistake. Sometimes when I think of the things I've done, I thought I'd done them right; but I didn't."

He said, "Sometimes we see you in this certain kind of dance. You are holding the precious flag.[6] That flag belongs to us. Before you speak or do anything, offer some tobacco. If you have no tobacco, you have to give the price for your tobacco." That's just what I do now. If I can't speak, I have somebody speak for me.

Then I went on from this place along the trail a little ways. I heard and saw some more. This man had his finger up in the air. He was talking. He was from the South. This was a different man. There was a thing about four feet high — just a stick sticking in the ground. The man took the stick and handed it to me. "If you lean on this stick," he said, "you'll use two of them later on, as you go along the road, if you do just what I tell you.[7] Go to your great adviser [Tom Badger] and tell him what you have seen."

As I was coming back along this trail, I saw a great big snake about this big around [about six inches]. He raised his head about this high [four feet] from the ground. "Don't be afraid of me," he said. "Just go and tell your adviser [Tom Badger] what you have seen. If you don't, you won't be able to walk." Then he pointed and said, "Look over there." I looked and saw myself lying flat on my back. Then the snake said, "But if you do what I tell you and tell all that you know, everything will be all right. I want to come into that place.[8] I like that place. It

6. A feather flag, used in the War Dance, which is now primarily a curing ceremony. A person who addresses the spirits holds the flag as he speaks.

7. Long life is highly valued among the Chippewa. Mide priests assert that if life is lived correctly, the person will "walk with two sticks" — that is, will live to be old and respected.

8. Later I asked Mrs. Badger what place the snake referred to, and she said, "He meant my home."

makes no difference how it looks. I'm coming there just the same. I'll go along now." Then I walked back home along the trail. That was all. Then I made preparations for going through the Midewiwin.

One afternoon, after I'd made all of my preparations for joining the Midewiwin again, I was all alone at home. The door was open about four inches. I looked at the door and saw this person coming in. I felt kind of scared. He was an unexpected visitor. He came in a few feet and said, "I have come at last." He looked around, turned over on his side, and made himself at home. Then he spoke to me: "If you take care of me like you should, I will do a lot of things for you, because I am the one that suggested all this to you. When you start, have the prettiest dress you've got. I know that I am welcome here. Don't be afraid of me, because I have come a long ways to see you." That's all he said. Then he became a snake and went out.

That's just the way that thing [the hide] looked. I got a snake hide that third time I joined.[9] He [the snake] is the one that put these things into my mind and set me to thinking. I'd wondered what was wrong, because I'd never kept thinking and seeing things like that before. He's the one that suggested I join the Midewiwin. He also asked me if I wanted a drink. I said No, not when I entered his house [the Mide lodge]. [Some sections omitted.]

When you join the Midewiwin the third time, they tell you that the snake is wrapped all around the earth. He may scare you, but he doesn't mean to.,

General Comments on Julia and Tom Badger's Fantasies

The parallels in these two fantasies are as follows: Bebukowe and the snake are generally fearsome beings, associated with evil and sorcery in Chippewa belief, but in these two accounts both play a reassuring, life-giving role. Bebukowe rescues Julia Badger from the road to the other world and returns her to the realm of the living, telling her that she is going to play with men in her life. The snake promises her that everything is going to be all right and says that he wants to come into that place, meaning her home. Later he appears in her home in the form of a man, speaks to her briefly, and then assumes the shape of a snake as he leaves.

As discussed in chapters 4 and 6, both Bebukowe and the snake may be seen as phallic symbols; here the symbolism also takes on a life-affirming aspect.

9. A snake hide is given to the candidate who joins the Midewiwin the third time.

Tom Badger's Bebukowe, in his prenatal recollections, does not seem to be either evil or phallic. All that we learn about him from the story is that he is a little man who wants to go sliding on the ice, and he seems to be connected with Tom Badger's birth.

Tom Badger's story calls to mind a remarkable Ojibwa tale collected at Nett Lake, Minnesota, by Paul Radin and A. B. Reagan in the 1920s. The parallels involve the descent of a frozen stream and an association with birth.

The tale deals with a period when women were already fully formed human beings, but the only male on earth was a man-god in a sort of cocoon state. "He had a large mouth and an elongated cigar-shaped body composed mostly of genital parts. . . . he had no eyes, no ears, no nose, no arms, no legs" (Radin and Reagan, 1928, p. 103). The man-god's wife had to take care of this helpless being, who was very large and heavy and had to be dragged around on a toboggan. The woman finally got tired of this burdensome task and decided to kill her husband. She wrapped him up well, took a sleeve from each arm of an old dress, and put one on each side of him, giving them magical powers so that they could answer his questions with her voice. She slid the toboggan, with her husband wrapped up on it, under the ice at an open pool near a waterfall. Then he started to slide down the stream beneath the ice. Soon this helpless man-god began to feel wet, and he asked why. The sleeves replied that a little water had splashed on him and he'd soon be all right. But the man-god continued to get wetter and wetter and to receive evasive answers from the two sleeves. Finally he could stand it no longer. In a rage the man-god wriggled loose, burst his bonds, smashed the ice, and broke out from his cocoon-skin as a fully developed male being with arms, legs, face, eyes, nose, and mouth. At once he looked around for his wife's tracks and chased after her.

In the end, however, the man-god is defeated by an old woman who shelters his wife. This old woman is a pike fish with sharp back fins upon which the huge god-man falls and is cut in two. The two women then cut up his body with knives and throw the pieces in all directions. These pieces become the human beings of our time.

The ties with Tom Badger's story are tenuous, but in both cases there is a birth associated with a frozen stream. Perhaps this symbolizes the descent of the birth canal and contact with the cold outer air. In the story of the man-god one wonders whether the cigar-shaped creature lashed to the toboggan represents a swaddled infant in a cradleboard. It could also be a phallic symbol: "an elongated cigar-shaped body composed mostly of genital parts."

CHAPTER TEN

General Comments
on the Myths and Tales

It is evident that the stories in our collection, excluding those of European origin, which will not be considered in this chapter, are congruent with and expressive of a nomadic or seminomadic hunting-gathering way of life. There are many tales involving animals, birds, fish, hunting, and fishing, and only two which mention corn (stories number 7 and 47). Some stories imply a specialization in hunting; there are men who hunt mainly turkeys, coon, or beaver (stories number 14, 17, and 47). In contrast to the folklore of such settled horticulturists as the Hopi and Zuni, there are few references to specific localities: only some references to Lake Superior ("the ocean") and one mention of Leech Lake.

In this concluding chapter some interpretations will be made about three main topics: (1) the nature of the social organization suggested by the tales, (2) inferences about personality patterns, and (3) belief systems which seem to be implicit in the narratives. My analysis will proceed on the assumption that there is apt to be an internal consistency within a culture in subsistence basis, social organization, and personality tendencies, and that this patterning will be manifest in some way in the folklore.

Social Organization

I think that the tales in our collection support the notion that the Chippewa social order of the past was atomistic, as discussed in chapter 1. Judging from the wide distribution of so many of the tales, this body of folklore is old and conservative. It must be significant, therefore, that there is no mention of clans in any of the myths or tales. The main function of Chippewa clans seems to have been the regulation of marriage. It seems likely that if clans had been more corporate in nature, they would have figured in Chippewa myths and tales; but our collection shows that they did not. This may be contrasted with the folklore of societies in which we know clans had important social functions. Zuni mythology, for example, concerns the migrations of clans and groups rather than the wanderings of an individual like Wenebojo. Frank Waters' *The Book of the Hopi* contains the following chapter headings dealing with origin myths: Migrations of the Bird Clans, The Snake and Lizard Clans, the Bow and Arrowshaft Clans. Tsimshian mythology is also much concerned with tales of clan traditions (Boas, 1916, pp. 411-19).

There is only one story in our collection which involves a social organization larger than a few families, that of Wakayabide, with its reference to a camp circle and a crier who makes announcements. There are no stories about chiefs who assume superordinate political status.

The Flambeau origin myth has no communal life except in its beaver and wolf episodes. Many of the stories are about two or three people living alone: Wenebojo and his wolf nephew; Wenebojo and his grandmother; Wenebojo and his daughters; Wenebojo, Madjikiwis, and their wives; the brother and sister at the beginning of "Bebukowe the Hunchback"; Matchikwewis and Oshkikwe in "Star Husband"; Matchikwewis and Oshkikwe at the beginning of "Oshkikwe's Baby"; the brother-sister pair in "The Little Boy and the *Windigog*"; the brother-sister pair in "The Boy, His Sister, and the Giant"; the husband-wife pair in "The *Windigo's* Hunting Ground"; the fox with his grandmother and the chief's daughter; the boy and his grandmother and the king's daughter; the three brothers in "The Bad Old Man"; the man and his nephew in "The Spell of the Wicked Uncle"; and Jidwe?e and his grandmother. In these stories we find the following combinations: two man-and-nephew, four man-and-grandmother, one man-and-daughters, two husband-wife, three brother-sister, two sister-sister, one brother-brother.

At the beginning of story number 14, "Bebukowe the Hunchback," the young man asks his sister if they are the only people in the world. Similarly, in story number 19, "Oshkikwe's Baby," Oshkikwe says to Matchikwewis, "I guess we're not really alone in the world." One would not expect to find such remarks in the folklore of a densely populated community such as the Zuni, but we can find them in Eskimo folklore, where the social order is more atomistic. For example, in one Nunivak Eskimo tale two brothers are living alone and one says to the other, "Are we the only people in the world? Are there others somewhere?" (Lantis, 1946, pt. 3, p. 270).

Cheyenne Social Organization and Mythology: A Contrast

A contrast to Chippewa mythology in the sphere of social organization may be seen in the mythology of the Cheyenne of the Plains. Between 1840 and 1860 the Cheyenne spent their summers camped in a large circle with five or six hundred lodges and a population sometimes numbering between two or three thousand persons. In winter the ten bands which made up the camp circle broke up and moved to different hunting grounds. When the circle was re-formed in the spring at an appointed place, each band returned to its traditional place in the circle. The headmen of the bands were also tribal chiefs. Each band had four representatives in the Council of Forty-Four along with four general chiefs. In addition to the chief's council there were six military societies making up a kind of police force which kept order when people moved camp and controlled the hunting of buffalo, which had to be done collectively. Lone hunters, who might drive off the herd, were punished. Apart from the Dog Soldiers, who belonged to a single band, the military societies were made up of men from all the various bands in the camp circle and therefore could function only during the summer months, which was also true of the Council of Forty-Four.

Although the tribe came together as a group only during the summer, it was considered a more important unit than the band. Hoebel states that this is reflected in Cheyenne mythology: "almost all the Cheyenne emphasis in the building of mythological accounts of the origins of their institutions is focused on the tribal structure and not on the bands" (1960, p. 32). Hoebel gives a long myth which accounts for the origin of the Cheyenne Council of Forty-Four, for the formation of the camp circle, and for the custom of exiling a murderer from the tribe. The story ascribes a supernatural origin to the tribal council, making it the oldest and most important source of political authority. The military societies were created later and made subordinate to the council (ibid., pp. 39-44). Chippewa mythology has no themes like these, since the Chippewa had no comparable social organization.

Personality Patterns

It is for their potential relevance to personality patterns that attention was drawn to oral and anal themes in our Chippewa tales. To review the oral themes, there are many references to the mouth or to food in the Wenebojo stories, including themes of oral frustration, such as Wenebojo's inability to eat the moosemeat and the ducks which he has killed. There is also the tempting strawberry which has to be avoided and references to seemingly unpleasant food substances, such as roots, intestines, and vomited food. There are some episodes in which feces come around the mouth. Oral themes, both gratifying and frustrating, appear in "The Bungling Host." Wenebojo (also Jidwe?e) is swallowed by a big fish or whale. Wenebojo and others are fed from a self-replenishing kettle. Other oral references include: drinking fat or tallow, a snake chewing up an animal's insides, swallowing trout, diving for cranberries, a hot rod being pushed down a man's throat, a mother demanding to eat whitefish, cooking and eating a son-in-law, a pup biting an old witch's hindquarters, a pup nursing at the breast, a man tasting an old witch's breast milk, an old witch's children being decapitated and having sugar cookies stuck in their mouths, a boy falling into a muskie's mouth, a cat swallowing a mouse, a woman eating her dead husband's genitals, a woman demanding to eat heart and livers, losers of a lacrosse game being killed and eaten by the winners, and men fighting cannibal giants. The hero who kills the giant temporarily assumes a *windigo* shape, and after his victory he must drink quantities of hot tallow to come back to his former size.

The themes of oral frustration and the *windigo* stories may be related to the former scarcity of food in the Chippewa region. People were said to turn into *windigog* as the result of prolonged hunger. The theme of oral frustration may also be related to the fasting experience which children went through until puberty. If food is symbolic of love, the prevalence of oral themes might express unsatisfied dependency needs, the satisfaction of which is projected onto the guardian spirit, who says, "My grandchild, I come to pity you."[1] A difficulty in assessing the psychological significance of oral themes in our Chippewa tales, however, is that the same sort of emphasis appears in North American Indian folklore in general, both among hunting-gathering peoples and sedentary agriculturists. Oral themes are common, for example, in Tsimshian mythology, especially in tales concerning Raven's voracity (Boas, 1916, pp. 64-86, 245-50, 350-54). Nunivak Eskimo folklore has many themes of an oral sadistic nature involving biting and eating, concerning which Margaret Lantis remarks: "the people always have before themselves images of both men and women cutting and biting some part of the animal. The cannibal woman cutting off human heads and boiling them is not hard for a Nunivaker to imagine, even though he has never known a case of cannibalism" (1953, p. 135). The folklore of the Zuni of New Mexico also contains many oral themes, including six references to cannibalism.[2] The prevalence of such themes in other bodies of

1. Oral themes appear frequently in the Thematic Apperception Test stories of Wisconsin Chippewa children; there are "constant references to eating or hunger or the descriptive emphasis of oral areas" (Caudill, 1949, p. 421).

2. For oral themes, see Benedict (1935, 1:79, 81-82, 90, 119, 125, 133, 143, 146, 150-51, 162, 170, 188, 213, 220, 229, 238; 2:6, 25, 33, 78, 80, 96, 103, 104, 109, 113, 150, 151, 169, 181, 193, 200, 209, 211, 213, 235; see also 1:20, 24, 27, 39, 84, 219; 2:1, 9, 21, 26, 41, 86, 143, 198). On cannibalism, see ibid., 1:13, 52, 59, 77, 174; 2:196.

American Indian folklore somewhat reduces the possible psychological significance of this emphasis in Chippewa folklore.

Perhaps a mere count of the numbers of "oral themes," however, is not the best way to assess their significance. There is also the question of what kinds of oral themes are involved. For the Chippewa we have both oral-frustration stories and compensatory tales of oral gratification, such as the self-replenishing kettle, which suggests that oral frustration and hunger were seen as live dangers. Some of the oral themes seem to be warnings against greed, for under conditions of scarcity, greed is antisocial and must be proscribed. We must keep in mind, too, the Chippewa pattern of fasting for a vision in the period before puberty.

Anal Themes

There does seem to be more emphasis on the anal zone in the folklore of the Chippewa and their neighbors than in those of most other North American Indian tribes.[3] Anal themes are also noticeable in the folklore of some Plains tribes.[4] Farther west, in Oregon, Melville Jacobs was struck by the prevalence of anal motifs in Clackamas Chinook folklore and went so far as to write that "very likely all northwest states peoples had an intense anal preoccupation (1959, p. 238).[5] Many collections of North American Indian folklore, however, have few anal references. There are very few, for example, in the extensive collection of Boas' Tsimshian texts. The few such references consist of an episode concerning talking excrements and one about a girl slipping on some bear's dung (Boas, 1916, pp. 68, 278).

Anal themes are not prominent in Nunivak Eskimo tales. There are several references to people going outdoors to defecate, but this is only incidental to some action that takes place outdoors and merely provides an explanation for the person's going outside. There are no themes of anal penetration, being engulfed in dung, or the other anal motifs found in the Chippewa material.

In Zuni folklore, likewise, there is no emphasis on anal motifs, although Benedict's collection of Zuni tales is much larger than ours. One such episode is given in the story of "Tail by Tail." This is about some coyotes who wish to get to the top of Corn Mountain to take ad-

3. For the neighboring Menomini, see Skinner (1915b, pp. 258, 271, 293, 297, 303). For the Winnebago, see Radin (1956, pp. 16, 17, 18, 25, 26, 27).

4. Kroeber (1907, p. 71), Dorsey and Kroeber (1903, p. 60n), Wissler and Duvall (1908, pp. 26, 38–89), William Jones (1907, pp. 279–89), Skinner (1916b, p. 351). See also Skinner (1911, pp. 89–92, 114–15).

5. See the numerous entries under the heading "Anality" in the index to Jacobs's work.

vantage of generous giveaways of corn provided by the *Kana·kwe*. In order to reach the mountain top, the coyotes plug up their anuses with corn cobs. The accumulated wind makes it easy for them to ascend. They are just about to get to the top, when one of the coyotes pulls out his corn cob and breaks wind. The coyotes then all fall down and die (Benedict, 1935, 1:49). Another story, "The Ahaiyute Recover the Dung Beetles' Wife," is about two humanlike kachinas who are really dung beetles, who defecate, put a human girl into the dung, and roll her to their home (ibid., 2:100). The theme of talking excrement appears in Benedict's volume 1, p. 174. These are the only stories with an anal theme that I found in her collection, apart from the Twin War Gods' creation of anuses in the emergence myth. The emphasis on the anal zone is therefore much less in Zuni mythology, especially considering the greater number and length of Zuni tales.

Freudians find an explanation for the "anal character" in severe early toilet training, but one would not expect to find strict toilet training in a nomadic hunting-gathering society. In its first year a Chippewa baby spent most of its time in the cradleboard, surrounded by dried padded moss which absorbed its urine and feces. The moss was thrown away and replaced when necessary. Thus there would seem to be no pressure on the child to develop self-restraint. Nevertheless, one informant said that sphincter control was instituted while the child was still on the cradleboard. She added in explanation, "Women never had as much soap to wash with as they do now." Another reason for continence was that the baby generally slept between its parents at night.

Urethral control, as Harriet Sharlow told Ernestine Friedl at Court Oreilles, was started early. "If you start early enough, the boys will be trained with their water by six months." One girl at Court Oreilles was said to have learned urethral control by nine months. There was a practical reason for such training in northern Wisconsin, for the temperature may drop to as much as forty degrees below zero in winter time, and wet clothing freezes and causes much trouble. In winter time children would probably have been discouraged from leaving the wigwam to urinate or defecate. Considering the foregoing circumstances, there may have been rather early toilet training among the Chippewa.

Moreover, there seems to have been a concern about constipation in the old culture. This is suggested by the fact that one of the few things created or discovered by Wenebojo in the Flambeau origin myth is a laxative grass. It is also notable that these Indians in aboriginal times independently invented an enema syringe (see Hallowell, 1935; Heizer, 1939).

Franz Alexander and William Menninger claim that there is a relationship between constipation, depression, and delusions of persecution. "The frequent constipation of patients suffering from persecutory delusions is mainly conditioned by their conflicts about anal sadistic tendencies which they deny and project. Their frequent deprecatory attitude and delusions about their food is another manifestation of the projection of their anal sadistic impulses" (1936, pp. 553-54).[6] This may provide an insight into possible reasons for the recurrent anal and oral themes, but we cannot say how prevalent constipation and depression were in the Chippewa area. There do, however, seem to have been culturally fostered delusions of persecution in many cases. In a discussion about fears of sorcery, Hallowell has written: "the ground is well prepared in this society for the development of paranoid or pseudo-paranoid trends in individuals" (1940, p. 402n).[7]

On the other hand, perhaps we should not see the presence of anal motifs as something surprising or pathological. After all, an interest in feces is natural and understandable. Modern industrialized man is more separated from his feces than are hunting-gathering people. In modern flush toilets, feces are quickly spirited away and disappear, but a hunter who defecates on the earth is literally closer to his feces, and they have more permanence for him. The most prominent of human excretions, feces pose a problem for classification: are they part of the self or part of the outside world? To quote Edmund Leach on this issue: "The child's first and continuing problem is to determine the initial boundary. 'What am I, as against the world?' 'Where is the edge of me?' " (1964, p. 38). As Leach points out, ambiguous intermediate categories, including human exudations, are often the subject of taboo: feces, urine, semen, menstrual blood, hair and nail parings. It is understandable that feces arouse curiosity and form a potential subject for myth-making. But since feces do not appear universally in myths, the recurrence of anal themes in Chippewa folklore still poses something of a problem. Besides, it is not a question of feces alone but also of recurrent references to the anal zone, including themes of penetration of the rectum.

6. Arnold Buss has noted an "invariable association" between constipation and psychotic depression. Buss (1968, p. 182). See also National Institute of Mental Health (1969, p. 349).

7. See also Jenness (195, pp. 87–88) and Landes (1937c, pp. 55, 57).

Concerning delusions of persecution Fenichel writes: "It is interesting that among the organs projected onto the persecutor, feces and buttocks play a prominent role." He refers to Bibring's case of a woman who believed that she was persecuted by a man named "Behind." "She attributed to this man a number of characteristics which were in fact true of her own gluteal region" (1945, p. 429). This personification is reminiscent of the episode in the Flambeau origin myth in which Wenebojo talks to his "rear end" as if it were another person, and then punishes it for its lack of cooperation.

In Europe we find parallel problems in the writings of Jonathan Swift and Martin Luther, both of whom emphasized anal themes. Both literary critics (John Middleton Murry, Aldous Huxley) and psychoanalysts (Sandor Ferenczi, Benjamin Karpman, Phyllis Greenacre) have related the anal emphasis in Swift's writings to his unhappy childhood, his poor relations with women, and his eventual insanity. Norman O. Brown, who has critically reviewed these analytic efforts (1959, p. 184),[8] has also discussed Luther's "anal" conception of the Devil, who was associated with blackness, filth, and evil smells. The climax of the Witch's Sabbath was to kiss the Devil's behind. In his own confrontations with the Devil, Luther threatened to throw him into his anus where he belonged. Brown comments: "The Devil is virtually recognized as a displaced materialization of Luther's own anality, which is to be conquered by being replaced where it came from" (ibid., p. 209). For our purposes it is interesting that Brown relates the Devil to the Trickster of primitive mythologies (ibid., pp. 220, 301-2). Certainly, anality provides a common link between the Chippewa Wenebojo and Martin Luther's Devil. Whether both were the products of early toilet training in the New World and in Europe cannot be judged from present data.[9]

Courtship Themes

Our Chippewa collection is marked by a rarity of courtship themes. Those that occur are apt to be told by the women, as in the Matchikwewis and Oshkikwe stories given in chapter 4, where we find the *Star husband* episode, the girls' courtship of the coon and whitefish men, and the story about Bebukowe the Hunchback. The animal tales also contain some courtship themes — in "Wakayabide," "The Fox and the Chief's Daughter," and "Jidwe?e the Sandpiper" — and there are courtship episodes in "The Spell of the Wicked Uncle" and "The Beaver Man." The courtship motif often plays only a minor role in these tales; the emphasis is on other matters. A marked difference in these respects appears when comparisons are made with Benedict's collection of Zuni folklore. There is a much greater proportion of courtship themes in the Zuni tales. Benedict gives thirty tales of courtship in volume 1 of her *Zuni Mythology*, which make up nearly 180 pages. Courtship themes also occur in eleven other tales (1935, 1:19, 53; 2:48, 91, 121, 154, 164-65, 228). Thus there are 41 tales dealing with courtship in a total of

---

8. The references to Murry, Huxley, Ferenczi *et al.* are given in Brown's bibliography.

9. There is some speculation on the topic of toilet training in Luther's time and more discussion of Luther's "anality" in Erikson (1962, pp. 244–50).

104 stories. The initiative in courtship may come from either the boy or girl; both kinds of tales are given. The emphasis on courtship themes is probably related to the fact that Zuni society is both matrilineal and matrilocal and had permissive attitudes toward sex. Courtship also forms a relatively prominent theme in Nunivak Eskimo tales, occurring in nineteen out of sixty stories. Courtship forms a fairly prominent motif in Tsimshian tales, but these are mostly about a man or woman who married a supernatural-animal lover. Boas gives six examples of the former and ten of the latter (1916, pp. 747, 759). The girls in these stories are sometimes described as "beautiful" (e.g., pp. 155, 166, 263, 273), a pattern not found in our Chippewa tales.

Implicit Ideals

Certain ideals of character and conduct are implicit in the tales, especially in those which seem to have cautionary elements. Respect for elders is stressed in stories 15, 17, and 45. At the same time, independence is valued. Wenebojo is happiest when he is all alone. The stories in chapter 7 express fear of being under the domination of others. There are themes about rapid growth from infancy in story number 1 (Wenebojo), number 19 ("Oshkikwe's Baby"), number 23 ("The Baby *Windigo*"), and number 48; but there are also themes of regression to an earlier state, as in the hero's return to the cradleboard in number 19 and perhaps in the symbolism of being swallowed by a big fish (numbers 6, 7, 24, 40).

Ideally, a man should be independent and a good hunter, like the turkey hunter in story number 14, the whitefish man in number 17, the gluttonous *windigo*-killer in number 21, Wagos in number 35, the young man in number 44, the beaver man in number 47, and the boy in number 48. Allied with hunting ability is the virtue of generosity, the sharing of meat with others, as is done by the turkey hunter and the beaver man.

The successful hunter, however, runs the risk of incurring the enmity of others, as in the case of Wenebojo's nephew and the gluttonous hunter in number 21.

The ideal man is not greedy, as the oral-frustration episodes in the Wenebojo series suggest. Nor is he readily provoked to anger or revenge, as number 45 indicates. He may be expected to take revenge eventually, however, as the latter story also makes clear. There are also other tales of revenge; for example, Wenebojo revenges himself on the two kings, and the beaver man punishes his wife. Sexual restraint is also implied as an ideal pattern, judging from the rarity of themes of courtship and references to sex.

Women are expected to be submissive, quiet, and obedient and not to ask foolish questions, as the stories about Oshkikwe and Matchikwewis make clear. They should not be greedy or demand too much of their husbands, as Wakayabide's wife did. They should tell the truth, as the wife of the beaver man failed to do; and they should not become too interested in sex, as story number 15 suggests.

Some Hypotheses Concerning Personality Patterns

Assuming that there is likely to be some relationship between the stories told by a group of people and the basic or modal personality type of that group, the following speculations are offered. There may be some connection between the rarity of courtship themes in Chippewa folklore and the abundance of oral and anal themes, which, from a Freudian point of view, would indicate a tendency toward regression in the old culture. The main reason for such a pattern, I suggest, is that aboriginal life instilled fearful attitudes toward the world. This fearfulness is implicit in the stories in chapter 7 about spells and magical powers and in such stories as "Wakayabide" and "The Village of Animals."

I think that cautious, ambivalent attitudes were developed in childhood in former times. Children were disciplined by scaring techniques, being warned about *windigog* and about giant owls which might carry them off. A menstruating girl was to be avoided, since her touch might kill or paralyze a child. The same was true of a person in mourning. Thus an older sister, who might play a rather maternal role at other times, became dangerous during her menstrual periods, and a friendly old uncle had to be avoided if his wife died. The dangers they caused were not intentional but stemmed from power which they could not control. Since human relations were generally uncertain, this applied to male-female relations and to courtship as well, leading to inhibitions in that sphere. Repression was probably a common psychological defense among the Chippewa — repression of both sexual and aggressive impulses.[10] This could partially account for the emphasis on oral and anal themes in Chippewa folklore.

In the section on social organization it was noted that the family units

10. In Chippewa folklore, water may be symbolic of the unconscious, and the underwater creatures may represent repressed impulses. When Wenebojo killed the underwater kings, this act of aggression led to a rising of the waters, which could be interpreted as a flooding of anxiety, the threat of being overwhelmed by the unconscious. Water is also said to rise when a giant horned snake is summoned by a sorcerer. I do not mean to suggest that such water symbolism is universal. Water must have a different and more positive symbolic significance in an agricultural society which depends upon irrigation, as among the Zuni or in ancient Egypt and Mesopotamia.

mentioned in the tales are small and often isolated. It is in keeping with this to find both incest themes and Oedipal themes. There is one tale of brother-sister incest (Wenebojo's grandparents), one father-daughter (after Wenebojo's feigned death), and one sister-sister (Matchikwewis and Oshkikwe). For a male, the Oedipus complex has two components: (1) mother fixation, and (2) hostility toward the father. Stories suggestive of mother-fixation include "Oshkikwe's Baby" (number 19) and "The Boy, His Grandmother, and the King's Daughter" (number 48). Stories about conflict between a son and a possible father-figure include "Wenebojo in the Whale and His Fight with an Ogre" (number 7), "The Bad Old Man" (number 44), and "The Spell of the Wicked Uncle" (number 45). To these may be added the *windigo* stories in which a boy or young man fights with a cannibal giant.

The ideal type for males suggested in the previous section set rather high standards of independence, self-control, and generosity. In the face of pressures to achieve such goals, it seems likely that there were undercurrent desires to be passive, uncontrolled, and selfish. Perhaps that was why Wenebojo's "foolishness" was regarded with sympathy. One could appreciate the trickster's self-centeredness and greed. Wenebojo was looked after by the wolves, who vomited up their food for him as for a wolf cub; his "nephew" hunted for him; and he played a passive, dependent role which was normally tabooed to adult males but perhaps secretly envied.

To conclude, a hypothetical personality picture of the Chippewa of former times suggests that there was a rather fearful, depressed attitude toward the world, involving some repression of sexual and aggressive impulses. There is some support for this in the characteristic patterns of Chippewa Rorschach responses collected in the 1940s. A characteristic feature of Chippewa Rorschach responses is avoidance of color. Out of a total number of 107 Rorschach records taken at Court Oreilles and Lac du Flambeau by Ernestine Friedl, Robert Ritzenthaler, and myself in the early 1940s, 53 records were without any color responses at all. Only nine persons gave more than two color responses. Dr. Bruno Klopfer, who commented on the Chippewa Rorschachs, concluded that this rarity of color responses implies that the individual is under pressure to become as emotionally independent of his environment as possible and to expect very little from others.[11]

11. Colors are not mentioned often in Chippewa tales, in contrast to those of the Hopi, Zuni, and Navaho, where different colors are related to the different directions and world layers. On the other hand, Wisconsin Chippewa were using gay face paints, reds and yellows, in the 1850s. See Kohl (1860, p. 16).

Chippewa Rorschach records are relatively high on human movement responses, averaging about three or four per record. This, combined with the low color percentage, suggests an introverted tendency, with fantasy and imagination playing an important role. Although the Nunivak Eskimo social order was also rather atomistic, the Nunivak seem to have been less repressed and less introverted. Commenting on the Rorschachs, Alice Joseph remarked: "Extroverts: probably ninety percent of the subjects," and she suggested that the Nunivakers were probably preoccupied with sex but without having a sense of conflict or guilt about it (Lantis, 1953, p. 143). Chippewa Rorschach analyses, on the other hand, emphasize their introverted tendency and their avoidance of color, which suggests a shying away from close emotional relationships with others.

Belief Systems Implicit in the Tales

Themes of Metamorphosis

A key concept, as we have seen, is the notion that visible forms are deceptive and that human and animal forms are interchangeable. A spirit may appear in either human or animal form, as in the guardian spirit vision and in stories about men with animal wives. Animals were believed to live in wigwams in villages under the earth or beneath a lake.

In the origin myth collected at Lac du Flambeau, Wenebojo assumes many different forms — a beaver, a snake, a tree stump, and an old lady. In other tales Wenebojo takes on the shape of a porcupine in the episode with Matchikwewis and Oshkikwe and the appearance of a dead caribou in the episode with the turkey buzzard. He also appears as a rabbit in the tale about the theft of fire.

A bad old man takes the form of a bear. In "The Village of Animals" and "Wakayabide" the people of a village can transform themselves into animals. Because of over-fasting a young man turns into a robin. In "The Spell of the Wicked Uncle" a man is transformed into a tree and his brother temporarily assumes the shape of a squirrel.

Apart from human-animal transformations, another change in visible form that appears in Chippewa folklore is the growth in size of a man who becomes a *windigo* and his reduction to normal size after swallowing hot tallow. One story suggests that even a small baby in a cradleboard can turn into a giant. Wakayabide's wolf-dog can make himself large or small at will. In two stories in chapter 7 a hero makes himself small enough to crawl into an oak ball, and a girl makes herself small enough to hide under a wooden bowl.

The interchangeability of human and animal forms was not just a literary convention, as in Aesop's fables or in much of African folklore; people believed these things. Tom Badger, who told me the story about the old man who was killed while in the form of a bear digging up a grave, concluded; "That's a true story told to me by my father-in-law at Lake Vieux Desert." Similarly, Prosper Guibord believed that when he shot the owl that had bothered his wife, the old man who subsequently died had been that owl. People at Court Oreilles believed that Mary Careful was able to make herself invisible and to appear in the form of a deer and a wolf. Julia Badger told of seeing a man turn into a snake.

Perhaps because of their human-like appearance, bears were particularly associated with human-animal transformations. I do not know whether or not Wisconsin Chippewa speech had the same pattern, but according to R. W. Dunning the terminology of the Canadian Ojibwa associated bears with menstruating girls. "Approaching the time of a girl's first period, she is known as *wemukowe* — literally, 'going to be a bear' — and during her seclusion she is known as *mukowe* — 'she is a bear.' " Contributing to this identification was a curious equation between hunting and courting. The same Chippewa term was used for both flirting and hunting game, while another Chippewa term "connotes both using force in intercourse and also killing a bear with one's bare hands" (Dunning, 1959, pp. 100, 129n, 101n). The symbolic relationship between hunting and sexual intercourse in a South American Indian hunting tribe is explored at length in Gerardo Reichel-Dolmatoff (1971). According to Reichel-Dolmatoff, the Desana Indians experience a good deal of sexual repression, partly because a hunter is expected to refrain from sexual relations before hunting, lest the animals whom he is "courting" become jealous and refuse to draw near. It would be interesting, and perhaps not too late, to inquire to what extent such concepts are or were present in North American hunting cultures. The stories about hunters with animal wives would fit into such a belief-system.

A. Irving Hallowell made the theme of metamorphosis the central focus of an article on the Ojibwa world view, relating it to other aspects of Ojibwa belief and culture (1960). I subscribe to Hallowell's insightful treatment of this subject, but I would like to point out that the cognitive approach he discusses is not limited to the Chippewa. Themes of metamorphosis are found in most collections of American Indian folklore. There are at least twenty such tales, for example, in Franz Boas' *Tsimshian Mythology* (1916, pp. 75, 83, 249, 747, 759). Although the Zuni did not have the vision quest shared by most North American Indians, they had the same ideas about the arbitrary nature of outward appearance and the ability of spirits to assume either human or animal form. Thus, kachinas become deer when killed. A man takes the shape of a coyote or an owl. A butterfly man has intercourse with eight girls, who are transformed into butterflies. A girl is transformed into a dove by a witch (Benedict, 1935, 1:72, 77, 199, 235-36; 2:19-20, 110-12, 157). In the Zuni tales, animals sometimes take off their coats or shirts and become humans. "The first eagle lay down his deer and took off his shirt and hung it on the wall, and he stood up a man" (ibid., 1:132, 173). Similar accounts are given of Lizard and Badger people (ibid., 2:44, 247). A girl has a turtle husband; a man has a parrot wife (ibid., 2:154; 1:185-89). Beliefs of this kind were generally characteristic of the Indians of North and South America and much of the Old World as well.

Lucien Lévy-Bruhl encountered opposition when he argued that "primitive" peoples though "prelogically" in ways different from modern Western man's. Those who criticized Lévy-Bruhl did so in the belief that his views implied or gave support to racist attitudes of superiority on the part of "civilized" Westerners. But Lévy-Bruhl did not deny rationality to "primitive" peoples; he mainly claimed that their basic assumptions and categories of thought were different from those of modern science. Themes of metamorphosis formed part of his argument. Lévy-Bruhl cited American Indian beliefs in the interchangeability of human and animal forms, mentioning the Jivaro of Ecuador, the Caribs of British Guiana, and the Central Eskimo, but also the Arunta and other tribes of Central Australia, the Trobriand Islanders, Malays, Sarawak, Nagas, the Ba-Ila of northern Rhodesia, and tribes of northern Nigeria (1966, pp. 36-55, 158-84).

Educated persons who read such accounts find it puzzling that people could believe something which seems to be counter to experience. After all, people do not normally turn into birds, animals, or trees. The point, though, is that persons may subjectively experience such transformations under certain conditions, such as fasting or the use of drugs. Hallowell gives an example of an Ojibwa boy who fasted for a vision and saw his guardian spirit as a golden eagle. "Glancing down at his own body as he sat there on a rock, the boy noticed it was covered with feathers. The 'eagle' spread its wings and flew off to the south. The boy then spread his wings and followed" (1960, p. 42).

For the boy this was a real experience. Hallowell remarks that when Westerners think autobiographically they include events that occurred while they were awake, but an Ojibwa remembers things that happened in dreams. In fact, dream experiences are all the more important for an Ojibwa, because that is when supernatural beings are encountered (1960, p. 40).

It is now becoming easier for us to take such considerations into account, since recent literature about hallucinogenic drugs has shown how metamorphoses may be experienced under the effects of LSD or other drugs. R. E. L. Masters and Jean Houston describe the experiences of an anthropologist who had taken LSD; he thought of himself as a tiger and saw himself as a tiger in the mirror. In another case a man identified himself with a tiger and later with a lion (1966, pp. 76-78, 293). After taking yage, one man felt himself being transformed into various animal forms: frog, sea lion, and snake; another man who took LSD saw his friend's face turn into that of a wolf (Aaronson and Osmond, 1970, pp. 52-55, 59-61).

Here is one subject's description of experiences under the influence of yage in an experimental setting: "I wasn't a fish anymore, but a big cat, a tiger. I walked, though, feeling the same freedom I had experienced as a bird and a fish, freedom of movement, flexibility, grace. I moved as a tiger in the jungle, joyously, feeling the ground under my feet, feeling my power; my chest grew larger. I then approached an animal, any animal. I only saw its neck, and then experienced what a tiger feels when looking at its prey" (Naranjo, 1973, p. 185).

Yage produces hallucinations of jaguars and snakes and human-animal transformations in South American Indians, including candidates for shamanism. Harner has suggested that the alleged European cases of lycanthropy are explainable in terms of hallucinogenic drugs being used by the men who believed that they turned into wolves (Harner, 1973, pp. 155-75, 140-45).

Weston La Barre has argued that the American Indian religions in general were based on shamanism and, since Upper Paleolithic-Mesolithic times, were related to the use of hallucinogenic drugs. He points out that New World natives knew between eighty and one hundred psychotropic drugs, while the Old World knew the properties of only about half a dozen, in spite of the fact that the Old World has a greater land mass, with great varieties of climate, and could well support a great proportion of psychotropic plants. Moreover, men had lived much longer in the Old World than in the New. La Barre's explanation for this discrepancy between the two hemispheres is that in the Old World, religion was modified by the Neolithic revolution and by the development of priesthoods, while in the New World the hunting base of shamanism was better preserved, even in the advanced civilizations of Mesoamerica and Peru (1972).[12]

It may be objected that not all American Indian cultures are known to have used hallucinogenic drugs. We have no evidence that such was a

12. See also La Barre's review of R. Gordon Wasson (1970).

custom, for example, among the Chippewa Indians, although in Appendix A I cite a possible case of a shaman's use of the hallucinogenic mushroom, *Amanita muscaria*. But La Barre's thesis makes it easier to understand the widespread belief in human-animal transformations, which could be promoted by other means as well, such as the fasting experience, which was undergone by most of the tribes in North America.

Instead of discussing Indian tribes in general in this connection, let us focus once again on the Chippewa Indians, the subjects of our study. Shamanism based on the guardian spirit quest was the heart of Chippewa religion. Perhaps one can say that the old shaman was the cynosure of Chippewa society (La Barre, 1946). "The mighty shamans are 'old' and always termed so in deepest respect and fear" (Landes, 1968, p. 37).

In aboriginal times shamans were not necessarily a small minority. When Hallowell did field work in the Berens River region in Canada, 10 percent of the adult males were known to have practiced conjuring, or tent-shaking. Hallowell estimated that under aboriginal conditions there would have been at least twice as many conjurers. There must have been at least one conjurer in every winter hunting group, for it was during winter that life was most hazardous and supernatural help most needed (1942, pp. 27-28).

In order to become a shaman one had to have the characteristic dream or vision, but all boys fasted for visions, whether they became medicine men or not. Hence there was a general encouragement to respond to inner psychological stimuli and projections of the unconscious. It may seem paradoxical that such an emphasis should exist in a hunting society in which men needed to pay realistic attention to their environment if they were to survive. But the frustrations of life also demanded some kind of supernatural resolution which a shaman could provide, and he had to cultivate his tendency to projection, if he were to function effectively in that role. While men were hunting, they had to be alert, focusing on the visible outer world, but at other times they could turn their attention fully to the inner world.

Under such circumstances, there may be experiences of metamorphosis. If educated Westerners, under the influence of LSD, have sensations of assuming animal form or of seeing others take on the appearance of animals, it would seem all the more likely that this would happen in a hunting society. In such a society, then, belief in human-animal transformations is not at all counter to experience but may actually be based upon memorate experience — if not upon one's own personal experience, then on the authority of a shaman. Chippewa shamans recited their fasting dreams or visions before embarking on a sucking cure or a conjuring lodge performance. These were apt to be emotionally charged times of crisis, and the shaman's story was probably listened to with rapt attention. For young children it may have provided a model for their own later fasting experience; it let them know what to expect.

Reversibility of Life and Death

Related to the interchangeability of human and animal form is the reversibility of life and death. Several of the stories in our collection are about bringing the dead back to life: "Bebukowe the Hunchback," "The Two Brothers and Oshkikwe," and "The Fox and the Chief's Daughter." The bear people in the story of "Wakayabide" kill one another, but everyone comes back to life. If one saves and assembles the dead person's bones, such a revival can be effected. The notion of return to life is implicit in the Midewiwin ceremony, in which members shoot one another with their medicine hides but come back to life again.

It is this belief which makes it possible for hunters to kill animals without guilt. Death is seen as only a temporary interruption. Animals do not mind being killed and eaten, provided that they are not treated with disrespect. Hence the conciliatory speeches made by successful bear hunters to the dead bear.

Like human-animal transformations, themes of restoration to life are not limited to the Chippewa Indians but were common in North American folktales and belief.[13] Memorate reinforcement of such notions came from the reports of people like Julia Badger who claimed to have traveled along the road to the other world. The experience of trance states, whether triggered or not by hallucinogenic drugs, can easily give persons the conviction of having died and come back to life. Readiness to enter into trance states constitutes a kind of death, and persons undergoing psychotic episodes may believe that they have died. To cite one example, Morag Coate, in a retrospective account of her psychosis, wrote that one night she was killed by two of the female nurses in the hospital to which she had been committed. "I came to life again next morning, but my confidence was gone. To die once and to come alive again by special arrangement was tolerable, but to run the risk of being killed over and over again was most disturbing" (1965, p. 104).

The acquisition of shamanistic power in some circumpolar hunting societies involved a kind of death and rebirth. A Tungus shaman described the visionary experiences of his novitiate as follows: "My ancestors appeared to me and began to shamanize. They stood me up

13. See, for example, Boas (1916, pp. 58, 214, 322–30), and Benedict (1935, 1:291, 317; 2:157, 292, 294).

like a block of wood and shot at me with their bows until I lost consciousness. They cut up my flesh, they separated my bones and counted them, and they ate my flesh raw."[14] This shaman said that only after such an experience could a man begin to shamanize.

A candidate for shamanism among the East Greenland Eskimo was believed to be swallowed up by a bear which came out of a lake beside which the candidate was sitting. The bear would spit him out again (Thalbitzer, 1931). Fasting, trance, and shamanism seem to provide a setting in which ideas about the reversibility of life and death may develop.

A body of folklore cannot be expected to present an altogether consistent world view, and there are some inconsistencies in the beliefs about death expressed in these tales. After all, Wenebojo's brother made a road to the other world which all must follow. If creatures can return to life, why was Wenebojo so upset by the death of his wolf nephew? Nothing is said about the revival of the latter or of the two kings whom Wenebojo killed.

Hierarchy of Power

A third concept of importance is the hierarchy of power. Some people such as medicine men and good hunters have more supernatural power than others, their powers being derived from their guardian spirits. In some tales (14, 32, 44, 45) a bad old man has power over people who are under his spell. The relativity of power is illustrated in the story of Wakayabide, when the hero bests his rivals, one of whom exclaims, "Ha ha ha! I've found a man who's better than I am. He's a *manido*. I won't bother him any more."

Not everyone can be a medicine man, but only those who have had the appropriate dream or vision. Not everyone can kill a grizzly bear or a *windigo*. In "The Man and the Grizzly Bear" a pipe is passed around to find out who has the power to kill the bear, and only one man takes it. Similarly, in "The Boy Who Defeated a *Windigo*" a pipe is passed about. The only one who can light the pipe without using a match is the young boy who goes out to fight the *windigo*.[15]

14. Quoted from a Russian work by G. V. Kenofontov in Joseph Campbell (1969, p. 171).

15. There are some other parallels in stories about grizzly bears and *windigog*, suggesting that these large creatures are functionally equivalent. As mentioned in chapter 2, William Jones gives a story about how Wenebojo kills a *windigo* by telling a weasel to run up into its anus, while in de Jong's collection there is a tale in which Wenebojo gets a weasel to run up into the anus of a bear. In another sense the two creatures are antithetical; the *windigo* is made of ice, while bears are rich in fat which is fed to *windigog* to melt their ice and reduce them to normal size.

The stories about the young boy and the little girl who kill *windigog* show, again, that appearances are deceptive and that one cannot tell who has power or how much. While it may be assumed that shamans and good hunters have much power, one cannot be sure how powerful other persons may be. A meek and humble individual may have great supernatural resources. That is why one should never be arrogant or laugh at anyone. In the story of Wakayabide, Madjikwis is warned by the old men, "Here, here, young man; don't talk that way. That's a *manido*. If you talk like that, he'll come and kill us some day."

If one man was known to have much power, feelings of inferiority and resentment might develop in others. Such attitudes are expressed in several of the stories in our collection. The underwater *manidog* kill Wenebojo's nephew because they are jealous of his success in hunting. For the same reason a hunter in story number 21 turns into a *windigo* to kill his more successful neighbor. Gabibonike in story number 39 becomes jealous of the hell-diver's success at fishing and closes up the hole in the ice to trap and kill him.

Expressions of similar attitudes have appeared in other sources. For example, Tanner wrote in his *Narrative:* "As I began to be considered a good hunter, Waw-be-be-nais-a became envious of my success, and often, when I was absent, he went slily into my lodge, and bent my gun, or borrowed it under pretence of his own being out of repair, and returned it to me bent, or otherwise injured" (1830, p. 94).

One man at Court Oreilles was reportedly "doped" or sorcerized by another man who was jealous of him for being such a good carpenter.

Any kind of success could attract the jealousy and hostility of others. Ruth Landes refers to two individuals who were outstandingly good at games and were consequently beaten up and wounded by jealous rivals (1937a, pp. 115-16). Fear of competition was felt by the women as well. One of Landes' female informants said that she alone in the village had no friends, because she was hated by all the women on account of her skill in beadwork and tanning (1939, p. 19). Landes remarks elsewhere, however, that women were not so sensitive about their self-esteem as men (1937a, pp. 114-15).

Supernatural power could be used for either good or evil; so ambivalent attitudes were felt toward persons with power. A shaman cures people, but he may also kill others through sorcery. An animal which is normally feared may act as a benevolent guardian spirit. Owls are associated with death and with sorcery, since evil old men may take the shape of owls, but in the story of "The Village of Animals" a guardian owl wraps its wings about the hero to keep him warm on a winter night. Wolves are dangerous animals, but a guardian wolf helps Wakayabide.

Bebukowe is an evil old sorcerer, but he appears in a friendly guise in the fantasies of Tom and Julia Badger. In his role of guardian spirit, a being may be protective toward his "grandchild" while remaining dangerous and hostile toward others.

In general, the folktales picture a dangerous world. Among the perils that threaten are starvation, sorcery and magical domination by others, and attacks by enemies, cannibal giants, and creatures like Bebukowe.

Ambiguities in the Analysis of Folklore

Opinions differ about the degree to which folklore reflects the beliefs and practices of a society. Clara Ehrlich so strongly believed that Crow folklore accurately reflected Crow Indian culture that she claimed: "If we were to lose the ethnological studies made of the Crow Indians and retain solely the folklore, we could still reconstruct with surprising accuracy the culture of the tribe" (1937, p. 396).

On the other hand, Ruth Benedict pointed out various ways in which Zuni mythology was at odds with Zuni culture. For example, polygamy occurs in Zuni tales, but the Zuni are thoroughly monogamous, in contrast to most other North American Indian tribes which allowed polygamous marriages. Benedict rejected the explanation that this was a folklore survival of earlier customs and expressed the view that such tales are compensatory daydreams of power (1935, 1:xvi). Another example of lack of fit between folklore and actual life is that sheepherding is an important activity in Zuni life today but is not mentioned in Zuni tales. Similarly, W. H. R. Rivers pointed out that pigs play a prominent part in Melanesian culture but do not figure in Melanesian mythology (1968, pp. 33-34).

Some of the stories we collected from Wisconsin Chippewa narrators tell about kings and queens. We do not conclude that the Chippewa once had kings and queens, since we know that these tales are of European origin. But this shows the difficulty of making inferences from a body of folklore about past forms of social organization, for folktales diffuse between societies with different cultures.

Lévi-Strauss not only made the point that folklore and culture often do not jibe but went further to say: "the institutions described in the myths can be the very opposite of the real institutions" (1967, p. 29).

If that is so, could one possibly draw any conclusions about former aspects of social organization from a body of folklore? Clans, tribal councils, and military societies are not mentioned in Wisconsin Chippewa myths and tales, but it could be argued that they were prominent but simply not mentioned in the folklore. Harold Hickerson, who has argued that clans were important institutions among the Chippewa of precontact times, has also made the claim that in the early nineteenth century the southwestern Chippewa, including those of Wisconsin, had military societies like those of the Plains (1962, pp. 52-64). I think that his evidence for this is slight, but together with the presence of village life, it leads him to assert that "the southwestern Chippewa in these facets of organization much more closely resembled the Indians of the Plains and Prairies than they did their northern congeners" (ibid., p. 63). If this view is correct, there would be an evident lack of fit between Wisconsin Chippewa institutions and their folklore, which would provide an apt illustration of Lévi-Strauss' viewpoint cited above.

My own view is that in societies where we know that clans play important corporate roles, as among the Hopi and Zuni, clans are mentioned in the mythology, including origin myths. We also know that tribal council, camp circle, and military societies were crucial institutions for the Cheyenne, and we do find them represented in their tales, including the origin myth given by Hoebel. It is granted that clans existed and that warfare took place, but Wisconsin Chippewa myths and tales provide no evidence that clans, tribal councils, or military societies of the Cheyenne type played significant roles in former times. As I see it, the folklore in our collection *does* reflect the past culture and social organization of the Wisconsin Chippewa.

Appendixes
Bibliography
Indexes

APPENDIX A

Possible Use of *Amanita muscaria* by a Chippewa Shaman

The use of hallucinogenic drugs by Chippewa medicine men has never been specifically reported, but there is a tantalizing indication of the possible use of *Amanita muscaria*, a hallucinogenic mushroom, in an educated Chippewa woman's account of native uses of fungi, an interesting study of ethnobotany. The Chippewa term for *Amanita muscaria* is *oshtimisk wajashauki*. Children were strongly warned to avoid this plant: "every Ahnishaba child was taught 'don't touch' to four things: flaming fire, animals with running sores, Grandfather Rattler, and the Oshtimisk (Red Top) Wajashauki." The author writes that the woman who was her sponsor in the Midewiwin and her teacher in herbal matters seemed to wage a personal war against the *oshtimisk*. "If the plants were immature or red, she smashed them. If they were old and dried, she gathered them and later burned them in a small stone slab oven. 'These are the worst of all,' she said" (Peschel, unpub. ms.).

She told this story: A wicked sorcerer, a tent shaker, had many wives, sometimes as many as seven at a time. He made a decoction from the *oshtimisk*. "Whatever was in it, it made them leave everything and anyone else and want to be with him. They said they saw colored lights and heard beautiful music and had at last found true happiness."

A young girl told her that she was in love with the chief's son and wanted some love magic to attract him. The woman refused, so the girl went to the shaman, who "gave her to drink of the Oshtimiskwabo and took her in his arms, and behold, he was more handsome than the chief's son . . . . Handsome! that rat had yellow teeth, a twisted body, and the eyes of a snake."

259

Biographical Sketches of Five Wisconsin Chippewa Informants

John Mink

A sketch of John Mink is given by Joseph B. Casagrande, from whose account the following information about him is drawn. John Mink, who lived to be ninety or more years old, was described by Casagrande as follows: "His large, almost massive head with its mat of unkempt grey hair dwarfed his stocky body and enfeebled legs which he supported with a walking-stick that now lay propped against the cot on which he sat" (1960, p. 469).

John Mink said that he was born near Rice Lake and remembered being tied up on a cradleboard and watching the charms that hung in front of it. He also claimed to remember the taste of his mother's milk, which was rich like bear fat, and he remembered crying for the breast. John stopped suckling when he was able to eat wild rice, venison, and blueberries. His mother's father became his godfather and gave him his name Shoniagizhik (Sky Money). His first toys were a little toboggan and a bow and arrow with which he killed squirrels and chipmunks. After he killed a partridge, his parents gave him a feast for the first kill. Another such feast was given later when John killed his first deer. He often fasted for a vision. "The spirits came to me in my dreams as I fasted and gave me the power to kill game and to cure people. They taught me songs and charms and how to suck the disease from sick people and make medicines" (Casagrande, 1960, p. 470).

John met his first wife at La Pointe, where the government made payments to the Indians. They first lived with her parents and later made their own wigwam. After five years she died in childbirth. John kept a mourning dish and prepared a mourning bundle for her which he gave to her parents at the end of a year. They combed his hair, painted his face, and gave a feast which marked the end of the mourning period. Two years later John married again and lived with his second wife for ten years. He had four wives in all, and many children, but all his children died early in life.

John Mink was a sucking doctor. He also acquired the power to call spirits into the conjuring lodge but never did so, for fear of possible bad consequences. He was also a Mide priest and leader of a Drum Dance group. John Mink was widely feared as a sorcerer,. One woman at Court Oreilles said of him: "Everybody's afraid of old Sonia now. You have to talk good to him when you see him any place. He's our terror around here. Working bad medicine is what keeps them up. That's why he's still alive. . . . The more they're paid (for sorcerizing people), the more they do, as long as they get their pay."

John Mink's bad reputation reached to Lac du Flambeau. Speaking after his death, Tom Badger said of John Mink: "He lived in Reserve, but he could be here (in Flambeau) at the same time. It wouldn't take him long. That's why people burned his house down three times — to get at his medicine."

Prosper Guibord

Prosper Guibord, aged sixty-seven in 1942, was the man who served as interpreter with John Mink for Joseph Casagrande and Robert Ritzenthaler, but he also narrated some of the tales in our collection: "The Bad Old Man," "The Magic Horse," and "The Magic Ox." The following information about him comes from field notes made by Robert Ritzenthaler in 1942.

Prosper Guibord was born in Barron County about seven miles east of Rice Lake. His father was a Frenchman who had come down from Canada for logging and married an Indian girl. She died in childbirth. Later he married another Indian girl, aged thirteen. Prosper was their fourth child. His mother could talk only Chippewa but understood French. Prosper was bilingual from an early age and was raised as a Catholic. The Guibord family lived in a cabin of hewn white oak logs until he was twelve. Then his father built a frame house, became a farmer, and raised wheat, oats, barley, corn, and timothy hay. Prosper went to school at the Catholic convent but did not get beyond the second reader, since he always had to help his father on the farm. Beginning to feel that he was being overworked, he left home and got a job cutting hay for lumber camp horses. Later he worked with teams of oxen, hauling logs.

Prosper courted a girl named Anna. They lay in bed all night with their clothes on, talking. "That is the way the old Indians courted," he

said. They were married when he was eighteen. Prosper continued to
work in lumber camps for forty-five years after his marriage and guided
fishing parties during the summer. He also went hunting and fishing in
fall and winter.

Prosper's wife, who could talk only Chippewa, gave birth to several
children. It happened that his wife and three of their children died
within a period of eight months. "For five years after I lost my wife, I
would sit in the evening without a light and think of her. I dreamed of
her every night. She would come and sleep with me in my dream, and
she appeared to be fleshy and healthy. After five years I started to go
with other women again, and she didn't come to see me any more."

The sickness and deaths in his family put him in debt up to $1400, but
Prosper finally paid it off. Then in 1923 he married a widow, who died
in 1929. For two years after that he lived with another widow. She
wanted to marry him in the Catholic church, but her father, a conservative Indian, wouldn't let her. So Prosper finally left her. Soon after
that he fell sick with a stiff arm, which John Mink diagnosed as being
due to sorcery from the widow's father. John Mink advised him to bathe
daily in water with cedar bough medicine and to take daily sweat baths,
heating rocks and throwing medicine on it. Prosper was tattooed on the
arm by a woman who also applied poultices, and his arm recovered. At
the time of field work in 1942 Prosper was living on a pension of $18 a
month, which he started to get at the age of sixty-five.

Delia Oshogay

Delia Oshogay was Ernestine Friedl's principal story-teller, the narrator of many tales in our collection. The following information comes
from Ernestine Friedl's notes, made in 1942.

Delia was born in 1864 at Jim Falls, Wisconsin. As in Prosper Guibord's
case, her father was a Frenchman working in a logging camp. Her
mother was a half-breed Chippewa girl from the Court Oreilles reservation. Delia's father started a farm, and they had cows, pigs, turkeys, and
geese; but after her father died, they lost all the land and property, which
was inherited by her father's brother.

Delia never went out to fast, for her people were Catholics. She never
lived in a wigwam either, until after she got married to an Indian.
Presumably, her large stock of Chippewa stories was acquired after that.

Tom Badger

The following account is culled from my article, "Reminiscences of a Chippewa Mide Priest" (1954), in which there is a good deal more detail.

In 1944 Tom Badger was a quiet level-headed man in his seventies, with a good sense of humor. He spoke a little English, but not quite enough for good communication, so most of the time we had an interpreter, principally Tom's wife Julia. Tom could not read and write and had never been to school. In telling me his life story, he began with the prenatal episode described in chapter 9. After that he continued as follows:

"There were seven in our family: three boys, four girls. I was the youngest. They were all a year or two apart; but I don't know exactly how many years. While we were at Sugar Camp Lake my father's mother and one of my sisters died. Then we left that place and moved about a thousand feet away, because of those two deaths.

"We used to travel a lot because my father had to keep on the move, looking for game. We used to travel from place to place by birchbark canoe. We had two canoes. Not everybody could get in, so some would walk along the shore. My brothers were old enough to carry the canoe on the portages. My mother and father carried the other canoe. I was just old enough to walk. I couldn't help carry.

"One time, when I was three or four years old, I wanted to nurse. My mother was cutting wood. It was in the winter time. So I went into the woods and told her there were some guests down at our log house. There really were no guests at all. But that's how I got her to nurse me. She left her work and came back to the house. . . .

"We picked berries every day. . . . Then we stopped picking berries and made a deer fence. I helped by clearing the leaves away, so that my father wouldn't make a noise on the leaves when he walked along. We made the fence by felling trees, lining them in a row. After the fence was laid, we cleared the pathway for my father. We made the fence about five miles long. The deer couldn't get across it. My father walked along the other side of the fence, along the cleared pathway.

"The fence at Clear Lake went for five miles down to the lake. My mother was waiting on the other side of the lake, and my father stayed on his side of the fence. When the deer came to the fence, they would follow it down to the lake and then start to swim across. I sat with my brother and sisters next to my mother. We'd warn her when we saw deer coming. Then she'd get into her canoe and paddle up to the deer and spear it with an iron-tipped spear. . . . We didn't go with her in the canoe, because it might tip over. We waited there two or three times a day, and my mother often got deer that way — more than my father got with his gun. After she speared the deer, she'd drag it to shore and skin it.

"My mother and father dried the deer meat and preserved it. They pounded it fine and kept it in birchbark containers. No bones were wasted. My mother split all the bones, kept them, and when she had enough she boiled them in an iron kettle. The grease was also stored in birch-bark buckets. . . .

"In winter time we fished through the ice. One time a fox barked at my uncle, my father's brother, while he was fishing. It's a bad sign when a fox barks; if you hear a fox barking, it means someone in your family will die. It was my uncle's little boy that died. . . .

"The same year, we went to Eagle River. There were quite a few Indians camping there in wigwams. They were being hired by people in the town to cut wood. While we were there they had a Medicine Dance and built a Mide lodge. They sometimes put up a Mide lodge in winter time, when somebody falls sick. That was the first one I'd seen. . . .

"That winter we used to fast, blacken our faces with charcoal, and go out into the woods, where we built a fire some place and played around. We weren't allowed to do any work around the house. We had to fast; there was no choice about it. In the morning our parents would put a little food in a bowl with a piece of charcoal on top. You had to take the charcoal and hand the food back to your parents. You couldn't eat the food. Then you'd take the charcoal in your hands and rub it good all over your face. That let other people know that you were fasting and that you shouldn't be given any food. . . .

"I didn't fast long enough. I stopped at noon every time. If I'd kept it up longer I'd have more power. My mother used to take pity on me and feed me at noon. She didn't want to see me go hungry. That broke the spell. That's why I never had a dream. Now I'm sorry. I don't know nothing now. But it was my mother's fault. . . .

"My brother made my first bow and arrow for me. I don't know how long I had those arrows or how old I was — just a small boy. My brother made me two arrows. I tried to get small birds with them, but I never got any. We used to shoot at small game while we were fasting. I always lost my arrows. Most of the time they landed up in a tree, and I couldn't get them down again. When I got one arrow caught in the branches, I'd shoot another one after it to get it down, and then both would get stuck up there. My brother had to make new arrows for me.

"One day I killed a little bird by the wood-pile, a little chickadee. It wasn't much bigger than my thumb. When I killed it, I was standing right next to it. My mother took that bird, took the feathers off, dried it, and kept it. She praised me for my first kill. She kept that little bird for a long time. Some time later I killed a big striped chipmunk. My mother singed off its hair and put it away too. Then she put the bird and chipmunk together in a pail and cooked them. They were all dried out. This was for my first feast. They had other food along with it, though.

"My mother and father sent tobacco around and called the Indians from round about to attend the feast. The feast was to announce the first two things I had killed: the bird and the chipmunk. After everyone was there, my father got up to make a speech. I didn't get any of the bird or the chipmunk to eat. I was awfully glad to be able to go out and play after the feast was over, since I had to sit so still at the time. This took place at Sugar Camp Lake. After that feast I killed lots of little animals and birds. . . .

"I went through the Midewiwin the first time when I was about five to seven years old. I don't know why I went through; don't know if it was due to sickness or what. I don't remember much about it, except that while we were setting around the heap of dirt in the lodge the Mide priest shouted at me and made me frightened. He was an old man wrapped up in a blanket — some relative of mine — and I guess he shouted so that I would remember what he said. I went through the Midewiwin twice. The second time was when I was about eighteen.

"I went with my brother to hunt, shining deer. We set out at about six o'clock one evening in a birch-bark canoe and went up the river about half a mile. There was a lake there. Then we came to a long boom stick — to hold the logs back — stretched across the river. We had to lift the canoe over the boom stick. As we were lifting the canoe, I felt a sharp pain in my side. I couldn't sit still in the canoe. Whichever way I turned, my side hurt. Before sundown my brother asked me why I couldn't sit still. I told him about the pain. He said, 'Why don't you go home then?' So we turned around and paddled home. After we got home I groaned in my sleep all night. My mother, who was in another tent close by, heard me groaning. They woke me in the morning to eat breakfast. I still had an awful pain. I ate a little breakfast, then went back to bed. My father went out and was gone all day. In the evening he came home again. He had gone to get some (Indian) medicine I could use. We boiled the stuff. Then I tried to drink it. It was bitter. The next morning my father set out again and was gone all day. Along about five o'clock he came back. He came with Old Man Hay and his wife this time. He had gone to the town of Eagle River to fetch them.

"In the evening Old Man Hay started to doctor me. He used those bones to doctor me. First he told me to lay on my left side. Then he put the bone right on the place where my pain was. He pushed his head down close and kept pushing as hard as he could on that bone. When he pulled the bone away finally, the skin there pulled back. That's when it hurt most of all. He started twice to doctor me. The second time he did the same thing he did the first time. When a sucking doctor starts to cure, he first tells the people there about the dream he had at the time that he was fasting. Old Man Hay did that. Then my father beat a War Dance drum. Old Man Hay shook a rattle while he doctored me. He put a little dish next to him, with a little water in it. The two bones were lying there. They were about one and a half to two inches long. He didn't touch them with his hands but picked them up with his mouth. He didn't even have to pick them up with his mouth. His power was so strong that when Old Man Hay leaned over the dish, the bones stood up and moved towards his mouth. He swallowed the bones twice and coughed them up again. Then he put the bone to my side. After he'd finished sucking, Old Man Hay drew out some stuff and spat it into a dish; it looked like blood. Old Man Hay showed it to me and to the others and then threw it into the fire. If he hadn't drawn the blood out, it would have turned to pus. And sometimes, when the pus bursts inside, the person dies. My father drummed all the time that Old Man Hay was doctoring me. He didn't sing, but Old Man Hay sang a little bit at the beginning of every time he doctored me. He put the bone to my side four times and got blood each time, but the last time he doctored me there was very little blood. It was the same every time he doctored me. All we gave him was a piece of cloth and some tobacco, and gave him his meals. After he had finished doctoring me, Old Man Hay said to my father, 'One time they had a medicine dance. You took the hide that Tom got in the medicine dance and gave it to someone else. You promised to give him another one in place of the one that you took from him. Sometimes he thinks about it. That's why he is sick now.' . . .

"During the next morning they doctored me again — same way as before. The two old people, Old Many Hay and his wife, stayed right there with us. Then my mother started cooking, and they were making preparations, and I heard my father say that I had to join the medicine dance. Soon after that we had a feast. At the feast they gave me a little shell to put around my neck. Old Man Hay stayed with us four days. Every morning and evening he doctored me with the bones. At the same time I kept drinking the bitter medicine. As a result I got a little better. Later we moved to Eagle River to stay with Old Man Hay and his wife.

"One day my father got sick. He was so sick he was pretty nearly crazy in a short time. He had bad headache spells. I called on one of the old men to doctor my father. This Indian doctor told him why he had those headaches. 'While you were at Flambeau somebody did something to your hat [sorcery]. There's nothing we can do to make you well.' This doctor didn't do any curing. He got his information from dreams. My mother thought of having my father go through the Midewiwin. We used everything we had — all of our blankets and goods we could get hold of. They had a medicine dance for my father. He felt good for a little while after that, but then he went blind. He could see a little, but not much.

"This all took place in the fall. I got to thinking. What can I do to help pull my parents through the winter? There were only three of us then. My sister had gotten married to Little Stone a while before that. My brother had married my oldest brother's wife and was living at Lake Vieux Desert. I got to thinking, I guess I'll take my parents away to some place where I can hunt in the woods and bring them through the winter. . . . . When winter came, I didn't know what to do. I thought of my brother at Lake Vieux Desert. One day I started off from camp to find out whether Lake Vieux Desert was frozen. My brother lived at the other end of the lake. On this side of the lake there were some Indians: my mother's brother lived there. My uncle told me that the lake had frozen over just two nights ago. So I took a chance and decided to cross the lake. The ice held all right. I carried a big long pole with me. When I got to the other side, I saw my brother's wife, and the rest of the people there, but my brother wasn't back from hunting yet. . . . Later that evening my brother got back from hunting. I told him where we were camping. The next morning I went back to my parents. I told them that we would go to stay at Lake Vieux Desert.

"My father was sick all the time. It took a day to get to my uncle's place. We stayed there. My uncle lived in a frame house, but we built a wigwam outside. After a while we moved across the lake. My brother helped me to take my father across the ice. We dragged him across on a hand sleigh, and my mother followed behind. It took about three quarters of an hour to get across. We went into my brother-in-law's home. . . .

"The rest of the people at the village were all hunting from different camps, which they'd set up in the fall, and were all scattered through the woods. We were the only ones living at the village. There were a lot of people out in the woods. In November they all came back to their homes at the village.

"My father was still very sick, so we called on Old Man Hay to doctor him. It was late in the evening. After he had doctored him, Old Man Hay said, 'I don't think it's sickness that's doing this to him. I think it's the work of someone.' He went on to say, 'Tomorrow evening we will put up a tipi, *jizikun* (conjuring lodge); then we will know if someone is doing this.'

"The next day we didn't go any place; we worked all day putting those sticks in the ground. The ground had frozen, so we had to work hard so that the stakes would be solid. In the evening we had a fire outside of the tipi. The old man went into it and had his pipe handed in to him. While he was smoking, the bells and the rattle on the tipi began to shake and make a noise. The old man was talking inside the tipi. He had a little War Dance drum, which he had given to the people outside the tipi. He told them to pound it. Then he began to sing inside the *jizikun*; pretty soon it began to swing back and forth. Someone was talking way up on top there, where there was a balsam bough about three feet long sticking out on top, above the other stakes. This was an open lodge — not covered on top. Some of the voices I heard were about four feet from the ground. . . .

"The person at the top of the tipi said that when my father went to this old man's house for a visit, the old man did something to my father's hat. The person up there also told Old Man Hay how to doctor my father. The spirit doesn't speak very well or very clearly. There are a lot of words he can hardly pronounce. . . .

"After a short time my father was pretty sick again. His head swayed from side to side. He couldn't see at all; he was completely blind. He had bad headaches. Another old man came to the village then. He had been hunting and was just coming home. At that time we used to sell meat to the logging camps, so I had a few pennies in my pocket. I went to that logging camp and bought a half pound of tobacco. Then I went to the home of that old man. I gave him the tobacco and said, 'You may doctor my father. That's why I'm giving you this tobacco. I will give you my horse too.'

"The old man didn't say anything for a while. Finally he said he would try to cure my father. The next morning the old man and his wife came over to our place. I didn't see anything that he was going to use to doctor my father. After he'd sat there a while, he asked for a tiny birchbark basket about an inch square. We made it right away. It wasn't supposed to leak. Then the old man asked for a little water. He poured a little of it into the basket. Then he took a little woven bag about four inches long and from it he took a little bundle. Then he took the end of a knife blade and took a little of the stuff the bundle was made of and put it into the tiny birchbark basket, which had a little water in it.

"Then the old man told me to take four hairs from the crown of my father's head. I took four hairs, just as he said, and tied them up as tightly as I could, in a little round bundle. When I'd done that, I handed it over to the old man, who put it into his little basket. That old man had some feathers that looked just like cotton. He made a tiny bundle of those too and put them into the little basket. Then the old man told me to cut some more hairs from the crown of my father's head — just as close to the scalp as I could cut them. After I'd done that, he handed me his pocket knife and told me to cut my father's head on top there. He told me to make a hole in his head clean down to the bone. I hated to do that, but the old man coaxed me to do it. I sat and thought about it a while. I thought, if he should get well, it would be worth it. So I did it. I took the knife and pushed it down in. I felt the knife go down through one layer, then through another one, until I hit that bone. Then I cut along a little ways, so that there was a hole in his head half an inch long. Then I pulled my knife out of there. My father didn't feel it at all.

"The blood came out of that hole just black. It kept pouring out of there for quite a while. After the blood had stopped flowing, I took the little bundle of four hairs out of the tiny basket and stuck them into the opening in my father's head. Then I stuck the bundle of feathers in there too. This was what the old man instructed me to do. On top of the little bundle of feathers the old man put some more medicine. Then he cut out a round piece of paper — about an inch across — and stuck that on top. Then he put a cloth or a white rag over my father's head and tied it under his chin. That's all that the old man did. Then he sat there for quite a while telling us stories. In the afternoon he and his wife left us and went home. We broke up our pair of horses then, so that we had only one left. That night my father slept good. From that time on he got better every day. We stayed at that place all winter.

"Soon after that I married one of Old Man Hay's daughters. I left my mother and father with my brother. He took care of them. I went to stay at my father-in-law's place. . . .

"The same winter I went to work in a logging camp at Land O' Lakes. That was my first job. I had a job sawing and cutting logs. I had to leave my wife at home and go to live in the camp. But I went home every Saturday and spent Sunday at home. . . .

"Then I went home again. We worked on the garden at my father-in-law's place, made it a little bit bigger. We planted potatoes and corn. . . .

"That summer, when I still had the canoe, they passed some tobacco for a Drum Dance across the lake. We paddled across the lake to the dance. After the dance I intended to hunt and shine deer on the way home. I went a long ways around the side of the lake, but I didn't see anything. My wife and my first child, a little boy in the cradle-board, were in the canoe with me. I quit shining and then we paddled home around the edge of the lake. I could see the ribs of the canoe, so I said to my wife that it must be getting to be morning. I turned my head and saw that the sky was getting light. When I turned to look behind me, the boat turned to the shore, and I had a hard time trying to steer the boat straight. The boat tipped way over to the left, for a limb sticking up from the bottom of the lake got caught on it. I jumped into the water and thought, I'm going to kick so that I can get up to the top. I thought that by jumping into the water I'd keep the canoe from tipping over. I did it to save the woman and the kid. When my head came up into the air again, I saw the canoe going ahead along on the water. I made a splashing noise with my hands and feet. That woman didn't even know that I had jumped overboard in the dark. She was just paddling ahead, and when she turned and heard me splashing behind her, she started to cry. I caught hold of the back end of the canoe, where I had been sitting, and asked that woman how the baby was. She was still crying. She said, 'The baby is all right.' Then I told her to paddle to shore. About a hundred feet from shore, when I could feel bottom with my feet, I towed the boat to shore. The canoe was already half full of water, since the limb had torn a hole in the bottom. That woman was still crying when I got to shore, but the baby was still asleep. We started to walk home then. It was getting toward dawn. That was the only time I ever went swimming so early in the morning.

"Most of the time in those days I hunted in the woods for food for my family. I stayed with my in-laws for one year. The next year I built a big log-house nearby for us to live in. In the spring of the year we made our own sugar — just my woman and me and our children. I had two boys then. The oldest was about four. The youngest was just learning to walk. . . .

"Two months after that my wife got sick. She had a baby. We built a wigwam for her, where she gave birth to a boy. She had to stay in that wigwam for a week or ten days before coming back into the home again. But she was up and around before she got well. While she was out in the wigwam, she had a visitor, a drunken man. She ran out and came back into the house. Her feet got wet from the dew on the grass, and the stuff that was in her from having the baby worked up to her head instead of out the other way. She died two days after that. At that time I had seven children living, but the little baby died two or three months later. There's only one boy and my daughter living now.

"I kept only two of my children — two boys, the first and the fourth. The other four were taken care of by grandparents. My wife's father and mother took care of them. They were all brought up at Lake Vieux Desert. After my wife died, her father and mother visited us at Robbins and took them back with them. I didn't see much of them after that. My brother took my smallest baby, the seventh; but it didn't live long. I moved to Flambeau a year after my wife died and put my oldest son in school there. I never went to see my kids at Lake Vieux Desert, because there were three of my wife's sisters living at that time, and they had a way of saying that if I went back there, they (my wife's sisters) would kill me. They thought I should have married one of the sisters, the youngest one. But she was going around with another man. That's why I didn't marry her. The men didn't mind so much. They didn't care. It was the women who were angry. I don't know if they really wanted to kill me. That's what I heard. So I stayed away. It was a long time — maybe ten years — before I saw my two youngest kids again. My boy was the first one to come down here. My daughter didn't come until after she was married.

"Two years after I moved down here, I put my third son in school. . . .

"I had a hard time for a while. There was no work at Flambeau then. The mill wasn't running any more. We made beadwork, little birch-bark canoes, moccasins, and stuff like that, and sold them to the tourists. We kept going all right, though."

Julia Badger

The following account is drawn from my *Acculturation and Personality Among the Wisconsin Chippewa* (1950, pp. 112-44).

Julia Badger, wife of Tom Badger, was a fat, bulky woman of thirty-four in 1944. She had gone through a great deal of sickness and misfortune in her life. Her father and mother were classmates at the Flambeau government school. Her father died when she was only five years old, but even before that time Julia had been transferred to her grandparents (father's parents), who brought her up. Julia always thought of her grandparents as her real parents and claimed that she did not know who her real mother was until she was fourteen years old.

Julia's grandfather, "Big Bill," was evidently the most influential person in her life. He was of huge stature, sometimes described on tourist postcards as "The Biggest Indian Alive." "Big Bill" had spent four years in jail for killing a white man in a brawl. In jail he made considerable progress in self-education along Western lines. After he got out, he bought a farm with his "timber money," according to Julia.

Julia Badger was always sickly. She was "wall-eyed" and suffered from eye trouble, had a bad gall bladder, and got severe headaches frequently. In infancy she contracted some kind of paralysis, so that she was unable to walk until she was two and a half years old. After that she wore a brace on her leg for several years. There is a possibility that some of these disturbances may have been hereditary, for her mother and grandmother had eye trouble as well, and her daughter suffered attacks of paralysis in childhood. Selected passages from her autobiography follow:

"I never wore glasses. I went through school without glasses. I can read all right, and I can do beadwork like the rest of them. But I never really did see well. The doctor says I have "inverted squint." I think that's what he called it. My eyes see out each way — not straight ahead.

"I was raised by my grandparents. I didn't get along very well with my grandfather at first, but after a while we got along all right. But my grandmother was mean. She used to whip us often, sometimes for nothing at all. . . .

"They used to scare us at night, so that we wouldn't go out to play, by drawing a face with chalk on a frying pan and sticking it in the window. Also, if we were playing while it was getting dark, they'd say, 'Oh, you don't see who you're playing with.' They'd make us think that there was a ghost playing with us, and we'd get frightened. . . .

"When I was about nine or ten, I was sick all summer with different things — mostly my legs, which were useless. I couldn't walk. I couldn't use either of my legs. My grandfather always carried me from place to place. That's how my paralysis is — it comes and goes. Sometimes I'm all right. At other times I can't walk at all.

"My ears, my legs, everything was wrong. My skin was just yellow — no color at all. I was like that all summer. I wasn't able to go to school until April, after Easter. My hair kept falling out. They didn't cut my hair, though. I didn't want anybody to do that. . . .

"When I was young, I never knew who my mother was. I thought of my grandmother as my mother; but she told me that I had a real mother somewhere. She didn't tell me where. I used to see my mother all that time, off and on, but I never knew that this woman was my mother until after 1923. Around then, one day, someone told me that this woman was my mother.

"One day this woman gave me some things to take to my grandmother. I took them along. I didn't know why she sent those things. That was my mother, but I didn't know it then. After I knew who my mother was, I used to visit her. I remembered who my father was, but I didn't know who my mother was. My father died in 1915. My mother married the second time in 1916 or 1917. I didn't like my step-father. He was mean.

"I started going to school in 1918. I didn't like it at first. . . .

[A long description of school follows, which I omit.]

"I missed a lot of school at Flambeau, because I got sick often, and I had that paralysis; so my grandfather kept me out of school. I used to have awful headaches and dizzy spells. So I stayed home.

"When I was thirteen I fasted for thirty-two days, a half a day every day, and stayed in a hut (a dome-shaped wigwam) specially built for that. My grandmother said that if I did that, I'd live to be an old lady. My grandmother cooked my food and brought it to me — right on the dot at noon every day. The sun was shining then. It never rained all that time. This was across the lake at the Indian Village. The hut was a birchbark-covered wigwam. It was fixed up real nice — with reed mats and everything. Just like a home. They had an extra place there for someone to stay. Other women came to stay there with me — my girl-friend, my cousin, and others. . . . I wasn't allowed to eat anything that comes from the ground — no vegetables, potatoes or anything. . . . My grandmother gave me canned corn. That's all right, since it comes from the can. But she couldn't give me fresh corn. . . . The first day I was there I felt kind of lonesome, because I didn't understand why I was doing it. But later I understood. Girls don't do that now. That's why you don't see berries on the trees now. My uncle's son — my mother's brother's son — was touched by a girl who didn't do that. It was the first time she was that way, and she hadn't gone out into the hut. When she touched that boy, he became paralyzed. Later on, he died. It's true. I always tell young people about these things. The more you hide, the worse it is. . . .

[Mrs. Badger went to boarding school in Pipestone, Minnesota, and gave a long account of her life then, which I omit.]

"In July, shortly after I came home, I went to the Indian wedding of my cousin in Rhinelander. Her husband was half Potawatomi and half Chippewa. Everybody had a good time at the wedding. It was there that I met my first husband, a Winnebago Indian.

"About a week later this man came up. He came up to ask my mother if he could live with me. I was sitting there. My mother made no objec-tions. She said, 'Yes, if you will take good care of her, because she ar-rived here only about a month ago. She hasn't spent the best part of her life yet.' Then he told me to go with him to Woodruff. He hired a car to take us down there. He was the age Tom is now when I married him. . . .

"My first husband was a leader in the peyote religion. We went to about four or five peyote meetings while I was down there with him. My husband worked in the factory, sometimes on the day shift, sometimes on the night shift. I didn't see very much of him. He used to ask to get off on Fridays. Then he'd have all day Saturday and Sunday free. At these times they'd have the peyote meetings, which started in the evening and lasted all night. He and his older brother were in charge of them, and they were held in a great big tipi, which must have held about fifty-six people. . . .

"I only lived with my first husband about three weeks. Then my grandmother (father's mother) and my aunt (father's sister) came down after me. They wanted me to leave him. They objected to his taking that herb (peyote). I don't know if it's bad for you to take peyote or not. I never took it. . . . But that religion is all right. We all worship the same god. It's all the same. . . .

"In November of the same year, my grandmother and my aunt got me to marry another man — Joe Bluebird. This is the time when I should have married my old boy-friend, the one who saw me off at the station when I first went to Pipestone. But he'd got married while I was at Pipestone. Later he said to me, 'That's where I made my big mistake.' . . .

"I didn't care much for Bluebird, but my people wanted me to marry him. He was a lot older than I was. I'd gone around with him a couple of years before that; so when he came and asked my mother if he could marry me, I didn't mind. I wasn't anxious to marry him, but I didn't care about it. So I said I'd marry him. My folks all wanted me to do it. Before then, when we were going around together, he'd once said something about living together or getting married, and I said, 'Live with you? I wouldn't go along with you to a dog-fight, if there was a dog-fight in town.' Later on, after we got married, he threw that all back at me, but I told him I'd never said it. You know, you have to say things like that. He treated me well, though. He was always good to me. He worked hard — guiding and different jobs.

"My daughter Christine was born while I was living with my second husband. I never found out I was going to have a baby until after I left my first husband. It's funny I didn't know. He must have known. He had preparations for me to go to the hospital and everything. I never went there, although he'd paid for it. . . .

"My grandfather died on April 15, 1930 . . . at a War Dance, at his brother-in-law's place. They had a War Dance at his funeral that lasted about a half an hour. . . .

"He died April 15th. My husband died April 28th, the same month. He died in his sleep of heart failure. When I woke up I thought he was just sleeping; but he was dead. That's why it hit me so bad. I couldn't talk. It was just like my tongue was made of lead. His mother was the same. She couldn't talk either. I just sat around. I couldn't do much. . . .

"At that time some of my first husband's folks came up and asked me to marry his younger brother, now that both of my husbands had died. But I didn't want to. Some other people told me that he was mean. He had a nice house, but he was mean. And I didn't want to marry him anyway, so I didn't do it.

"I didn't want to marry anybody then; I was so blue. I made up my mind that I'd never marry again. I decided that I'd go into church work and go around telling people about Jesus. That way I could get away from people and I could do some traveling. That's what I wanted to do — travel. When I get to feeling bad, I want to get on a train. . . .

"The first time I met Tom was at a War Dance on New Year's Eve. Oh, I'd seen him before then, but I never paid any attention to him before that, and he never paid any attention to me. So this New Year's Dance was really the first time we met. I had a lot of liquor in me, and you know how liquor will make you act foolish. I was pretty crazy that evening. . . .

"I went with Tom, April, May, June, and July — four months. Eddy [a friend of Tom's, who called Tom his brother] always used to come along. . . . When Tom asked me to live with him, I said my intentions were different, and I didn't intend to get married again, because maybe I couldn't find a man like the one I lost.

"He didn't say anything until about four days later. The second time he asked me, I told him, 'If you can do as my second husband intended to do and be good to us, I'll do just as you tell me to do. But in the first place I want to know what you're going to do with that other one you're going to leave behind [Tom's second wife, still living at that time].'

"He said, 'I'm not going to do anything. I'll just leave.'

"What are you going to do about the papers you made out with her?

"He said, 'I never made out any papers with her.'

"Eddy was standing about twenty yards away. He clapped his hands then and shouted, 'Hooray! Oh boy!' . . .

"I went to live with Tom in the country. We camped in a tent, and Tom went hunting. I left Christine with my mother-in-law. Living in the country brought the color back to my face, and I got fat in a short time. . . .

"I told Tom that what worried me most was that I couldn't help him much. I was too weak. I said, 'I can't help you get meals the way I did for my other husband. I can't begin all over again.' "

References Cited

AARNE, ANTTI, AND STITH THOMPSON
    1961. *The Types of the Folktale: A Classification and Bibliography.*
    Helsinki: Suomaleinen Tiedeakatemia. Academia Scientiarum Fen-
    nica.

AARONSON, BERNARD, AND HUMPHREY OSMOND (eds.)
    1970. *Psychedelics: The Uses and Implications of Psychedelic
    Drugs.* New York: Doubleday.

ALEXANDER, FRANZ, AND WILLIAM MENNINGER
    1936. "The Relation of Persecutory Delusions to the Functioning
    of the Gastro-Intestinal Tract." *Journal of Nervous and Mental
    Diseases,* 84:541–54.

BALLARD, ARTHUR C.
    1929. "Mythology of Southern Puget Sound." *University of Wash-
    ington Publications in Anthropology,* 3:31–150.

BARNOUW, VICTOR
    1949. "The Phantasy World of a Chippewa Woman." *Psychiatry,*
    12:67–76.
    1950. *Acculturation and Personality Among the Wisconsin Chip-
    pewa.* American Anthropological Association Memoir no. 72. Me-
    nasha, Wis.
    1954. "Reminiscences of a Chippewa Mide Priest." *The Wisconsin
    Archeologist,* 35:83–112.
    1955. "A Psychological Interpretation of a Chippewa Origin Leg-
    end." *Journal of American Folklore,* 68, pt. 1, no. 267, pp. 73–86;
    pt. 2, no. 268, pp. 211–23; pt. 3, no. 269, pp. 341–55.
    1960. "A Chippewa Mide Priest's Description of the Medicine
    Dance." *The Wisconsin Archeologist,* 41:77–97.
    1961. "Chippewa Social Atomism." *American Anthropologist,* 63:
    1006–13.
    1973. *Culture and Personality.* Rev. ed. Homewood, Ill.: The
    Dorsey Press.

BARTLETT, F. C.
    1932. *Remembering. A Study in Experimental and Social Psy-
    chology.* Cambridge, Eng.: The University Press.

This bibliography concerns references made in the text and is not intended to cover all available references to Chippewa folklore. More references may be found in the bibliographies given by Fisher, 1946, Haywood, 1961, and Tanner, 1976, cited below.

BENEDICT, RUTH
   Zuni Mythology. 2 vols. Columbia University Contributions to Anthropology, vol. 21. New York: Columbia University Press.
BISHOP, CHARLES A.
   1970. "The Emergence of Hunting Territories Among the Northern Ojibwa." *Ethnology,* 9:1–15.
   1974. *The Northern Ojibwa and the Fur Trade: An Historical and Ecological Study.* Toronto: Holt, Rinehart and Winston of Canada, Ltd.
BLACKBIRD, ANDREW J.
   1887. *History of the Ottawa and Chippewa Indians of Michigan.* Ypsilanti, Mich.: Ypsilantian Job Printing House.
BOAS, FRANZ
   1888. *The Central Eskimo.* Bureau of American Ethnology Annual Report no. 6. Washington, D.C.: Smithsonian Institution.
   1895. *The Social Organization and Secret Societies of the Kwakiutl Indians.* Report of the U.S. National Museum. Washington, D.C.
   1912. "Notes on Mexican Folklore." *Journal of American Folklore,* 25:204–60.
   1916. *Tsimshian Mythology.* Bureau of American Ethnology Annual Report no. 31. Washington, D.C.: Smithsonian Institution.
   1918. *Kutenai Tales.* Bureau of American Ethnology Bulletin 59. Washington, D.C.: Smithsonian Institution.
   1925. "Romance Folk-Lore Among American Indians." *The Romanic Review,* 16:199–207.
   1935. *Kwakiutl Culture as Reflected in the Mythology.* Memoirs of the American Folklore Society, vol. 28. New York.
   1940. *Race, Language and Culture.* New York: Macmillan.
BOBERG, INGER M.
   1938: "The Tale of Cupid and Psyche." *Classica et Mediaevalia,* 1:177–216.
BØDKER, LAURITS
   1957. "The Brave Tailor in Danish Tradition." In *Studies in Folklore.* Edited by W. Edson Richmond. Bloomington: Indiana University Press. Pp. 1–23.
BOYER, L. BRYCE
   1964. "An Example of Legend Distortion from the Apaches of the Mescalero Indian Reservation." *Journal of American Folklore,* 77: 118–42.
BROWN, CHARLES E.
   1941. *Sea Serpents: Wisconsin Occurrences of These Weird Water Monsters in the Four Lakes, Rock, Red Cedar, Koshkonong, Geneva, Elkhart, Michigan, and Other Lakes.* Madison, Wis.: American Folklore Society.

BROWN, JENNIFER
    1971. "The Care and Feeding of Windigos: A Critique." *American Anthropologist,* 73:20–23.

BROWN, NORMAN O.
    1959. *Life Against Death. The Psychoanalytical Meaning of History.* Middletown, Conn.: Wesleyan University Press.

BUSS, ARNOLD
    1968. *Psychopathology.* New York: John Wiley and Sons.

CAMPBELL, JOSEPH
    1969. *The Flight of the Wild Gander. Explorations in the Mythological Dimension.* New York: Viking Press.

CARSON, WILLIAM
    1917. "Ojibwa Tales." *Journal of American Folklore,* 30:491–93.

CASAGRANDE, JOSEPH B.
    1960. "John Mink, Ojibwa Informant." In *In the Company of Man. Twenty Portraits by Anthropologists.* Edited by Joseph B. Casagrande. New York: Harper and Brothers. Pp. 467–88.

CAUDILL, WILLIAM
    1949. "Psychological Characteristics of Acculturated Wisconsin Ojibwa Children." *American Anthropologist,* 51:409–27.

CHAMBERLAIN, A. F.
    1889. "Tales of the Mississaguas." *Journal of American Folklore,* 2:141–47.
    1891. "Nanibozhu Amongst the Otchipwe, Mississagas, and Other Algonkian Tribes." *Journal of American Folklore,* 4:193–215.
    1892. "A Mississaga Legend of Nä'nibōjū: *Journal of American Folklore,* 5:292–93.

COATE, MORAG
    1965. *Beyond All Reason.* Philadelphia: J. B. Lippincott Co.

COOPER, JOHN M.
    1933. "The Cree Witiko Psychosis." *Primitive Man,* 6:20–24.

COSTELLO, PETER
    1974. *In Search of Lake Monsters.* New York: Coward, McCann and Geoghan.

DAWKINS, RICHARD M. (ed. and trans.)
    1953. *Modern Greek Folktales.* Oxford: Clarendon Press.

DE JONG, J. P. B. DE JOSSELIN
    1913. *Original Odžibwe-Texts.* Leipzig and Berlin: Baessler Archiv.

DELARUE, PAUL (ed.)
    1956. *The Borzoi Book of French Tales.* New York: Alfred A. Knopf.
    1957. *Le Conte Populaire Français.* Vol. 1. Paris: Éditions Érasme.

DELARUE, PAUL, AND MARIE-LOUISE TENÈZE
    1963. *Le Conte Populaire Français.* Vol. 2. Paris: Éditions G.-P. Maisonneuve et Larose.

DEWDNEY, SELWYN
1975. *The Sacred Scrolls of the Southern Ojibway.* Toronto: University of Toronto Press.

DORSEY, G. A., AND A. L. KROEBER
1903. *Traditions of the Arapaho.* Field Columbian Museum Publications, no. 81, vol. 5. Chicago.

DORSEY, J. OWEN
1892. "Nanibozhu in Siouan Mythology." *Journal of American Folklore,* 5:293-304.

DORSON, RICHARD M.
1952. *Bloodstoppers and Bearwalkers.* Cambridge, Mass.: Harvard University Press.
1963. "Current Folklore Theories." *Current Anthropology,* 4:93-112.

DUCATEL, TIMOLEON
1846. "A Fortnight Among the Chippewa." *U.S. Catholic Magazine,* vol. 5.

DUNDES, ALAN
1962. "Earth-Diver: Creation of the Mythopoeic Male." *American Anthropologist,* 64:1032-51.
1963. "Structural Typology in North American Indian Folktales." *Southwestern Journal of Anthropology,* 19:121-30.
1964. "The Morphology of North American Indian Folktales." *Folklore Fellows Communications,* no. 195. Helsinki.

DUNDES, ALAN (ed.)
1965. *The Study of Folklore.* Englewood Cliffs, N.J.: Prentice-Hall, Inc.

DUNNING, R. W.
1959. *Social and Economic Change Among the Northern Ojibwa.* Toronto: University of Toronto Press.

EHRLICH, CLARA
1937. "Tribal Culture in Crow Mythology." *Journal of American Folklore,* 50:307-408.

ERIKSON, ERIK H.
1962. *Young Man Luther. A Study in Psychoanalysis and History.* New York: W. W. Norton & Co.

FENICHEL, OTTO
1945. *The Psychoanalytic Theory of Neurosis.* New York: W. W. Norton.

FENTON, WILLIAM N.
1962. "This Island, the World on the Turtle's Back." *Journal of American Folklore,* 76:283-300.

FISHER, MARGARET
1946. "The Mythology of the Northern and Northeastern Algonkians in Reference to Algonkian Mythology as a Whole." In *Man*

in Northeastern North America. Edited by Frederik Johnson. Andover, Mass.: Papers of the R. S. Peabody Foundation for Archeology. Vol. 3, pp. 226-62.

FOGELSON, RAYMOND D.
1965. "Psychological Theories of *Windigo* 'Psychosis' and a Preliminary Application of a Models Approach." In *Context and Meaning in Cultural Anthropology.* Edited by Melford E. Spiro. New York: The Free Press. Pp. 74-99.

FOX, MICHAEL W.
1971. *Behavior of Wolves, Dogs, and Related Canids.* London: Jonathan Cape.

GATSCHET, ALBERT S.
1899. "Water-Monsters of American Aborigines," *Journal of American Folklore,* 12:255-60.

GERBER, A.
1893. "Uncle Remus Traced to the Old World." *Journal of American Folklore,* 6:245-57.

GILLE, JOHANNES
1939. *Der Manabozho-Flutzyklus der Nord-, Nordost- und Zentralalgonkin.* Göttingen: C. Trüte.

GRANT, PETER
1890. "The Sauteux Indians: About 1804." In *Les Bourgeois de la Compagnie du Nord-Ouest.* Edited by L. R. Masson. Quebec: Coté et Cie.

GRINNELL, GEORGE BIRD
1892. *Blackfoot Lodge Tales. The Story of a Prairie People.* New York: Charles Scribner's Sons.
1926. *By Cheyenne Campfires.* New Haven, Conn.: Yale University Press.

HALL, ROBERT L.
1976. "The Archaeology of Life Metaphors from Kinnickinnick to the Sun Dance." Typescript in author's possession.

HALLOWELL, A. IRVING
1926. "Bear Ceremonialism in the Northern Hemisphere." *American Anthropologist,* 28:1-175.
1935. "The Bulbed Enema Syringe in North America." *American Anthropologist,* 37:708-10.
1940. "Aggression in Saulteaux Society." *Psychiatry,* 3:395-407.
1942. *The Role of Conjuring in Saulteaux Society.* Philadelphia: University of Pennsylvania Press.
1946. "Concordance of Ojibwa Narratives in the Published Works of Henry R. Schoolcraft." *Journal of American Folklore,* 59:136-53.
1947. "Myth, Culture, and Personality." *American Anthropologist,* 49:544-55.

1955. *Culture and Experience*. Philadelphia: University of Pennsylvania Press.

1960. "Ojibwa Ontology, Behavior, and World View." In *Culture in History. Essays in Honor of Paul Radin*. Edited by Stanley Diamond. New York: Columbia University Press. Pp. 19–52.

HARNER, MICHAEL J. (ed.)

1973. *Hallucinogens and Shamanism*. New York: Oxford University Press.

HARRIS, JOEL CHANDLER

1880. *Uncle Remus. His Songs and Sayings*. New York: D. Appleton & Co.

1883. *Nights With Uncle Remus. Myths and Legends of the Old Plantation*. Boston: Houghton Mifflin Co.

HASTINGS, JOHN (ed.)

1911. *Encyclopaedia of Religion and Ethics*. New York: Scribners.

HAWLEY, FLORENCE

1937. "Kokopelli, of the Prehistoric Southwestern Pueblo Pantheon." *American Anthropologist*, 39:644–46.

HAY, THOMAS E.

1971. "The Windigo Psychosis: Psychodynamic, Cultural, and Social Factors in Aberrant Behavior." *American Anthropologist*, 73:1–19.

HAYWOOD, CHARLES

1961. "Chippewa (Ojibway) Folklore." *A Bibliography of North American Folklore and Folksong*. New York: Dover Publications, Vol. 2, pp. 835-43.

HEIZER, R. F.

1939. "The Bulbed Enema Syringe and Enema Tube in the New World." *Primitive Man*, 12:85–93.

HICKERSON, HAROLD

1962. The *Southwestern Chippewa: An Ethnohistorical Study*. American Anthropological Association Memoir no. 92. Menasha, Wis.

1967. "Some Implications of the Theory of the Particularity or 'Atomism' of Northern Algonkians." *Current Anthropology*, 8: 313–43.

HOEBEL, E. ADAMSON

1960. *The Cheyennes. Indians of the Great Plains*. New York: Henry Holt & Co.

HOFFMAN, W. J.

1891. *The Midewiwin, or "Grand Medicine Society" of the Ojibwa*. Bureau of American Ethnology Annual Report no. 7, 1885-86. Washington, D.C.: Smithsonian Institution.

1896. *The Menomini Indians*. Bureau of American Ethnology, Annual Report no. 14, 1892-93. Washington, D.C.: Smithsonian Institution.

HONKO, LAURI
    1964. "Memorates and the Study of Folk Beliefs." *Journal of the Folklore Institute,* 1:5–19.

HORSLEY, J. STEPHEN
    1943. *Narco-Analysis.* Oxford: Oxford University Press.

HULTKRANZ, AKE
    1961. "The Owners of the Animals in the Religion of the North American Indians. Some General Remarks." In *The Supernatural Owners of Nature.* Edited by Ake Hultkranz. Stockholm: Almqvist and Wiksell. Pp. 53–64.

JACOBS, MELVILLE
    1959. *The Content and Style of an Oral Literature. Clackamas Chinook Myths and Tales.* Chicago: University of Chicago Press.

JAMES, BERNARD J.
    1954. "Some Critical Observations Concerning Analyses of Chippewa 'Atomism' and Chippewa Personality." *American Anthropologist,* 56:283–86.

JAMES, EDWIN (ed.)
    1956. *A Narrative of the Captivity and Adventures of John Tanner.* Minneapolis: Ross and Haines, Inc.

JENKS, ALBERT E.
    1902. "The Bear Maiden. An Ojibwa Folk-Tale From Lac Courte Oreille Reservation, Wisconsin." *Journal of American Folklore,* 15: 33–35.

JENNESS, DIAMOND
    1935. *The Ojibwa Indians of Parry Island, Their Social and Religious Life.* Ottawa: Canada Department of Mines, Bulletin 78, National Museum of Canada Anthropological Series no. 17.

JONES, ERNEST
    1948. *Papers on Psychoanalysis.* Baltimore: Williams and Wilkins.

JONES, WILLIAM
    1907. *Fox Texts.* Publications of the American Ethnological Society, vol. 1. Leyden.
    1915. *Kickapoo Tales.* Publications of the American Ethnological Society, vol. 9. Leyden.
    1916. "Ojibwa Tales From the North Shore of Lake Superior." *Journal of American Folklore,* 29:368–91.
    1917, 1919. *Ojibwa Texts.* Publications of the American Ethnological Society, vol. 7, pts. 1 and 2. Leyden.

JUNG, C. G.
    1956. "On the Psychology of the Trickster Figure." In Radin, 1956, pp. 195–211.

KINIETZ, W. VERNON
    1947. *Chippewa Village. The Story of Katikitegon.* Cranbrook
    Institute of Science Bulletin no. 25. Bloomfield Hills, Mich.
KIRK, G. S.
    1973. *Myth. Its Meaning and Functions in Ancient and Other
    Cultures.* Berkeley: University of California Press.
KNIGHT, JULIA
    1913. "Ojibwa Tales from Sault Ste. Marie, Michigan." *Journal of
    American Folklore,* 26:91–96.
KNIGHT, ROLF
    1965. "A Re-examination of Hunting, Trapping, and Territoriality
    Among the Northeastern Algonkian Indians." In *Man, Culture, and
    Animals. The Role of Animals in Human Ecological Adjustments.*
    Edited by Anthony Leeds and Andrew P. Vayda. American Asso-
    ciation for the Advancement of Science, Publication no. 78. Wash-
    ington, D.C. Pp. 27–42.
KOHL, J. G.
    1860. *Kitchi-Gami: Wanderings Around Lake Superior.* London:
    Chapman and Hall.
KÖNGAS, ELLI KAIJAL
    1960. "The Earth-Diver (Th A812)." *Ethnohistory,* 7:151–80.
KROEBER, A. L.
    1907. *Gros Ventre Myths and Tales.* Anthropological Papers of the
    American Museum of Natural History, vol. I, pt. 3. New York.
    1939. *Cultural and Natural Areas of Native North America.* Berke-
    ley: University of California Press.
LA BARRE, WESTON
    1946. "Social Cynosure and Social Structure." *Journal of Personality,*
    14:169–83.
    1970. Review of R. Gordon Wasson, *Soma: Divine Mushroom of
    Immortality,* in *American Anthropologist,* 72:368–73.
    1972. "Hallucinogens and the Shamanic Origin of Religion." In
    Flesh of the Gods. The Ritual Use of Hallucinogens. Edited by
    Peter T. Furst. New York: Praeger. Pp. 260–78.
LAIDLAW, G. E.
    1914–25. "Ojibwa Myths and Tales." *Annual Archaeological Report,*
    1914: 77–79; 1915: 71–90; 1916: 84–92; 1918: 74–110; 1921–23:
    84–99; 1924–1925: 34–80. Toronto: Ontario Provincial Museum.
LANDES, RUTH
    1937a. "The Ojibwa of Canada." In *Cooperation and Competition
    Among Primitive Peoples.* Edited by Margaret Mead. New York:
    McGraw-Hill Book Co. Pp. 87–126.
    1937b. *Ojibwa Sociology.* Columbia University Contributions to
    Anthropology, no. 29. New York: Columbia University Press.

1937c. "The Personality of the Ojibwa." *Character and Personality,* 6:51–60.

1938. "The Abnormal Among the Ojibwa." *Journal of Abnormal and Social Psychology,* 33:14–33.

1939. *The Ojibwa Woman.* Columbia University Contributions to Anthropology, no. 31. New York: Columbia University Press.

1968. *Ojibwa Religion and the Midewiwin.* Madison: University of Wisconsin Press.

LANTIS, MARGARET

1946. *The Social Culture of the Nunivak Eskimo.* Transactions of the American Philosophical Society, vol. 35, pp. 153–323. Philadelphia.

1953. "Nunivak Eskimo Personality as Revealed in the Mythology." *Anthropological Papers of the University of Alaska,* 2:109–74.

LAUBSCHER, B. J. F.

1937. *Sex, Custom, and Psychopathology. A Study of South African Pagan Natives.* London: Routledge and Kegan Paul, Ltd.

LAUGHLIN, WILLIAM S.

1968. "Hunting: Its Evolutionary Importance." In *Man the Hunter.* Edited by Richard B. Lee and Irven De Vore. Chicago: Aldine Publishing Co. Pp. 304–20.

LEACH, EDMUND R.

1964. "Anthropological Aspects of Language: Animal Categories and Verbal Abuse." In *New Directions in the Study of Language.* Edited by Eric H. Lenneberg. Cambridge, Mass.: M.I.T. Press. Pp. 23–63.

LÉVI-STRAUSS, CLAUDE

1967. "The Story of Asdiwal." In *The Structural Study of Myth and Totemism.* Edited by Edmund Leach. A.S.A. Monographs 5. London: Tavistock Publications, pp. 1-47.

1963. *Totemism.* Translated by Rodney Needham. Boston: Beacon Press.

1970. *The Raw and the Cooked. Introduction to a Science of Mythology I.* Translated by John and Doreen Weightman. New York: Harper & Row.

LÉVY-BRUHL, LUCIEN

1966. *The "Soul" of the Primitive.* Translated by Lilian A. Clare. New York: Frederick A. Praeger.

LLEWELLYN, KARL N., AND E. ADAMSON HOEBEL

1941. *The Cheyenne Way.* Norman: University of Oklahoma Press.

LOCHER, G. W.

1932. *The Serpent in Kwakiutl Culture.* Leyden: E. J. Brill.

MALINOWSKI, BRONISLAW

1926. "Myth in Primitive Psychology." *Psyche Miniatures.* General series, no. 6. London: Kegan Paul, Trench, Trubner and Co. Reprinted in *Magic, Science and Religion and Other Essays*. Edited by Robert Redfield. New York: Doubleday Co., 1954. Pp. 93-148.

MASLOW, ABRAHAM H., AND JOHN J. HONIGMANN
  1970. "Synergy: Some Notes of Ruth Benedict." *American Anthropologist*, 72:320–33.

MASSIGNON, GENEVIÈVE (ed.)
  1968. *Folktales of France*. Chicago: University of Chicago Press.

MASTERS, R. E. L., AND JEAN HOUSTON
  1966. *The Varieties of Psychedelic Experience*. New York: Holt, Rinehart & Winston.

McKENNAN, ROBERT A.
  1959. *The Upper Tanana Indians*. Yale University Publications in Anthropology no. 55. New Haven, Conn.

MECH, DAVID
  1966. *The Wolves of Isle Royale*. Fauna of the National Parks of the United States Fauna Series 7. Washington, D.C.: U.S. Government Printing Office.

MORRISEAU, NORVAL
  1965. *Legends of My People the Great Ojibway*. Edited by Selwyn Dewdney. Toronto: Ryerson Press.

NADEL, S. F.
  1937. "A Field Experiment in Racial Psychology." *British Journal of Psychology*, 28:195–211.

NARANJO, CLAUDIO
  1973. "Psychological Aspects of the Yagé Experience in an Experimental Setting." In Harner, 1973, pp. 176–90.

NATIONAL INSTITUTE OF MENTAL HEALTH
  1969. *Recent Advances in the Psychology of the Depressive Illnesses*. Washington, D.C.

OSBORN, CHASE S., AND STELLANOVA OSBORN
  1942. *Schoolcraft, Longfellow, Hiawatha*. Lancaster, Pa.: Jacques Cattell.

PARKER, SEYMOUR
  1960. "The Wiitiko Psychosis in the Context of Ojibwa Personality and Culture." *American Anthropologist*, 62:603–23.

PARSONS, ELSIE CLEWS
  1917. "Tales from Guilford County, North Carolina." *Journal of American Folklore*, 30:168–200.
  1918. "Pueblo-Indian Folk Tales, Probably of Spanish Provenience." *Journal of American Folklore*, 31:216–55.
  1925. "Micmac Folklore." *Journal of American Folklore*, 38:55–133.
  1938. "The Humpbacked Flute Player of the Southwest." *American Anthropologist*, 40:337-78.

PESCHEL, KEEWAYNAH, MARGARET M.
n.d. "*Kawin-Ojashwash-Mashkossiwan*. A Narrative Account of Some Uses of Fungi Among the Ahnishnawbekog." Typescript in author's possession.

PLAUT, A.
1959. "A Case of Tricksterism Illustrating Ego Defenses." *Journal of Analytic Psychology*, 5:35–54.

PROPP, VLADIMIR
1968. *The Morphology of the Folktale*. 2nd ed. Publications of the American Folklore Society, Bibliographical and Special Series, vol. 9. Austin, Tex. [First published in Russian in 1928.]

RADIN, PAUL
1945. *The Road of Life and Death: A Ritual Drama of the American Indians*. New York: Pantheon Books, Bollingen Series, no. 5.
1956. *The Trickster. A Study in American Indian Mythology*. New York: Philosophical Library.

RADIN, PAUL, AND A. B. REAGAN
1928. "Ojibwa Myths and Tales." *Journal of American Folklore*, 41:61–146.

RANDALL, BETTY UCHITELLE
1949. "The Cinderella Theme in Northwest Coast Folklore." In *Indians of the Urban Northwest*. Edited by Marian W. Smith. New York: Columbia University Press. Pp. 243-85.

RANDS, ROBERT L.
1954. "Horned Serpent Stories." *Journal of American Folklore*, 67:79–81.

RANKE, KURT
1934. *Die Zwei Brüder*. Folklore Fellows Communications, vol. 44, no. 114. Helsinki.

RASMUSSEN, KNUD
1929. *Intellectual Culture of the Iglulik Eskimos*. Report of the Fifth Thule Expedition, 1921–24, vol. 7, no. 1. Copenhagen.

REICHEL-DOLMATOFF, GERARDO
1971. *Amazonian Cosmos. The Sexual and Religious Symbolism of the Tukano Indians*. Chicago: University of Chicago Press.

RICKETTS, MAC LINSCOTT
1966. "The North American Indian Trickster." *History of Religions*, 5:327–50.

RITZENTHALER, ROBERT E., AND PAT RITZENTHALER
1970. *The Woodland Indians of the Western Great Lakes*. Natural History Press. New York: Doubleday & Co.

RIVERS, W. H. R.
1968. "The Sociological Significance of Myth." In *Studies on Mythology*. Edited by Robert A. Georges. Homewood, Ill.: The Dorsey Press. Pp. 27–45.

ROGERS, EDWARD S.

   1962. *The Round Lake Ojibwa*. Royal Ontario Museum, University
   of Toronto, Occasional Papers, Art and Archaeology Division, no. 5.
   1966. "Subsistence Areas of the Cree-Ojibwa of the Eastern Sub-
   arctic: A Preliminary Study." National Museum of Canada, Bulletin
   no. 204, *Contributions to Anthropology, 1963–64*, pt. 2, paper no. 3.
   Ottawa.

ROHEIM, GÉZA

   1952. "Culture Hero and Trickster in North American Mythology."
   In *Indian Tribes of Aboriginal America*. Edited by Sol Tax. Selected
   Papers of the 29th International Congress of Americanists. Chicago:
   University of Chicago Press.

ROHRL, VIVIAN J.

   1970. "A Nutritional Factor in Windigo Psychosis." *American
   Anthropologist*, 72:97–101.

SCHMERLER, HENRIETTA

   1931. "Trickster Marries His Daughter." *Journal of American
   Folklore*, 44:196–207.

SCHOOLCRAFT, HENRY ROWE

   1825. *Travels in the Central Portions of the Mississippi Valley*.
   New York: Collins and Hannay.
   1834. *Narrative of an Expedition Through the Upper Mississippi
   to Itasca Lake*. New York: Harper & Brothers.
   1839. *Algic Researches*. New York: Harper & Brothers.
   1848. *The Indian in His Wigwam*. New York: W. H. Graham.
   1956. *Indian Legends*. Edited by Mentor L. Williams. East Lan-
   sing: Michigan State University Press.

SKINNER, ALANSON

   1911. *Notes on the Eastern Cree and Northern Saulteaux*. Anthropological Papers of the American Museum of Natural History, vol.
   9, pt. 1. New York.
   1913a. "European Folk-Tales Collected Among the Menominee
   Indians." *Journal of American Folklore*, 26:64–80.
   1913b. *Social Life and Ceremonial Bundles of the Menomini Indians*. Anthropological Papers of the American Museum of Natural
   History, vol. 13, pt. 1. New York.
   1915a. *Associations and Ceremonies of the Menomini Indians*. Anthropological Papers of the American Museum of Natural History,
   vol. 13, pt. 2. New York.
   1915b. With John V. Satterlee. *Folklore of the Menomini Indians*.
   Anthropological Papers of the American Museum of Natural History,
   vol. 13, pt. 3. New York.
   1916a. "European Tales from the Plains Ojibwa." *Journal of
   American Folklore*, 29:330–40.

1916b. "Plains Cree Tales." *Journal of American Folklore*, 29:341–67.

1919. "Plains Ojibwa Tales." *Journal of American Folklore*, 32:280–305.

1921. *Material Culture of the Menomini*. New York: Heye Foundation.

1925. "Traditions of the Iowa Indians." *Journal of American Folklore*, 38:425–506.

1928. "Sauk Tales." *Journal of American Folklore*, 41:147–71.

SMITH, EDWIN W., AND ANDREW MURRAY DALE
1968. *The Ila-Speaking Peoples of Northern Rhodesia*. 2 vols. New Hyde Park, N.Y.: University Books.

SMITH, ERMINNIE A.
1883. *Myths of the Iroquois*. Bureau of American Ethnology Annual Report no. 2, 1880–81. Washington, D.C.: Smithsonian Institution.

SPECK, FRANK G.
1915a. "Some Naskapi Myths from Little Whale River." *Journal of American Folklore*, 28:70–77.

1915b. *Myths and Folk-lore of the Timiskaming Algonquin and Timagami Ojibwa*. Canada Department of Mines, Geological Survey, Memoir 71, no. 9, Anthropological Series, Government Printing Bureau, Ottawa.

SWAHN, JAN-OJVIND
1955. *The Tale of Cupid and Psyche*. Lund: Håkan Ohlssons Boktryckeri.

SWIFT, ERNEST
1946. *A History of Wisconsin Deer*. Madison: Wisconsin Conservation Dept.

TANNER, HELEN HORNBECK
1976. *The Ojibwas: A Critical Bibliography*. Bloomington: Indiana University Press.

TANNER, JOHN
1830. *A Narrative of the Captivity and Adventurers of John Tanner*. Edited by Edwin James. New York: Carvill.

TEICHER, MORTON I.
1960. *Windigo Psychosis. A Study of the Relationships Betweeen Belief and Behavior among the Indians of Northeastern Canada*. Proceedings of the American Ethnological Society. Seattle.

THALBITZER, W.
1931. "Shamans of the East Greenland Eskimo." In *Source Book in Anthropology*. Edited by A. L. Kroeber and T. T. Waterman. New York: Harcourt, Brace. Pp. 430–36.

THOMPSON, STITH
1919. *European Tales Among the North American Indians*. Colorado

College Publications, General Series nos. 100 and 101, Language Series, vol. 2, no. 34. Colorado Springs.

1946. *The Folktale.* New York: Dryden Press.

1955-58. *Motif-Index of Folk Literature.* 6 vols. Copenhagen: Rosenkilde and Bagger.

1965. "The Star Husband Tale." In Dundes, 1965, pp. 414–74. *Studia Septentrionalia,* 4(1953):93–163.

1973. *Tales of the North American Indians.* Bloomington: Indiana University Press.

TITIEV, MISCHA
1939. "The Story of Kokopele." *American Anthropologist,* 41:91–98.

VAN LAWICK-GOODALL, HUGO AND JANE
1971. *Innocent Killers.* Boston: Houghton Mifflin.

VOTH, H. R.
1905. *The Traditions of the Hopi.* Field Columbian Museum Publication no. 96, Anthropological Series, vol. 8. Chicago.

WARREN, WILLIAM G.
1885. *History of the Ojibways.* Collections of the Minnesota Historical Society, vol. 5. St. Paul, Minn.

WATERS, FRANK
1969. *The Book of the Hopi.* New York: Ballantine Books.

WATROUS, BLANCHE G.
1949. *A Personality Study of Ojibwa Children.* Ph.D. dis., Northwestern University, Evanston, Ill.

WELLMAN, KLAUS D.
1970. "Kokopelli of Indian Paleology. Hunchbacked Rain Priest, Hunting Magician, and Don Juan of the Old Southwest." *Journal of the American Medical Association,* 212:1678–82.

WHEELER-VOEGELIN, ERMINIE, AND REMEDIOS W. MOORE
1957. "The Emergence Myth in Native North America." In *Studies in Folklore.* Edited by W. Edson Richmond. Indiana University Press. Pp. 66–91.

WISSLER, CLARK, AND D. C. DUVALL
1908. *Mythology of the Blackfoot Indians.* Anthropological Papers of the American Museum of Natural History, vol. 2, pt. 1. New York.

WOODS, RALPH L. (ed.)
1947. *The World of Dreams.* New York: Random House.

YOUNG, EDGERTON R.
1903. *Algonquin Indian Tales.* New York: Eaton and Mains.

Index of Motifs

General Index

DESIGNED BY EDGAR J. FRANK
COMPOSED BY FOX VALLEY TYPESETTING, MENASHA, WISCONSIN
PRINTED BY MALLOY LITHOGRAPHING, INC., ANN ARBOR, MICHIGAN
TEXT IS SET IN CALEDONIA, DISPLAY LINES IN GARAMOND

ᛒᛒ

Library of Congress Cataloging in Publication Data
Barnouw, Victor.
Wisconsin Chippewa myths & tales and their relation to
Chippewa life.
Bibliography: p.
Includes index.
1. Chippewa Indians—Legends. 2. Indians of North
America—Wisconsin—Legends. 3. Chippewa Indians—
Social life and customs. 4. Folk-lore, Indian.
I. Title.
E99.C6B34   398.2'09775   76-53647
ISBN 0-299-07310-6